## Critical Acclaim for MODELS OF REVELATION

"MODELS OF REVELATION addresses the most fundamental issues theology must face, more fundamental even than the mystery of the church. If the God of theology is real, is that God also knowable? . . . As in his earlier *Models of the Church*, Dulles offers herein five models of revelation: as doctrine, as history, as inner experience, as dialectical presence, and as new awareness. But unlike *Models of the Church*, this latest book does more than synthesize what others are saying and instead tries to surmount the conflicts . . . No brief summary can do justice to a work so careful in its argumentation and so systematic in its construction, nor can one adequately identify and draw out the implications for Christian spirituality. Whatever effort is required to study this book will be amply rewarded. No one who has read Avery Dulles in the past will need to be convinced."

—*Spirituality Today*

"Fr. Dulles strips the doctrine/theology of revelation of all the ecclesiastical pronouncements and refinements encumbering our understanding, and returns to the Biblical and Christian context in which the fundamental topic is fixed . . . This is a carefully and clearly structured text, illuminating the foundations of Christian faith and the Roman Catholic tradition."

—*Best Sellers*

"This is probably Avery Dulles' most representative work to date . . . it shows the breadth of scholarship, clarity of thought and soundness of judgement we have come to expect from its author. But it also offers a theological maturity that is deceptively simple, yielding its full measure of insight only on a second reading."

—*America*

"As both a comprehensive overview of modern technologies of revelation and an index of the direction in which contemporary thought is moving forward the book will prove enormously useful."

—*New Catholic World*

"Dulles' book deserves serious attention by scholars concerned with the current debate on theological epistemology. While his own solution can be questioned, his analysis of competing views is stimulating and, on the whole, accurate."

—*The Christian Century*

"Superbly crafted, crammed with practical information, and an incentive for future directions in thought, Dulles's study is one of the most important books of theology published so far in the 1980's. It succinctly tackles a vast amount of material, and it helps all of us sort out both where we are in the theological journey of life and where we are going."
—Religious Book Club *Bulletin*

"Though not spiritual reading in the strict sense, Dulles' wide-ranging and important views always make for a sharpened spiritual mind ready for meditation and prayer."
—*Spiritual Book News*

"MODELS OF REVELATION . . . gathers together the contemporary debate on the theology of revelation in a most readable format. This new book by Dulles, the mature reflection of an experienced teacher, brings together into a creative synthesis an enormous amount of theological material on revelation that is scattered around in different books and articles. As of now, it is the most comprehensive treatment of revelation available in the English-speaking world . . . [and] . . . a most welcome contribution."
—*The Living Light*

". . . one cannot help but think that Dulles has produced a minor classic that will constitute a 'basic text' for many years to come."
—*Emmanuel*

"This is a rich book, any one section of which could lead to extended discussion . . . the study is highly to be commended."
—*Expository Times*

# MODELS OF REVELATION

# AVERY DULLES, S.J.

**IMAGE BOOKS**
A Division of Doubleday & Company, Inc.
Garden City, New York
1985

Image Books edition published September 1985 by special arrangement with
Doubleday & Company, Inc.

*Imprimi potest*
   Reverend Vincent M. Cooke, S.J., Provincial New York Province, Society
      of Jesus
*Nihil obstat*
   Reverend Walter J. Schmitz, S.S. *Censor Librorum*
*Imprimatur*
   ✠Reverend Monsignor John F. Donoghue, Vicar General Archdiocese of
      Washington, August 31, 1982

The *nihil obstat* and *imprimatur* are official declarations that a book or
pamphlet is free of doctrinal or moral error. No implication is contained therein
that those who have granted the *nihil obstat* and *imprimatur* agree with the contents, opinions or statements expressed.

Quotations from Vatican II documents are from *The Documents of Vatican
II*, Walter M. Abbott, S.J., General Editor, and Very Rev. Msgr. Joseph
Gallagher, Translation Editor, America Press, New York, New York, 1966.

Library of Congress in Publication Data
Dulles, Avery Robert, 1918–
Models of revelation.
Includes index.
   1. Revelation—Comparative studies.   I. Title.
BT127.2.D78   1983      231.7′4
ISBN 0-385-23235-7
Library of Congress Catalog Card Number: 82–45243
*Copyright © 1983 by Avery Dulles*
Biblical quotations are from the Revised Standard Version of the Bible
Grateful acknowledgment is made to the following for permission to reprint
their copyrighted material.

Excerpts from *Church Dogmatics* by Karl Barth. Reprinted by permission of
T. & T. Clark Ltd.

Excerpts from *God, Revelation, and Authority*, Volumes I, II, III, IV, by
C. F. H. Henry. Volume I copyright © 1976 by Word Inc. Volume II copyright
© 1976 by Word Inc. Volume III copyright © 1979 by Word Inc. Volume IV
copyright © 1979 by Word Inc. Reprinted by permission of Word Books, Pub-
lisher, Waco, Texas 76796.

Excerpt from *Paths in Spirituality* by John Macquarrie. Reprinted by permission of SCM Press Ltd.

Excerpt from *A Theological Anthropology* by Hans Urs Von Balthasar.
Copyright © 1967 by Sheed and Ward, Inc. Reprinted by permission of Andrews
and McMeel, Inc. All rights reserved.

# CONTENTS

# Part Two

# PREFACE

The prehistory of this book goes back more than two decades. I have been teaching courses on revelation nearly every year since 1960. In the first few years, seeking to establish the possibility of revelation and its factual occurrence in Jesus Christ, the Son of God, I taught an essentially apologetical course. But as I continued to teach I became progressively more interested in the theological questions: What is revelation, how is it communicated? These questions were only lightly touched on in the standard scholastic treatises.

René Latourelle's monumental monograph of 1963 was the first major Catholic contribution to these theological questions, and it remains to this day one of the best.[1] Although it does not omit the speculative questions, its approach is predominantly historical and dogmatic. It admirably summarizes the official Catholic teaching on revelation up to Vatican Council II (1962–65), which is analyzed in the revised edition translated into English in 1966.[2]

As I have taught and lectured on revelation, I have been increasingly concerned with the question of method. The apologetical treatise assumed that the existence and nature of revelation were already known; it sought simply to convince the unconvinced. The dogmatic treatise assumed that the nature of revelation could be sufficiently known by the acceptance of official church teaching. But there were further questions: How does the Church itself find out what revelation is? How can one know things about revelation on which the Church has made no pronouncement? How are church pronouncements on revelation related to revelation itself?

These questions, easily asked, are hard to answer. For responsible investigation one needs a method. Theological method generally presupposes a doctrine of revelation and uses revelation as a norm. But to employ a doctrine of revelation in the very investigation of revelation would be to presuppose the answer to the very question one was asking. Thus the standard theological method seems inapplicable.

Could one establish the nature of revelation nontheologically, by the methods of some other discipline, such as philosophy? Philosophy can always be of help for avoiding certain mistakes, but as usually understood, it knows nothing of revelation. If God alone can speak well of God, as Pascal said, it is also true that only revelation can speak well of revelation. The circle, then, would seem to be unbreakable.

A glimmer of light came to me when I was able to see, with Michael Polanyi's help, the distinction between tacit and explicit knowing. All Christian believers, it could be said, tacitly know what revelation is simply by virtue of adherence to a revealed religion. But they do not yet have a formulated concept or theory of revelation. The theological problem is how to move from tacit to explicit knowledge. The primary criterion is the predominantly tacit norm of faith itself. The theology of revelation seeks, with the help of this norm, to spell out what is implicitly known by all who can say, in a religious context, "I believe."

A further enlightenment occurred when I began to see the value of models for theology. In various writings on ecumenism, on the Church, and on faith, I found it profitable to survey the opinions that had been held, to see where they agreed and disagreed, and in this way to identify the questions that needed attention. The opinions, I found, could usually be grouped in certain major constellations—not more than half a dozen. Distinctive to each constellation was an angle of approach that predetermined the answers to many particular questions. The basic unity in each constellation could be clarified by reference to a root metaphor that was shared by all members of the group. Theologians of different orientation often disagreed because they were working on the basis of different metaphors which they took for granted and did not subject to serious questioning.

In the theology of revelation, as I explain in Chapter II, the approaches may conveniently be grouped under some five headings. Based on different root metaphors, these approaches can be called models.

The method of models was excellent for identifying the basic questions at issue, but it did not greatly help to solve the questions. To say that the models were compatible was to fly in the face of the persistent judgment of the theologians, who rejected one another's models as inadequate and misleading. To choose one model and reject the rest seemed arbitrary. To concoct a new model would only add to the confusion by entering one more candidate into the race.

In this book I try to get beyond these seeming impasses. My method, as the reader will see, is to reflect on the process by which the original tacit knowledge of revelation arises. It comes about, in my opinion, through a form of communication which I call symbolic. If this be true, symbolic communication may serve as a dialectical tool for transcending the differences between the models, correcting some of their deficiencies, and establishing a coherent theology not wedded to any one model. The symbolic epistemology employed in this book is consciously theological, rather than merely literary or anthropological. My conception of symbol is partly determined by my beliefs as a Christian.

To some readers the disputes about revelation may seem excessively abstract and arid. They might be tempted to think that theology would do better not to become embroiled in these questions. The term "revelation" does not appear in the creeds and is not central in the Scriptures. Treatises on revelation did not begin to be written until the Enlightenment period, in controversies with the Deists. But since that time theologians have recognized that an implicit doctrine of revelation underlies every major theological undertaking. The great theological disputes turn out, upon reflection, to rest on different understandings of revelation, often simply taken for granted. The controversies that have raged in our own century about the divinity of Christ, the inerrancy of the Bible, the infallibility of the Church, secular and political theology, and the value of other religions would be unintelligible apart from the varying convictions about revelation.

Revelation has been a major theme in twentieth-century Protestant theology. Karl Barth, Emil Brunner, Rudolf Bultmann, H. Richard Niebuhr, and Paul Tillich, among others, wrote what have by now become classics on the subject, but their views call for reexamination in the perspectives of our own day.

In Catholic theology prior to Vatican Council II what little was written on the subject was chiefly apologetic. Vatican II made revelation the theme of one of its two dogmatic constitutions (*Dei Verbum*), the other (*Lumen gentium*) being on the Church. Since the Council many historical and critical monographs on revelation and many commentaries on *Dei Verbum* have been published, but we still lack a comprehensive study of revelation, especially from the point of view of fundamental theology. In the present work I am seeking to fill this gap.

Two limitations of the present work should be borne in mind. First, I have confined my attention in this work to the contemporary theological scene, and have deliberately avoided historical questions about what is to be found in the earlier theological tradition. I am aware of the importance of these historical issues, but their study would involve inquiries into the past that would be distracting in a work focusing on contemporary questions. Secondly, this work, as a contribution to fundamental theology, is predogmatic. Once the approach to revelation has been clarified in fundamental theology, there remains the task of studying revelation in the context of a total theological system. Such a study can only be undertaken in the light of positions taken regarding other theological questions, such as the doctrine of the Trinity, Christology, and the theology of grace. As far as possible I have avoided taking positions on controverted issues in these other theological treatises, since the effort to justify such positions would far exceed the scope of the present work.

More than a decade ago I published a brief work, *Revelation Theology: A History* (1969). When I wrote it I had in mind to follow it up with a systematic study, but in the intervening years my attention has been taken up more with ecclesiological questions. My later work, *Models of the Church* (1974), anticipates to some extent the methodology used in the present book. But the parallelism is not complete. In this work I am more concerned to surmount the conflicts than I was in *Models of the Church,* which was designed rather as a synthesis of what others had been saying.

I began work on this book in 1977, when I was awarded a fellowship at the Wilson Center in Washington, D.C. At the end of that year I presented a paper, "The Symbolic Structure of Revelation," published in *Theological Studies,* March 1980. Since 1977 I did not find time to do further work on the project until the academic year 1981–82, when I was given a one-year appointment as Thomas I. Gasson Professor at Boston College. With a light teaching load and no departmental responsibilities I found time to complete the project begun at the Wilson Center.

I should like to express my profound gratitude to the Director and Board of Directors of the Wilson Center for my fellowship and to the Jesuit Community of Boston College, which generously founded and endowed the Gasson chair. I am especially indebted to four colleagues who have read the manuscript of this book and have assisted me with their comments. They are: Gabriel Fackre, Abbott Professor of Christian Theology, Andover–Newton Theological School, Newton, Massachusetts; Gerald O'Collins, S.J., professor of theology at the Gregorian University in Rome; Lucien J. Richard, O.M.I., professor at the Weston School of Theology, Cambridge, Massachusetts; and Professor Frans Jozef van Beeck, S.J., of Boston College. I express my thanks to Walter J. Burghardt, S.J., editor of *Theological Studies,* for permission to reproduce sections of my article,"The Symbolic Structure of Revelation," in Chapter IX. My genial editors at Doubleday, first John B. Breslin, S.J., and then Robert T. Heller, have offered valuable advice in the development of this book. I am also grateful to my secretary at Boston College, Ruth J. G. Michelson, for her patient typing and retyping of this manuscript.

In preparing the paperback edition I have introduced no significant changes except for the addition on page 128 of a new final paragraph, which seemed necessary in order to prevent the misunderstandings reflected in several reviews. I have also reworked the Index to make it, in my opinion, more serviceable. The pagination remains unchanged.

AVERY DULLES, S.J.

# PART ONE

# Chapter I

# THE PROBLEM OF REVELATION

## 1. *The Function of Revelation in Modern Christianity*

In every civilization there have been thinkers concerned with the ultimate basis of reality, meaning, and value. In some traditions this basis has been viewed as an invisible and transcendent order in which our empirical world is somehow rooted. This view, which may be called metaphysical or religious, is held in common by many of the Greek philosophical systems, the Eastern religions, and the Western religions.[1]

The great Western religions—Judaism, Christianity, and Islam —are based on the conviction that the existence of the world and the final meaning and value of all that it contains ultimately depend on a personal God who, while distinct from the world and everything in it, is absolute in terms of reality, goodness, and power. These religions profess to derive their fundamental vision not from mere human speculation, which would be tentative and uncertain, but from God's own testimony—that is to say, from a historically given divine revelation.

Christian faith and theology, for nearly two thousand years, have been predicated on the conviction that God gave a permanently valid revelation concerning himself in biblical times—a revelation that deepened progressively with the patriarchs, Moses, and the prophets, until it reached its unsurpassable climax in Jesus Christ. The Christian Church down through the centuries has been committed to this revelation and has sought to propagate it, defend it, and explain its implications.

The idea of revelation is pervasive in the Bible and in the theology of the early centuries, but because revelation was taken for granted, little effort was made to prove the existence of revelation or to define the concept in contradistinction to whatever might be opposed to it; for example, naturally acquired knowledge. The category began to achieve prominence in the sixteenth century, when orthodox theology, both Protestant and Catholic, appealed to revelation as justification for its confessional positions. In the seventeenth and eighteenth centuries the doctrine of revelation was further developed in opposition to the Deists, who held that human reason by itself could establish all the essential truths of religion. The apologetic notion of revelation which had been excogitated at the time of the Enlightenment was attacked and defended in the nineteenth century, when evolutionists held that all religious truth was the fruit of human inquiry and when positivists denied that the human mind could have knowledge of the divine.[2]

By the end of the nineteenth century the Christian churches were equipped with a systematically complete doctrine of revelation as a deposit of truth built up in biblical times and reliably transmitted through the Bible and church teaching. Among Christians who still adhere to this doctrine, revelation is seen as foundational to the religious life of the individual, to the mission of the Church, and to the method of theology. Let us briefly consider revelation under each of these three aspects.

In the personal life of the believer, the fundamental Christian attitude is faith in the sense of a believing response to God's revealing word. This concept of faith, common to most Christians, was expressed by Vatican Council I in 1870:

> The Catholic Church teaches that this faith, which is the beginning of human salvation, is the supernatural virtue whereby, inspired and assisted by the grace of God, we believe the things which he has revealed as true, not because of their intrinsic truth as perceived by the natural light of reason, but because of the authority of God himself who reveals them, and who can neither be deceived nor deceive.[3]

Without a prior act of revelation on God's part, faith—it is held—would have no basis and no object; and without faith the whole edifice of Christian existence would collapse.

The Church sees itself as commissioned to safeguard and herald the revelation committed to it by Christ. Called into being by divine revelation, the Church claims to address its own members and all humanity in the name of the revealing God. In 1941 Emil Brunner, a distinguished Swiss Reformed theologian, wrote: "All that the Church proclaims and teaches is an attempt to express in human language the truth which she has received. Hence the divine revelation alone is both the ground and the norm, as well as the content of her message."[4] From this it evidently follows that revelation is the ultimate criterion for resolving disputes among Christians.

Theology, as contrasted with the philosophy of religion, is commonly defined as a disciplined reflection on faith, and thus also on revelation. Anselm, the eleventh-century Archbishop of Canterbury, described himself as "one who strives to lift his mind to the contemplation of God, and seeks to understand what he believes."[5] Thomas Aquinas, in the thirteenth century, spoke of "sacred doctrine" (which we would today call theology) as "doctrine about God according to divine revelation."[6] Karl Rahner, a ranking contemporary Roman Catholic theologian, offers the following definition of theology: "Theology is the *science* of faith. It is the conscious and methodical explanation and explication of the divine revelation received and grasped in faith."[7] According to many of its practitioners, theology seeks to serve the Church and its members by examining current doctrine and practice in the light of divine revelation, by exposing the error of tenets at variance with revelation, by giving an intelligible account of the contents and significance of revelation, and by vindicating the beliefs of the Christian community on the basis of revelation. In all of these phases—critical, polemical, speculative, and apologetical—theology presupposes the existence and knowability of divine revelation.

In the light of these three functions of revelation, one can readily understand how Christian theologians of many different schools and traditions can agree on the centrality of revelation. Early in the twentieth century the Dutch Calvinist, Herman Bavinck, asserted: "With the reality of revelation, therefore, Christianity stands or falls."[8] Especially is this true, he held, for theology:

> As science never precedes life, but always follows it and flows from it, so the science of the knowledge of God rests on the reality of his revelation. If God does not exist, or if he has not revealed himself, and hence is unknowable, then all religion is an illusion and all theology a phantasm.[9]

As recently as 1970 a German Catholic theologian, Walter Kasper, could speak no less emphatically. For modern theology, he asserted, revelation describes "the final presupposition, basis, means, and norm of everything that purports to be Christian."[10]

## 2. Contemporary Difficulties Against Revelation

The concept of revelation as a permanently valid body of truths communicated by God in biblical times, preserved and commented on by the Church, is still accepted by many Christians, but is widely questioned in the twentieth century. While the objections cannot be fully enumerated or expounded at this point, a selective listing may help situate the theology of revelation in its contemporary context.

1. *Philosophical agnosticism,* already widespread in the nineteenth century, continues to question the capacity of human reason to go beyond the phenomena of worldly experience. God, even if he exists, is held to be utterly incomprehensible, with the result that all statements about God and his actions are devoid of cognitive value. Revelation itself is viewed as a myth or metaphor that cannot be taken literally.

2. *Linguistic analysis,* reinforcing the philosophical agnosticism just mentioned, calls attention to the paradoxical and symbolic character of God-talk. Many analytic philosophers question whether language about the divine can have a definite cognitive content such as was implied by the classical doctrine of revelation.

3. *Modern epistemology,* probing into the genesis of knowledge, tends to undermine the seemingly clear distinction between revealed and acquired knowledge. The idea that the human mind could passively receive information by some kind of transfusion from the divine mind is widely rejected. As a product of the knower's own powers, all human knowledge must in some sense be "acquired" and must be subject to the conditions and limitations of the human subject. This realization, where accepted, puts an emphatic question mark against the divine authority usually attributed to revelation.

4. *Empirical psychology* has destroyed any naive confidence that visions and auditions, purportedly received by seers and prophets, can be credited as coming from on high. Ecstatic states can be induced by hypnosis or by drugs. Involuntary hallucinations are frequently attributable to pathological states of mind. Some authors

surmise that revelation in an age of rational thought is nothing but a vestige of a primitive mentality in which the subconscious or trans-marginal regions of the psyche were more easily activated than they normally are today.

5. *Biblical criticism* has exposed the difficulty of attributing particular words and deeds to the divine agency. According to many modern Scripture scholars, the prophets and apostles formulated and expressed their own thoughts with the help of the conceptual and linguistic tools available in the place and time. The oracular form of certain statements ("God says . . .") is attributed in some cases to expanded states of consciousness and in other cases to literary convention (the so-called messenger-form). Attempted proofs of revelation from biblical miracles and prophecies have been abandoned by many scholars, who regard the accounts of such divine interventions as historically unreliable.

6. *The history of Christian doctrine* demonstrates that many beliefs formerly viewed as divinely revealed truths have been reclassified as human and even fallacious opinions. For example, the doctrine of Copernicus that the earth revolves about the sun and that of Darwin that man was descended from the lower animals were once rejected as contrary to God's own word in Scripture. Today the Bible is not used as a source for scientific information, except by certain Fundamentalist thinkers not representative of the Church as a whole. The question therefore arises whether doctrines still taught as divinely revealed—such as the virginal conception of Jesus, the Incarnation, and the Resurrection—may not in the course of time be set aside as myths and legends. The fact that certain central Christian doctrines, such as the Trinity and the divinity of Christ, did not become established Christian doctrine until several centuries after the apostles also prompts skepticism about their claim to revealed status. If the dividing line between revealed and nonrevealed is in flux, the category of revelation itself appears questionable.

7. *Comparative religion* requires Christianity to relate itself to other religions which in some cases claim contrary revelations and in other cases recognize no such thing as divine revelation. Can biblical religion, or Christianity alone, credibly announce itself as the revealed religion, thus setting itself on a lonely peak above all others? Many tensions and suspicions could be relieved if it were conceded that all religions, including Christianity, were noble but

merely human attempts to probe the depths of truth and goodness. Such a concession, it is claimed, would greatly facilitate dialogue not only among the religions but also between religions and secular ideologies.

8. *Critical sociology* has exposed the ideological component characteristic of belief systems. In many cases appeal to divine authority can be a hidden way of obtaining conformity and of suppressing doubt and dissent. The question has therefore been raised: Is this the real, though perhaps unconscious, motivation behind official declarations that certain truths are divinely revealed? When church authorities define a doctrine as taught by God, are they secretly aspiring to enhance their own authority as oracles of revealed truth?

These objections are merely illustrative. Others, more closely related to specific aspects of revelation, such as the authority of Scripture and the autonomy of reason, will be treated in future chapters.

## 3. *Christianity Without Revelation?*

In view of the many and serious objections against the idea of revelation it must be asked whether it might not be possible to excise it from Christianity. In theory it seems possible to esteem and adhere to Christianity as a human faith founded on a long tradition of spiritual experience and reflection. The Christian religion could thus be seen as embodying a rich heritage of acquired wisdom concerning the ultimate nature of reality and the proper conduct of human life, but not as conveying God's own testimony.

In a reconstructed Christianity, one could imagine, "revelation" could be conceived as a mythical way of describing sudden and transforming insights that arise from the exercise of the latent powers of the human mind. In such a perspective the Scriptures would be valued as preserving the memory of the struggles and discoveries of a religiously gifted people. Jesus would be understood not as God incarnate but rather as a remarkable religious leader whose teaching could be revered as uniquely disclosive of God, at least to the community of his own disciples. The Church would then be seen as the place in which the memory of Jesus is specially preserved, in which the Scriptures are read with veneration, and in which efforts are made to cultivate a life conformed to the wisdom contained in the Jewish and Christian traditions. Christian faith would mean an attitude of mind characterized by special confidence in the biblical heritage as being a reliable path to spiritual growth.

The existentialist philosopher Karl Jaspers presents a position not wholly unlike that sketched in the preceding paragraph. In his *Philosophical Faith and Revelation,* among other books, he categorically rejects the idea of revelation, by which he understands "a direct manifestation of God by word, command, action, or event, at a definite time and place. . . . All this happens by an objective invasion from without."[11] In Christian theology, he adds, revelation means the special and unique manifestation of God given in Scripture and tradition.[12] "I do not believe in revelation," he writes; "to my knowledge I have never believed in the possibility."[13] "I myself cannot but hold with Kant that if revelation were a reality it would be calamitous for man's created freedom."[14]

Within Christianity, Jaspers acknowledges, there are believers who adhere to revelation as the personal manifestation of God, confirmed and warranted by ecclesiastical authority. But there are other believers whose faith, though grounded in the biblical tradition, does not accept revelation in the usual sense of the word. Christians of this second class, with whom Jaspers associates himself,[15] accept the biblical symbols, including prophecy, apostleship, and inspiration, as "ciphers" to be tested by their capacity to light up human existence and point to the inaccessible depths of transcendence. This second form of faith, he holds, is in its way biblical. "The Bible is as rich as life. It does not document one faith; it is an area in which possibilities of faith vie with each other for the depth of the divine."[16] In some sort this biblical faith without revelation is Christian. "All of us are Christians in the sense of biblical faith, and whoever claims to be a Christian should be so considered. We need not let ourselves be thrown out of the house that has lodged our fathers for a thousand years."[17]

Jaspers therefore pleads with the Christian community and its authorities to abandon the ecclesiastical concept of revelation and to translate revelation into a cipher.[18] If this were done, he believes, the Christian churches could forego their exclusive claims and relate peacefully to other religious communities.[19] But at the present time, Jaspers concedes, this hope appears utopian. The churches appear to be committed to fixed and absolute revelations enforced in an authoritarian way.[20]

In framing his criticism Jaspers no doubt has in mind some particularly obnoxious examples of rigid, authoritarian, and exclusivist presentations of the word of God. One can easily share his concern for freedom and religious tolerance. If this were Jaspers' only concern, he might be content to espouse some of the more liberal and ecumenical concepts of revelation that are current in modern theology. One suspects, however, that Jaspers' difficulty is more fundamental. He rules out even the possibility of revelation. God for him is not a personal being but a mere cipher for transcendence, and thus God cannot be said to speak and act in history except in a mythological sense.[21] The doctrine of Incarnation for Jaspers is both a "philosophical impossibility"[22] and, "if philosophy allowed us to use the language of believers in revelation," would have to be called blasphemous.[23] Jaspers denies, moreover, that there can be any special presence of God in the Church or the sacraments—views which he characterizes as magical.[24] The Church for him can have no authority to establish the canon of Scripture or to compose binding creeds or confessions.[25] All such beliefs, for Jaspers, must be translated into ciphers—that is to say, into a language that "has no real speaker, nor even a real relation between cipher and meaning."[26]

It would be beyond the scope of this work to criticize Jaspers on philosophical grounds. Philosophers have already addressed themselves to this task.[27] As a theologian Karl Barth has pointed out the deficiencies of Jaspers' position in the perspectives of Christian faith. In an apparent reference to Jaspers, Barth warns against any tendency to equate God with "the unsubstantial, unprofitable, and fundamentally very tedious magnitude known as transcendence," which would be far better interpreted "as an illusory reflection of human freedom, as its projection into the vacuum of utter abstraction." He then comments: "It is characteristic of this transcendence that it neither has a specific will, nor accomplishes a specific act, nor speaks a specific word, nor exercises specific power and authority. It can neither bind man effectively nor effectively liberate him. It can neither justify nor satisfy him. It cannot be for his life either a clear meaning or a distinct purpose."[28]

The theologian will have many reservations about Jaspers' contention that the Christian idea of revelation is static and objectivistic; that it precludes freedom and personal thought; that it leads to idolatry, fanaticism, exclusivity, and intolerance. Yet the forceful critique of Jaspers against certain expressions of Christianity cannot be lightly set aside. By calling attention to deformities sometimes found in revelation theology, Jaspers prompts the theologian to speak cautiously. Jaspers' ciphers of transcendence, even though they do not fully coincide with what we shall describe as revelatory symbols, call attention to certain aspects of the elusive process whereby the hidden God manifests himself to the human spirit while still remaining transcendent mystery.

The example of Jaspers tends to confirm rather than invalidate the hypothesis that the Christian theologian cannot dispense with the category of revelation. There are, he maintains, two ways of thinking about realities that lie beyond the scope of scientific research. "If this thinking springs from, and is defined by, a historically determined revelation we call it theology; if it springs from the source of essential humanity, we call it philosophy."[29] Jaspers does not write as a theologian or as one who accepts the faith of the Church. As a philosopher he uses biblical symbols only to transform them into ciphers that speak to the depths of human *Existenz*.[30]

For a more theological argument against the notion of revelation one may turn to the work of F. Gerald Downing, *Has Christianity a Revelation?* Underlying the entire work is a theory of religious language heavily influenced by R. B. Braithwaite, among others. The creedal statements, "I believe in God . . . and in Jesus Christ . . . and in the Holy Spirit," Downing concurs, "should be taken as a declaration of an intention to live in a particular way; it is well summarized by his [Braithwaite's] coined [term] 'agapeistically.' "[31] The Christian way of life, then, is essentially one of altruistic love (in Greek, *agape*). As the creed implies, Christian love is a response to a perfect love which is believed to be prior to itself. This belief, however, does not imply any real knowledge about God, but only an acceptance of what Downing calls "the 'myth' of the prior love of 'real God in Christ.' "[32] Holding that God "still insists on hiding himself, and leaving us unsure,"[33] Downing regards faith as a leap into the unknown.[34]

From the standpoint of this understanding of faith, Downing mounts his critique of the notion of revelation. His principal objections are two: first, the absence of any sufficient biblical basis, and second, the difficulty of using the word "revelation" logically and coherently.[35]

In his biblical chapters Downing gives a very helpful analysis of the terminology of both the Old and New Testaments. He shows convincingly that the biblical notion of faith is not a merely intellectual assent, but also an act of obedient and trustful surrender. He likewise adduces a multitude of texts to prove that the biblical writers regard the full and manifest revelation of God as something to be given in the eschatological future. What Downing fails to establish, in my judgment, is that the biblical authors question or deny that God has really manifested something of his power, his fidelity, and his intentions in "the terms of the obedience that he requires of men."[36] How could we obey a God who had not made his will known? How could we love him if he had not disclosed his love for us? How could we proclaim salvation by a God who had not manifested himself as our Savior?

With regard to the theological usage, Downing marshals a considerable amount of evidence that seems detrimental to his own position. Downing is probably justified in holding that the concept of revelation first became focal with the disputes against Deism in the seventeenth century;[37] but he is less than successful in maintaining that the concept is not a valid one. Indeed, he provides excellent material for establishing the importance of revelation to the patristic writers.

Downing argues in part from a rather idiosyncratic notion of revelation. The term, he contends, normally implies direct vision, effecting a disclosure that is both clear and complete.[38] If this were admitted, scarcely anyone would deny that the ordinary believer, in this earthly life, is without revelation. But Gerald O'Collins, in a penetrating analysis of Downing's argument, raises some telling objections:

> There is good reason for disquiet over this argument. Does common usage support Downing's case? Revelation can occur between persons without there being an utterly complete disclosure of personalities. Take the following statement: "He revealed to me his wishes in the matter." No full, continuing, personal communion is asserted. But something has been disclosed and that too in a context which affords some insight into the other's per-

sonality. To see something of his personality is not equivalent to seeing nothing at all. May we not use "reveal" in some such qualified sense of God, and speak of a genuine experience of God which communicates something and yet falls short of being full disclosure?[39]

Downing argues also from the disagreements among theologians about the precise nature of revelation. That there is a multiplicity of opinions on this score will become quite evident as the present study proceeds. But Downing tends to exaggerate the differences.[40] Also, his argument is one that could be turned against himself. He contends that the Christian receives not revelation but salvation; yet theologians fail to agree about the exact meaning of salvation. Downing's more stringent demands for agreement about revelation seem to rest upon his prior position that the term "revelation" is applicable only to perfectly clear and complete knowledge.

We shall return to Jaspers and Downing in our final chapter in order to supplement these preliminary criticisms on the basis of the theory of revelation that emerges from the intervening investigation. For the present, we shall proceed on the assumption that biblical and Christian faith should not and indeed cannot be divorced from belief in revelation. The Jewish and Christian view of God, the world, and human life is inseparably intertwined with the conviction that God is free and personal, that he acts on behalf of those whom he loves, and that his action includes, already within history, a partial disclosure of his nature, attributes, attitudes, and intentions. The acceptance of revelation, therefore, is of fundamental importance to the Christian faith.

Contemporary theology cannot and does not ignore the difficulties against revelation set forth above. The responses fall into two general types. Some theologians, adhering to the classical concept of revelation, attempt to show that the objections are unfounded and that they prove nothing against the reality of revelation. Other theologians admit that the objections, or some of them, have telling force against the naive conceptions of revelation purveyed by many theological manuals of the past few centuries. But going back to the biblical and patristic sources, or moving forward to a more modern theological outlook, these authors attempt to develop a doctrine of revelation that can stand up against objections such as those here considered. Before showing how the objections are met in the various theories, we shall have to examine how revelation is understood in recent Christian theology. After having considered the various options, we shall in our final chapter return to consider the force of the objections.

## 4. *Method and Criteria*

As a preamble to the theory of revelation, which will be the principal theme of the present volume, some consideration of method is evidently called for. The theology of revelation offers peculiar methodological problems. It is not a part of doctrinal theology (or dogmatics) as ordinarily understood, for doctrinal theology, as we have already seen, customarily tests its assertions by their conformity with what is already recognized as revelation. Without falling into a vicious circle, one could not test a theory of revelation by its conformity to revelation. We cannot at this point presuppose any given theory of revelation as established.

Could the doctrine of revelation, then, be established by reason alone, without appeal to revelation? If revelation were not necessary to know what revelation was, revelation, it would seem, would not be necessary at all. It would disclose nothing that could not be known without it. Since this restrictive understanding of revelation is manifestly contrary to the biblical and Christian understanding, we shall not impose this philosophical straitjacket. We shall be open to a properly theological idea of revelation, provided that this idea is not demonstrably at odds with what philosophy can establish.[41]

Our method, then, will be to start from a position within a faith-tradition that does appeal to revelation. More specifically, we shall write from a Christian, and indeed a Roman Catholic, perspective. Dwelling within the tradition of faith that is common to the Christian churches, and more specifically, within the Roman Catholic phylum of that tradition, we shall be guided by the tradition and by its classical and binding expressions of faith. We shall, as previously stated, provisionally assume that revelation is implied in biblical and Christian faith, but we shall not presuppose that any given doctrine of revelation is the right one. We shall examine a multiplicity of doctrines that have been put forth by believing Christians, and seek to assess which, if any, are satisfactory. The various theories partly confirm and partly oppose one another, thus providing input for critical evaluation.

For our present purposes it does not seem necessary to take a position regarding the disputed question whether the theologian who conducts this type of inquiry must be a person of faith.[42] Faith in the sense of the divinely infused virtue described by Vatican I and quoted earlier in this chapter, could perhaps help one to recognize what truly comes from God, as the theologian must do, but it could hardly serve to identify the theologian, for there is no empirical way of testing the presence or absence of this virtue in oneself or others. Nor does it seem to be strictly essential that the theologian be personally committed to the Christian (or, as the case may be, Catholic) tradition in order to construct a Christian (or Catholic) theology. The theologian does need the capacity to perceive, at least by empathy, what beliefs are implied in (or compatible or incompatible with) commitment to the tradition of the Church. Tradition, like the body and its organs, is best known in a subsidiary way by dwelling in it, rather than in a focal way, by looking at it.[43] Hence the doctrinal implications of the tradition will presumably be clearer to one who is existentially committed to the tradition than to the outsider. But many other factors besides existential commitment enter into the equipment of the theologian, and thus the absence of this one factor could perhaps be compensated for by other factors.

What is being attempted in this book may be described as a fundamental theology of revelation. By fundamental theology I do not here mean a pretheological discipline that proceeds, as the classical apologetics aspired to do, by the "unaided light of reason." Rather I mean a properly theological discipline which is, however, predogmatic. Fundamental theology is theological because it is not a mere preamble but an integral part of the critical and methodic reflection on Christian faith. Beginning from within the Christian tradition, it seeks to spell out what is implied by the stance of faith. Fundamental theology, however, is predogmatic because, as stated above, it does not rest on a finished theory regarding revelation and its mediation through tradition and ecclesiastical pronouncements. Rather, by fashioning such a theory, it contributes to the foundations for dogmatic theology. The fundamental theology of revelation deals with one of the principal areas of fundamental theology, other areas being concerned with the Church and with theological method.[44]

It remains for us to discuss the question of criteria. Theologians of different schools differ not only in their views about what revelation is but in the criteria whereby they assess theories of revelation. By accepting any given set of criteria one would inevitably prejudice to some extent the decision as to what theory or theories were sound.

There is no set of perfectly neutral criteria that would be equally acceptable to all Christians or even to all Catholics. But the theological literature offers some helpful indications. It seems reasonable to suppose that if God has revealed himself, his revelation could best be known through the testimony of those who profess to adhere to it. Since believers have discussed the nature of revelation for a considerable period of time, it would be irresponsible to try to construct a theory without having carefully examined the opinions that command respect and influence in the community of faith. Progress in theology, as in other disciplines, is generally achieved not by ignoring but by critically assimilating the work of one's predecessors. To the Christian it will seem highly improbable that all existing theories of revelation are so deficient that they cannot significantly help the contemporary theologian.

While writing as a Catholic, the author considers that the present official stance of his own church not only permits but requires careful and sympathetic attention to the theology of other Christian traditions. From the recent theological literature it seems that many of the divergences regarding revelation are theological rather than confessional. The theological schools in the field of revelation cut right across the lines between denominations. For this reason the Catholic can expect to profit from the work of non-Catholic theologians and can offer the results of his own reflections to Christians of other communions.

Within a commitment to Christianity as understood in a broadly Catholic and ecumenical framework, certain criteria can be identified as promising. A fair sample of theologians who belong to different schools would acknowledge criteria such as the following seven:[45]

1. *Faithfulness to the Bible and Christian tradition.* Anyone who intends to do Christian theology will seek to stand in continuity

with what believers of previous generations have recognized as compatible with faith.

2. *Internal coherence*. The notion of revelation must be capable of being conceptually formulated in an intelligible manner and be free from internal self-contradiction. Self-contradictory positions are self-destructive.

3. *Plausibility*. The theory must not run counter with what is generally thought to be true in other areas of life, unless it is capable of providing an alternative explanation of the phenomena responsible for the general state of opinion.

4. *Adequacy to experience*. An acceptable theory of revelation will illuminate the deeper dimensions of secular and religious experience both within and beyond the Christian community.

5. *Practical fruitfulness*. The theory will commend itself to Christians if, once accepted, it sustains moral effort, reinforces Christian commitment, and enhances the corporate life and mission of the Church. Various psychological and social benefits may also be included under this rubric.

6. *Theoretical fruitfulness*. The theory of revelation must satisfy the quest for religious understanding and thus be of assistance to the theological enterprise.

7. *Value for dialogue*. The theory will be more acceptable if it assists in the exchange of insights with Christians of other schools and traditions, with adherents of other religions, and with adherents of the great secular faiths.

These seven criteria, while genuinely theological, are relatively "neutral" since their acceptance does not presuppose a prior choice of any particular type of revelation theory, though members of certain theological schools might see little or no value in one or another of these criteria. By the same token, the criteria are rather abstract. When one attempts to specify exactly what is meant by fidelity, coherence, and plausibility, or precisely what is adequate to experience and fruitful, or what kind of dialogue is to be desired, disagreements break out. The criteria, therefore, contain certain ambiguities.[46]

The ambiguities do not mean that the criteria are vacuous. In point of fact most theories are defended on the ground that they meet some of the criteria better than rival theories, and that they are not unacceptable when judged by the other criteria. Thus the criteria, if not decisive, are at least provocative. They serve to raise certain questions and thus to focus the debate. Anyone seeking to make an intelligent choice among theories will carefully weigh the answers given to the questions, and will decide how convincing these answers are.

## 5. Plan of the Book

The chapters that follow can be grouped into two major parts, the first more descriptive in character, the second more speculative. Chapters III–VII, constituting the substance of Part One, will present currently popular theories of revelation schematically under five major headings. These chapters will be primarily expository, secondarily critical. Chapter II will introduce the method of models as applied to revelation theology, and Chapter VIII, concluding Part One, will draw some conclusions.

Chapter IX is transitional between Parts One and Two. It will attempt to propose a theory—that of symbolic mediation—as a dialectical tool for integrating some of the best positive insights in rival theories, overcoming some of the impasses between opposed schools, and showing up the deficiencies in certain positions.

Part Two will be more systematic in character. In Chapters X–XV, constituting the substance of this Part, we shall consider six central problems that must be dealt with in any comprehensive theory of revelation. These chapters will further illustrate the tensions among the models and the value of the symbolic approach for achieving a balanced solution.

As a conclusion to the entire work, Chapter XVI will return, in the light of the preceding analysis, to the questions raised in Chapter I. We shall there reexamine the function of revelation in relation to the faith of the individual, the mission of the Church, and the practiceof Christian theology. We shall at that point consider more closely whether and how the objections to revelation in Chapter I can be answered.

## Chapter II

# THE USE OF MODELS IN REVELATION THEOLOGY

## 1. *Recent Trends in Revelation Theology*

For several reasons no attempt will be made in this volume to give a survey of the ideas of revelation found in the Bible and in the history of Christian theology. The present author has already published a brief history of the theology of revelation,[1] and although there would be much to add to that sketch, the additions would involve rather lengthy inquiries that could be distracting in a study devoted to current systematic questions. Furthermore, as indicated in that work, the biblical authors and theologians prior to the sixteenth century rarely used the term "revelation" in the modern sense as a technical concept to designate whatever is needed to make something a matter of divine and Christian faith.

In the older authors revelation (in Latin, *revelatio,* and in Greek, *apocalypsis*) is usually understood as an extraordinary psychic occurrence in which hidden things are suddenly made known through mental phenomena such as visions and auditions. Revelation, in that restricted sense of the term, is an ingredient of many religions, from the most primitive to the most sophisticated, and continues to attract the attention of those interested in what is today called "private revelation."[2] In the Bible and in church teaching revelations in this latter sense are frequently mentioned, but they are hardly central to the faith of Israel as a people or to the self-understanding of the early Church. What we would today call revelation is connected rather with God's self-manifestation through historical events and persons, and especially, for Christians, with Jesus Christ. Although these events and persons may not be revelation except when interpreted in a particular way, the power so to interpret the events is not commonly called revelation by the biblical writers or by the classical theological tradition. If we today say that the events together with their interpretation are revelation, that is because we are drawing on certain modern conceptions of revelation, which must first be justified. For a systematic treatment, therefore, it seems best to begin with contemporary theology. In the light of a systematic conception of revelation the biblical scholar or the church historian can then find elements of a theology of revelation in the Bible and in the ancient and medieval theologians.

A word may perhaps here be said about the emergence of the technical concept of revelation in modern times. With some foundation in fourteenth-century Scholasticism, the scholastic theologians of the sixteenth century began to use the term "revelation" by preference not to designate a specific action on the part of God but rather an objective deposit of truth which Christians accepted as simply given to the Church. For the Catholics of the Counter Reformation this deposit included everything that the Church taught as requiring acceptance in the name of Christ. For their Protestant contemporaries, this "given" was rather the word of God in Holy Scripture. Because the controversies of the time focused attention primarily on the content of revelation, and on the means whereby revelation was transmitted, neither the Protestants nor the Catholics of the sixteenth century showed any great interest in analyzing the process by which revelation initially occurred. The theological treatise on divine revelation had yet to be born.

Whereas in the sixteenth century Protestants and Catholics had been in polemical confrontation with each other, in the following two centuries the treatise on revelation was developed apologetically by Protestants and Catholics as they joined forces to resist the rationalism of the Deists. The Deists held that all the essential truths of religion were knowable by reason unassisted by supernatural revelation. Orthodox Christians were concerned to stress the insufficiency of the natural religion derived by analysis of the order of creation, and to insist on the necessity of a supernatural revelation given by God at particular times and places. While bringing greater clarity to the distinction between the natural and supernatural orders, the apologetics of this period did not notably advance the systematic understanding of revelation.

In the nineteenth century the battle for the orthodox concept of revelation was joined on two fronts. The first set of adversaries were the agnostics who, under the influence of Immanuel Kant, argued that human knowledge was necessarily restricted to the phenomenal order and that the transcendent could not be known, even through revelation. In the Kantian tradition—represented in some ways by Friedrich Schleiermacher—there was a tendency to stress faith rather than revelation and to depict faith as a sentiment or practical decision having little or no cognitive import.

The second set of adversaries, represented by J. G. Fichte, G. F. W. Hegel, and others, held that revelation, rather than being a free, supernatural intervention of God, was a necessary phase in the immanent progress of the human spirit toward the fully rational truth of absolute philosophy. In opposition to both sets of adversaries, the orthodox theologians, both Protestant and Catholic, defended the idea of revelation as authentic knowledge gratuitously bestowed on the human race through divine interventions, accredited by prophecy and miracle. For Roman Catholics Vatican Council I (1869–70) was an official endorsement of this theology on the highest level.

In the late nineteenth and twentieth centuries, the theology of revelation, no longer viewed as a department of mystical psychology or as an apologetical prolegomenon to theology, took shape as a comprehensive systematic treatise, foundational for the whole of dogmatics. But as this new treatise emerged, the theologians who specialized in it began to separate into different schools having radically different conceptions of revelation. So numerous are the schools and movements, and so subtle the shades of difference among them, that it is difficult to make general statements about this exceptionally fertile period. While recognizing the crudeness of the categories, we may call attention to the following eight major movements.

1. The first major tendency, which culminated in the early decades of the twentieth century, may be called liberal. Liberal theology, in the Kantian tradition, was antimetaphysical and agnostic as regards the transcendent order. Liberal Protestants such as Wilhelm Herrmann, Julius Kaftan, and Adolf von Harnack looked upon the

appearance of Jesus in history as the datum that enabled practical reason to recognize the obligatory character of the gospel message of love. The gospel in its significance for practical reason was sometimes regarded as revelation. In historians of religion such as Ernst Troeltsch, Rudolf Otto, and Nathan Söderblom, revelation was equated with the experience of the holy. For Christians this experience was most intensely aroused by Jesus Christ, but religiously inclined non-Christians might experience the holy in connection with other symbols.

2. At the turn of the century the Roman Catholic Modernists (Alfred Loisy, George Tyrrell, and others) were influenced by liberal Protestants such as Auguste Sabatier and by Hegelian idealists such as Edward Caird. They tended to look upon revelation as a quasi-mystical experience such as that which occurred in the consciousness of Jesus and in the lives of the apostles who consorted with him. Doctrine, they maintained, is a kind of sedimentation that occurs when revelation is made the object of human reflection. Dogma, for these authors, is always historically and culturally conditioned by the situation in which it is formulated.

3. The novel tenets of liberal and modernist theology, quite predictably, provoked or gave added impetus to conservative movements in the theology of revelation. The strongest reactionary movement on the Protestant side was Fundamentalism, which achieved great popularity in the early decades of the twentieth century. The Fundamentalists insisted that the Bible alone is revelation, that it is to be interpreted in its obvious literal sense, and that it is totally inerrant. Although not adequately described as a Fundamentalist, the Princeton professor, Benjamin B. Warfield, gave intellectual leadership and respectability to the movement.

On the Roman Catholic side, the reaction against Modernism took the form of a number of strongly worded decrees from the Holy See insisting on the supernaturality of revelation and on the sufficiency of the objective signs (miracles and fulfilled prophecies) by which revelation is authenticated. Rome insisted likewise that revelation had a determinate content and that this was faithfully enshrined in the dogmas of the Church. The neo-Scholastic seminary theology of the first half of the twentieth century, heavily influenced by the anti-Modernist documents, supported their teaching and in some cases enriched it with insights drawn from St. Thomas Aquinas and the medieval Scholastics.

4. In the period between the two world wars Karl Barth exercised an extraordinary influence on revelation theology. For Barth and those close to him revelation is an eschatological event in which the eternal is paradoxically present in the historical, the infinite in the finite, the word of God in human words. The great German exegete, Rudolf Bultmann, developed a more existential word-theology, stressing the call to personal decision that comes through the proclamation about Jesus. The work of Barth, Bultmann, and their associates, frequently labeled "dialectical theology," will be examined in Chapter VI.

Paul Tillich, although he had affinities with the dialectical theology of Barth and with the existentialism of Bultmann, was more heavily indebted to the nineteenth-century German idealists, notably Friedrich Schelling. For Tillich symbol rather than word was the primary bearer of revelation.

5. In the years immediately preceding and following World War II, Protestant revelation theology was enlivened by a flowering of biblical theology. Scripture scholars particularly stressed the idea of revelation through certain historical events whereby God addressed his people. As a result many biblical theologians spoke, as did Oscar Cullmann, of revelation through salvation history. Efforts were made to show that the biblical idea of history, as linear and progressive, stood in sharp contrast with the cyclical ideas of history current in pagan antiquity.

6. In the period following World War II, Roman Catholic theology in Western Europe consciously strove to overcome the narrowness of the official Scholasticism. Theologians such as Henri de Lubac, Jean Daniélou, and Hans Urs von Balthasar enriched the theology of revelation with insights derived from the Greek Fathers. Other Catholic theologians developed the theology of revelation in close connection with biblical theology (J. L. McKenzie, L. Alonso Schökel), the theology of preaching (J. A. Jungmann, O. Semmelroth), and the liturgical movement (R. Guardini). All of these tendencies were to prepare for the very positive and forward-looking statements of Vatican II, notably in its Constitution on Divine Revelation (1965).

7. Since the early 1960s the theology of revelation has been affected by a multitude of movements, most of which have not been primarily concerned with revelation as a theme. Particularly significant for our purposes has been the secular theology that seeks to discern the revelation of God not simply in the "sacred" history set forth in the Bible but in the entire cosmos and in the whole of human history. With some indebtedness to Pierre Teilhard de Chardin, Vatican II incorporated aspects of this secular theology into its Pastoral Constitution on the Church in the Modern World. Contemporary theologians such as Edward Schillebeeckx, Johann Baptist Metz, Wolfhart Pannenberg, and Jürgen Moltmann, while differing among themselves on many points, are at one in stressing the relationship of revelation to public and political life. The same may be said of some Latin American Liberation theologians.

8. These progressive trends, however, have been met with a resurgence of conservative theology, especially in biblical Protestantism, during the 1970s. Conservative Evangelicalism, which will be more extensively treated in Chapter III, generally seeks to distance itself from Fundamentalism, while perpetuating some of the concerns of that movement.

## 2. *From History to Typology*

In practice all theologians build on, and at the same time modify, the work of their predecessors. Often they follow, with some variations, the thought of a professor under whom they have studied. In some cases the same individual becomes successively disciple, collaborator, and continuator, as did Thomas Aquinas with regard to Albert the Great, and Melanchthon with regard to Luther.

Not infrequently the theologian combines in an original way the key insights of several predecessors, known to him either personally or through books. Karl Rahner, for example, integrates certain themes from his older Jesuit confrere, Joseph Maréchal, with others derived from Martin Heidegger, under whom he later studied. Paul Tillich synthesized ideas from Friedrich Schelling, on whom he did his doctoral work, with ideas from his own teachers, such as Martin Kähler.

Valuable though these continuing associations sometimes are, they do not necessarily prevent the theologian's fundamental principles from being a matter of chance rather than deliberate choice. When they are free to do so, theologians may wish to make an informed decision whether to locate themselves in any specific theological tradition and, if so, what tradition to opt for. So, too, the student of revelation may wish to make a considered choice between alternative theological positions. This may best be done if, in addition to having a wide exposure to a variety of traditions, one reflects carefully on the agreements and disagreements, arguments and counterarguments propounded in the literature.

Most theologians can be classified according to the way they answer a whole set of interrelated questions. Underlying any theological system is a kind of basic option which predetermines to some extent what answers will be given to a number of particular problems. When a theologian is described as a Liberal, Modernist, Fundamentalist, or whatever, an effort is being made to indicate such a basic option.

In order to sharpen the issues between different tendencies in the theology of revelation it may be helpful at this point to shift from a chronological account, which tells the story, to a typological survey, which attempts to classify the main varieties of revelation theology. Such a typology, abstracting from the particularities of time, place, and circumstance, focuses rather on the structural features of the systems. Although historical contacts among theologians will often, in point of fact, influence them to adopt the same type (or an opposed type), typological similarities and dissimilarities may be noted among theologians who are unaware of one another's work.

Typology has been extensively used in theological literature since the epoch-making work of Ernst Troeltsch, *The Social Teachings of the Christian Churches*.[3] The method is brought to high perfection in H. Richard Niebuhr's classic, *Christ and Culture,* an investigation of how theologians of different ages have assessed the impact that Christian faith should have on a person's relationship to human culture. The method of types, as pursued by Troeltsch and Niebuhr, is extremely valuable for pointing out the issues and choices to be made and the theoretical implications of pure positions. On the other hand, as Niebuhr himself recognizes, the method of types does not do full justice to the complexities of individual positions, many of which cannot be neatly pigeonholed. To quote Niebuhr on this point:

> A type is always something of a construct, even when it has not been constructed prior to long study of many historic individuals and movements. When one returns from the hypothetical scheme to the rich complexity of individual events, it is evident at once that no person or group ever conforms completely to a type. Each historical figure will show characteristics that are more reminiscent of some other family than the one by whose name he has been called, or traits will appear that seem wholly unique and individual. The method of typology, however, though historically inadequate, has the advantage of calling to attention the continuity and significance of the great *motifs* that appear and reappear in the long wrestling of Christians with their enduring problem.[4]

Inasmuch as the types are free theological constructions one cannot give definitive status to any given typology. Most typologies are empirically based in the sense of being derived from actual cases rather than aprioristic considerations. One notes that theologians wrestling with similar questions can be classified in groups according to the answers they give, not only to individual questions but to a whole series of questions, as a result of a certain mindset. The theologians thus fall into clusters with certain common characteristics. Although every major type can be broken down into smaller subtypes, it is usually desirable, in an initial exposition, to propose a relatively small number of types, all of which can be kept simultaneously in mind. The typology will be more successful if the types are sharply delineated, so that their differences are evident, and if each is capable of being characterized by a single orientation or metaphor that gives the key to the positions taken on a large number of questions.

It would be possible to construct a typology of revelation theologies from any of several points of view. One might seek to categorize them according to the epochal changes that marked the transition from one age to another—for example, the patristic, the monastic, the scholastic, the idealistic, the positivistic, and the existentialist.[5] Or one could construct the types according to certain permanent features of human thinking, such as the historical, the rational, and the mystical.[6] Then again, one could classify theologies of revelation in terms of types constructed with a view to another branch of theology—for example, by exploring the implications of various ecclesiological options for the understanding of revelation.[7] In the present work, I should like to propose a set of types specifically adapted to the theology of revelation in the twentieth century. Contemporary systems, in my opinion, may be divided into five major classes according to their central vision of how and where revelation occurs. These five types, to be studied in more detail in the next five chapters, may here be set forth in summary fashion.

1. *Revelation as Doctrine.* According to this view revelation is principally found in clear propositional statements attributed to God as authoritative teacher. For Protestants who accept this approach, revelation is generally identified with the Bible, viewed as a collection of inspired and inerrant teachings. For Catholic representatives of this approach, revelation is to be found, at least most accessibly, in the official teaching of the Church, viewed as God's infallible oracle. The truth of the teaching is held to be recognizable by external signs (miracles and the like), but some proponents of this position, both Protestant and Catholic, regard interior grace as a necessary precondition not only for the response of faith but even for perceiving the force of the evidence.

2. *Revelation as History.* This type of theory, proposed in conscious opposition to the preceding, maintains that God reveals himself primarily in his great deeds, especially those which form the major themes of biblical history. The Bible and the official teaching of the Church are considered to embody revelation only to the extent that they are reliable reports about what God has done. Although some adherents of this approach look upon biblical and ecclesiastical teaching as revelation in a derivative sense, most prefer to say that the Bible and church teaching are rather *witnesses* to revelation.

3. *Revelation as Inner Experience.* For some modern theologians, both Protestant and Catholic, revelation is neither an impersonal body of objective truths nor a series of external, historical events. Rather it is a privileged interior experience of grace or communion with God. Although this perception of the divine is held to be immediate to each individual, some proponents of this position

say that the experience of grace depends on the mediation of Christ, who experienced the Father's presence in a unique and exemplary way.

4. *Revelation as Dialectical Presence.* A number of European theologians, especially in the years following World War I, repudiated both the objectivism of the first two types of revelation theology and the subjectivism of the third. God, they insisted, could never be an object known either by inference from nature or history, by propositional teaching, or by direct perception of a mystical kind. Utterly transcendent, God encounters the human subject when it pleases him by means of a word in which faith recognizes him to be present. The word of God simultaneously reveals and conceals the divine presence.

5. *Revelation as New Awareness.* Especially since the middle of the twentieth century, an increasing number of theologians have felt that the prevalent theories of revelation were too authoritarian, and that the "inner experience" model, which tries to correct this, is too individualist and unworldly. These thinkers hold that revelation takes place as an expansion of consciousness or shift of perspective when people join in the movements of secular history. God, for them, is not a direct object of experience but is mysteriously present as the transcendent dimension of human engagement in creative tasks.

Each of these five typical positions situates the crucial moment of revelation at a different point. For the doctrinal type, the pivotal moment is the formulation of teaching in clear conceptual form. For the historical type, the decisive point is the occurrence of a historical event through which God signifies his intentions. For the experiential type (i.e., the type emphasizing *inner* experience), the crux is an immediate, interior perception of the divine presence. For the dialectical type, the key element is God's utterance of a word charged with divine power. For the awareness type, the decisive moment is the stimulation of the human imagination to restructure experience in a new framework.

The preceding types, although they cannot pretend to cover all possible or actual theological positions, suffice, in my opinion, to indicate the principal issues debated in current revelation theology. By studying the tendencies here signalized, one can gain a sufficient grasp of contemporary theological opinion to check any given proposal against a significant number of alternative points of view. Unless the view can be accommodated by some of these schools, and meet the objections raised by the others, it cannot be regarded as reliable.

The typology here proposed does not rest on the assumption that every living theologian can be neatly pigeonholed within one and only one of the five types. Some of the greatest modern theologians have developed highly personal positions that are difficult to classify. Others combine elements from two or more different types. For example, it is possible to hold that revelation was originally given in ecstatic experiences or in historical events, but that it subsequently became embodied in inspired propositions, the form in which revelation is accessible to posterity. Or one many hold that revelation is never found except in a combination of external events and interpretative words. To understand hybrid positions such as these, it would be advisable first to study the pure positions.

These five types, consciously based on recent Protestant and Catholic theologies of revelation in Europe and the Americas, are not all-inclusive. If the present work had been written in 1900, greater attention would have had to be given to the ethically oriented theology of revelation characteristic of liberal Protestantism. At that time there would have been no possibility of presenting the dialectical model described above. One may reasonably conjecture that fifty years hence the present typology will need to be modified in ways not now foreseeable. Although the types to some extent reflect anthropological constants, they also depend on particular historical trends, and are thus culturally conditioned. A timeless typology based on the invariant structures of God, nature, and history is probably not attainable, since there is no agreement about exactly what is invariant. Even if attainable, such a timeless typology would be too remote from the existing theological proposals to serve our present purposes.

Among the currently developing theological movements, liberation theology holds particular promise of being able to articulate a distinctive theology of revelation. The few references to liberation theology in the following chapters will fall under the rubric of the fifth model. But there is evidence that the conflictual and praxis-oriented character of this theology will cause it to become rather sharply differentiated from the disclosure-oriented evolutionary humanism characteristic of many type-five theologians. Liberation theology is a wide and loosely knit phenomenon that includes Latin Amtrican, Asian, African, Feminist, American Native, American Hispanic, Black, and Ecological variants. Common to them all, as Matthew Lamb says, "is an uncommon attentiveness to the victims of widespread contemporary injustice."[8] These theologians have not as yet elaborated a systematic theology of revelation, though they have made major contributions to the theology of faith and hermeneutics. They seem to assume that God preeminently reveals himself when believers enter into solidarity with the victims of "racism, sexism, classism, militarism, and ecological pollution" and engage in the struggle to transform the social structures responsible for these evils.[9]

## 3. The Types as Models

In constructing types on the basis of the expressed views of individual theologians one is moving from the particular to the universal, from the concrete to the abstract, from the actual to the ideal. The type does not exactly correspond to the thought of the theologians whom it allegedly includes. For one thing, the type is simplified: it omits many qualifications and amplifications which the theologians make. Secondly, the type is schematic: it represents a pure position or ideal case from which any given theologian will presumably diverge at certain points, especially if one considers the full output of the individual over a span of years.

As an ideal case, the type may be called a model. That is to say, it is a relatively simple, artificially constructed case which is found to be useful and illuminating for dealing with realities that are more complex and differentiated. A theological model might in some ways be compared to a tailor's dummy, which represents a woman or man of more or less average stature and build, and therefore assists in the manufacture of clothes. But the clothes, when marketed, do not fit as perfectly as if individually tailored. They usually have to be adjusted to the measurements and tastes of particular customers, who may be judged tall or short, fat or thin insofar as they depart from the normative model. The five types of revelation theology represent five styles which serve to characterize theologians in a rough and approximate way. In using these typical cases as reference points one is treating them as models by which one can submit an indefinitely large class of individual theologians to simultaneous consideration.

Notwithstanding its limitations, a typology of this kind has enormous advantages. Intelligible as a unit, each model can readily be grasped holistically, in such a manner that the details easily fall into place. Not only is this true of the thought of an individual theologian, but the same may be said of all the members of the class to the extent that they are faithful to the model. But great care must be taken in passing from the evaluation of a typical position to that of a particular thinker, who may not be exactly true to type, or to the type as schematically portrayed. The very broad and comprehensive typologies in this book can by no means dispense the reader from more specific study, but they may nevertheless serve to open up issues and alternatives in a helpful way.

Our five types, then, are models in the sense of being schematic prototypes of revelation theology. But there is also a second sense in which they may be called models: At the core of each type is a theoretical model of revelation itself. The model explains, and in some degree conditions, the characteristic theses of the theologians who rely on it.

The concept of theoretical model may be elucidated with the help of Ian Barbour, an author trained both in physics and in theology. A model, he maintains, is an "organizing image" which gives a particular emphasis, enabling one to notice and interpret certain aspects of experience.[10] A distinction must be made between experimental models, which can actually be constructed and used in a laboratory, and theoretical models, which are excogitated with the help of creative imagination, have a merely mental existence, and are used for the development of theories. Experimental models may be either scale models, which reproduce the same structural features as the original, or working models, which do not purport to bear a physical resemblance to the realities of which they are models. Theoretical models are more like working models than scale models, for they do not claim to give a literal picture of the reality under investigation. They are "imagined mental constructs invented to account for observed phenomena" and are used to "develop a theory which in some sense explains the phenomena."[11] Each model suggests a possible and consistent way of thinking about a certain set of problems, but it in no way guarantees the validity of the hypotheses it suggests. If a model has been judged viable by a number of reputable thinkers, the hypotheses it suggests may enjoy a certain presumption in their favor, but any such hypothesis must then be appraised by the methods and criteria proper to the discipline in question.[12]

Theoretical models provide "limited and inadequate ways of imagining what is not observable."[13] The fact that they fail to represent the reality literally and comprehensively does not deprive them of cognitive value. On the contrary, Barbour argues persuasively that theoretical models yield limited but valid knowledge concerning the reality itself.

Theological models are for religion, in an analogous way, what theoretical models are for science. Their purpose is not to present replicas of God or of the divine action, but to suggest ways of accounting for theologically relevant data and for explaining, up to a point, what Christians believe on a motive of faith. The intelligibility of the revealed mysteries depends on their mutual interconnections and upon the analogies between them and what we know without dependence on faith.[14] Like theoretical models in science, theological models cannot prove the truth of what they suggest, but they help to generate hypotheses which are then tested by theological criteria, including the criteria for fundamental theology set forth in Chapter I.

If we credit the widely accepted idea that theology is an attempt to gain some limited understanding of the mysteries of faith,[15] we shall readily concede that no theological model can lead to comprehensive knowledge of its subject matter. Rather, theological systems, with the help of theoretical models, illuminate certain aspects of a reality too complex and exalted for human comprehension. A given system, even though correct in what it affirms, will inevitably fall short of fathoming the mystery of the divine being or the divine activity. The classical theological tradition, with its doctrine of analogy, has consistently maintained this position. Revelation, as a divine mystery, surpasses all that theology can say about it.

If every theological system relies on inadequate theoretical models, the same must be said of our five types of revelation theology. Their differences may partly be ascribed to the facts that they take their departure from different aspects of human cognition and employ different creaturely analogies. More specifically:

In the doctrinal model revelation is understood on the analogy of authoritative teaching. God is seen as an infallible teacher who communicates knowledge by speech and writing. The recipients, as pupils, are expected to be attentive and docile.

In the historical model revelation is depicted as a series of historical events which have given the community of faith its corporate identity. God is represented as the transcendent agent who brings about the revelatory events and by means of them makes signs to his people. Their task is to discern and interpret the signs given in salvation history.

In the experiential model revelation is interpreted on the basis of an immediate interior experience. God is viewed as the divine visitor, the guest of the soul. He communicates by his presence, to which the recipient must be prayerfully open.

In the dialectical model revelation occurs through a powerful, transforming word, such as the proclamation of the Cross and Resurrection. God is the merciful judge, who pronounces an efficacious sentence of condemnation and of pardon. The recipients are obliged to submit obediently to the power of the word, which simultaneously convicts and justifies.

In the awareness model revelation takes the form of a breakthrough in the advance of human consciousness. God reveals by luring the imagination to construe the world in a new way. The recipients of revelation are those who dare to dream new dreams, responding to the call to build a fully human world.

It would be a mistake to suppose that the models differ primarily by reason of the images employed. Within a given model a certain range of images may be appropriate. For example, a theologian using the doctrinal model could depict God as whispering words into a writer's ear, as guiding the hand of an inspired scribe, or as pouring ideas or intelligible representations in the mind of a seer. Just as different images are compatible with a single model, so, conversely, the same imagery can be used in different models. For example, the image of God as speaker is common to both the doctrinal and the dialectical models.

What is constitutive of the models, therefore, is not the imagery but the structural relationships represented as obtaining between the revealer, the recipient, and the means of revelation. These structural relationships constitute what Stephen Pepper has called a "root metaphor."[16] By this term he means a basic analogy chosen as a clue for thinking about a complex or unfamiliar reality. The root metaphor is "the concrete evidential source of the categories" used in framing hypotheses or theories.

The categories in any given theory hang together in sets and mutually corroborate one another through the evidence they gather up. The more adequate root metaphors, according to Pepper, are those that have greater powers of expansion and adjustment to the data. In his study of world hypotheses, Pepper maintains that there have been six prevalent root metaphors—animism, mysticism, formism, mechanism, contextualism, and organicism. Each of these hypotheses generates its own criteria of truth (intellectual authority, immediate certainty, correspondence, nominalism, operationalism, and coherence). The first two hypotheses Pepper judges to be inadequate in terms of comprehensiveness and determinateness. The other four, which are deemed relatively adequate, are in Pepper's estimation reciprocally illuminative and mutually corrective.

What Pepper says of metaphysical models raises a further question about theological models: Are they mutually exclusive or compatible? Are they contradictory or complementary? This question has been much debated with regard to the theoretical models employed in physics. Niels Bohr, as is well known, defended the view that light could be properly, though inadequately, understood with the help of each of two models—the particle theory and the wave theory—though these two models could not be systematically reconciled. "A complete elucidation of one and the same object," he wrote, "may require diverse points of view which defy a unique description."[17] Bohr himself attempted to defend this pluralism of models by appeal to a Kantian agnosticism regarding the relationship between concepts and things.

It would be beyond the scope of this book to take a position regarding the pluralism of models in metaphysics or physics, but in view of what we have said about the divine transcendence, it would seem that something akin to Pepper's or Bohr's pluralism ought not to be antecedently excluded in theology. If all theological models are deficient representations of limited aspects of the mysteries of faith, a variety of models might well prove the best route to theological understanding. For purposes of systematic theology, one may settle on a certain model as being the most fruitful, but this will not require one to deny the validity of what other theologians may affirm with the help of other models. A good theological system will generally recognize the limitations of its own root metaphors and will therefore be open to criticism and correction from other points of view.

These general observations, however, do not imply that all five of our models of revelation are of equal value. Each of them must be studied for itself and assessed with the help of the criteria already laid down. Then a comparison will have to be made among the models to assess their relative strengths and weaknesses in illuminating what may be called the "data" of faith.

As a concluding reflection, it may be noted that the typological approach to revelation has some of the characteristics of a new model, distinct from any of the five we have considered. Recognizing a certain disparity between revelation itself and the articulation of revelation, the typologists point out that all theories of revelation are deficient in comparison with revelation itself, inasmuch as they rely on analogies or metaphors taken from ordinary experience in the world. Revelation, in their judgment, can remain identical with itself, even when being understood and formulated in irreducibly different ways. When asked to speak about revelation itself, they reply that it is in some degree ineffable: every effort to say what revelation is must rely on inadequate metaphors, and therefore falls short of the reality. Revelation is known when it occurs, but this knowledge, given in the depths of the human spirit, should never be confused with statements about revelation. In explaining the relationship between revelation and theories of revelation, the typologists appeal to analogies such as the pluralism of models used in the physical and social sciences.

Typological thinking is characteristic of periods when cultural and ideological pluralism abounds. It tends to go with a somewhat skeptical and critical mentality—one that sees the limitations of every theory and commitment. Characteristically reflective by temperament, typologists seek to avoid the fray and reconcile the warring parties. Conscious of the partial perspectives of others, they wish to keep their options open. In their efforts to mediate, typologists are likely to find themselves rejected by all who are firmly committed to one or another of the particular models.

## Chapter III

# MODEL ONE: REVELATION
# AS DOCTRINE

It seems appropriate to begin with the theory that is most familiar because of its long history and its unchallenged predominance in the recent past. Elements of the doctrinal, or propositional, model of revelation may be traced back to the rabbinic theories of inspiration in late Judaism and to the early church Fathers, some of whom were influenced by rabbinic lore. But it would be too much to claim that this theory was dominant in patristic times or in the Middle Ages, for during these periods revelation was often depicted in more dynamic and less verbal terms. In the late Middle Ages, propositionalism was stimulated by the excessive application of syllogistic logic to theology. In the sixteenth century the tendency was further abetted by the Humanists' enthusiasm for textual criticism and for antiquity, with the result that humanistic theologians came to look upon revelation as a verbal deposit to be reconstituted by antiquarian research. In the seventeenth and eighteenth centuries, when revelation was denied by the Deists and defended by orthodox Christians, the propositional concept was chiefly at issue. Infected somewhat by the very rationalism they were seeking to refute, the orthodox commonly portrayed revelation as a body of clear and distinct ideas from which conclusions could be deduced, as the Westminster Confession put it, "by good and necessary consequence." In the nineteenth and twentieth centuries, when nonpropositional theories of revelation became widespread, Christians who adhered to the propositional view came to be known as conservatives. They frequently deplored Liberalism and Modernism as subversive of the true faith.

In this chapter we shall examine two forms of the propositional model current in the twentieth century: Conservative Evangelicalism and Catholic neo-Scholasticism.

## 1. *Conservative Evangelicalism*

During the nineteenth and twentieth centuries the propositional view of revelation was expounded at Princeton Seminary by a series of brilliant Presbyterian theologians, most notably Benjamin B. Warfield (1851–1921). Today the theory is defended in the English-speaking world by a large number of Evangelical theologians, including Gordon H. Clark, James I. Packer, John Warwick Montgomery, and Carl F. H. Henry. The views of this school are aggressively propagated by organizations such as the International Council on Biblical Inerrancy, which in 1978 sponsored the four-thousand-word "Chicago Statement on Biblical Inerrancy."

While fully recognizing the great variety of schools that can be included under the rubric of Evangelicalism, we shall here use the term "Conservative Evangelical" to designate primarily theologians of the orientation just described.[1] Terms such as "biblical orthodoxy" and "evangelical orthodoxy" are sometimes used as virtual synonyms for the system of which we are speaking.

Notwithstanding some individual variations, these Conservative Evangelicals would generally subscribe in broad outline to the following summary, based chiefly on Warfield. In principle God makes himself known through nature, so that one may speak in a certain sense of natural (or "general") revelation, available always and everywhere. But because of the transcendence of God and the devastating effects of original sin, human beings do not in fact succeed in attaining a sure and saving knowledge of God by natural revelation or natural theology. The self-manifestation of God through nature has as its principal result that those who fail to know and worship God are without excuse (cf. Rom 1:20). For effective knowledge of the salvific truth, supernatural (or "special") revelation is necessary. This supernatural revelation was imparted in early biblical times by theophanic phenomena and prophetic visions, but as the revelation progressed it took on to an increasing degree the form of doctrine. In the final period, revelation characteristically occurred through a "concursive operation" whereby the Holy Spirit inspires and controls human powers as they are exercised in historical research, logical reasoning, and literary composition.[2]

Jesus Christ brings to a climax supernatural revelation in all its forms. In his incarnate life he is the appearance of God par excellence, and in that sense a divine epiphany. Prophecy is supereminently his, from whom the Father withholds no secrets. And he reasons and speaks with the assistance of the Spirit of Truth, given to him in fullness.[3]

The apostles received revelation most determinately in the teaching of Jesus himself—a teaching they were later able to interpret by the assistance of the Spirit given at Pentecost. We today no longer receive revelation through the prophets, through Jesus Christ, or through the apostles as living mediators, but we are not for that reason left without revelation. The prophetic and apostolic teaching has been gathered up for us in the Scripture. The Bible, according to Warfield, contains the whole of revelation and is itself the final revelation of God.[4]

The inspiration of Scripture, although not synonymous with revelation, is closely connected with it. Revelation, in the sense of occurrence, is the initial communication of information or understanding to the original recipients, whereas inspiration is the divine impulse and assistance accorded so that revelations previously received may be suitably and accurately consigned to writing. For Warfield "revelation is but half revelation unless it be infallibly communicated; it is but half communicated unless it be infallibly recorded."[5] The Bible as a whole and in all its parts is so inspired that, in the original manuscripts, it is entirely free from error and is God's written word. For us who come in postbiblical times the Bible is objectified revelation. Read as a whole, the Bible interprets itself, and thus there is no need of any infallible norm or organ of interpretation outside the Bible.

It might seem that the propositional theory of revelation could stand if only some assertions of Scripture were the word of God, but with near unanimity the Conservative Evangelicals affirm plenary verbal inspiration. If a single statement of the Bible were not covered by inerrancy, the whole doctrine of inspiration on which the theory rests would be called into question, and a new criterion for revelation would have to be sought. Thus Clark Pinnock, as recently as 1971, could say that limited inerrancy is a slope rather than a platform on which to stand.[6] Some centuries earlier, Johann Andreas Quenstedt formulated the "domino argument" very sharply:

> If anything had been written in the canonical books in a human manner or by human industry, and not by divine inspiration, then the reliability (*firmitas*) and certainty of the Scriptures would be endangered, and the authority of the Scriptures, which is *uniformiter divina,* would be lost, and our faith would be shaken.[7]

Similarly, Abraham Calov argued in the seventeenth century that if the Bible were not infallible in its totality, the source of theology would have only probable value, and hence all theological conclusions would be thrown into doubt.[8]

Revelation, for these orthodox Evangelicals, is thus equated with the meaning of the Bible, taken as a set of propositional statements, each expressing a divine affirmation, valid always and everywhere. What God has revealed, they insist, is truth and is capable of being communicated to human minds through articulate speech. Carl Henry, for example, states that God is revealed "in the whole canon of Scripture which objectively communicates in propositional-verbal form the content and meaning of all God's revelation."[9] Elsewhere he states: "God's revelation is rational communication conveyed in intelligible ideas and meaningful words, that is, in conceptual-verbal form."[10] He approvingly quotes Gordon Clark as asserting: "Aside from imperative sentences and a few exclamations in the Psalms, the Bible is composed of propositions. These give information about God and his dealings with men."[11] Francis Schaeffer agrees: "God has spoken in a linguistic propositional form, truth concerning himself and truth concerning man, history, and the universe."[12] Clark Pinnock similarly affirms: "Revelation is enshrined in written records and is essentially propositional in nature."[13] James I. Packer insists that this position is well grounded in the theological tradition: "From the earliest days of Christianity, the whole Church regarded the Bible as a web of revealed truths, the recorded utterances of God bearing witness to himself."[14] Elsewhere Packer asserts that "the biblical position is that the mighty acts of God are not revelation to man at all, except in so far as they are accompanied by words to explain them."[15]

Conservative Evangelicalism, in the sense in which the term is here used, may almost be defined by its commitment to the Bible as the only infallible guide for Christian belief and practice. Within the movement, however, there are various views about inerrancy.[16] Some representatives, such as Harold Lindsell, hold for the inerrancy of the original manuscripts (called "autographs") and also for a grace of preservation whereby the Holy Spirit protects certain received texts from error. Others, such as Carl Henry, insist on the inerrancy of the autographs, but grant that there can be minimal errors of an unessential kind in the transmission of the texts. A third position, taken by Clark Pinnock, defends the inerrancy of the textual intention but not that of the specifics of the text. A fourth view, typified by Bernard Ramm, holds for inerrancy only in "soteric knowledge," but not in historical and scientific matters. A fifth school, somewhat marginal to Conservative Evangelicalism, holds that the Bible is inerrant in its major theological assertions but not in all matters of religion and morality, let alone science and history. Donald G. Bloesch and Paul K. Jewett fall essentially in this last category. None of these five positions understands inspiration as strict verbal dictation from God.

Thanks to the process of "inscripturation," according to theologians of this orientation, revelation is embodied in definite written statements which can make a determinate claim on our assent. Faith they interpret primarily in intellectualist terms as an assent to revelation. "Faith in all its forms," writes Warfield, "is a conviction of truth, founded as such, of course, on evidence."[17] Gordon Clark is even more emphatic: "Christianity cannot exist without the truth of certain definite historical propositions. . . . [B]y faith we *understand* that God created the universe; by faith we *assent* to the proposition that God is a rewarder of those that diligently seek him; by faith we know that Jesus rose from the dead."[18] Carl Henry is of the same mind. "Faith divorced from assent to propositions," he declares, "may for a season be exuberantly championed as Christian faith, but sooner or later it must become apparent that such mystical exercises are neither identifiably Christian nor akin to authentic belief."[19]

Coming principally out of the Calvinist tradition, Conservative Evangelicals do not overlook the role of the Holy Spirit in the inspiration and interpretation of the Bible, but they are on guard against the tendencies of some neo-Calvinists to pit the Spirit against the biblical word. The inner testimony of the Spirit, they maintain, enables the biblical books to be identified as the word of God, and assists in the interpretation of difficult passages. "But to make the fact of illumination and the need of appropriation a reason for compromising the perspicacity of scriptural teaching is," according to Henry, "unjustifiable."[20] "Revelation," he asserts, "is derived from the Bible, not from experience, nor from the Spirit as a second source alongside and independent of Scripture, unless we presume to share the office and gifts reserved for prophets and apostles."[21]

## 2. *Catholic Neo-Scholasticism*

In the Roman Catholic theology of the period from about 1850 to about 1950, a theory of revelation having many points of similarity with the Conservative Evangelicalism just examined became all but universally dominant. Most fully set forth in the neo-Scholastic textbooks of the period, this type of theology is exemplified by authors such as Reginald Garrigou–Lagrange, Christian Pesch, and Hermann Dieckmann. The conciliar and Roman documents of the period, drafted by leading theologians of the Roman school, gave official support to neo-Scholasticism, as may be seen from the Constitution on Catholic Faith issued by Vatican Council I (1870), the anti-Modernist documents issued from Rome in the years 1907–10, and Pius XII's encyclical letter, *Humani generis* (1950). As we shall see in subsequent chapters, the Second Vatican Council backed away from some of the characteristic emphasis and tenets of neo-Scholasticism.

Like the Protestant Evangelicals, the neo-Scholastics distinguish between two kinds of revelation, natural and supernatural. "Natural revelation," says Pesch, "is given by deeds (*per facta*); supernatural by words. By deeds even things manifest themselves, but only persons do so by words."[22] When they use the word "revelation" without qualification, these authors are referring to supernatural revelation.

Contemplating the order of nature (and thus on the basis of what some call "natural revelation"), it is possible for human beings, even in their present fallen condition, to know by reason the existence of the one personal God, creator and last end of all things. But because it is very difficult for unaided reason, since the Fall, to achieve certain and accurate knowledge concerning God and the truths of natural religion, supernatural revelation of these truths is for most people a practical necessity. Such revelation, moreover, is absolutely necessary in order for anyone to know strict mysteries, such as the doctrines of the Trinity and the Incarnation. Without revelation, therefore, the human race would remain ignorant of its true end and of the means whereby that end is to be achieved. Revelation, consequently, is necessary for salvation.[23]

A cardinal tenet of neo-Scholasticism, as of Protestant Evangelicalism, is that supernatural revelation transmits conceptual knowledge by means of words (or speech). Dieckmann, following Pesch, asserts that in revelation God "communicates to men something of what he knows."[24] "Speech," Dieckmann goes on to say, "is the act whereby one directly manifests to another one's own thought. . . . This manifestation of the divine thought (*mentis divinae*) is by its nature *intellectual* and conceptual; it has truths as its object and cannot be perceived by man except through the intellect, although perhaps it may be proposed to him by means of certain images."[25] Revelation, Dieckmann concludes, cannot be a mere experience of feelings aroused by the innate religious sense, nor can it be given through inarticulate groans or interjections, for these signs do not convey conceptual or intellectual knowledge.[26] Revelation, therefore, may be defined as "God's speech to men" (*locutio Dei ad homines*).[27]

In revealing, Dieckmann then asserts, God acts as authoritative witness and in that sense as teacher. God asks for assent to his word on the basis of his authority.[28] Other manualists in the same tradition agree. Unlike illumination or infused knowledge, they assert, revelation implies acceptance of the ideas of another, manifested through intelligible speech.[29]

Many neo-Scholastic authors, like Dieckmann, derive the verbal-conceptual nature of revelation primarily from an abstract analysis of the concept of revelation in general. Others, however, proceed more positively on the basis of what church documents have to say about supernatural faith. They quote, for instance, the statements of Vatican Council I about the "word of God" as offering the content of faith: "All those things are to be believed with divine and Catholic faith which are contained in the word of God, written or handed down (*in verbo Dei scripto vel tradito*), and which the

Church, either by a solemn judgment, or by its ordinary and universal magisterium, proposes for belief as having been divinely revealed."[30] The Anti-Modernist Oath (1910) likewise asserts that faith is "a genuine assent of the intellect to truth externally communicated by hearing, whereby, on the authority of the all-truthful God, we believe as true what has been said, attested, and revealed to us by the personal God who is our Creator and Lord."[31]

In their discussions of faith, these authors analyze how the individual achieves certitude regarding the fact of revelation. They insist that the decision to believe is a reasonable one, even though the contents of word-revelation cannot be directly proved to be true. As the principal grounds of credibility, they point to miracles and fulfilled prophecies.[32]

The external signs of revelation, the neo-Scholastics generally concede, cannot give more than a moral certitude (sometimes called "probable certitude") regarding the fact of revelation, even for believers who have sufficient intelligence and education to appreciate the force of the evidence. How then can the act of faith be supremely certain, even in the case of uneducated believers? To answer this vexing question, many of the neo-Scholastics go back to the teaching of the medieval Scholastics, especially Thomas Aquinas, on the working of interior grace in the soul of the believer. God, they assert, produces in the will a supernatural "instinct" or connatural inclination toward the divine. Those who follow this supernatural dynamism receive an infused "light of faith" enabling them to discern what is truly of God.[33] Although the light of faith plays a vital role in bringing revelation home to the individual believer, this illumination, according to the neo-Scholastics, is not speech and consequently is not revelation. Not distinctly perceived by introspection, the light of faith is a theological postulate to account for the certitude of faith. If this light can in any sense be said to be revealed, the revelation of it is contained in the verbal testimonies of Scripture and tradition.

Revelation, in this system of theology, is taken both in an active and in an objective sense. Actively, it means the whole process by which the deposit of faith was built up in biblical times, including prophecy, inspiration, and the teaching of Jesus. Secondarily, or by extension, revelation means the process by which the revealed deposit is communicated to believers in postapostolic times (mediate revelation). Objectively, revelation signifies the deposit itself—that is to say, the body of propositional truth contained in Scripture and apostolic tradition. This revelation was committed to the Church, and is authoritatively taught by pastors of the Church, who speak in the name of Christ himself and are to be implicitly believed, according to the biblical maxim, "He who hears you hears me" (Lk 10:16). The ecclesiastical teaching office (or "magisterium") is the proximate and universal norm for determining what is of revelation.[34] When the universal magisterium (consisting of the pope and the bishops who teach in unison with him) teaches something as a dogma, its teaching is infallible, since Christ has promised not to desert his followers in their exercise of their ministry. One must therefore believe the dogmas as though they were uttered by Christ himself. In equating the dogmas of the Church with divine revelation the neo-Scholastics are faithful to their propositional understanding of revelation. The concept of dogma as a divinely revealed truth serves in turn to reinforce the propositional view of revelation.

The magisterium, in its official teaching of the faith, is bound to the apostolic deposit of revelation, contained in Scripture and tradition. It teaches authoritatively what is to be found in the deposit, so that there is normally no need to verify whether the magisterium has correctly understood the deposit. Scholars themselves must defer to the official magisterium.[35]

With regard to the status of Scripture, the Catholic neo-Scholastics essentially agree with the Conservative Evangelicals. They take their departure from the declaration of the First Vatican Council (1870) that the books of the Old and New Testament, "with all their parts . . . are held to be sacred and canonical because, having been written by the inspiration of the Holy Spirit, they have God for their author and as such were entrusted to the Church."[36] It would be quite impossible, they hold, for God to be the author of any error.[37] A representative manualist can therefore propound the following thesis as one that all Catholics are bound to accept on a motive of divine faith: "All declarations (*sententiae*) of Scripture are infallibly true."[38] Even when a biblical writer, moved by the charism of inspiration, writes down something previously learned by him through natural means without revelation, the literary product becomes the written word of God, and is revelation to those who read it. God speaks to the Church and its members through the Bible as his written word.[39]

Rejecting the Protestant view that the Bible is self-sufficient and complete, the neo-Scholastics generally hold that revelation is contained in two sources, namely the Bible and apostolic tradition—both of which are to be esteemed, in the phrase of the Council of Trent, "with the same sense of devotion and reverence."[40] Tradition is held to supplement and clarify the truths contained in the Bible. A typical neo-Scholastic manualist defines tradition as "the collection of revealed truths which the Church has received through the apostles in addition to inspired Scripture and which it preserves by the uninterrupted continuity of the apostolic teaching office."[41] The magisterium, drawing on tradition as well as on Scripture, can dogmatically define truths that are not given, or at least not clearly given, in Scripture.

## 3. Summary

In summary, then, the propositional theory maintains that supernatural revelation is given in the form of words having a clear propositional content, and that such revelation is necessary for salvation, since it enables us to know about God's saving dispensation in Jesus Christ and thus, as the neo-Scholastics put it, to choose apt means to our last end. Objectively considered, the revelation is identical with the prophetic-apostolic deposit committed to the Church. This deposit is held to consist, at least partly, of the canonical scriptures which, as a collection of inspired and inerrant propositions, are to be accepted with implicit faith. To this doctrine of Scripture, which it shares with Evangelical Protestantism, Catholic neo-Scholasticism adds that there is a second apostolic source, namely tradition, which both supplements and interprets the Bible. For the neo-Scholastics, the authoritative magisterium of the Church can proclaim as divinely revealed certain propositions not clearly taught in the Bible, but found in the apostolic deposit with the help of living tradition.

The appropriate response to revelation, according to both Conservative Evangelical and neo-Scholastic theologians, is faith in the sense of a firm assent to the revealed truths contained in the authori-

tative sources. For both groups, that faith is the work of the Holy
Spirit in the hearts of believers. The neo-Scholastics and very many
Evangelicals hold in addition that faith is not blind but is a reason-
able act resting on external signs of credibility.

## 4. Merits of the Propositional Model

Before turning our attention to other perspectives on revelation
we may weigh some of the strengths and weaknesses of the model
just considered, keeping in mind the criteria proposed in Chapter I.
The propositional model stands up well in terms of its faithfulness to
tradition, its internal coherence, and its practical advantages, but
less well when judged by other standards.

In the first place, the theory may be said to have a certain foundation in the Bible, which frequently speaks as though God deliv-
ered messages in human language. In the Old Testament, the Law
and the prophets are treated as God's word. At many points in the
New Testament, statements from the Old Testament are cited as the
word of God. While there is no cogent proof that every passage
from Scripture is regarded as God's word, many biblical passages
are quoted as if God said what the Bible said. Whenever the Bible is
cited, it is treated as a peremptory authority.

Further, the propositional understanding of Scripture can claim
some basis in tradition. In their use of Scripture the Fathers and
doctors of the Church show a tendency to treat individual biblical
statements without reservation as the word of God. From the Reformation until the nineteenth century, both Protestants and Catholics
were almost unanimous in accepting propositional views of revelation and in treating the Bible as a collection of divine oracles.

The propositional theory does not lack internal coherence.
Once the premises are granted, the whole theory follows with a certain inevitability. This, in turn, makes for a measure of theoretical
fruitfulness. The propositional model provides firm doctrinal standards, so that the orthodoxy and heterodoxy of theological opinions
can be measured with relative ease by reference to agreed and objective standards of revealed truth. Partly for this reason, the propositional model was cherished by the polemical theologians of the sixteenth and seventeenth centuries, when deductive argumentation was

much in favor. The Bible was seen as a "divine armory" of revealed truths.

The propositional model, especially in its Protestant Evangelical form, provides the basis for a rather simple theological method. In the words of Carl Henry:

> Christian theology is the systematization of the truth-content explicit and implicit in the inspired writings. It consists essentially in the repetition, combination, and systematization of the truth of revelation in its propositionally given biblical form. The province of theology is to concentrate on the intelligible content and logical relationships of this scripturally given revelation, and to present its teaching as a comprehensive whole.[42]

Theology, then, has the task of systematizing the data of revelation, defending them against adversaries, and spelling out their logical implications. Speculative theology becomes a "science of conclusions," with premises taken from Scripture or, in the case of neo-Scholastics, from church dogma. Such a theology was particularly well suited to the era of rationalism, when the Church found itself under external attack from defiant unbelievers. Theology in this mode has a certain "scientific" appearance and is not subject to the ambiguities of a discipline without solid premises.

Among the most striking advantages of this model are its practical fruitfulness for the unity and growth of the Church. It encourages loyalty to the foundational documents and traditions of the Church and thus gives the members a clear sense of identity. The propositional model also promotes a sense of solidarity, drawing all true believers into manifest unity by their acceptance of the same divinely revealed doctrines. Churches which accept the propositional model are in a good position to maintain orthodoxy, since their doctrines are considered immune from human contestation, and they are also able to exclude dissenters, who are considered to deviate from the divinely given rule of faith.

Finally, this model fosters a lively sense of mission. It underscores what is unique and distinctive about Christianity and consequently does not leave the faithful in doubt about what they have to proclaim. For those who accept it, the propositional model facilitates full commitment to biblical and ecclesiastical teaching and makes it relatively easy to give a clear account of one's faith. Inasmuch as the conservative churches adhere to this model, it is not surprising that these churches have been able to grow, in some cases rapidly, while many of the more liberal branches of Christianity, having less clarity about revelation, have been losing adherents.[43]

## 5. Criticisms of the Propositional Model

Notwithstanding these considerable strengths, the propositional model has been waning in popularity, except perhaps in Conservative Evangelical circles, where the propositional inerrancy of the Bible is currently a matter of debate. In Roman Catholicism the neo-Scholastic theology that was dominant in the late nineteenth and early twentieth centuries has gone into a severe and possibly irreversible decline. Commenting on the general theological scene, an ecumenically open Protestant, writing a little more than a decade ago, felt entitled to assert: "No proposition would gain wider acceptance than the following one: the *content* of revelation is not a body of propositions to be accepted as the condition of faith."[44] Let us examine some of the reasons that have contributed to this state of opinion.

Although the propositional model claims to be well grounded in Scripture and in the constant beliefs of the Christian community, one may question whether it is truly faithful to either Scripture or the pre-Reformation tradition. The Bible, in this approach, is viewed principally as a collection of propositions, each of which can be taken by itself as a divine assertion. In spite of the efforts made to prove the contrary, the Bible does not seem to claim such propositional infallibility for itself. Nor did the ancient and medieval exegetes, for the most part, hold to the narrowly literalistic views espoused by twentieth-century conservatives. The church Fathers and their medieval followers, by and large, were open to a great variety of allegorical and spiritual interpretations that went well beyond the literal meaning of isolated propositions, and sometimes even bypassed the literal sense.

Essential to the propositional model, in the form here considered, is the thesis that every declarative sentence in the Bible, unless the contrary can be shown from the context, is to be taken as ex-

pressing a revealed truth. To this the neo-Scholastics add that whatever the Church, by its universal magisterium, declares to be
revealed is in fact revealed. These theses, in an age of critical thinking, are commonly felt to lack plausibility.

Modern biblical criticism calls attention to the great variety of
literary forms and conventions in Scripture. It has reclassified many
of the so-called historical books of the Bible under rubrics such as
saga, drama, and historical fiction, and points out the close relationship between the Gospels and the preaching of the early Church.
Critical scholarship establishes that even passages that profess to be
historical are shot through with poetic, legendary, and mythical elements, and that the biblical authors differ considerably among themselves in their religious views. Modern advances in science and historiography make it well-nigh impossible to use the Bible any longer
as an authoritative source of scientific and historical information, as
was done in the precritical era.[45]

The neo-Scholastic form of the propositional theory, since it
concurs with the conservative Protestant estimate of the Bible, is in
no better position to meet the mounting evidence against the propositional inerrancy of Scripture. In some ways it makes the problem
more acute by adding two other infallibilities—those of tradition
and of the magisterium. In the light of serious historical study it is
hard to maintain that popes and councils, even when solemnly
defining articles of faith, have escaped the limited horizons of their
day.[46] If one admits that the definitions cannot be accepted at face
value, but are subject to reinterpretation, one has already abandoned
the objectivist concept of truth that underlies the propositional
model. Contemporary hermeneutics, without necessarily abandoning
every kind of inerrancy or infallibility, seeks to achieve fidelity to
the given without rigid adherence to the approved verbal-conceptual
formulations.

More generally, one may say that the propositional model rests
on an objectifying theory of knowledge that is widely questioned in
our time. In communications, propositions play a rather modest
part. Even declarative sentences often communicate more by their
suggestive power than by their logical content. What is more important, even propositions depend for their meaning upon a host of circumstances that can never be adequately stated in propositional

form. I cannot tell what a person means by a statement unless I know something of the person and the situation in which he or she is speaking.

The neo-Scholastic version of the propositional model has the apparent advantage over Protestant biblicism in that it recognizes the importance of tradition as an interpretative medium. But tradition was restrictively understood by the neo-Scholastics as though it consisted primarily in explicit oral teaching. Maurice Blondel rightly protested against this concept.[47] According to the usual conception, he protested, tradition is the transmission, principally by word of mouth, of information and doctrines that happen not to have been written down. If this were the case, tradition would gradually become superfluous as more and more recollections came to be codified in writing. Further, tradition would continually lose credibility with the ever-widening time-gap between the cessation of revelation and the present. To use an example not given by Blondel himself, one might ask how a dogma such as that of the Assumption of the Blessed Virgin, defined in 1950, could be plausibly grounded in explicit oral testimonies coming down from the apostles.

Blondel rightly questioned two presuppositions of this theory of tradition: that "tradition only reports things explicitly said," prescribed, or done, and that "it furnishes nothing which cannot or could not be translated into written language."[48] Such a concept of tradition, Blondel objected, did not account for the esteem in which the Church continues to hold tradition. As a preferable alternative, Blondel presented a dynamic and expansive notion of tradition, in which believers are prepared to achieve new insights through the pursuit of discipleship and engagement in the practices characteristic of committed Christians. More recently Michael Polanyi has emphasized the necessity of tradition as a means of passing on tacit or unspecifiable knowledge. "A society which wants to preserve a fund of personal knowledge," he writes, "must submit to tradition."[49] His concept of tradition, like Blondel's, is diametrically opposed to that found in neo-Scholasticism.

Further objections to the propositional model are made under the heading of its inadequacy to experience. The model is a highly authoritarian one, requiring submission to concepts and statements that have come out of situations radically different from those of the contemporary believer. The propositions in the Bible and in the

Church's tradition are held to be revelation, irrespective of whether they actually illuminate the believer's own situation. In this approach, little appeal is made to the evocative power of the biblical images and symbols; little motivation is given to seek signs of God's presence in one's own life and experience; little allowance is made for the kind of faith that probes and questions.

For reasons such as these the propositional model, in the estimation of many critics, fails to satisfy the quest for religious understanding. It gives theology an assignment and a scope that some regard as far too narrow. The theologian is required to operate within a set of verbal-conceptual formulations that are regarded as divinely revealed. This leads to the kind of theology described by Pius XII in *Humani generis:*

> It is also true that theologians must continually return to the sources of divine revelation, for it is their role to show in what manner the things taught by the living magisterium are found either explicitly or implicitly in Sacred Scripture and in Divine Tradition. . . . For this reason our predecessor of immortal memory, Pius IX, in teaching that the noblest task of theology is that which shows how the defined doctrine of the Church is contained in the sources, was moved by grave reasons to add the words: "in that very sense in which it is defined."[50]

Although no one would deny that theologians may properly bring out the continuity between the ancient sources and the current teaching of the Church, it is widely felt that theology should be open to the possibility that certain teachings of the modern Church are not propositionally in the sources "in that very sense in which they are defined." Theology has a critical task to expose deficiencies in past and present formulations, and a creative task in seeking better ways of expressing the ancient revelation for a new age. In seeking to perform these functions, theologians must give closer consideration to the experience of contemporary Christians than the propositional model encourages them to do.

Finally, it must be mentioned that the doctrinal understanding of revelation has not shown itself favorable to dialogue with other churches and religions. Convinced of possessing the pure and complete deposit, the theologian looks on members of other groups as heretics or infidels. Non-Christians, insofar as their doctrines cannot be traced to sources that Christians recognize as divinely authoritative, are presumed to be deprived of revelation. If Christians are made to feel complacently superior to all others, they can hardly enter into constructive and respectful dialogue with other faiths.

In this chapter we have taken as the target a rather rigid form of the propositional model. In showing the shortcomings of this style of theology we should not be taken as implying that God's revelation is devoid of cognitive value or that the clear teachings of Scripture and the creeds are without grounds in revelation. In later chapters we shall have occasion to retrieve various elements of value that the propositional model has rightly defended, even though perhaps not by the most apt arguments. We shall maintain, as does this model, that revelation does effectively reach the human mind and that it can be grasped, at least in some degree, by human convictions and affirmations.

# Chapter IV

# MODEL TWO: REVELATION
# AS HISTORY

The propositional theories of revelation already examined do not deny that revelation is in some sense historical. Evidently, it occurs in history, for there is nowhere else for revelation to occur. Furthermore, revelation is handed down as a memory from generation to generation, and by treasuring the memory a people can dispose itself to receive an increment of revelation. Finally, the revelation attests and interprets certain historical events, such as the Exodus and the career of Jesus Christ. Still, the propositional model is not in the fullest sense historical, for it denies that the events of sacred history are by themselves revelation, at least for modern Christians. Nothing is revelation unless it is contained in the word of God, understood as propositional speech. God's word, moreover, is held to convey many truths that are not historical facts. It imparts eternal truths concerning God, the soul, and immortality. It tells us not only about the past but about things to come.

Finding the propositional model of revelation too authoritarian and abstract, some theologians of the nineteenth century, followed by a great throng of twentieth-century theologians, have maintained that revelation occurs primarily through deeds, rather than words, and that its primary content is the series of events by which God has manifested himself in the past. John Baillie, writing in 1956, noted "a remarkable breadth of agreement" to the effect that "God reveals himself *in action*—in the gracious activity by which he invades the field of human experience and human history which is otherwise a vain show, empty and drained of meaning."[1] David Kelsey, in 1975, spoke of "a wide-spread consensus in Protestant theology in the past four decades that the 'revelation' to which scripture attests is a self-manifestation by God in historical events, not information about God stated in divinely communicated doctrines or concepts."[2] Looking into the future, James Barr, in 1963, ventured to predict: "Historians of theology in a future age will look back on the mid-twentieth century and call it the revelation-in-history period."[3]

## 1. *Revelation as Event in Anglo-American Theology*

A recurrent theme in this new approach is the priority of event over interpretation. The Anglican archbishop, William Temple, put the case as cogently as anyone.[4] God, inasmuch as he is personal, cannot be adequately revealed through nature but only through persons—that is to say, through actors on the stage of human history. The historical persons and events are the source of any truths which the mind may derive from them. Creeds and doctrines depend upon the prior events of revelation from which they are derived. The events, moreover, are always richer than what can be said about them. An event, definite in itself, can be revelation even though it cannot be adequately represented by propositions about it. Strictly speaking, for Temple, there are no revealed truths. Doctrinal and creedal formulations, for him, are but signposts indicating where revelation is to be found. The same may be said of the Bible itself: it is not revelation but rather the record of revelation. The Bible, moreover, should not be regarded as an inerrant book. For God to preserve all the human authors from error would be contrary to what we otherwise know about the workings of divine providence.

While insisting that revelation occurs primarily in historical events, Temple avoided any crude reduction of revelation to objective history. For the events to be revelation, he held, they must be understood as disclosures of God. Secondarily, then, revelation consists in the illumination of the minds of the prophets to discern what has been manifested. In Temple's words, "The essential condition of effectual revelation is the coincidence of divinely controlled event and minds divinely illumined to read it aright."[5]

A less philosophical but more biblically oriented analysis of revelation, agreeing substantially with Temple's, was offered by the American Presbyterian scholar, G. Ernest Wright, in several books on Old Testament theology. For one of these he chose the title, *God*

*Who Acts,* with the express intention of pointing up the contrast with the more customary expression, "God Who Speaks."[6] Wright deplored the prevalent tendency to think of revelation as infallible doctrine. "The primary means by which God communicates with man," he declared, "is by his acts, which are the events of history."[7] The Bible is thus not primarily the word of God but the record of the acts of God, together with human responses elicited by those acts.

In its core the biblical narrative is a confessional recital of an extraordinary series of saving acts which reveal God's purposes for the whole of human history. Following Gerhard von Rad, Wright traces in Deuteronomy and Joshua the earliest confessions on which the developing faith of Israel was founded. In the New Testament he finds, with the help of C. H. Dodd, primitive kerygmatic sermons which embody the earliest faith of the Church.

In some passages, Wright acknowledges, the Bible does speak of God and his attributes. It celebrates God as holy, righteous, merciful, faithful, and the like. But it does not do so in the style of later Christian dogmatics. Abstract ideas should never be substituted for the living God as the content of revelation. The so-called attributes of God, Wright insists, are concrete descriptions of the ways in which God has directed history.[8] It is the task of biblical theology to bring the Church constantly back to the simple recital of the acts of God as set forth in the biblical narrative.

On the basis of Scripture Wright concludes that God has revealed himself not through diffuse or mystical experiences but by objective historical events.[9] The saving acts of God in biblical history reveal God's purposes for the whole of humanity. This revelational history is not a bare chronicle but an interpreted account in which the interpretations are so basic that they become "integral parts of the acts themselves."[10]

As various critics have noted, Wright's approach, suggestive and stimulating as it is, leaves many questions unanswered. Nowhere does he explain what he means by an "act of God," which he presents as the very kernel of revelation. He leaves rather unclear the process by which the biblical authors moved from the events to the interpretation. The events, he concedes, need interpretation before their true meaning can be understood, and for this reason God "provides each event with an accompanying Word of interpretation."[11] But Wright explicitly asserts that the interpretations are inferences from the events and even that they are the "only possible explanation" available to the Hebrews for the great things that had happened to them.[12] If so, it would hardly seem necessary for God to provide a word of interpretation.

Finally, Wright speaks as though the contemporary reader could establish the nature and attributes of God by the same process he ascribes to the biblical authors. The Bible describes God as gracious, loyal, and forgiving. "We know God is like this," says Wright, "because it is what we infer from what he has done."[13] What is the basis for any such inference? If we cannot trust the biblical interpretation, what resources do we have for asserting the fact that God was active in this history? Wright gives no clear answer.

## 2. Cullmann on Revelation and Salvation History

One of the outstanding biblical theologians of the twentieth century, Oscar Cullmann, holds that the doctrine of revelation is an aspect of what he calls "salvation history"—a term derived from J. C. K. von Hofmann (1810–77) and the Erlangen school. Biblical revelation is the story of God's redemptive dealings with his elect people, issuing in a message of salvation to be carried to the ends of the earth. In dialogue with other contemporary theologians Cullmann has attempted to clarify how the saving events are ascertained and interpreted, and in so doing he has considerably nuanced the idea of revelation as history.[14]

Cullmann distinguishes three moments in the revelation process: the naked event, which is seen by believer and nonbeliever alike; the disclosure of the divine plan to the prophet through the event; and the association of the new event, again in the mind of the prophet, with the earlier revelations in salvation history.[15] Cullmann seems to vacillate between two senses of the term "revelation." Sometimes it means for him the event together with its inspired interpretation, or even the whole chain of events together with their total interpretation.[16] At other times Cullmann uses the term "revelation" more narrowly to signify the enlightenment given to the prophet to recognize and interpret a given event or series of events as disclosive of the divine. The biblical selection and interpretation of events, Cullmann is convinced, has been "Spirit-directed" and thus divinely determined.[17]

Although he allows that the events are, humanly speaking, prior to the interpretation, the interpretation is for Cullmann essential. He denies that the events of salvation history are self-interpreting. For him, as for Temple, the events yield their supernatural significance only when contemplated from the point of view of faith. The faith by which the events are interpreted is something not open to testing by the mere historian; it rests not on historiography but on prophetic revelation. The central affirmations of the Old and New Testaments —that Israel is chosen by God and that Jesus is the Son of God— remain concealed to the historian as such. The Bible, therefore, is not sheer history but rather "revealed prophecy concerning history."[18] The Bible is revelation not because it accurately recounts history from a human point of view but because it narrates and interprets the action of God in history. Where the biblical authors make use of myth, they do so in the service of salvation history, in order to convey the meaning of the historical events.

The books of Wright and Cullmann, in combination with other similar works, made an enormous impact on the theology of revelation, both Protestant and Catholic, throughout the 1950s. Abandoning the framework of scholastic metaphysics, many took up the cry for a return to the concrete, historical, and personalistic categories of the Bible and of the ancient Semitic mentality. We shall later have more to say of the "biblical theology" movement.

A balanced Catholic approach, combining many insights from Cullmann with others derived from the Greek patristic tradition, was developed by Jean Daniélou, who wrote, in his popular *The Lord of History:*

> Thus the substance of the Christian revelation is not in a knowledge of God's existence (which other religions have as well), but in the perception of his activity on the scene of time, his effective interventions in the world of human history. From the Creation to the Resurrection, by way of the choosing of our father Abraham, the Christian revelation is a sacred history, the chronicle of the wonderful works of God, a documentary narrative: alone among the sacred books, the Christian's Bible is not a collection of doctrine but a story.[19]

Building on Cullmann's conception of Christ as the midpoint of salvation history, Daniélou defended the typological exegesis of the Greek Fathers as consonant with the biblical dialectic of prophecy and fulfillment and as in line with the interpretation of the Old Testament given by the authors of the New Testament. In the light of his Catholic understanding of tradition, Daniélou, as we shall later see, differed from Cullmann on the relationship between the Church and revelation.

Since the theory of salvation history was initially broached by the Erlangen school, it has met with persistent criticism from certain schools of historiography. Early in the twentieth century, Ernst Troeltsch objected that the theory unwarrantably postulated, alongside of ordinary history, a second stream of history in which God was supernaturally at work.[20] This second history, according to Troeltsch, was unjustifiably removed from the probings of historical criticism and protected by the security of faith. Modern historical thinking, however, makes it impossible to absolutize any particular portion of history and to isolate it from organic connection with the rest. History, said Troeltsch, is a seamless web in which each event is reciprocally interconnected with all the others. Troeltsch's philosophy of history has proved a fertile source of objections against the supernaturalism of certain recent theories of salvation history, such as those of Wright and Cullmann.

## 3. *Pannenberg: Revelation as History*

In the mid-twentieth century Wolfhart Pannenberg, pressing for a consistently historical understanding of revelation, objected that the nineteenth-century salvation-history school stopped halfway. His critique is more theological than that of Troeltsch:

> The conception of a redemptive history severed from ordinary history, as in Hofmann's view or in the sense of Barth's "primal history," is hardly acceptable on theological grounds, and is judged not to be so in the first instance because of historical presuppositions. It belongs to the full meaning of the Incarnation that God's redemptive deed took place within the universal correlative connections of human history and not in a ghetto of redemptive history, or in a primal history belonging in a dimension which is "oblique" to ordinary history (and intersects it only at that notorious mathematical point which is without extension on the intersected plane), if, indeed, it has not remained in an archetypal realm above the plane of history.[21]

For the reasons just given Pannenberg finds fault also with Cullmann's thesis that "a supplementary, added interpretation is constitutive for the quality of an event as a salvation event and thus for the isolation from profane history of a qualitatively unique *Heilsgeschichte.*"[22]

In opposition to the "salvation history" school, Pannenberg argues for a still closer identification of revelation with history. Revelation, he holds, is not to be found in a special segment of history but rather in universal history—the history of the whole world as it moves to its appointed consummation. The revelatory events do not have to be subjected to a peculiar kind of historiography in order to yield their redemptive meaning. According to Pannenberg the events are self-interpreting: they bear their meaning intrinsically in themselves, and have no need to be elucidated by a supplementary prophetic disclosure. When the events "are taken seriously for what they are," he writes, "and in the historical context to which they belong, then they speak their own language, the language of facts."[23] Hence no special illumination is needed for their meaning to be understood. It suffices that people be able to use their reason in a perfectly natural way. Faith, therefore, does not precede the recognition of revelation, but revelation, as a self-manifestation of God in the public arena of history, elicits the response of faith in the sense of a lively trust and hope in God's saving power.[24]

Holding that revelation never occurs except indirectly through events, Pannenberg denies that God directly manifests himself either through theophanies or by word-revelation. Relying on the biblical scholarship of colleagues such as Rolf Rendtorff and Ulrich Wilckens, Pannenberg insists that God's self-revelation in the Bible is always indirect. The totality of God's activity in history indirectly discloses God himself.

In opposition to the word-theologians, Pannenberg argues that the word of God is revelation only when seen as an aspect of, and in conjunction with, revelatory events. The word may point forward to a future revelation; it may embody a precept which presupposes revelation; or, finally, it may proclaim or record a revelation, as we can see from the kerygma in the New Testament. In none of these cases, however, does word-revelation add anything extrinsic to event-revelation. Historical events have a linguistic dimension, apart from which they would lack determinate significance. In this way Pannen-

berg tries to overcome the dichotomy between event and interpretation, between historical fact and verbal commentary. History,
for him, is essentially the interweaving of events and meanings
within the history of traditions, which is continually being modified
in the process of transmission.[25]

Against Pannenberg it might still be objected that the events are
not of such a character that they establish the reality of the God in
whom Christians place their faith. Pannenberg concedes that this is
true of the events of the history of Israel, such as the Exodus and
the Conquest of Palestine. If we had no more than this to go on,
Yahweh the God of Israel might be regarded as one of a number of
the tribal deities studied in the history of religions. In the Old Testament, therefore, we have only a provisional revelation of the God
who must, so to speak, still prove his full divinity and universal
lordship. This he does in the Resurrection of Jesus—an event which,
taken in the context of prophecy and apocalyptic expectation (the
actual context in which the ministry of Jesus unfolded), cannot be
reasonably interpreted as anything except the anticipation of the end
of the world.[26] Pannenberg can therefore maintain, in opposition to
the historical relativism of Troeltsch, that the Resurrection of Jesus
has universal and unsurpassable significance insofar as in Jesus the
glorious transformation of the cosmos already enters proleptically
into history. Hegel was fundamentally correct in maintaining that
the meaning of universal history cannot be grasped except from the
final outcome. Christian revelation, however, gives us knowledge of
the outcome by its anticipation in the fate of Jesus.

## 4. Summary

The "historical event" approach to revelation may be summarized in terms of content of revelation, its form, the response for
which it calls, and its relationship to salvation. The content is the
great deeds of God in history—events which, seen in their mutual
connection, manifest God as the lord and goal of history. The form
of revelation is primarily that of deeds or events, especially the climactic events of the death and Resurrection of Jesus, in the light of
which the previous history of revelation in God's dealings with Israel is at once confirmed and reinterpreted. The appropriate response is unwavering trust and hope in the God who has conclu-

sively shown his power, goodness, and fidelity to his promises. Those who put full trust in the saving mercies of this God will not be disappointed.

## 5. Merits of the Historical Model

The historical model, as set forth in the preceding pages, has both assets and liabilities. On the credit side we may note the features which its advocates regard as making this model preferable to the propositional. It has the pragmatic religious value that, by virtue of its relative concreteness, it brings the faithful into a more palpable relationship with God. Just as actions are said to be the proper language of love, so the deeds of God manifest his attitudes more powerfully than mere words could ever do, and evoke a deeper personal response. In times of fear and confusion, this type of theology inspires trust in God's providential care.

Secondly, the historical approach picks up certain biblical themes that were underplayed in the propositional model. The historical and prophetic books of the Old Testament, the apocalyptic writings seen as interpretations of history, the Gospels, and the Acts of the Apostles all focus attention on the great deeds by which God has manifested himself to his elect people. It is not surprising, therefore, that the idea of revelation as historical event has appealed to many distinguished biblical scholars such as Wright and Cullmann, Rolf Rendtorff, Klaus Koch, and Ulrich Wilckens. Theologians committed to the historical model have made effective use of certain kinds of biblical theology, and have in turn stimulated biblical theologians to make further progress in their own discipline.

Thirdly, the historical model is more organic than the propositional. The doctrinal theories tend to present revelation as a body of discrete propositions all having identical value as "revealed truths." The event theory, by contrast, points to the total pattern of a history in which the succeeding phases are dynamically linked. The meaning of the events is capable of being formulated in many ways, according to the perspectives and thought-forms of varying cultures, and is constantly subject to reconceptualization. The flexibility, however, does not lead to relativism. Believers of every age and culture can find their identity in relationship to revelatory events that have objectively occurred and have brought with them a new horizon of interpretation. The theory thus preserves the Church's roots in the past and its sense of continuity with its own origins.

Finally, the historical model is less authoritarian than the propositional and consequently more plausible to many of our contemporaries. Believers are not told to submit uncritically to whatever statements appear in the Scriptures, the creeds, and the dogmas of the Church. They are invited to test the traditional doctrines against the events which these doctrines report and interpret. Hence the theory makes room for a moderately critical approach to the data of revelation. The acceptance of revelation is seen not as a blind leap but as a fully reasonable act. Biblical faith commends itself to reason insofar as it gives to history an intelligibility for which philosophy, unaided by revelation, would search in vain. In an age dominated by historical consciousness, historical revelation can offer an answer to a widespread quest for meaning and purpose in history.

## 6. Criticisms of the Historical Model

Measured by the kind of criteria set forth in our first chapter, the historical model of revelation must be said to exhibit some weaknesses, not all of which, of course, are equally present in all versions of the historical approach.

The common affirmation in this approach to the effect that in the Bible revelation is primarily event and only secondarily word has been widely questioned. Benjamin Warfield, writing long before the recent enthusiasm for revelation through events, emphasized the primacy of word over event. The Scriptures, he held, are not content to represent revelation as a constant accompaniment of the redemptive acts of God "giving their explanation that they may be understood. It occupies a far more independent place among them than this, and as frequently precedes them to prepare their way as it accompanies or follows them to interpret their meaning."[27]

Granting this, it may still be asked, of course, whether the prophetic words are revelation in themselves or only call attention to revelation by deed. The Bible represents God as freely communicating with human beings and thereby bestowing knowledge of himself.[28] For example, God is reported as saying to Aaron and Miriam: "Hear my words: If there is a prophet among you, I the Lord make myself known to him in a vision, I speak with him in a dream. Not so with my servant Moses: he is entrusted with all my house. With him I speak mouth to mouth, clearly, and not in dark speech; and he beholds the form of the Lord" (Nm 12:6–8). God's self-disclosure in words and visions is not unrelated to his self-disclosure by deed, but there seems to be no cogent reason for unilaterally subordinating the former to the latter, as though the former could not be revelation in its own right.

While the word of God in the prophetic and historical books is closely related to historical events, this is less true of the Wisdom literature, which Wright himself acknowledged as founding a difficulty against his own theory. In works such as Job, Qoheleth (Ecclesiastes), and the Wisdom of Solomon, history can scarcely be regarded as the controlling category. Sirach (Ecclesiasticus) ranks wisdom as a divine gift higher than prophecy (39:1) and applies to it the vocabulary of revelation (39:6–8; cf. 1:1–6).

It must be acknowledged that much of the biblical material pertaining to God's actions can be called history only in a very extended sense.[29] Stories such as those of the creation, the flood, and the Exodus cannot all be contained under the rubric of history as commonly understood in our time. Even the historical passages pertaining to the kings of Israel and the public ministry of Jesus are so heavily charged with doctrinal and doxological overtones that they scarcely deserve the same name as history in the modern academic sense.

A further difficulty against the historical model is its relatively meager grounding in the earlier theological tradition. The model could scarcely have arisen prior to the emergence of "historical consciousness" as a result of the development of scientific historiography in the nineteenth century. Barr calls attention to this difficulty when he writes:

A theology which organizes itself too exclusively around the idea of revelation through history has some difficulty in establishing its own continuity and identity, in this respect, with earlier stages of the church. For it is certain that our forefathers, emphatically as they understood that Christian faith was implanted in earthly reality, in space and time, flesh and blood, were able to do this without accepting "history" as an organizing bracket in their theology at all.[30]

Barr likewise questions the value of the historical model for ecumenical and interreligious dialogue. The Eastern Orthodox
churches, in his opinion, attach little importance to history as a category. The great religions of the East, he goes on to say, find it
difficult to credit the idea of revelation through history. In seeking to
foster better relationships with these religions, Christians must be on
guard against what might turn out to be yet another form of cultural
imperialism, if the biblical evidence were filtered through the
thought-forms currently in vogue in the West.[31] To this comment of
Barr's one may add that the Eastern heritage might help Western
theology to regain a sense of the permanent and the universal and
thus to prevent the idea of revelation from being swallowed up in
historical relativism.

Turning now to other criteria, we must ask whether the
identification of revelation with historical events is plausible and coherent. Langdon Gilkey, in a probing article, charged that Wright
and others fail to assign any clear meaning to the term "act of God,"
which holds a crucial position in their theories.[32] They apparently
do not believe, as did the older orthodox theologians, that God in-
tervenes to break the normal sequence of created causality, yet they
insist on retaining biblical terminology that arose when it was held
that God did so intervene. After castigating the liberal theologians
for neglecting the objective element in revelation, the salvation history theologians leave the idea of God's mighty deeds as an empty
phrase without specifiable meaning.

Gilkey's objection has some force against authors such as
Wright and Cullmann, who were unconcerned with philosophy, but
one could not rightly conclude from this that the concept of revelation through history, as it functions in modern theology, is incoherent. Among the authors we have mentioned, Temple and Pannenberg have labored to give philosophical precision to the concept of
God's action in history. The same may be said for theologians such
as Adolf Darlap and Karl Rahner, who develop a distinctive concept
of salvation history on the basis of transcendental philosophy.[33]
Gilkey's alternatives of "orthodoxy" and "liberalism" are by no
means the only options.

Pannenberg's case for revelation rests ultimately on the factual
occurrence of the Resurrection as known to historical reason without reliance on faith. In his efforts to prove this, he subjects the bib-

lical testimonies to severe historical and literary criticism. For example, he comments: "The appearances reported in the Gospels, which are not mentioned by Paul, have such a strong legendary character that one can scarcely find a historical kernel of their own in them."[34]

Not surprisingly, Pannenberg's critics express dissatisfaction. Jürgen Moltmann objects:

> The thesis that this event of the raising of Jesus must be "historically" verifiable in principle, would require us first of all so to alter the concept of the historical that it would allow of God's raising of the dead and would make it possible to see in this raising of the dead the prophesied end of history. To call the raising of Jesus historically verifiable is to presuppose a concept of history which is dominated by the expectation of a general resurrection of the dead as the end and consummation of history. Resurrection and the concept of history then contain a vicious circle for the understanding.[35]

From the point of view of Evangelical word-theology, Carl Henry complains about Pannenberg: "His radical criticism of the biblical testimony, including rejection of the virgin birth of Jesus, leaves no secure basis for regarding the resurrection as historical."[36] And from a perspective generally sympathetic to Pannenberg, Carl Braaten observes: "The critique of historical reason, which theologians like Pannenberg and R. R. Niebuhr propose, seems calculated to secure for theology a high degree of objective probability, but at the high cost of complete subjective uncertainty."[37]

Under pressure of criticisms such as these Pannenberg has somewhat modified his position, at least by a change of emphasis. The Resurrection has occurred, but the eschatological transformation of the world is still to come. Within history we have only pointers to the Resurrection. "Only in connection with the end of the world that still remains to come," writes Pannenberg, "can what happened in Jesus through his resurrection from the dead possess and retain the character of revelation for us also."[38] The horizon of eschatological expectation is for us, as for those who lived before the first Easter, a promise to be accepted in trust. If promise is only the *anticipation* of revelation, as Pannenberg sometimes asserts, it would seem that so long as history lasts we are doomed to be deprived of revelation itself. At the moment that Jesus becomes the fulfillment of the promise he passes beyond the limits of history, and is accessible only through signs and testimonies. To complete his theory of revelation, it would seem, Pannenberg must give more explicit attention to the theology of signs, of testimony, and of faith.

Temple and many salvation-history theologians, while insisting that events are primary in revelation, acknowledge that the events are not self-interpreting, even in context, but must be interpreted by a prophetic word which is the result of a special divine illumination. If this be true, it is no longer apparent why primacy must be given to the event. Would it not be better to say that revelation is a complex reality consisting of the inspired word as the formal element and of the historical event as material element? This has been the opinion of many modern Catholic theologians,[39] and seems to be favored by Vatican II, which states in its Constitution on Divine Revelation:

> This plan of revelation is realized by deeds and words having an inner unity: the deeds wrought by God in the history of salvation manifest and confirm the teaching and realities signified by the words, while the words proclaim the deeds and clarify the mystery contained in them.[40]

In the complex theory here proposed neither word nor event is revelation apart from the other. The relationship between the two could be conceived as merely extrinsic, as though each were required in order to supply for a deficiency in the other, whether in credibility or in clarity. According to the Council, however, the two have an "inner unity."

Even philosophically, a strict dichotomy would have to be ruled out. Whenever a person performs a human act, a meaning is expressed, so that the action takes on the character of word. Whenever a person speaks or writes, the body is involved and an impact is made on the world. Word and deed thus participate in one another. "Speech is at once an operation of the intelligence and a motor phenomenon."[41]

In the case of divine revelation, the word of God is never empty. God's word is a creative power that calls being into existence. Any act of God, expressing a divine intention, possesses features of word and of deed alike. Most of all is this true of the act whereby God posits himself in the world as a man: the Incarnation. The Johannine expression, "the Word became flesh" (Jn 1:14), expresses the word-character of the event. And the further statement that the disciples have heard, seen, and touched the "word of life" (1 Jn 1:1) expresses the event-character of the word.

All revelation, inasmuch as it has the two dimensions of intelligibility and embodiment, is both manifestation and accomplishment. The Hebrew term *dabar,* meaning both word and event, suggests this duality.[42] Thanks to the intrinsic correlation between the two dimensions, revelation has a sacramental structure, as we shall see more fully when we turn to the symbolic aspects of revelation in the systematic portion of this work.

# Chapter V

# MODEL THREE: REVELATION
# AS INNER EXPERIENCE

The two previous models have certain common features. Both concentrate on the objective aspects of revelation, which is seen as a divine message communicated either through propositional speech or
through facts having a clear religious significance. In either case, the
revelation terminates in a body of articulate knowledge built up
cumulatively in the course of the history of the people of Israel
down to, and including, the apostles who followed Jesus. This understanding of God's words and deeds was then committed, at least
in part, to writing and was passed down to posterity by the Church.
God's revealing activity, according to both models, came to an end
with the Christ event of the first century.

For various reasons, these models of revelation have met with
mounting criticism since the early nineteenth century. For one thing,
they were felt to offer no satisfactory account of the religious heritage of nonbiblical peoples. Further, they failed to make sufficient
allowance for the immediacy of each generation's religious access to
God. And finally, they seemed to tie the Christian faith too closely
to acceptance of the prophetic and apostolic testimonies reported in
the Bible. These testimonies were felt by some to be unreliable and
by others to be irrelevant to the contemporary religious scene.

## 1. Theologians of the Experiential Type

Not surprisingly, therefore, a number of theologians of the
twentieth century have turned to the religious experience of the

believer as the point of insertion of God's revelatory activity. The concept of religious experience is notoriously pliable and hard to define. What is characteristic of the tendency to be considered in this chapter is the view that revelation is not only to be found in experience but that it consists in an immediate experience of God who inwardly communicates with each believer. The self-revealing God is regarded as making himself present to the consciousness of the individual in a way that minimizes the need for mediation through created signs. Under this heading we shall include theologians of a number of different schools.

One such school is the liberal Protestantism that developed in Germany under the influence of Friedrich Schleiermacher and Albrecht Ritschl. Wilhelm Herrmann, a distinguished representative of this school in the early twentieth century, found revelation primarily in the inner sense of communion with God that is aroused by the image (*Bild*) of Jesus in the New Testament. At the turn of the century, the French liberal Protestant, Auguste Sabatier, developed a more modernistic theory, according to which revelation is the positive manifestation of God in the piety which he himself inspires. Some of the Catholic Modernists of the early twentieth century, such as George Tyrrell, partly influenced by Sabatier, equated revelation with an immediate inner experience of God's redeeming presence. Tyrrell's friend, the Baron Friedrich von Hügel, wrote eloquently of the mystical element in religion, but sought to hold this in balance with the institutional and rational elements.

In the succeeding decades several prominent Anglicans, such as Evelyn Underhill and Dean W. R. Inge, closely identified revelation with the mystical component which they saw as the basis of all religion. The Swedish Lutheran Archbishop, Nathan Söderblom, who was a personal friend of von Hügel, explored the typology of mysticism in various religions. In the United States the idealist philosopher William Ernest Hocking likewise held that all religions are based on a mystical experience, revelatory in character.

In England several prominent Scripture scholars, influenced by liberal Protestant thought, attempted to spell out, on the basis of the biblical accounts, the experiential dimension of prophetic revelation. H. Wheeler Robinson and C. H. Dodd (in his early work) reflected this tendency.

Among contemporary philosophical theologians, the English

Presbyterian John Hick is notable for the cognitive importance he attaches to mystical experience. The great founders of religions, he holds, are persons on whose consciousness the Transcendent has impinged in new ways with special intensity and power. Since the same infinite Spirit presses in continually on every individual, it is possible, Hick contends, for others to find meaning and credibility in what the mystics claim to have experienced.

While avoiding the individualism of the Modernists, Catholic transcendental theology, in the mid-twentieth century, locates revelation primarily in an experience of grace. For Karl Rahner revelation initially occurs in a mysterious experience of communion with God, called in his system "transcendental revelation." The Belgian Jesuit, Piet Fransen, applying Rahner's thought to the theology of grace, holds that inner experience is the focal point where revelation concretely occurs. Rahner and Fransen, since they insist that the transcendental experience of God is nonobjective and is correlative with revelation through word and history (Rahner's "predicamental revelation"), are not typical representatives of the model that equates revelation with inner experience. We shall have to return to Rahner in connection with our fifth model.

## 2. The Form of Revelation

Although the authors just mentioned approach the question of revelation from a variety of perspectives, they speak with surprising unanimity with regard to many of the typical questions discussed in the theology of revelation.

A fundamental principle for all these thinkers is that God is both transcendent and immanent. As absolute and unconditioned, God is immediately present to creation at every point, for "in him we live and move and have our being" (Acts 17:28). Through religious experience (ascribed by some of our authors to a "religious sense" or a "religious a priori") it is possible for the human person to perceive the presence of the divine. The experience of God, insofar as it is God's transforming work in us, may be called grace, and grace, insofar as it brings about a new awareness of the divine, is revelation.

With virtual unanimity these authors reject any dichotomy between natural and revealed religion. Religion, they maintain, always arises out of some particular experience of the divine. Sabatier accordingly contends that the ideas of religion and revelation are correlative and mutually inseparable. "Religion is simply the subjective revelation of God in man, and revelation is religion objective in God."[1] According to Söderblom, "A revelation of God is found wherever a real religion is found."[2] Tyrrell, however, points out that only the passive element of religion is to be ascribed to revelation. The active response, whereby we fashion representations and express them, pertains not to revelation but to religion. Supernatural revelation, Tyrrell maintains, is an exceptional heightening of the normal and universal experiences of the moral and mystical life.[3]

Since experience is always had by particular persons in a here-and-now situation, the experiential model is unfavorable to any sharp distinction between general and special revelation. Initially, Sabatier asserts, revelation comes individually to particular persons and peoples (as special revelation), but it gradually achieves a measure of generality by entering into the mainstream of the common religious vocation of humanity as a whole.[4]

It is almost tautologous, in the view of these theologians, to affirm that revelation is interior. "It will be interior," writes Sabatier, "because God, not having phenomenal existence, can only reveal Himself to spirit, and in the piety that He Himself inspires."[5] Dean Inge insists that revelation is chiefly inner and personal. "All that can be done from outside is to quicken and confirm the revelation in the soul."[6] Herrmann, although he links the experience of revelation to the historical person of Jesus, speaks in somewhat similar tones. The image (*Bild*) of Jesus, he maintains, is not revelation until it acts upon us as something indubitably real.[7] "Any communication whatever we can call a revelation only when we have found God therein. But we find and have God when He so undoubtedly touches and seizes us, that we are compelled to submit ourselves entirely to Him. We experience the revelation of the Almighty in the moment in which we bow ourselves with deep joy under His power," which "is His love."[8]

Rahner, since he insists on the historical and doctrinal aspects of revelation, makes no simple identification between revelation and inner experience. But he does speak of a transcendent moment or dimension of revelation. By this he means the self-communication of God in divinizing grace, insofar as that grace modifies the perspectives in which we view the world. "Revelation," he asserts, "is not possible in the original bearer of revelation without the occurrence of what may be called 'mysticism as the experience of grace.' "[9] Even in those who believe on the testimony of such original recipients, Rahner goes on to say, there must be some experience of grace, for if faith were supported only by an external word, it could not rise above the level of human opinion.[10] Although not distinctly perceived by mere introspection, such illuminating grace deserves to be called revelation even prior to the acceptance of any particular message as divinely revealed.[11]

## 3. *The Content of Revelation*

What is the content of revelation as inner experience? "The object of the revelation of God," writes Sabatier, "can only be God Himself, and if a definition must be given of it, it may be said to consist of the creation, the purification, and the progressive clearness of the consciousness of God in man—in the individual and in the race."[12] "Let us boldly conclude, against all traditional orthodoxies," he adds, "that the object of the revelation of God could only be God himself, that is to say the sense of His presence in us, awakening our soul to the life of righteousness and love."[13]

Hocking, in his discussion of mystical knowledge, speaks in much the same terms. The mystic's chief concern, he asserts, "is not to find things new to men at large, but only to find the Ancient of Days as a God revealed personally to him. . . . What the mystic knows is, first of all, that which he intends to know, namely God: and insofar as he is a mystic pure and simple knows nothing else than God."[14] Yet this experience of God, Hocking adds, "illuminates everything else. All other things are lit up with an unfamiliar light, shining out strange and reborn" so that the whole of reality becomes new.[15] Thus the mystic's revelation cannot stop with the absolute, because it has bearing on other experiences.

Emphasizing the element of immediacy, theologians of this orientation generally deny that there are such things as revealed doctrines. They draw a sharp distinction between faith, as the acceptance of revelation, and belief, as subscription to doctrine. "Belief," Schleiermacher declares, "which is to accept what another has said or done, or to wish to think and feel as another has thought and felt, is a hard and base service" unworthy of true religion.[16] Whatever value is to be found in doctrine arises from the fact that religious emotions spontaneously break forth into speech, which symbolically communicates the inner affections of the speaker.[17]

Sabatier's position is close to that of Schleiermacher. The inner experience of revelation, he declares, naturally translates itself into speech and writing, and in this way all civilized religions present revelation in the form of sacred writings.[18] Doctrines have a symbolical truth insofar as they appropriately express and effectively awaken the religious consciousness.[19] But dogma, as an intellectual datum, cannot without idolatry be identified with revelation itself. Authentic religion is deformed when faith is misconstrued as "an intellectual adherence to an historical testimony or to a doctrinal formula."[20]

Tyrrell, for whom revelation is a passive impression made by the experience of the divine, continually insists that there can be no revealed statements or doctrines, since these could only be constructions of the mind. But he adds that such constructions, though human, can powerfully suggest the truth of revelation inasmuch as they are produced under the impact of revelation. The apostolic deposit of faith, for Tyrrell, has religious but not scientific truth. As an avowedly symbolic presentation of the apostolic experience, it has abiding value in shaping and directing the spiritual life of Christians.[21]

The dogmas of the Church, Tyrrell holds, are "a protective husk wrapped round the kernel of apostolic revelation"—a husk eminently useful for the preservation of the apostolic revelation but still not identical with revelation itself.[22] If there is any revealed truth in dogma, Tyrrell maintains, that is because dogma perpetuates the inspired symbolism by which the original witnesses expressed their revelatory experience.[23]

Just as the Modernists distinguished between scientific and symbolic truth, so Hocking distinguishes between empirical and esoteric truth. When the mystic makes statements about things other than his personal experience of God, "he writes esoterically, that is, for the reader who has the sense and good-will to supply the cautions and conditions for his statements." The statements, measured by ordinary empirical criteria, may be untrue, but they convey a deeper truth to the reader of insight and goodwill. So too with the "valid doctrines" of the Church. "Their truth is literal, but esoteric."[24]

The experientialist approach is somewhat ambivalent about the distinctive value of what is specific to any given religious tradition. If the essence of revelation is thought to consist in an ineffable encounter with the divine, the particular symbols and doctrines of any given religious tradition will be regarded as secondary and accidental. Evelyn Underhill is quite explicit:

> So we may say that the particular mental image which the mystic forms of his objective, the traditional theology he accepts, is not essential. Since it is never adequate, the degree of its inadequacy is of secondary importance. . . . We cannot honestly say that there is any wide difference between the Brahman, Sufi, or Christian mystic at their best.[25]

On the other hand, the assumption that religious differences are merely accidental to the religious experience is not shared by all representatives of this type of theology. Herrmann, as already noted, holds that the assured experience of personal communion with God, which is the true meaning of revelation, is available only to those who open themselves to the inner life of Jesus as communicated in the Bible and in the Christian tradition.[26] Herrmann, like his master Ritschl, was profoundly suspicious of mysticism on the grounds that it sought to bypass the human Jesus in his terrestrial condition and lay claim to a direct, unmediated union with the deity.[27]

Nathan Söderblom, seeking a middle position, censured the Ritschl school for overlooking "important phenomena of essential mysticism within revealed religion, in the Christian era and before Christ as well."[28] He distinguished therefore between two types of mysticism: a mysticism of nature or of infinity, which he found in pagan religions, and a mysticism of personality, which is characteristic of biblical faith. Dean Inge and others, Söderblom believed, were too eager for ecstatic experiences which reach out to the divine darkness as "the nameless, formless nothing."[29] More proper to revealed religion, Söderblom contended, is the personal authority of the chosen men of God through whom communion with God becomes available to others. For the Christian revelation is to be found in a special way in the "soul life of the prophets."[30] It reaches its perfection in the person of Jesus Christ, who mediates to us his own communion with God. True Christianity, therefore, knows only one authority, that of personality.[31]

## 4. *Authority and Criteria*

Somewhat along these lines C. H. Dodd, in an early work, defended the authority of the Bible. He was not interested in holding that the propositions written in the book are themselves revelation or that the oracles of the prophets were divinely protected against all error. The mystery of revelation, he declared, is "the mystery of the way in which God uses the imperfect thoughts and feelings, words and deeds, of fallible men, to convey eternal truth, both to the men themselves and through them to others."[32] The Bible, he contended, taken as a whole, is a revelation of God—a revelation that comes to its apex in the life and teaching of Jesus.[33] It mediates divine truth, first, through the prophets, who possess "the authority of religious genius";[34] then, through the appropriation of the insights of the prophets by the whole community, "whose experience through many generations tests, confirms and revises them";[35] and finally through the life of Jesus, "in whom religious genius reached its highest point and passed into something greater still."[36]

Although revelation occurred to the fullest extent in the personal life of Jesus, it continued, according to some authors of this tendency, beyond the first century of our era. In the words of Sabatier, "The divine revelation which is not realized in us, and does not become immediate, does not exist for us."[37] Revelation, therefore, although it presupposes a certain human and historical preparation, comes directly to every individual, "for the least in the kingdom of heaven, as for the greatest of the prophets."[38] Söderblom agrees. "There is a measure of revelation," he holds, "that is, of a divine self-disclosure, wherever there is found a sincere religiousness." Thus it is impossible "to hold fast to faith in revelation without extending it beyond the times of the Bible."[39] In its acceptance of continuing revelation this experiential type of revelation theology contrasts with the two preceding models.

What, for these authors, is the criterion of authentic revelation? With one accord they reject any rational demonstration through prophecies, miracles, and the like. The criterion, they assert, is the quality of the experience itself. For Sabatier it is evident that revelation does not need any proof—for the proofs would show nothing to the irreligious person who has not had the experience and would be superfluous to the pious person who has experienced revelation.[40] "Only one criterion," he writes, "is sufficient and infallible: every divine revelation, every religious experience fit to nourish and sustain your soul, must be able to repeat and continue itself as an actual revelation and an individual experience in your own consciousness."[41] Tyrrell, in like manner, appeals to what he calls "criteria of life, of spiritual fruitfulness."[42] "The reasons we give to our mind," he writes, "are but after-justifications of an impulse that derives not from reason but from the sympathetic intuitions of the spirit of holiness."[43]

For Dean Inge the criterion of validity is the way in which the message of revelation awakens a response in our hearts. "It is the indwelling Christ," he says, "who is the primary authority."[44] Söderblom, too, is convinced that we achieve certainty "by an experience of communion with the life of God."[45] Dodd, concerned to minimize the external aspects of authority, asserts: "The criterion lies within ourselves, in the response of our own spirit to the Spirit that utters itself in the Scriptures." In this connection he refers to the classic Protestant theme of *testimonium Spiritus Sancti internum*.[46]

Mention of the inner testimony of the Holy Spirit might seem to suggest that orthodox Calvinists would find in the Holy Spirit a direct, experiential source of revelation in addition to the biblical word. This does not seem to be generally the case. Pointing out that Calvin, like Luther, was opposed to the "enthusiasm" of the radical Reformers, modern Calvinists are wary of Pentecostal phenomena. Carl Henry, whom we have already quoted as holding that the Spirit reveals only what the Bible says, takes great pains to align his position with Calvin's.[47]

## 5. Summary

To summarize the experiential approach to revelation, we may place our usual questions regarding the form, the content, the salvific power, and the appropriate response. The form is of course an immediate interior experience. For most of our authors this consists in a direct, unmediated encounter with the divine, although some affirm, with the biblical and Christian tradition, that this experience is to be found in communion with the prophets and especially with Jesus, whose familiarity with God was unsurpassably intimate. Thus faith possesses a kind of "mediated immediacy."

The content of revelation, in this model, is neither information about the past nor abstract doctrinal truth. Rather, the content is God as he lovingly communicates himself to the soul that is open to him. As Hocking says of the mystic's revelation, its chief burden "is that religion must exist as experience and not as idea only."[48]

The saving power of revelation is identical with revelation itself. Revelation imparts a blessed experience of union with God, which may be called "eternal life." Although nothing in this model requires one to deny life beyond death, the model does not accept immortality or resurrection as divinely revealed dogmas, nor does it make the saving power of revelation depend on such doctrines.

The appropriate response to revelation, as understood in this model, is neither an adherence to a definite body of truth nor a commitment to a particular course of action, but rather, as Dodd puts it, "a religious attitude and outlook"[49] characterized by what Schleiermacher would call "pious affections" and what Sabatier designates as "the prayer of the heart."

## 6. Merits of the Experiential Model

After several centuries of arid and decadent Scholasticism, which had sought in vain to ward off the advances of rationalistic infidelity, the experiential model of revelation came as a great boon to the churches. In an age dominated by the Kantian critique of knowledge, this model made it possible to accept that critique without falling into skepticism. By underscoring the difference between revelation and conceptual or factual knowledge, the experiential approach relieved Christians of the burden of having to justify the whole system of inherited beliefs. Since revelation existed in a different dimension than science, and had a different kind of truth, the problem of collisions between revelation and scientific thought was prevented from even arising.[50] Within the context of Kantian agnosticism and pragmatism, therefore, this approach to revelation had a certain plausibility.

Further, this model gave striking support to the life of devotion.

It stimulated the kind of religious piety that is so palpably present in the authors we have cited. New links began to appear between systematic and ascetical theology. The life of prayer and mystical experience, which had been shunted off from the main thoroughfare of theology, appeared once again as central themes. Works of devotion and spiritual autobiography became primary loci for the study of revelation.

Partly as a result of the distinction between revelation and doctrine, adherents of this approach felt authorized to take a more positive attitude toward the nonbiblical religions than had been customary for Christians. It became possible to hold that not only Christianity but all religions, with varying degrees of purity and intensity, bore witness to the self-revelation of the living God. This attitude resulted in great gains for interreligious dialogue.

## 7. Criticisms of the Experiential Model

The experiential model, in the form here studied, is not free from serious weaknesses. For one thing, it makes rather selective use of the Bible and even contradicts many biblical texts. All the passages from Scripture which are used to support either of the first two models constitute objections to the third. By shifting from the biblical categories of the deeds and words of God to the psychological categories of religious genius and mystical experience, this model rejects the self-understanding of the prophets, many of whom, from Moses to Jeremiah, insist on their ineptitude for the task to which they have been called.

Dodd, who made considerable use of the category of religious genius in his earlier work, came increasingly to see its limitations for interpreting the prophetic and apostolic message. In his later writings he accented the category of the "word of God" and showed a deeper appreciation for history as a medium of revelation. Criticizing the concept of religious genius, he wrote:

> We do not however gather from the prophets the impression that they supposed their people to possess a natural genius for religion. "Ah, sinful nation! a people laden with iniquity! a seed of evil-doers! rebellious sons!" (Is 1:4). These are only a few specimens of the rich vocabulary of vituperation with which the prophets assailed their contemporaries. Nor is the case different

in the New Testament. It is never suggested that the Church of God's "elect" consists of people with a natural genius for religion. Quite the contrary. "The Son of Man came not to call the righteous, but sinners" (Mk 2:17). And there have always been Christians, and those not the worst sort, who would confess that they had a natural genius for atheism—but for the grace of God. We cannot eliminate that suggestion of a free act of God which is inherent in the idea of "choice."[51]

Another difficulty in making revelation the prerogative of the religious genius is that it substitutes a natural elitism for the biblical idea of election. Interior spiritual experience, especially on the higher levels, is seen as falling within the province of those who have, as Schleiermacher puts it, "a talent for religion,"[52] and are naturally endowed with what Schleiermacher characterizes as vivid God-consciousness. But many persons seem to be, as Max Weber said of himself, "religiously unmusical." If revelation has to be an immediate interior experience, is not revelation, and consequently faith, restricted to a privileged minority? Can we admit a doctrine that would tie divine grace so closely to native endowment?

Because the theory of inner experience was fashioned in opposition to the views that revelation essentially consists in external deeds or divine doctrines, it stands in considerable tension with traditional church teaching. Not surprisingly this view of revelation, at least in its acutely modernistic form, was officially condemned by Roman Catholicism and by many conservative Protestant churches. It was also profoundly alien to Eastern Orthodoxy, which remained strongly traditionalist. Yet it must be conceded that the experiential model can claim some support from the mystical traditions of Eastern and Western Christianity.

By divorcing revelation from doctrine this model pays a price. It disappoints many of the expectations with which people ordinarily approach religion. It says in effect that there are no divine answers to the deep human questions about the origin and ultimate destiny of humanity and the world. A church that can acknowledge no revealed doctrine can hardly offer the kind of heavenly wisdom which revealed religion is commonly supposed to supply. The human quest for meaning thus remains unsatisfied.

The practical values of the experiential model, though real, are rather limited. The search for private religious experience has sometimes resulted in excesses of interiority, individualism, and pietism, with a corresponding loss of concern for the wholeness of the Church and for the healing of the social fabric. In some authors, such as Sabatier, one finds an overly sentimental emotionalism. Such emotionalism can easily drift off into vague syncretism or agnosticism.

William James, whose philosophy of religion relied heavily on feelings associated with a sense of Presence, acknowledged the ambiguity of the evidence. "The mystical feeling of enlargement, union, and emancipation," he wrote, "has no specific content whatever of its own. It is capable of forming matrimonial alliances with material furnished by the most diverse philosophies and theologies . . ."[53] It can appear as world-affirming or world-denying, as pantheistic, theistic, or atheistic. The visions and the ecstatic revelations of the prophets, since they corroborate incompatible theological positions, "neutralize one another and leave no fixed results."[54]

Some exponents of this model, committed to the thesis that all religious experience is essentially the same, hold that the differences between theists and pantheists, monists and pluralists, are unimportant. Abraham Maslow, for example, argues that "to the extent that all mystical or peak experiences are the same in their essence and have always been the same, all religions are the same in the essence and have always been the same." All religion, according to Maslow, can be subsumed under the heading of "peak experiences" and hence it is no longer necessary to refer to God or any other supernatural source. Peak experiences can serve as a bond of union not only among religious people but between the religious and the atheist.[55]

Maslow, of course, is not a theologian. But if one wishes as a theologian to retain a theistic, not to say a Christian, understanding of religious experience, and to avoid humanistic reductionism, one will find it necessary to take the doctrinal and historical dimensions more seriously than does, for instance, Evelyn Underhill in the passage quoted above.

Quite apart from the conflicting interpretations as to what is disclosed in revelatory experiences, there is the problem whether the experiences themselves are to be credited. Do they really signify anything except the self's experience of the self? William James, at the end of his careful analysis of numerous testimonies, concludes that religious experience arises out of a transmarginal or subliminal region of the psyche, but he thinks it probable that this region is closely attuned to the higher part of the universe, and in that sense with God. *"If there be* higher spiritual agencies that can directly touch us, the psychological condition of their doing so *might* be our possession of a subconscious region which alone should yield access to them."[56]

In terms of his own empirical presuppositions, James's reserve is amply justified. The quality of a religious experience, considered as an isolated psychological occurrence, can never establish that God is in fact experienced. Religious phenomenology, so long as it confines itself to empirical descriptions, cannot pronounce on the reality of revelation.[57] To decide on the question of truth or illusion one must go beyond the methods of psychological description and ponder evidence from many other channels.[58]

If there is one characteristic defect in the third model, it is not its emphasis on experience but rather its excessively narrow concept of experience. British and American empiricism had a tendency to look upon experience as immediate, individual, instantaneous, and self-evidencing, and to set experience, so understood, above all other forms of cognition. When this concept of experience is applied to revelation, revelation comes to be seen as a bare, unanalyzed datum that imposes itself on the human spirit as a *tabula rasa*. God becomes a strange phenomenon perceived without any reliance upon community, tradition, or other forms of worldly mediation.

In recent decades, numerous philosophers have pointed out the inadequacy of this view of experience.[59] In any experience the subject contributes a host of socially acquired memories and anticipations, hopes and fears, which in great part shape the experience itself. The richer the experience the more abundant will be the required input. Experience is ongoing and cumulative; it grows gradually out of the past and moves toward the future. It is constituted not by lonely individuals but by groups who share and interact. It is mediated by gestures, by language, and by numerous other signs. It is subject to interpretation and appraisal in the light of many criteria.

The observations about experience in general hold also for religious and revelatory experience. Religious empiricism tended to concentrate on certain rarified experiences of a quasi-mystical order involving intense personal emotions. The human and historical context were rather neglected. But the context is of constitutive importance. Any meaningful religious experience, according to John E. Smith, involves mediating elements, so that consequently "every alleged experience of God would also be experience of something else at the same time."[60] Taking the human and social context into account, Smith can say that specific disclosures such as the biblical events can figure as revelation. The rootedness of a religion in an ongoing tradition does not make it less experiential. "For revelation represents a further development of the experiential matrix of religion, since experience is the only medium through which anything can be revealed to man."[61]

Edward Schillebeeckx, in several recent works, has grappled with the relationship between revelation and experience. There can be no revelation without experience, he holds, but revelation transcends any human experience.[62] It never exists without an interpretation. In conscious opposition to the empiricists and modern theologians who are influenced by them, Schillebeeckx asserts that every experience includes, and is modified by, interpretative elements.[63] Interpretative elements that are intrinsically connected with the experience of salvation given in Jesus, but no others, pertain to Christian revelation.[64] When the original experience is overlaid by alien interpretations extrinsically imposed upon it by subsequent reflection, the revelation can be obscured, so that the contemporary believer is hindered from finding salvation in Jesus.[65]

To this basically acceptable position, the philosopher Louis Dupré adds two important reservations. In the first place, Schillebeeckx unduly subordinates interpretation to experience, as though the former were always derived from the latter. According to Dupré the original Jesus-experience could not convey any revelation unless it were accompanied by a primary interpretation that enjoyed equal status with the experience itself. Both the experience and the basic interpretation, enjoying the same privileged status, must be preserved.[66]

Secondly, according to Dupré, neither the experience nor the interpretation should be understood as completely given in the initial encounters of the disciples with Jesus, or even in the Easter events. "Instead of a single, privileged Jesus experience at the beginning, I would rather posit a continuing process of interpreted experience, of which with respect to later generations the first stage was not completed until it was codified, long after most eyewitnesses had died, in what later became the canonical text."[67] This second qualification is important, as we shall see, for the status of Scripture as revelation.

Once the dichotomy between experience and interpretation has been overcome, the experiential approach ceases to stand in stark contrast with the approaches through word and deed examined in previous chapters. Before comparing these approaches, however, we shall turn our attention to two other models of revelation theology.

# Chapter VI

# MODEL FOUR: REVELATION AS DIALECTICAL PRESENCE

## 1. *Leading Representatives*

Liberal theology, which tended to look upon revelation as an inner experience exemplified by the prophets and by Jesus, reached its zenith between the turn of the century and the outbreak of World War I. After 1914, however, this position began to appear less satisfying. By then New Testament scholarship had shown the difficulty of reconstructing the historical Jesus according to the presuppositions of the liberal school. Further, the calamity of the war and the ensuing economic and political chaos seemed to require a theology that gave greater recognition to sin, to the fragility of human enterprises, to the distance between human beings and God, and to the divine mercy extended to us in Jesus Christ. Preachers such as Karl Barth, during World War I, found that the liberal theology could not be proclaimed with the needed power. Did not Christianity, they asked, have a more potent message about God's work on our behalf in Jesus Christ?

These critics of the liberal theology, however, felt unable to go back to the older orthodoxies, which would have identified revelation with fixed doctrines (Model 1) or with a miraculous history (Model 2). Educated by great liberal theologians such as Harnack and Herrmann, the new theologians were acutely aware of the obscurities in biblical history and the variations in biblical and ecclesiastical doctrine. They therefore sought a theology of revelation that could honestly accept the results of critical scholarship without falling into the insipidities of liberalism.

Karl Barth, Emil Brunner, Rudolf Bultmann, and several others, though they never constituted a school in the strict sense, developed a common approach often called "crisis theology" or "dialectical theology." Profoundly conscious of the divine transcendence and of human sinfulness, they denied that God's presence and activity could ever be discovered within the realms of historical fact, doctrinal statement, or religious experience. And yet they were convinced, in faith, that God was present and active in human history, language, and experience. To express the paradoxical reality of God's presence and absence they had recourse to a succession of affirmations and denials, statements and counterstatements, which seemed to them to respect the mystery of God. Only a simultaneous yes and no, they held, could be adequate to that mystery. The dialectic, therefore, was one of unresolved diastasis. Unlike Hegel's, it never came to a synthesis.

The leading representatives of the dialectical school differed significantly from one another. Barth was in his dialectical period strongly influenced by the existentialism of Kierkegaard and Dostoevsky. He gradually moved through an actualist theology of the word of God toward a more incarnational theology centered on God's self-gift in Jesus Christ. In his later theology he moderated the dialectical thinking that had been prominent in his work prior to 1940. Brunner developed a theology of encounter and communion influenced by the personalism of Ferdinand Ebner and Martin Buber. Bultmann, finally, excogitated a theology of human self-understanding heavily influenced by Heidegger's existential philosophy.

Notwithstanding these differences, our three theologians shared a common interest in the theme of revelation, which they concurred in viewing as a mysterious salvific encounter with the living God. They leaned toward an existential and actualist theology of the word, thus preparing the way for later word-theologies such as those of Ernst Fuchs, Gerhard Ebeling, and Eberhard Jüngel. Without seeking to do justice to the individual variations we shall in the following pages present a synthetic sketch of the dialectical model of revelation.

## 2. Revelation, God, and Christ

Our three authors agree that revelation is a highly mysterious thing, since it has to do with the self-communication of God, who is absolute mystery. Barth can therefore say: "According to Scripture God's revelation is God's own direct speech which is not to be distinguished from the act of speaking and therefore is not to be distinguished from God Himself, from the divine I which confronts man in this act in which it says Thou to him. Revelation is *Dei loquentis persona*."[1] Consistently with this position, he holds that every revealing is at the same time a concealing, for it discloses the absolute inscrutability of God. "Revelation in the Bible means the self-unveiling, imparted to men, of the God who by nature cannot be unveiled to men . . . It is the *Deus revelatus* who is the *Deus absconditus* . . ."[2]

For Bultmann, "God the mysterious and hidden must at the same time be the God who is revealed."[3] The kind of knowledge that occurs in revelation, he holds, "cannot be directly mediated by reports about the Revealer, but can only be attained by man allowing himself to encounter the word of the Revealer, which at once reveals and conceals him.[4] He is the concealed Revealer."[5]

Brunner likewise maintains that God, as absolute subject, makes himself known as absolute mystery and hence as nonobjectifiable.[6] The truth of revelation, he writes, "is neither subjective nor objective, but it is both at once: it is the truth which may be described, in other words, as the encounter of the human 'I' with God's 'Thou' in Jesus Christ."[7]

As this last sentence suggests, the content of revelation is not God in his abstract essence, but God who turns toward his creatures in judgment and forgiveness—that is to say, in Jesus Christ. Of Christ, Barth says: "He is the light of God and the revelation of God."[8] And again: "Jesus Christ is the revelation because He is the grace of God made manifest to us—*grace* in the full sense of the conception."[9] "If God were not *gracious* (and this means if He retained the majesty of His Godhead for Himself), if He did not of his own free decision turn toward men, there would be no revelation."[10] Bultmann speaks in similar terms: "Thus revelation consists in nothing other than the fact of Jesus Christ."[11] For Brunner, too, revelation is Jesus Christ, in whose personal presence the personal presence of God has become a reality.[12] It is especially in the mystery of the Cross and Resurrection, say these authors, that God reveals himself in Jesus Christ.

The Christological concentration of these authors involves a rejection of the revelatory capacities of nature, of religious experience, and of non-Christian religious traditions.[13] Barth, in holding that the revelation of Jesus Christ frees us from the illusion of natural theology, defines the latter as "the doctrine of a union of man with God existing outside of God's revelation in Jesus Christ."[14] Brunner takes sharp issue with Goethe, who in his poetry celebrated the revelation given always and everywhere. On the contrary, says Brunner, revelation for the Christian occurs only in Christ, beside whom no other name is given.[15] And for Bultmann, "God meets him [the believer] only in Christ. . . . To put it another way, Christ is God's eschatological deed, beside which there is no room for any other deed claiming or promoting faith."[16]

Viewing revelation as inseparable from the living self-communication of God, these authors hold, quite logically, that revelation is intrinsically salvific. "To the extent that God's revelation as such accomplishes what only God can accomplish," writes Barth, "namely, restoration of the fellowship of man with God . . . revelation is itself reconciliation."[17] Since God comes to us in revelation, Brunner agrees, "revelation and forgiveness are the same."[18] Commenting on the text, "I am the way" (Jn 14:6), Bultmann observes: "This is the pure expression of the idea of revelation. The Revealer is the access to God which man is looking for, and what is more . . . the only access."[19] Thus he can use the composite term *Heilsoffenbarung* (salvific revelation).[20]

## 3. *The Word of God*

Identifying revelation with grace, these authors maintain that even after the time of the apostles, who first received the revelation, revelation still remains God's free decision and his gift. The Bible and the preaching of the Church bear witness to divine revelation but are not themselves revelation. In Barth's well-known terminology, Bible and proclamation as such are not the word of God, but they can become God's word and his revelation if and insofar as Jesus Christ, the revealed Word of God, is pleased to speak to us through these chosen witnesses.[21] The event of Christ speaking through these agencies occurs when and as God so chooses.

While the written and spoken word are media of revelation, the content of revelation, for these authors, is not the conceptual meaning of the language. The truth of revelation, Barth insists, is not what the preacher or the theologian conceptually asserts, but rather the very truth of God who asserts himself. God's word is only paradoxically or dialectically identified with word of man.[22] The human and conceptual errors in the testimonies to revelation therefore leave intact the truth of God's revelation. Barth unequivocally affirms that because the authors of the Bible, including the prophets and apostles, were real historical men, they cannot have been immune from all error, but "being justified and sanctified by grace alone, they have still spoken the Word of God in their fallible and erring human word."[23] Brunner is of the same opinion: "God can, if he so wills, speak his Word to a man even through false doctrine."[24] The truth of revelation, he says, is not propositional; it is not an "it-truth" or, in other words, is not information about something.[25]

Bultmann is equally emphatic. "The truth does not exist as a doctrine, which could be understood, preserved, and handed on, so that the teacher is discharged and surpassed. Rather the position a man takes vis-à-vis the Revealer decides not whether he *knows* the truth, but whether he is 'of the truth.' "[26] Elsewhere Bultmann puts this still more memorably:

> What, then has been revealed? Nothing at all, so far as the question concerning revelation asks for doctrines—doctrines, say, that no man could have discovered for himself—or for mysteries that become known once and for all as soon as they are communicated. On the other hand, however, *everything has been revealed, insofar as man's eyes are opened concerning his own existence and he is once again able to understand himself.*[27]

Through revelation, then, we know in actual encounter the event of revelation itself; and that event means total newness of life even though it has no informational content.[28] The Bible itself is not an infallible book, but a book to be judged by the revelation God communicates through it. "Therefore the New Testament itself is revelation," Bultmann writes, "only insofar as it is kerygma or insofar as it 'preaches Christ' (Luther)."[29]

When does revelation occur? For the dialectical theologians, revelation occurs whenever God's word is effectively proclaimed and is received in faith, and revelation is never revelation except when it is occurring. Barth, as we have already seen, holds that the Bible and the preached word become revelation when and insofar as God is pleased to speak through them. For Brunner, too, the Bible becomes the word of God to me in the moment of revelation when I become contemporaneous with Christ.[30] Bultmann in similar fashion holds that the Scriptures become the word of God only when I hear them "as a word which is addressed to me, as kerygma, as a proclamation."[31] Thus he can say: "Revelation encounters man in the word—in a word that sounds forth in his present."[32] Far from being a past historical event, revelation occurs now. "Each generation has the same original relation to revelation."[33]

## 4. *Faith and Its Grounds*

From this the dialectical theologians move on to a further assertion—that the act of faith, whereby revelation is actually received, is an integral part of the revelation itself. Revelation, according to Barth, is never complete with the objective element of God's self-disclosure through his Son, for the fact of that disclosure is not apparent without the subjective transformation by which the Holy Spirit renders us capable of acknowledging what has happened. "Therefore this receiving, this revealedness of God for us, is really itself revelation."[34] Brunner protests against the tendency to think of revelation as an objective fact set over against the subjective act of its reception in faith. "The fact of the illumination" which makes the fact known, he says, is "an integral part of the process of revelation; without this an event is no more revelation than light is light without the seeing, illuminated, eye."[35] Elsewhere he declares: "Faith and revelation are correlatives";[36] they reciprocally depend on each other. Bultmann is of the same mind. "Outside of faith," he writes, "revelation is not visible; there is nothing revealed on the basis of which one believes. It is only in faith that the object of faith is disclosed; therefore, faith itself belongs to revelation."[37]

This last quotation from Bultmann brings us to the rational grounding of faith. On this question the dialectical theologians have a characteristic view—that revelation cannot be authenticated by arguments available to human reason, apart from faith. In a celebrated essay on Schleiermacher, Barth ridicules the apologist, who has to go forth from theology carrying a white flag and seeking to parley with unbelief on neutral ground.[38] From such a neutral ground,

Barth maintains, revelation cannot be seen. "According to Holy Scripture God's revelation is a ground which has no higher or deeper ground above or below it, but is an absolute ground in itself, and therefore for man a court from which there can be no possible appeal to a higher court."[39]

For Emil Brunner, likewise: "Revelation, as the Christian faith understands it, is indeed, by its very nature, something that lies beyond all rational arguments."[40] Elsewhere he writes: "Therefore all means of verification and of proof are taken out of our hands. Revelation is grasped only by faith, and what faith believes is foolishness to thought, for it is the opposite of all thinking that moves outward from ourselves."[41] According to Bultmann, the testimony of Jesus as reported in the Fourth Gospel presupposes the self-sufficiency of faith:

> Apart from his witness he [Jesus] offers no other proof of his authority which might provide a man with the *means* of believing in that witness. The hearer who asks can be referred only to the very thing whose validity he is questioning, to the object of faith itself. There are no criteria for determining the validity of the claim of revelation, whether it be the reliable witness of others, or rational or ethical standards, or inner experiences. The object of faith is known only to faith; and this faith is the only means of access to its object.[42]

It might seem that the Christocentrism of these authors would compel them to admit that apologetics must at least defend the historicity of the central events of the career of Jesus, but in contrast to the salvation history school considered above, the dialectical theologians ingeniously shelter faith from the vicissitudes of historical knowledge. Barth, in his commentary on Romans, spoke of a "primal history" (*Urgeschichte*) whereby God's action, without ever becoming identified with worldly history, meets it from above. In this connection Barth used his famous metaphors of the perpendicular, the tangent, the mathematical point, the crater, and the vacuum. The Resurrection of Jesus, he maintained, is "the 'nonhistorical' happening, by which all other events are bounded, and to which events before and after Easter Day point."[43] Because all historical events are irremediably involved in the seesaw of human relativity, with its "obscurity, error, and essential questionableness,"[44] the Resurrection cannot be properly brought within the sphere of ordinary history.

Brunner, in his dialectical period, spoke of "primal-and-ultimate history" (*Ur-End-Geschichte*) as a theological category by which to refer to the paradox of the Eternal becoming present in history without assuming the historical extension of other events. The revelation, he asserts, is invisible and has no extension in time. For this reason the human life of Jesus cannot constitute the revelation. The revelatory dimension is nothing other than the divine word, which is present in the history without ever being identical with it.[45] In contrast to the liberals, the dialectical theologians profess no interest at all in the "Founder of Christianity" in his personal religious attitudes.[46]

Bultmann, in his well-known "demythologizing" program, emphasized the existential significance of the biblical testimony to Jesus, sharply distinguishing this from the historical facticity, which is a matter of indifference to the believer as such. Nothing that the historian can prove or disprove about Christian origins, Bultmann maintains, can either ground or imperil faith, for "faith being a personal decision, cannot be dependent on the historian's labor."[47]

The cardinal theses of dialectical theology, which we have surveyed in the work of Barth, Brunner, and Bultmann, continue to have impact upon their disciples. "Post-Bultmannian" theologians, such as Ernest Fuchs and Gerhard Ebeling, drawing on the philosophy of the later Heidegger, have developed a highly sophisticated theory of the historical occurrence of God's saving word in the form of what Fuchs calls the "language event" (*Sprachereignis*) and Ebeling the "word-event" (*Wortgeschehen*).[48] Closer to Barth than to Bultmann, and closer to the mature work of Barth than to his dialectical phase, theologians such as Jürgen Moltmann and Eberhard Jüngel have continued to probe the paradox of God's presence and absence in the world and its history. For all these theologians, as for their dialectical forbears, revelation is the self-attestation of the revealing God who comes through his powerful word of judgment and of grace.

## 5. Summary

Disregarding these later variations, we may summarize the dialectical theology of revelation by responding to our usual four questions: What are the form of revelation, its content, its salvific value, and the appropriate response to it?

Since revelation comes through the word, its proper form is Christ, the Word in person. Nothing finite is revelation except insofar as the Word speaks through it. For all these authors, the Bible is not revelation itself but rather the primary witness to the revelation which is Christ. Both the Old and the New Testaments, for Barth and his followers, bear witness to Christ.[49] But the word of Scripture cannot be equated with the word of God. It must ultimately be judged by Christ, the revealed Word, according to the dictum of Luther, Christ is King and Lord of Scripture.[50]

In a secondary way, Church proclamation bears witness to Christ, but the word of the Church must always be critically measured against the word of God as given in Scripture. When the Holy Spirit is pleased to speak through the ministry of the Church, the preached word and the sacraments become bearers of revelation.

The content of revelation for these theologians is God, who as speaker reveals himself. Especially for Barth, the Word and the Spirit, as complementary aspects of revelation, manifest God as triune. For Jüngel and Moltmann, no less than for Barth, revelation, as the self-interpretation of God, cannot be understood except in trinitarian terms. The Bultmannians, while agreeing that God reveals himself, emphasize that in so doing God reveals us to ourselves, giving us authentic self-understanding. Rightly understood, this insight can be harmonized with the Barthian accent on the primacy of God. Barth too would insist that God's word in Christ enables us to perceive ourselves as sinners, as powerless, as called to live, and as forgiven.

Although Barth does not clearly exclude the possibility of redemption without revelation, the connection between revelation and salvation, for these authors, is intrinsic. They assert, as we have seen, that revelation is not just a doctrine about salvation but a saving transaction. Ebeling is faithful to this model when he declares: "Revelation, as an event that bears on the fellowship between God and man, does not consist merely in its happening to transmit a doctrine of salvation but rather in its bringing God and man together and reconciling them."[51] Revelation, for Ebeling, does not increase human knowledge except by first changing human existence.

The appropriate response to revelation, in the dialectical model, is faith. Since it belongs to the essence of revelation that it be received, the response of faith is included in the very definition of revelation. As a response, faith is in the first instance personal obedience and only secondarily a matter of formal assent. Yet faith does impart a new understanding of God and of self, for believers come to see themselves as sinners mercifully welcomed into fellowship by God.

## 6. *Merits of the Dialectical Model*

The dialectical model of revelation does not lack a biblical basis. Barth and Bultmann, in different ways, were steeped in the Bible. Their theology of revelation echoes the judging, healing proclamation of the prophets and the "word of the Cross" heralded by Paul (1 Cor 1:18). It also takes up many characteristic themes of the sixteenth-century Reformers, notably Luther. Biblically centered, the dialectical theology of the 1920s and 1930s anticipated some of the principles by which the theologians of the "New Hermeneutic" (E. Fuchs, G. Ebeling, and others) were to give fresh vitality to biblical theology in the middle of the century.

At a time when the idea of revelation was under severe attack from positivists and liberals who regarded all truth as a merely human achievement, dialectical theology made it possible for Christian preachers and teachers once again to speak confidently in the name of the revealing God. They were able to give new force to the biblical and traditional notions of sin and redemption. Dialectical theology had a clear Christological focus, since it looked exclusively to Christ as the revelation of God. In the case of Barth, the twofold emphasis on Word and Spirit made the doctrine of revelation the starting point for a renewed theology of the Trinity. Taking the Bible and the theological tradition more seriously than they had been taken since the Reformation, dialectical theology spearheaded a major revival in Protestant systematic theology.

By denying the need to make faith plausible, dialectical theology in fact removed many objections based on the alleged implausibility of the Christian message. The very rejection of apologetics proved apologetically fruitful. Insofar as it refused to tie the word of God to any particular historical facts or biblical statements, this model liberated believers from feeling threatened by the new hypotheses of liberal and radical scholarship. Bultmann's demythologizing program could be launched from within the framework of dialectical theology.

Finally, the dialectical theology of revelation, while it deemphasized the category of religious experience, made it once more possible for many believers to have a sense of encounter with the transcendent God as absolute mystery. Even when speaking against religion, the Barthians ministered to the need felt by many Christians to submit ot a God of unlimited sovereignty. In a curious way, the very disavowal of religion was made to serve the purposes of religion.

## 7. Criticisms of the Dialectical Model

Great as its impact was, the new dialectical model of revelation did not win universal approbation. Conservative and orthodox theologians were displeased with the way this model circumvented the clear teaching of many biblical texts and church pronouncements, as well as its casual approach to biblical history.[52] Liberals, on the other hand, found fault with the model for its effort to rehabilitate the authority of Scripture and the themes of traditional dogmatics.

The most persistent charge against this style of theology was that it lacked inner coherence. David Kelsey says: "There is a convergence of critical judgment from otherwise quite different theological perspectives that the allegedly 'biblical' doctrines of 'revelation' developed in the neo-orthodox era were conceptually incoherent."[53] With apparent boldness, these theologians insist on the word of God as the norm that judges all human words, but then they add that the word of God is never accessible except in deficient human words. The preacher, according to Barth, is faced by the impossible task of having to speak about that which cannot be uttered, and thus of using words which are false unless contradicted. But the two sides of the contradiction cancel each other out, leaving a mere void in place of God. "How can this emptiness," asks Hans Urs von Balthasar, "be a real signpost? Why can't it signify the opposite, nothingness, just as well?"[54] The dialectical method thus affords no bridge across the "infinite qualitative difference" between God and creatures; it leaves God unrevealed.

Langdon Gilkey turns against Barth and the neo-Orthodox the same dilemma with which we have seen him confronting G. E. Wright and the salvation-history theologians. The biblical and traditional understanding of God as creator and sovereign Lord, according to Gilkey, is incompatible with the modern secular understanding that underlies the scholarship of these theologians. "The modern side of neoorthodoxy," writes Gilkey, "seemed to make impossible what its orthodox side required, namely a direct relation with an objective divine Word of revelation."[55]

When the dialectical theologians speak of God's self-disclosure through his acts in history, their paradoxical language becomes especially opaque.[56] They refer in glowing terms to God's mighty deeds in delivering the Israelites from their captivity in Egypt and in Babylon, and in raising Jesus from the dead. But at the same time they repudiate the received idea of salvation history, denying that there is any inherent quality that distinguishes the special history of revelation from ordinary historical events.[57] At this point they have recourse to categories such as "primal history" and "eschatological event," which allegedly distinguish the "transhistorical" action of God from the events accessible to ordinary academic history. Faith, they insist, is in no way dependent upon what the profane historian, using the techniques of historical science, can recover. But if faith is grounded only in itself, how does it differ from an arbitrary and irresponsible fanaticism? What is the objective reality of a deed of God which cannot be discerned except by the faith which so interprets it?

Problems such as this become particularly pressing in the realm of Christology. The dialectical theologians unanimously affirm the identity of revelation with Jesus Christ, but they are far from clear as to how the Christ of faith is related to the Jesus of history. If the Christ of faith and proclamation is totally sealed off from the results of historical investigation, a chasm opens up between faith and factual history, and it is difficult to see how commitment to the Christian kerygma differs from commitment to a myth. In the late 1950s and early 1960s, certain younger theologians of the Barth and Bultmann schools proposed the thesis that Christ is a mere symbol by which a certain faith-community chooses to express its understanding of the authentic existence to which all human beings, including the unevangelized, are called.[58] About the same time another group of theologians, sometimes called "post-Bultmannians," asserted the importance of a "new quest" for the historical Jesus, precisely to establish that the Christ of faith was not a mere projection of the pious imagination.[59] Whether one chooses to acknowledge that Christ is a Christian myth or to revive the quest for the historical Jesus, one is departing dramatically from the dialectical model and moving back toward the liberalism of Ritschl and Troeltsch.

For a variety of reasons, the dialectical model of revelation seems unfavorable to interreligious dialogue. Barth and other members of the movement were given to making very negative statements about religion in general and the non-Christian religions in particular. They also indulged in a certain "Christomonism" (as George Ernest Wright called it),[60] denying that revelation could come in any other form than that of Jesus Christ, the Word of God.

These difficulties, however, are perhaps not insuperable. When Barth speaks of religion in disparaging terms, he is pressing only one aspect of his dialectic. He can likewise say: "Revelation can adopt religion and mark it off as true religion."[61] The relationship between revelation and religion is paradoxical. Barth wants to "sublate" religion through revelation, not simply to abolish it.

The common charge that the dialectical model is incoherent leaves its partisans unperturbed. If revelation could totally coalesce with any human system, they ask, would it still be revelation? If it could be proved from a standpoint outside of faith, why would revelation be needed at all? Only by keeping the word of God unconfused with any human word can the integrity of revelation be preserved. The main function of revelation in its encounter with human systems is to expose their inadequacy inasmuch as they proceed from finitude and sin. In dialectical theology the Reformation themes of humanity's total corruption and God's free grace are consistently applied to the doctrine of revelation.

The dialectical model raises insistently the problem of religious language. It seeks to communicate by metaphor and paradox what lies beyond the reach of direct propositional discourse, and thereby suggests that there are nonpropositional modes of cognition of crucial importance for theology. The rhetorical style of Barth and his associates (but especially Barth) is no mere ornament to their theology, but rather its very life and substance. Only by means of dialectical language, these theologians hold, can one speak of the divine without imprisoning it in human conceptual structures.

The dazzling rhetoric of these theologians, with its clashing contrasts, remains one of the most arresting achievements of theology in the twentieth century. But can such a tapestry of incompatibles claim to be a theology of revelation? If men and women lack the capacity to receive the word of God, can there be revelation at all? And if the word can be received, must it not be distinguishable from its own contradictory? The simultaneous yes and no cannot be final.

In view of these difficulties it is not surprising that dialectical theology, in its acute form, was only a phase in the career of its own authors. When they sought to reflect further on the meaning of the gospel, they moved beyond dialectical thinking into a more affirmative theology of proclamation. Without renouncing the sheer event-character of the word of God, and the radical negation of human presumption therein implied, these theologians took up something like the analogous discourse of the classical tradition.[62] Brunner's personalism, Bultmann's existentialism, and Barth's theology of reconciliation ultimately broke out of the frail framework of dialecticism. Within these systems, a strong negative moment persists, calling attention to the inadequacy of all human affirmations about God. But the classical doctrine of analogy likewise contained a negative ingredient reflecting the realization that any similarities between the creature and God are qualified by a much greater dissimilarity.[63]

Whenever theology is tempted to forget its own limitations and to claim mastery of the revealed message, the vehement negations of dialectical theology remain a valuable corrective. Whether and how far these negations can be harmonized with the more positive thrust of the other models is a question we must reserve for later consideration.

## Chapter VII

# MODEL FIVE: REVELATION
# AS NEW AWARENESS

In the models so far considered, revelation is seen as something given from outside, descending from above upon the human subject. The recipient of revelation is viewed as passive. The content of revelation is regarded as being beyond the reach of human experience and human heuristic powers.

## 1. *Origins and Representatives*

A different approach to revelation, having roots in the subjective idealism of the nineteenth century, has become popular in many circles in the past generation. According to this approach revelation is a transcendent fulfillment of the inner drive of the human spirit toward fuller consciousness. Far from reducing the subject to passivity, revelation occurs when human powers are raised to their highest pitch of activity. Rather than going beyond experience, revelation is itself an experience of participation in divine life. It does not, however, disclose God as object. It gives a new perspective or point of view on the self and on the world as they are experienced in the whole of life. To the transformed subjectivity of the recipient of revelation, the objects of experience become symbols mediating a contact with the divine. A theology of revelation following these general lines has been developed by a variety of English-speaking theologians such as Gregory Baum, Leslie Dewart, Gabriel Moran, Ray L. Hart, and William M. Thompson. Elements of this approach may be found in eminent theologians such as Paul Tillich and Karl

Rahner, although each of them combines elements belonging to several different models.

The consciousness or awareness model, as I shall call it, has its philosophical ancestry in the transcendental idealism of Kant and the subjective idealism of Fichte. It comes into Catholic theology partly through the influence of Maurice Blondel, who was in some respects followed by Teilhard de Chardin. It can legitimately appeal to certain texts of Vatican II, though the Council was not dominated by this approach. This model also has points of contact with the evolutionary humanism represented, for example, by Julian Huxley, though Huxley himself advocated "religion without revelation."

In the present chapter I shall seek to set forth the main features of this model schematically, with citations from a variety of authors, whose individual positions cannot, of course, be adequately presented here. As in other chapters, my interest is in presenting a typical position rather than in assessing the work of any particular theologian.

## 2. *The Anthropological Shift*

Pierre Teilhard de Chardin, concerned with the apparent irrelevance of a revelation given from on high, developed a theory in which revelation, while still conceived in line with classical faith-assertions, was essentially related to humanization and psychic growth. Revelation, for him, was "a reflection of God in our consciousness."[1] In Christian revelation, he held, "the transcendent has made itself in some degree immanent." God's presence can bring certitude not through a merely external contact but through "contact between two centers of consciousness." Teilhard asserted: "It is no longer an act of *cognition* but of *recognition*: the whole complex interaction of two beings who freely open themselves to one another and give themselves—the emergence, under the influence of grace, of theological faith."[2] Accordingly, "God never reveals himself from outside, by intrusion, but *from within,* by stimulation and enrichment of the human psychic current, the sound of his voice being made recognizable by the fullness and coherence it contributes to our individual and collective being."[3] In Teilhard's estimation, revelation is necessarily linked to progress, and progress, conversely, demands revelation. Against secular humanists such as Julian Huxley, Teilhard steadfastly maintained that human consciousness by its inherent powers could not provide the irreversible center and the transcendent focus needed for convergence.[4] Progressive revelation, he contended, is to be found in an axis that points toward the future. It results in "orthogenesis" rather than orthodoxy, in convergence rather than intolerance.[5] Revelation, he argued, cannot be encountered except through an ascending movement toward the Omega, the ultimate goal of the process of evolution.[6] Until the final Parousia the process of revelation will continue,[7] but the terminal stage of "pleromatization" has already begun with the Incarnation of the divine in Jesus Christ.[8] Although revelation continues after the Ascension, it takes the form of a further development of what has already been objectified in Christ.[9]

Possibly influenced by Teilhard de Chardin, Karl Rahner in several essays presents his theory of revelation in terms of an evolutionary view of the world. For him revelation is a particular instance of a more general phenomenon—that of the self-transcending movement of created reality toward ever greater freedom and self-possession. Self-transcendence in the direction of spirit can occur, Rahner maintains, because the Absolute is Spirit. God is always and everywhere present as "the living, permanent, transcendent ground of the self-movement of the world itself."[10] Revelation, then, should not be understood as an insertion of fully articulated divine truths into the continuum of human knowledge, but rather as the process by which God, working within history and human tradition, enables his spiritual creatures to achieve a higher level of consciousness. Jesus Christ is for Rahner the unsurpassable high point of God's transcendental self-communication and of its historical acceptance.[11]

For Rahner, as we have seen, grace itself implies revelation, for it is God's self-communication to a spiritual and self-conscious subject. Grace discloses God as communicating himself and the human subject as tending toward transcendent self-fulfillment in union with God. Viewed under this aspect, revelation may be seen as a new mode of human consciousness in which the human spirit perceives itself as finalized toward the divine in a new way, and perceives the divine as drawing the human spirit into closer union with itself. Transcendental revelation, as Rahner calls it, is simultaneously anthropocentric and theocentric.[12]

Rahner's theology of revelation cannot be adequately understood on the basis of the transcendental alone. For him it is essential that revelation come to expression in conceptual language having a permanently valid content. Rahner keeps the two dimensions—the transcendental and the predicamental—in a dialectical balance. For purposes of this chapter, the transcendental dimension is of greater interest, since it has been taken up by theologians of the consciousness model.

While cautioning against subjectivism, Thomas O'Meara notes in recent Roman Catholic theology a departure from the previous tendency to begin with God and with the objective mediation of revelation through events and doctrine. The newer tendency, with which he identifies himself, is to begin with the human and with the presence of God surrounding every personality. He calls for a "theopsychology of revelation"[13] in which revelation is regarded as occurring primarily in the inner bestowal of grace. He quotes Rahner to the effect that God's self-revelation in the depths of the spiritual person occurs primarily as a "state of mind—not knowledge but a consciousness."[14]

The religious educator, Gabriel Moran, makes use of the category of intersubjectivity to describe the interweaving of the divine initiative and the human response in revelation. Already in his *Theology of Revelation* (1966) he spoke of revelation as "an interpersonal communion of free individuals."[15] More recently he speaks of a "personal and social communion,"[16] a lived relationship, a "continuing process of interaction in which each party plays both an active and a passive role."[17] The interrelationship involves both a subject and an objective pole, each of which is indispensable.

Building on the work of Blondel and Rahner, the Canadian theologian, Gregory Baum, typifies the distinctive emphases of the awareness model. "Since divine revelation," he writes, "is not information about another world but God's self-communication to man, and hence his gracious entry into the dynamic process of man's becoming fully human, it is possible to express what the Church believes by describing the new self-consciousness created by faith."[18] "The Christian message," for Baum, "is not information about the divine, to be intellectually assimilated. It is, rather, salvational truth; it raises man's consciousness; it constitutes a new awareness in man through which he sees the world in a new light and commits himself to a new kind of action."[19] Faith, as the acceptance of divine revelation, is "an entry into a new self-consciousness and a new orientation toward the world."[20] Church doctrines, according to Baum, function as revelation not because they correspond to some sacred reality beyond the human but because they are, as symbols, coconstitutive of human experience. Religious symbols, by focusing on the ultimate meaning of life, channel and reshape our experience.[21]

Although this model like our third, highlights experience, it differs from the latter in that it views God as the horizon, rather than the object, of religious experience and finds revelation not in withdrawal from the world but rather in involvement. This model repudiates the individualism and sentimentalism· of modernist mysticism; it insists on the secular and historical context as constitutive of revelation. Although Edward Schillebeeckx cannot be fitted easily in the "new awareness" model, his critique of the empiricist view of experience would be generally accepted by adherents of this model.

Paul Tillich, whose work has been enormously influential, advocated "an existential understanding of revelation, that is, a creative and transforming participation of every believer in the correlation of revelation."[22] Revelation, for him, did not derive from experience as a source, but it could not occur unless mediated by experience. As a manifestation of the holy, revelation implied experiences in which nature or history became transparent to the divine ground. Rejecting the Barthian view that revelation is cast "like a stone" into the human situation, Tillich emphasized that it is always correlated with human questions arising out of a specific cultural and historical context. Revelation speaks to man's ultimate questions, and may be defined as "the manifestation of what concerns us ultimately."[23] Revelatory events, he added, are always "shaking, transforming, demanding, significant in an ultimate way."[24]

According to Langdon Gilkey, who in many respects follows Tillich, the ultimate never intrudes as a foreign element into the human situation but is, in fact, a dimension of all experience. Revelation does not supply new information that could possibly compete with the findings of history or science, but provides a new source, ground, limit, and horizon within which we think and act.[25] Gilkey tries to show that ultimate questions are present in ordinary secular experience, and that revelation, mediated through religious symbols, meaningfully answers those questions. Religious discourse, he concludes, is not, directly, talk about God but is talk about the finite with regard to its divine ground. "It is not talk about heaven, but about earth—with regard to its ultimate and sacred ground and limits."[26]

## 3. *Revelation as Cognitive*

Theologians of this model generally reject the fideism of the dialectical school; they insist on the involvement of reason in the appropriation of revelation. Further, they reject the view that revelation is a matter of religious sentiment—a view they commonly attribute to the Modernists. Yet they also deny that revelation is discerned by discursive reason, in the sense that it could be proved from a position outside of revelation. Many like to speak with Tillich of "ecstatic" or "theonomous" reason—reason that somehow overleaps itself to discover a meaning beyond all assignable meanings. Gilkey, following Tillich, holds that revelation occurs in a special experience that symbolically manifests ultimate reality.[27] Teilhard de Chardin saw a close parallelism between discovery and revelation.[28] Revelation, in Teilhard's system, may be described as the light that "increases the dim light of reason so that it can see the depths of the future and know where to go to attain its goal."[29] Eulalio Baltazar, who thus summarizes Teilhard, holds that revelation liberates reason and enables it to advance beyond its immature, undifferentiated state.[30]

An American Protestant theologian, Ray L. Hart, stresses the involvement of the imagination in the revelatory process. He shares with many of the thinkers already quoted the idea that revelation is given in order to expand our humanity and give wholeness to our being.[31] Since the imagination is the power by which we anticipate and construct our own future, revelation must actuate the symbolic imagination. God, in revealing, solicits the human imagination to exist out of the potential contained in the paradigmatic events carried by the religious tradition.[32] "Imaginative discourse proceeds *from* the speaking subject who participates the paradigmatic event in genesis of meaning . . ."[33] Schleiermacher was right, Hart believes, affirming that revelation implies founding, original events. "Against Schleiermacher, it must be contended that these founding, original events have the potency to operate upon man as a cognitive being; and that this precisely does *not* make revelation 'originally and essentially doctrine.' "[34]

The American pragmatist philosopher, Eugene Fontinell, prefers to say that revelation is essentially noncognitive. The symbolic language of revelation, he asserts, stimulates the mind to construct symbols that convey a deeper sense of responsibility for the creation of ourselves and our world.[35] The imagination, he holds, is the organ through which ideals are constructed and possibilities are apprehended. The truth of revelation, for Fontinell, is not propositional but pragmatic. Revelation is true if it enriches the quality of individual and community life.[36]

Gabriel Moran, recognizing the difficulty of identifying revelation with knowledge, makes a sharp dichotomy between two meanings of "knowledge":

> If the word "knowledge" connotes the gathering in of objective data and the quantitative increase of facts about the world, then God's revelation cannot be identified with knowledge. God does not compete with infinite [*sic*] objects for man's attention; he does not fit into our schema of known things.
>
> On the other hand, if "knowing" can designate man's primordial receptiveness to being and man's thrust forward to the fullness of life, then the Christian would claim that he knows and is known by God. Man's quest for some ultimate meaning has been met by God's loving gift of himself.[37]

## 4. *Past, Present, and Future*

Revelation for these authors can never be confined to the past. Teilhard de Chardin wrestled with the problem of reconciling the completeness of revelation in Christ with the processive character of all human reality. He maintained that revelation is fully given in the Incarnation, but that the Incarnation continues to occur as the Body of Christ is being built up in the world. The revelation of Christ will reach its culmination at the Parousia.[38] In his study of Teilhard, Baltazar concludes: "Revelation, then, which is none other than Christ, is a sure guide to the land of truth. It is immutable—not as an idea, not as a content, but as a direction."[39]

This general approach is followed by a number of the theologians who identify revelation with new awareness. Baum, for instance, interprets Vatican II as holding that divine revelation continues to occur when the worshiping community reads the Scriptures, proclaims the word, and engages in spiritual conversation.[40] "Divine revelation," he asserts, "has to do with the transformation of man now."[41] Unlike some Teilhardians, Baum does not believe that revelation tells us that humanity will necessarily evolve into a more blessed future as the Parousia approaches. He holds that the gospel assures us that "greater humanization is offered to men in every historical situation."[42]

For nearly all representatives of this model, the revelation once given in Christ continues to be given. Leslie Dewart, a Canadian Catholic philosopher of religion, holds that revelation was completed with the apostles in the sense that through them the age of the "new and eternal testament" began.[43] But "revelation has not ended and indeed never shall as long as God continues to deal personally with man and be present to human history."[44] Through revelation, according to Dewart, God communicates not messages about himself but his own reality. The Christian experience of God, given by God's free initiative, stimulates one to produce concepts and thereby to relate oneself to the reality in which one believes.[45]

Gabriel Moran has repeatedly returned to the theme of revelation as present, but his thought on this subject is by no means easy to follow. Revelation exists today, he contends, as present event, for "a happening is a happening only when it is happening."[46] In *The Present Revelation* he puts the matter very starkly: "Admonitions to keep a balance among past, present and future make no sense. One must choose from the beginning: either the present is everything or it is nothing."[47] Moran's position thus seems to diverge from the futurism of the Teilhardians, but like them he identifies revelation with awareness, accenting experience.

Past history, according to many awareness theologians, retains a certain importance, but not because the events actually took place as related. History is revelatory insofar as it provides paradigms for human self-transcendence that continue to function in the present. According to Hart, paradigmatic events have extraordinary importance in that they manifest patterns by which other events can be coordinated. By participating in paradigmatic events, one is imaginatively stimulated to use signs in a creative way so that the paradigmatic events can convey meaning to those who collaborate in the imaginative mode.[48] Every religious tradition has master images which provide a horizon for the interpretation of contemporary experience[49] and for the fashioning of the future.[50]

Theologians of this orientation tend to assert that Scripture, creeds, and dogmas are of interest not (or not primarily) because they supply information or knowledge about God but because they provide what Fontinell calls "a 'meeting-place' of the continuing and ever-new dialogue between man and God."[51] Believers ought not to worry about whether a biblical story happened as it has been written down, for as Baum puts it, "what counts, after all, is the revealed story's symbolic power and creativity."[52] William M. Thompson, who relies on Baum for some of his insights, calls for an "imaginative hermeneutics" in which "the text serves as a catalyst for our own imaginative capacities."[53]

## 5. The Human Condition

What, if anything, does revelation tell us? The theologians cited in this chapter are almost unanimous in declaring that there are no revealed truths. Gilkey, Dewart, Moran, and Fontinell explicitly say as much. Tillich, Baum, and Hart deny that the truth of revelation is propositional. Yet many theologians of this orientation hold that revelation illuminates our experience in such a way as to enable us to find new meaning in it. Enlightened by God, the believing individual and the believing community are able to speak with new confidence about the human situation, for as Vatican II said in its Pastoral Constitution on the Church in the Modern World, "faith throws a new light on everything, manifests God's design for man's total vocation, and thus directs the mind to solutions which are fully human."[54]

Twentieth-century transcendental theology, according to Baum, has seen faith not as new knowledge but as new consciousness created by the Christian message. Theologians of this school, he remarks, "regarded the whole of human history as being under the influence of God's grace and tried to present the Christian faith as the explication and specification of the redemptive mystery that takes place everywhere."[55] Revelation, he adds, does not tell us about what God is in himself but about God as he is present to human consciousness. Every sentence about God in the traditional creeds, according to Baum, may properly be translated "into a sentence dealing with human possibilities promised to man and changes of consciousness offered to him."[56] In similar fashion, Moran declares: "The professions of faith of the community are not truths revealed by God but they are of special importance in helping to unveil the God who reveals himself in all human life."[57]

Because revelation is seen as clarifying the universal human condition, it is seen as universal in intent. To the extent that any individual or community, empowered by God's presence, experiences itself as grounded in the divine, God's revelation may be found in it. Vatican II encouraged this universalism when it asserted, in its Pastoral Constitution: "All believers of whatever religion have always heard His [God's] revealing voice in the discourse of creatures."[58] O'Meara, summarizing the thought of Rahner, declares: "The Catholic tradition holds that grace is universally offered to mankind— before Moses and Christ, beneath explicit faith. *If grace is universal, so is revelation.*"[59] Moran is of the same mind. In Judaism, he writes, "there was only one God to be believed in and he was not the Jewish god but the God of mankind. A God who has involved himself in partnership with all men is revealed wherever there are men."[60]

Thompson, accepting Moran's universalism, affirms that the Christian consciousness is called in our planetary age to expand itself with the help of interreligious dialogue.[61] From a similar point of view, John Hick calls upon Christians to be prepared to recognize "the tremendous revelatory moments which lie at the basis of the great world faiths."[62] All such faiths, he contends, are "encounters from different historical and cultural standpoints with the same infinite divine reality and as such they lead to differently focused awarenesses of that reality."[63] Hick's recognition of revelation in the non-Christian religions rests on the premise that revelation does not essentially consist in doctrine but in encounter and awareness.

## 6. *Revelation and Faith*

A final question to be answered within this model of revelation theology concerns the relationship between revelation and faith. In the models previously examined, faith is generally understood as a response to revelation. Authors commonly refer to revelation as an objective datum calling for faith, as *le donné révélé* (to quote from the title of a famous book by Ambroise Gardeil). In the present model, this view is regarded as an oversimplification.

Moran, while he gives a certain priority to revelation, defines both revelation and faith in an unusual way. By faith he seems to mean "a searching, open trust that is necessary for all human beings"[64] and by revelation "the underlying reality which gives sense to faith as an open-ended search."[65] Taken in its full context, "revelation is the structure of all experience and faith is an element or basic component of the revelational process."[66]

In contrast to the general opinion, some exponents of the awareness model give priority to faith over revelation. James P. Mackey, for instance, holds that the language of faith, spoken from man's side, is first-order language, expressing a commitment which we directly experience as our own. Revelation talk, spoken as it were from God's side, is second-order language; it adds no new content to faith talk, but invests the latter with a claim to divine authority.[67] "Faith," moreover, "is literal, revelation talk metaphorical. All revelation talk is a metaphorical or mythical description of the literal truth of faith, as necessary and justified as myth itself is necessary and justified, as in fact the only way we have of talking about God at all."[68]

Thompson, who aligns himself with Mackey, puts the matter a little differently. Revelation language, he asserts, is the kind of language that Israelites and Christians spontaneously spoke after their respective expansions of consciousness.[69] When they became aware of the historicity of their own consciousness, they recognized that revelation language is secondary, and that it presupposes the speaker's own experience of faith. For Thompson, faith and revelation are two ways of talking about the same thing. "'Faith,'" he asserts, "*is* the 'revelation,'" or, in our terms, revelation primordially means our expansion of consciousness."[70] The "available God," he further states, "is our expansion of consciousness."[71] Thompson in this last statement is perhaps influenced by Baum, who maintains: "Because of the change in the understanding of man and his world, it has become impossible to think of God as a being over against and above human history."[72] God, for Baum, would seem to be another name for the transcendent dimension of human consciousness, the "new horizon" disclosed in revelation.

## 7. *Summary*

In summary, the consciousness model of revelation may be described in terms of the form of revelation, its content, its salvific power, and the required response.

The form of revelation in this model is that of a breakthrough into a more advanced stage of human consciousness, such that the self is experienced as constituted and empowered by the divine presence. Revelation mediates itself through paradigmatic events which, when recalled, stimulate the imagination to restructure experience.

As an ongoing process, revelation has no fixed content. Its continuity is to be found in its dominant intention, which is always in the direction of greater integration, freedom, and self-possession. Past events and doctrines are revelation only insofar as they have illuminative power for the present. They are subject to continual reinterpretation in the perspectives of contemporary awareness.

Revelation has salvific power insofar as it is a participation in God's creative-redemptive activity leading toward universal reconciliation and fulfillment. Its truth is not merely theoretical but is intrinsically practical and salvational. It activates the imagination and thereby contributes to the restructuring of experience and to the transformation of self and world.

Faith, which may be equated with the new consciousness, arises from revelation in the sense that it is elicited by God's transcendent self-communication. But faith is not a response to revelation in the sense that it apprehends and reacts to a fully constituted objective datum. On the contrary, the process of revelation completes itself when it terminates in the new consciousness which is faith. When they speak and act in faith, individuals and communities use revelation language. But only through mature reflection do they become aware that their concepts of revelation are conditioned and shaped by their own faith. Revelation language is a limping human effort to describe the process by which faith is brought into being through the transcendent activity of God.

## 8. *Merits of the Consciousness Model*

The strengths of the consciousness model of revelation theology are apparent when it is studied in relation to the weaknesses already noted in the previous types of revelation theory. As against the propositional model, it avoids rigidity and authoritarianism; it provides a great flexibility in the reinterpretation of Scripture and Tradition. As against the historical model, it escapes the problem of having to reconstruct the events of biblical history in a convincing way and having to find in them the fullness of revelation. In contrast to the mystical approach, it avoids a withdrawal into sentimentalistic religiosity; it places revelational experience in the full context of human history and progress.[73] Finally, in opposition to the dialectical model, it respects the active role of the human subject in the constitution of the revealed datum.

In terms of the criteria set forth in Chapter I, the consciousness model comes out especially well when judged in terms of plausibility, practical fruitfulness, and value for dialogue.

From Teilhard de Chardin to Gregory Baum, many proponents of this model show a deep concern to present the idea of revelation in a form acceptable to the contemporary mind. According to Vatican II's Pastoral Constitution on the Church in the Modern World, the human race today is passing through a new state of its history; it is passing "from a rather static concept of reality to a more dynamic, evolutionary one."[74] This epochal transition has vast repercussions in the religious sphere. Modes of thinking handed down from the past are often felt to be unsuited to the present age. People find it necessary to distinguish true religion from a magical or superstitious view of the world.[75] More than ever before, human beings find themselves saddled with responsibility for their own future. A theory of revelation and faith which fails to help believers to rise to the new challenges of the day will, in good conscience, be rejected.

The "new awareness" model harmonizes with an evolutionist or transformationist understanding of history, such as is intimated in Vatican II's Pastoral Constitution. By separating revelation from particular statements and doctrinal formulations, it avoids all danger of conflict between faith on the one hand and history or science on the other. By situating revelation within the individual psyche, in its sociocultural context, this model escapes an unwelcome authoritarianism and appeals to minds enamored of freedom and progress.

For many who were becoming disenchanted with the apparent irrelevance and inadequacy of the Bible and of time-honored ecclesiastical formulations, the approach to revelation in terms of stages of consciousness made these ancient sources come alive. The paradigmatic value of the classic texts could be retrieved through a "new hermeneutic" that captured their dynamism toward the future and placed them in the service of a contemporary imaginative vision. The true meaning of the text was no longer sought so much behind the text as before it.

If other models are in danger of focusing attention on the unworldly and of reducing the Christian to passivity before God, these charges cannot be fairly directed against the consciousness model, which includes human responsiveness and creative imagination within the concept of revelation itself. It underscores the responsibility of the believer for the concrete actuality of revelation itself and evaluates revelation pragmatically in terms of its contribution to the making of a more human world. Because of its affinity with the Blondelian philosophy of action, and with various forms of pragmatism, this model of revelation may be said to meet the criterion of practical fruitfulness.

By reason of its widely ecumenical or universalistic horizons, this model of revelation theology is particularly well adapted to dialogue with great religions and secular faiths other than Christianity. It is open to the idea that revelation is present unthematically, or is otherwise thematized, in the consciousness of those who do not belong to the biblical religious tradition. It encourages Christians to believe that their own faith could undergo a further development in the direction of universality by appreciating the perspectives of other human faiths.

## 9. Criticisms of the Consciousness Model

Measured against some of the other criteria, the merits of the awareness model appear more problematical. The most persistent objection has to do with the fidelity of this model to Scripture and tradition. In repudiating the "outsider God," does not this model reject a central biblical theme? The prophets and apostles sharply distinguish between divine revelation and the deliverances of their own consciousness. For them revelation is closely identified with a specific message, which is to be proclaimed as the word of God. In their efforts to reinterpret the Bible to fit into the epochal shifts of modern philosophers of history (Hegel, Jaspers, Teilhard de Chardin, Voegelin . . .), the awareness theologians may be suspected of doing violence to the text.

When confronted with the data of tradition, this model faces similar difficulties. The official teaching of the Christian churches—whether Protestant, Catholic, or Orthodox—has generally taken at face value the biblical reports of determinate revelations given by divine intervention. When immanentistic theories of revelation have been proposed—whether by Hegelian philosophers or by Modernistic theologians—the reaction of church authority has been swift and vehement. Mackey is well aware that the anti-Modernist Oath of 1910 taught that faith is an intellectual assent to truth acquired extrinsically, by hearing, and that faith accepts as true those things said, testified, and revealed (*dicta, testata, revelata*) by a personal God, crediting them on the authority of the One who can never deceive or be deceived.[76] Mackey, however, dismisses the Oath Against Modernism as a "compendium of all that was crudest in nineteenth-century theology."[77] To some critics, however, the consciousness model of revelation might seem to reflect some of the cruder elements in twentieth-century anthropocentrism and historicism.

By its insistence on the continuation of revelation since the apostolic age, the awareness model raises further problems. It seems to imply that Christians today can no longer be satisfied by the revelation given in biblical times, and that the early Christians had only a preparatory revelation in comparisons with modern Christians. This problem is further compounded when it is asserted that Christ reveals himself not only through the Church but also through the signs of the times, through non-Christian religions, and through secular ideologies. One wonders in some cases whether Christ is being made into a mere cipher for an epochal advance in human consciousness. Theories such as these are hard to reconcile with the traditional insistence of Christianity—Protestant, Catholic and Orthodox—on the fullness of the revelation communicated once and for all in Jesus Christ, the Incarnate Word, as witnessed by the apostolic Church.[78]

Christian theologians who accept the consciousness model, therefore, are in an uncomfortable position. They find it hard to appropriate the teaching of the Bible without radically reinterpreting it in their own sense. Catholics, in particular, are burdened with having to reconcile their position with many official documents of their church. The theory of truth characteristic of this model stands in some tension with the kind of teaching authority that popes and bishops have consistently attributed to themselves. Adherents of our fifth model often have ambivalent feelings toward their own ecclesiastical authorities, and thus find it difficult to give a fully coherent account of their position.

Whether the consciousness model is adequate to experience may be disputed. It corresponds to certain kinds of experience, in which people have a lively sense of the presence and activity of God in their own labors and in the great movements of current history. But it would be a mistake to dismiss other types of religious experience which are less well served by this model—for example, that of classical theologians, who tend to find God in a realm above and beyond history, and that of dialectical theologians, who encounter the divine as *mysterium tremendum,* totally other than self and world. It is scarcely surprising, therefore, that a modern Thomist such as Jacques Maritain should have accused Teilhard de Chardin of "genuflecting before the world"[79] and of forging "a new Christian gnosis" which at heart is mere "theology-fiction."[80] Karl Barth, for his part, dismissed Teilhard as "a giant gnostic snake."[81] Gregory Baum, then, does not speak for all contemporary women and men when he declares that it is no longer possible to "think of God as being over against and above human history."[82]

By the tests of theoretical fruitfulness, the awareness model would meet with a mixed judgment. For persons committed to the philosophy of action, pragmatism, or historical relativism, the advantages of this model may seem decisive. But thinkers of a more speculative bent will be dissatisfied with an approach that restricts or denies the cognitive value of revelation. They will find small comfort in Fontinell's assurances that God is not a problem-solver and that authentic faith includes risk and doubt. Many will be reluctant to settle for a church which, like Dewart's, has no message to proclaim, or one which, like Moran's, proclaims its own word and not that of God.

Nowhere is it more evident than in our consideration of this fifth model that the criteria for choosing among models are ambiguous. Each model seeks to defend itself by criteria similar to the seven listed in our first chapter. But they apply the criteria in different ways. The criteria, then, are more useful for focusing the debate than for adjudicating among the models. For an attempt to arrive at a balanced judgment, which takes proper account of all aspects of the problem, it will be helpful to make a comparative review of our five models. Such a review may perhaps pave the way for a constructive theory of revelation.

# Chapter VIII

# THE MODELS COMPARED

## 1. *The Common Point of Reference*

From the models we have considered one could distill different and competing definitions of revelation, such as the following five:

—Revelation is divinely authoritative doctrine inerrantly proposed as God's word by the Bible or by official church teaching.

—Revelation is the manifestation of God's saving power by his great deeds in history.

—Revelation is the self-manifestation of God by his intimate presence in the depths of the human spirit.

—Revelation is God's address to those whom he encounters with his word in Scripture and Christian proclamation.

—Revelation is a breakthrough to a higher level of consciousness as humanity is drawn to a fuller participation in the divine creativity.

The diversity among the conceptions of revelation reflected in these definitions raises a problem. Do all the concepts in fact refer to the same reality? It might appear at this point that theologians are misled by language. The term "revelation" might be equivocal. If so, it might be pointless to ask what revelation really is. All of the models could be correct in the sense that they express realities which in certain theological traditions are termed "revelation." Debates about the nature of revelation could be viewed as senseless feuding about words.

This easy solution, however, ignores the fact that the partisans of the various models have been convinced that their preferred model is the right one. They have been acquainted with, and have polemically argued against, rival models as untrue to the Christian reality. Questions of terminology are intimately connected with questions of truth. Different languages, as Michael Polanyi points out, represent different conclusions; they sustain alternative conceptual frameworks, expressing mutually opposed convictions about the way things are.[1] To borrow an example from Polanyi, the act of classifying a hitherto undiscovered bird as an owl rather than a sparrow is to make a statement about owls and sparrows, which may be either true or false, depending on whether the linguistic decision was correct or incorrect. So, likewise, to call a given idea, experience, or event "revelation" is to make an affirmation about the real order.

How does it happen that Christians who are committed to the same faith can differ in their views of revelation and meaningfully discuss their differences? In addition to their formal or conceptual meaning, common nouns refer to multiple realities, not all of which are clearly and simultaneously present to one's consciousness. When one uses general terms of great human significance, such as truth, justice, courage, and the like, one evokes an unfathomable fund of subsidiary connotations generally shared by those who use the words. In view of this shared fund of tacit knowledge, Socrates was entitled to challenge Thrasymachus, who defined justice as the interest of the stronger. To construct or appraise a definition, one must focus one's attention not on the term being defined but on the reality to which the term refers. To concentrate on the term, as Polanyi points out, would be to destroy its meaning. To study the correct use of terms we must be jointly aware of both the term and the subject matter. The result of the investigation will be both a better understanding of the reality and a more correct and confident use of the term.

Revelation, as a term of great religious significance in the Jewish and Christian traditions, is no more subject to arbitrary definition than is justice. Justice is a term that needs to be known and accepted if the good society is to endure. The same may be said, in a religious context, about revelation. In their commitment to the biblical and Christian understanding of reality, Christians are implicitly committed to a concept of revelation that rightly articulates what the term connotes. Because some properties of revelation are not readily specifiable, it is possible for Christians to disagree about the concept, but because of their common commitment to the shared fund of tacit meaning out of which the concept arises, Christians can meaningfully discuss which definitions are correct. In any such discussion they must be attentive to the realities in which they believe, even though these are not known with full conceptual clarity. The definitions are intended to bring into focus what is subsidiarily and implicitly known in faith, or at least attested in the Christian sources.

In spite of the wide discrepancies already noted, the concepts of revelation implied in the five models are not totally disparate. Certain properties of revelation are readily specifiable, and as a result a solid majority of theologians adhering to any one of our models would probably subscribe to statements such as the following:

—Revelation is God's free action in turning to his spiritual creatures. In revealing, God bestows a gift over and above the fundamental gift of creation, and perfective of the latter.

—By revelation God communicates truth concerning himself and concerning humanity as related to him. Revealed truth is, at least in part, beyond the capacity of the human mind to discover by its own connatural powers.

—The truth of revelation is spiritually important. It has value for salvation (that is to say, for the total and final good of the individual and the community). Most would regard revelation as essential for salvation.

—Revelation, for Christians, comes in a finally decisive way in Jesus, the incarnate Word of God.

—For Christians, the normal way of access to revelation is through the Church which reads and proclaims the biblical message.

—Revelation demands a positive reception on the part of those to whom it comes. This reception or response is usually designated by the term "faith."

Summarizing these agreed points, one could propose a common definition which would probably be acceptable to many adherents of each model: Revelation is God's free action whereby he communicates saving truth to created minds, especially through Jesus Christ as accepted by the apostolic Church and attested by the Bible and by the continuing community of believers.

## 2. Divergences

Compared with this major consensus, the differences are relatively limited. They relate more to the theological understanding of revelation than to the fundamental idea. In the summaries at the end of each exposition we have already noted divergences among the five theories regarding the form, content, and salvific power of revelation, and the appropriate response to revelation.

With respect to the form or process whereby God communicates revelation, the differences may be summarized as follows.

According to the first model, revelation takes the form of divinely authoritative doctrine, sealed by prophecy and miracle. According to the second model, it comes in the form of historical deeds accessible, at least in part, to historical inquiry. For proponents of the third model, revelation comes as a direct interior experience of God's self-communication. In the fourth model, it is seen as taking the form of God's word of address through Jesus Christ and through the fallible human words that bear witness to him. According to the fifth model, God reveals by raising human consciousness through an inner attraction and through external paradigms.

Since form and content are correlative, it should not be surprising that the content of revelation is differently understood in each of the five models. For the first model, revelation consists of suprarational truths concerning God's inner nature, his will, and his plan of salvation. The second model perceives the content of revelation as comprising rather the actual deeds of God in history—deeds which indirectly reveal the attitudes and "relative attributes" of God as loving, merciful, powerful, and the like. According to the third model, the direct content of revelation is God himself, who communicates himself to the soul as utterly transcendent and ineffable. The fourth model agrees with the third on the ineffability of the content, but holds that God himself transcends immediate experience. The word of God reveals God as sovereign and unapproachable; it also reveals the utter sinfulness of all who would seek to approach God or know him by means of merely human resources. The fifth model, finally, designates no specific content for revelation. The content might be said to be whatever anticipations of the final Kingdom are discernible from the new perspective afforded by the higher stage of self-awareness in which the revelation essentially consists.

The third principal point of divergence has to do with the connection between revelation and salvation. The fact of such a connection is not in dispute, but the nature of it is. From the point of view of our first model, revelation is salvational because it informs human beings about the blessings of heaven and the way to inherit them. For the neo-Scholastics, revelation concerns God, as man's supernatural end, and the supernatural means by which that end may be attained. As seen in the second model, revelation is connected with salvation because it inspires trust in the power and goodness of God, who comes to the help of those who rely on him. In the perspectives of the third model, revelation and salvation coincide. To the extent that God's loving presence is experienced, one already enjoys eternal life. According to the fourth model, the saving efficacy of revelation necessarily involves the destruction of human self-confidence. By communicating God's judgment of condemnation and pardon (two dialectically intertwined aspects of the same judgment), revelation cancels out the creature's guilt before God. In the fifth model, finally, revelation is seen as salutary insofar as it involves its recipients in the building of God's Kingdom, in which the old creation is brought to a transcendent fulfillment, and thus "saved."

Since the form and content of revelation are different in the different models, it follows that the response to revelation must also be differently conceived. Adherents of all five models agree that revelation calls for faith, but they have different understandings of faith and of its relationship to revelation. In the first model faith is an assent to fully constituted revealed truths contained in the written or transmitted word of God. The motive of faith is the authority of the divine teacher, who can neither deceive nor be deceived. In the second model, faith is understood as trust in God as the Lord of history, who has repeatedly proved his goodness and faithfulness to those who rely on him. In the third model faith is understood rather in the sense of "pious affections" (Schleiermacher), the "prayer of the heart" (Sabatier), or some such loving and devout response. In the fourth model faith means personal acceptance of one's status as a forgiven sinner thanks to God's mercy in Jesus Christ. In the fifth model, finally, faith is understood as a commitment to, and participation in, the movement whereby the encompassing divine Spirit continually leads creation forward to its ultimate and surpassing fulfillment.

In the first three models revelation is seen as prior to faith. In the fourth, the priority of revelation is still stressed, but revelation is seen as somehow including the response of faith. In the fifth model, as we have noted, the active role of the believing subject is so emphasized that revelation tends to be subordinated to faith, which formally constitutes revelation by affirming it.

## 3. *Apparent Contradictions*

From these contrasts it is not immediately apparent whether the models are complementary or mutually exclusive. While it would be tempting to hold that the models are fully compatible, at least in their positive assertions, there are questions to which partisans of the different models generally give contradictorily opposed answers. Five illustrations may be given.

1. Does revelation communicate any factual data over and above what can be known apart from it? Proponents of the first two models hold that revelation is inseparably connected with the knowledge of specific statements or deeds attributed to divine agency. Proponents of the last three models commonly assert that revelation gives no factual information. Revelation and secular knowledge, they contend, lie in different dimensions, and thus can neither confirm nor contradict each other.

2. Does revelation give infallible certitude? The first model replies with an unequivocal yes. The other models are unfavorable to the idea of infallible statements, but in their own way profess the certainty of revelation. The second model acknowledges that God's interventions in history are clearly perceptible; the third, that the experience of God is self-attesting; the fourth, that the Holy Spirit gives full assurance of God's word; and the fifth, that the Spirit implants within the faithful a sure instinct for discerning the direction in which God's purposes are moving.

3. Is the truth of revelation demonstrable to reason? The first model suggests an affirmative answer—namely, that the arguments from miracle and prophecy extrinsically certify the trustworthiness of the divine messengers, and hence indirectly authenticate the mes-

sage before the bar of reason. The second model affords two different answers. In its "salvation-history" form, this model shuns apologetics and relies on the pure gift of faith, which is seen as over and above, but not contrary to, reason. Pannenberg and his circle, on the other hand, hold that revelation, while necessarily indirect, is demonstrable to historical reason. The third model denies that revelation, as an ecstatic experience, is accessible to discursive reason. For the fourth model, revelation is absolute paradox, scandalous and repugnant to natural reason. Advocates of the fifth model, for their part, characteristically assert that revelation is apprehended by a transformed or "theonomous" reason.

4. Did revelation reach its completion in the apostolic age? The first and second models hold that revelation culminated with Christ and the apostles, and that nothing can be added to the deposit except by way of interpretation or clarification. According to the third model, every age is equally close to the revealing God, who communicates himself afresh to every recipient. The fourth model sees the event of revelation as occurring here and now, but the gospel message as unchanging. According to the fifth model, revelation continues and even increases as the world draws nearer to its final consummation.

5. Is revelation given outside the biblical religions? To this question the first and second models generally respond in the negative, though many proponents of these models speak of a "general" or "natural" revelation which is preparatory to the "special" or "supernatural" revelation of the Old and New Testaments. The third model holds that all peoples have access to revelation on the same basis as Jews and Christians. The fourth model rejects even the idea of general or natural revelation, insisting that Christ alone is God's revealing Word. The fifth theory holds that all humanity is affected by the offer of revelation, for God is everywhere at work, in various stages, in the history of creation.

These five questions may suffice to illustrate the difficulty of simultaneously adhering to different models. The point could be further emphasized by considering additional questions such as the following: Is revelation clear (as in models one, two, and three), paradoxical (as in model four), or obscure (as in model five)? Is it direct (as in models one and three) or indirect (as in models two, four, and five)? Is revelation immediate (as in model three) or mediated (as in all the others, which however, differ among themselves regarding the process of mediation)?

## 4. *Values and Disvalues*

The seven criteria set forth in Chapter I call attention to positive values to be sought in any theology of revelation. Some of these values are found preeminently in one or another of the models. For instance:

Model one safeguards the meaning and authority of revelation, which is here seen as providing clear, firm answers to deep and persistent questions concerning God, humanity, and the universe, and thus as offering sure guidance through the confusions of life.

Model two is outstanding for its vindication of the realism of revelation. Not satisfied with a merely verbal or interior style of revelation, it perceives manifestations of God's love and power in historic deeds such as the Exodus and especially, for Christians, the event of Jesus Christ. In events such as these, which are richer than all that can be said about them, God by making signs "signifies" his will and intentions.

Model three is to be valued for its insistence on the immediacy of revelation and on the fact that the true content of revelation is God himself, rather than any words or ideas about him. Revelation, it tells us, can never be simply a report about what others heard and saw; it must contain the element of immediacy between the believer and God.

Model four reminds one of the abiding distance between God and sinful creatures such as ourselves. It instills deep reverence and gratitude to the Lord who, in judging us, forgives. Dissuading us from any Promethean endeavor to wrest God's secrets from him, it prompts us to rely humbly on God's powerful and redemptive Word.

Model five emphasizes the meaningfulness of revelation to the human task. It arouses commitment to peace, justice, and to all that can make human beings participate more fully in the blessings of God's Kingdom.

Corresponding to these assets there are specific shortcomings in each of the five models taken alone. The first model treats meaning too narrowly as a matter of explicit propositional teaching. It is authoritarian and extrinsicist, for it does not assure that the content of revelation address any human need or aspiration, or that it fit in with the order of reality as commonly experienced.

The second model raises in acute form the question, how can historical knowledge, which deals with contingent phenomena, detect the presence of the divine? It commonly neglects the factors that control the selection and interpretation of past events on the part of the biblical writers or the Church.

The third model raises, and perhaps fails to solve, the question whether human consciousness can immediately perceive God, who is transcendent and nonobjective. If any such perception is possible, it would seem to be incommunicable and thus incapable of sustaining the Church or its teaching.

In the fourth model, the almost exclusive concentration on the negative phase of the dialectic gives rise to a serious problem regarding coherence. How can the clash of contradictory statements result in a message that is intelligible and credible?

The fifth model seems particularly subject to the charge of relativism. It fails to explain how a breakthrough that occurs at a particular point in the evolution of consciousness can retain its validity for other times and places. How does revelation become constitutive of an abiding, transcultural community committed to definite scriptures and creeds?

Turning more specifically to the seven criteria, we may now observe that different models have different strengths and weaknesses. In terms of faithfulness to the Bible (criterion 1a), the first, second, and fourth models come out better than, probably, the third and fifth. In terms of faithfulness to tradition (criterion 1b), the first and fourth models fare better than the third and fifth, or possibly the second. In terms of internal consistency (criterion 2), the first three models would seem more satisfactory than the fourth and fifth. In terms of plausibility (criterion 3), the second, third, and fifth models appear to have the advantage over the first and fourth. In terms of adequacy to experience (criterion 4), the third, fourth, and fifth models have more to recommend them than the first and second. In terms of practical fruitfulness (criterion 5), distinctions must be made. The first model is especially serviceable to the Church as institution; the third, to the individual spiritual life; and the fifth, to the general advancement of human society. In theoretical fruitfulness—our sixth criterion—the first, second, and fourth models have proved their ability to sustain prominent theological schools, whereas certain other models, such as the third, are relatively less concerned with theory. In terms of the final criterion—value for dialogue—the third and fifth models would seem superior to the first, second, and fourth.

# 5. *Theological Options*

If we take it as evident that there are at least some irreconcilable points of difference between different models, it is logically impossible to accept them all. For practical purposes, then, the theologian is left with only four options: first, to accept one theory, rejecting all the others; second, to follow different models in dealing with different questions; third, to combine or harmonize models, adjusting the differences so that contradictions are eliminated; and, fourth, to construct a new model differing from the five we have studied.

## (a) *Election of One Model*

The first option is a definite possibility. Each of the models represents the characteristic positions of a number of theologians whose competence is generally acknowledged. Many living theologians fall predominantly into one of our five models, although others combine the positions of two or more models. To elect some one of the five alternatives is to adopt a clear and consistent stance.

In deciding which, if any, model to choose, one will inevitably be influenced by certain "nontheological factors." A given individual will approach the question of revelation with a whole complex of prior attitudes shaped by temperament, upbringing, education, social contacts, and experiences. All such factors have power to sharpen one's perceptions but also to blind. Theological reflection will not necessarily lead one to abandon these prior considerations, but it should lead to a more responsible choice, which will frequently modify one's previous commitments while partly reaffirming them.

In view of the strengths and weaknesses to be found in all five models the choice of any one to the exclusion of the rest is by no means easy. The strengths in the models that have to be rejected and the weaknesses in the one chosen for acceptance alike militate against this first option.

### (b) *Eclecticism*

What, then, of our second option, eclecticism? On the principle that all the models have certain strong points, it might seem proper to use one model in dealing with one problem, other models for other problems. Such a procedure, however, would scarcely be permissible in theology, which must strive for consistency and intelligibility. Each model of revelation theology represents a "Gestalt," implicitly committing its adherents to specific answers to a whole gamut of questions. Conversely, any particular answer to a given question—for example, whether revelation is fully given in the Christ-event—commits one to a model of revelation theology that supports such an answer. By implication it commits one to compatible answers to all other questions that might be asked. Thus the question of models or types cannot be evaded. No theological question can be approached as though it were an isolated unit, unconnected with other questions. Consistency demands that the theologian seek answers not simply to individual questions, taken one by one, but to the "meta-question" of a comprehensive approach to revelation theology. A purely eclectic approach would be superficial and irresponsible.

### (c) *Harmonization*

The third option would be to harmonize two or more models, perhaps all five. It might seem that a relatively more adequate theory of revelation could be constructed by putting together the best in every model. Why should it not be possible to combine the givenness of revelation, as held in Model one, with its contemporary relevance, as stressed in Model five? Cannot the immediacy of revelation, brought out by Model three, be reconciled with the abiding distance between God and ourselves, accented in Model four? Perhaps by making appropriate distinctions one might be able to find that the values of all five models could be integrated.

We have already noted, however, that the various models give apparently contradictory answers to many fundamental questions. Since it is impossible to hold contradictories at the same time, any harmonization of the models will require an overcoming of the weaknesses of the models as usually understood, and thus the creation of something new. To compose an intelligible unity out of two or more models requires that the models be modified by integration into a larger complex. Thus we are led to our fourth option.

### (d) *Innovation*

If innovation were not possible, systematic theology would no longer be a living discipline. All past theories of revelation, including the five models we have considered, arose through innovation. Some have arisen in rather recent times. Our fourth and fifth models, for example, can hardly be said to have existed, except in germ, before the twentieth century. Further innovation may yet be called for if we are to overcome the conflicts among the existing models. But, once again, we must take account of the working principle that the theological opinions of a large number of intelligent and reflective Christians may not lightly be set aside. The history of theology seems to prove that creative innovation generally comes about through profound immersion in the tradition. The outstanding theologians have normally respected their predecessors and have sought to preserve the insights handed down by them. Radical and disruptive shifts in theology have rarely produced lasting fruits. Change does occur, but the new models emerge gradually, often almost imperceptibly. Without setting bounds to what the inspiration of the Holy Spirit or the genius of the human mind may bring about, we may surmise that new models of revelation theology, if they prevail, are likely to be modifications of theories already in currency.

As a case in point one may cite the work of H. Richard Niebuhr. In his *The Meaning of Revelation* he set out to mediate between the liberalism of Ritschl and Troeltsch, on the one hand, and the dialectical theology of Barth, on the other. In this way he concocted a novel theory of "confessional history" as revelation. Separating "inner history" (concerned with values) from "outer history" (concerned with facts), he held that revelation occurs in the former, inasmuch as people's shared memories provide them with images "by means of which all the occasions of personal and common life become intelligible."[2] Revelation, for H. R. Niebuhr, was an open-ended process in which human thoughts "are caught up in the great turmoil of a transvaluation."[3] The end-product of Niebuhr's synthesis in many ways foreshadowed what we have described as the "new awareness" model.

## 6. Dialectical Retrieval

What seems to be required at this point is the kind of process described by Bernard Lonergan under the heading of "dialectic."[4] In its initial phase, corresponding approximately to the content of this chapter, dialectic seeks to identify the fundamental conflicts between diverse interpretations, past and present. Then, by reference to certain critical standards (such as Lonergan's own preferred standard of conversion to the transcendent), the dialectician seeks to bring to light the positive values (which Lonergan calls "positions") and the disvalues (which he calls "counterpositions") in the mutually opposed theories. Dialectic thus points the way to a new proposal that can "sublate" the previous theories. Referring to Rahner's *Hearers of the Word,* Lonergan adds:

> I would use this notion [sublation] in Karl Rahner's sense rather than Hegel's to mean that what sublates goes beyond what is sublated, introduces something new and distinct, puts everything on a new basis, yet so far from interfering with the sublated or destroying it, on the contrary needs it, includes it, preserves all its proper features and properties, and carries them forward to a fuller realization within a richer context.[5]

In a sublation of this sort, it is not sufficient to make a static comparison between existing theories. A theologian who lacked personal familiarity with revelation would be totally at the mercy of reports from others, and would be incapable of transcending them. To validate, invalidate, or transcend existing theories one needs independent acquaintance with what the theories purport to explore. The seven criteria with which we have worked are merely presumptive signs of conformity between a theory and revelation itself. The supreme criterion, above and behind all seven, is adequacy to that revelation. A theory of revelation is sound and acceptable to the extent that it measures up to, and illuminates, the reality of revelation.

As mentioned in the opening pages of this chapter, the theology of revelation could not arise at all except that a certain prethematic awareness of the reality of revelation is given to all in faith. Theology, then, becomes fruitful when it returns to its original source and seeks to trace, with the help of the work that other thinkers have done, the process whereby revelation takes hold of the human consciousness and engenders speech about itself. A sublation of the existing models can be achieved only from an independent standpoint which gives personal contact with the reality with which the models purport to deal.

In spite of what one might expect, such an independent standpoint is not achieved by ignoring the tradition of Christian speech about revelation. On the contrary, revelation as apprehended by Christians cannot be known except by allowing oneself to dwell confidently in the clues that point to Christian revelation. For the Bible, or the traditional statements of faith, or the contemporary existence of the Church, to serve as clues, one must dwell within them as extensions of one's own body and allow them to provide lenses wherein God's revelation can be apprehended.[6] At this point in our investigation, it will be helpful to examine more closely the process by which created media of this kind can disclose the reality of the revealing God.

In the following chapter I shall contend that revelation is given and transmitted by symbolic communication. Symbol, I shall maintain, is a pervasive category that functions, sometimes more dominantly and sometimes more recessively, in each of the five models. The idea of symbolic communication, I believe, can be of great value as a dialectical tool for bringing out the strong points and overcoming the weaknesses in the typical theories we have hitherto examined. Chapter IX will therefore be pivotal for everything that follows in this book.

A word of caution may be needed here. I am not proposing a sixth model, the "symbolic," to be played off against the other five The variety of models has advantages that should not be sacrificed by the adoption of a single model, however apt. The five models already analyzed give a sufficient panorama of the elements to be included in a sound theology of revelation. By recourse to symbol as a dialectical tool it will be possible, I believe, to enrich and correct the existing models and to achieve a fruitful cross-fertilization.

# PART TWO

PART TWO

# Chapter IX

# SYMBOLIC MEDIATION

## 1. *The Meaning of Symbol*

The poets have long been familiar with the connection between symbol and revelation. Samuel Taylor Coleridge affirmed very simply: "It is by Symbols alone that we can acquire intellectual knowledge of the Divine."[1] William Butler Yeats, using the concept of revelation in a wide sense, declared: "A symbol is indeed the only possible expression of some invisible essence, a transparent lamp about a spiritual flame; while allegory is one of many possible representations of an embodied thing, or familiar principle, and belongs to fancy and not to imagination: the one is revelation, the other an amusement."[2]

In twentieth-century theology the idea of revelation as symbolic disclosure has achieved wide popularity. This approach is represented, with important nuances and variations, by such esteemed thinkers as Paul Tillich, H. R. Niebuhr, Karl Rahner, Paul Ricoeur, Langdon Gilkey, Ray Hart, John Macquarrie, Louis Dupré, and Gregory Baum. I shall seek to present the theory in my own way, without binding myself to the precise epistemology or terminology of other authors.

According to this approach, revelation never occurs in a purely interior experience or an unmediated encounter with God. It is always mediated through symbol—that is to say, through an externally perceived sign that works mysteriously on the human consciousness so as to suggest more than it can clearly describe or define. Revelatory symbols are those which express and mediate God's self-communication.

The notion of symbol utilized in this theory calls for some

elucidation. In agreement with many modern authors, I shall hold that symbol is a special type of sign to be distinguished from a mere indicator (such as the shadow on a sun dial) or a conventional cipher (such as a word or diagram). A symbol is a sign pregnant with a plenitude of meaning which is evoked rather than explicitly stated. Ricoeur uses the examples of defilement, which in religious literature serves as a symbol for the effects of sin and guilt.[3] The literary critic Philip Wheelwright speaks in this connection of "tensive symbols"— that is to say, symbols which "draw life from a multiplicity of associations, subtly and for the most part subconsciously interrelated," and which thereby derive the power to tap a vast potential of semantic energy.[4] Wheelwright contrasts these "tensive symbols," with what he calls steno-symbols, which are practically the same as what other authors call mere signs. Steno-symbols, for Wheelwright, have an exact identity of reference, thanks to their abstract quality or simply as a matter of human stipulation. When I speak of symbols in the following pages, I shall be following the more common terminology, and thus referring to what Wheelwright would call tensive symbols.

With terminology different from Wheelwright's, Michael Polanyi distinguishes between indicators and symbols.[5] Indicative signs, in his view, are those which function in a purely subsidiary way, so that without being attended to they direct our attention to other objects which are focally known. When, for example, we read a letter, we hardly notice the print or even the language, since our attention is directed to the meaning. The indicative signs lack intrinsic interest. We interpret them as mere observers, without being deeply moved by th signs themselves.

In symbolic communication, the clues draw attention to themselves. We attend to them, and if we surrender to their power they carry us away, enabling us to integrate a wider range of impressions, memories, and affections than merely indicative signs could enable us to integrate. Thanks to symbols, we can bring an indefinite number of diffuse memories and experiences into a kind of focus. As examples of symbolic communication Polanyi refers to the reactions of a patriot in the presence of a national flag or the tombstone of a fallen hero.

No clear dichotomy can be drawn between the symbolic and the nonsymbolic. All comprehension demands that we go out of ourselves and dwell in the subsidiaries in order to perceive their joint meaning. But in symbolic knowledge a deeper degree of indwelling is required. To enter the world of meaning opened up by the symbol we must give ourselves; we must be not detached observers but engaged participants.

For all that follows, it will be important not to restrict the idea of symbol to the literary sphere. Natural objects, historical persons, visible artifacts, and dreams can all be symbols. In the sphere of religion it is helpful to distinguish between cosmic or natural symbols (such as the sun), personal or historical symbols (such as David and the Davidic monarchy), and artistic symbols (such as temples and icons). Thus the figurative speech of sacred literature is only one species within the genus of religious symbolism.

It would be impossible in this chapter to do justice to the complex relationships between literary symbols and other forms such as analogy, myth, metaphor, allegory, parable, and ritual. A few observations may, however, be in order. An analogy is an affinity or proportional likeness between objects which are fundamentally dissimilar; for example, life on the human, animal, and vegetative levels (or, improperly speaking, life in a tire). Analogues, being rooted in the nature of things, are self-interpreting. Symbols, although frequently based on analogy, may require explanation if they derive not from intrinsic similarities but from historical associations (e.g., the Cross as a symbol of redemption).

According to many authors any symbol-sentence is a metaphor, in the sense that it transfers to one subject what is proper to another.[6] If I say "man is a thinking reed" or "Napoleon was a wolf," I am making a statement that is grammatically a proposition. The metaphor, however, is not really a proposition, because the figurative character of the predication precludes its use in syllogistic argument.

The relationship between metaphor and symbol is much discussed. When a metaphor is used simply to illustrate what is already known in a nonsymbolic way, it does not function heuristically as a symbol. Going further, some literary critics, such as Wheelwright (with whose position Ricoeur in substance agrees), hold that every living metaphor is too personal and evanescent to be called a symbol—a term which in their view connotes greater objective density and firmer rootedness in the stable forms of biological and communal existence.[7] Although their view of symbol may be too narrow, we may agree with these authors that the power of metaphor depends on the prior presence of meaningful structures in the events and realities to which the metaphor refers.

Myths, allegories, and parables are literary entities replete with symbolic elements. According to some authors, myth is presymbolic, inasmuch as mythical thought fails to distinguish between the literal and the nonliteral—a distinction they regard as essential to symbolic discourse. These authors acknowledge, however, that "the mythical origin of the primary symbols of religious expression is beyond question."[8] It is increasingly common to use the term myth in a wider sense to designate any symbolic story that underlies and shapes the collective life of a group.

Allegory, on the contrary, may be called "postsymbolic." It uses symbols to convey meanings that have already been grasped in an explicit, reflective way. In allegory, symbolism operates rhetorically but not heuristically.[9]

Parables, according to Norman Perrin, can function either as similes or as metaphors. If the parable is a simile, it "teases the mind into recognition of new aspects of reality," often by using symbols or myths, such as, in the parables of Jesus, the Kingdom of God. If the parable is metaphorical, it "produces a shock which induces a new vision of world and new possibilities . . . for the experiencing of that existential reality which the myth mediates."[10] Many of the biblical parables are primarily oriented toward evoking a decision, but they contain symbolic elements which serve to mediate revelation. We shall presently consider how the symbol of the Kingdom of God functions in the teaching of Jesus as a medium of revelation.

Ritual, finally, is a symbolic or mythic narrative in action. It dramatically renews the sacred events which it recalls. By participation in the ritual the worshiper is able to discern ultimate meaning, to integrate the negative elements of existence, and to experience the power of the sacred. Ritual symbolism, according to Mircea Eliade, "effects a permanent solidarity between man and the sacred" and is thus "able to carry on the process of hierophanization."[11] These observations bring us back to our theme of revelation and symbol.

## 2. Revelatory Symbolism in Scripture

As a preliminary indication of the connection between revelation and symbol, it is worth noting that the great revelations of which we read in the Bible are replete with symbolic ingredients:[12] for example, in the Old Testament, the miracles of the Exodus, the theophanies of Sinai, the "still, small voice" heard by Elijah, the inaugural visions of the major prophets, and the ecstasies of the apocalyptic seers. In the New Testament the life of Jesus is introduced by the highly symbolic circumstances of his conception and birth. His public life is inaugurated by numinous phenomena such as the heavenly voice and the descent of the Holy Spirit in the form of a dove. His ministry is marked by sign events such as the transfiguration and the miracles of healing, and is closed by the symbolic act of his death upon the Cross. The glorious life of Jesus and the history of the Church are initiated, once again, by symbolic occurrences such as the Resurrection and the descent of the Holy Spirit. The presence of these symbolic events at the major turning point of biblical history lends support to the thesis, sometimes proposed, that redemptive history consists of a series of "disclosure situations."[13] The sign-events comprising this history have been impressively depicted "as symbols fraught with meaning and as the point of entry through which salvation emerges into language."[14]

Not only the events of biblical history but the central themes in the teaching of the prophets, of Jesus, and of the apostles are likewise symbolic in form. This point can be illustrated by an examination of nearly any of the key themes of the Old and New Testaments, such as that of the Kingdom of God. As Norman Perrin points out, the Kingdom of God in the preaching of Jesus is not a clear concept or idea with a single, univocal significance. Rather, it is a symbol that "can represent or evoke a whole range or series of conceptions or ideas"[15] and thus bring the hearer into the very reality borne by the preaching of Jesus. Perrin profusely illustrates the symbolic nature of this language as found in the proverbial sayings of Jesus, in the Lord's Prayer, and especially in the Gospel parables. The constant factor in these diverse materials, he maintains, is the symbol of the Kingdom of God, which had for Jewish audiences the power to evoke the faith-experience of God's dramatic action on be-half of his people and to elicit an appropriate response. To seek to pin down some one definite meaning of the term "Kingdom of God," according to Perrin, would be to overlook the polysemic character of symbolic communication, which always suggests more than it clearly states. By virtue of this symbolic dimension, the revelatory language of Scripture is capable of grasping and trans-forming the responsive hearer.

## 3. *Common Properties of Symbolism and Revelation*

The argument from Scripture, to be sure, does not prove that revelation must by its very nature be symbolic. To establish this, one would have to construct a theoretical argument based on the nature of revelation itself. The validity of such an argument would not be universally admitted, for the reasoning would appeal to theological and anthropological assumptions that are not self-evident. While ac-knowledging these inevitable limitations, I shall seek to propose an argument based on the parallelism between the properties of sym-bolic communication and of revelation. Four such properties may be singled out.[16]

First, symbolism gives not speculative but participatory knowl-edge—knowledge, that is to say, of a self-involving type. A symbol is never a sheer object. It speaks to us only insofar as it lures us to situate ourselves mentally within the universe of meaning and value which it opens up to us. As Nathan Mitchell says, "A symbol is not an object to be manipulated through mime and memory, but an en-vironment to be inhabited. Symbols are places to live, breathing spaces that help us discover the possibilities that life offers." "To put the matter succinctly," he continues, "every symbol deals with a new discovery and every symbol is an open-ended action, not a closed-off object. By engaging in symbols, by inhabiting their environment, people discover new horizons for life, new values and motivation."[17]

Hence the second property: Symbol, insofar as it involves the knower as a person, has a transforming effect. The healing capacity of symbolism is dramatically illustrated by psychotherapy. Victor White, a theologian disciple of Carl Jung, writes as follows:

A symbol, as we say, "does something to us," it moves us, shifts our center of awareness, changes our values. Whether it is just looked at or heard, acted out, painted out, written out, or danced out, it arouses not only thought, but delight, fear, awe, horror, and the rest. . . . Jung saw . . . that it was the very instrument which, just because it was polyvalent, transformed consciousness itself and thereby the sick personality. This is what Jung means when he calls the symbol the psychological machine which transforms energy into work, much as a turbine transforms the untamed, useless energy of a torrent into power that can be controlled and applied.[18]

Thirdly, symbolism has a powerful influence on commitments and behavior.[19] It works on people like an incantation. It stirs the imagination, releases hidden energies in the soul, gives strength and stability to the personality, and arouses the will to consistent and committed action. For this reason all important social and political movements have felt the need to equip themselves with appropriate symbols. A national flag or anthem, for example, has symbolic power to instill sentiments of patriotism and motivate citizens to heroic deeds on behalf of their country.

Fourthly, symbol introduces us into realms of awareness not normally accessible to discursive thought. As Tillich puts it, a symbol "opens up levels of reality which otherwise are closed to us . . . and also unlocks dimensions and elements of our soul which correspond to the dimensions and elements of reality."[20] This process always involves an ingredient of mystery. Thomas Carlyle rightly observed: "In the symbol there is concealment and yet revelation."[21] The symbol discloses not by presenting its meaning for inspection but by drawing us into its own movement and (as we have learned from Polanyi) by carrying us out of ourselves.[22] The meaning of the symbol, therefore, cannot be precisely nailed down in terms of categorical thought and language. Yet the symbol is not without value for the serious quest of truth. It "gives rise to thought," according to Ricoeur's famous phrase.[23] By putting us in touch with deeper aspects of reality symbolism can generate an indefinite series of particular insights.

This multivalent quality of symbolic knowledge is closely connected with the healing power previously referred to. Symbols, according to Eliade, are able to "identify, assimilate, and unify diverse levels and realities that are to all appearances incompatible."[24] Or, as he says in another place, "The symbol is thus able to reveal a

perspective in which heterogeneous realities are susceptible of articulation into a whole,"[25] thus enabling human life to be integrated
into the totality of being.

These four qualities of symbolic knowledge make it apparent
how symbol can be uniquely apt as a medium of revelation; for the
qualities of revelation correspond, on a transcendent level, to those
just noted in symbolic communication. In the first place, revelation
gives participatory awareness. To accept the Christian revelation is
to involve oneself in a community of faith and thus to share in the
way of life marked out by Jesus. "He who does not love does not
know God; for God is love" (1 Jn 4:8).

Secondly, revelation is transformative, for its introduces us into a
new spiritual world, shifts our horizons, our perspectives, our point
of view. Christians come to perceive themselves as personally related to God. In biblical and traditional language, they become
adopted members of God's family and household, called to repentance, forgiveness, and newness of life.

As a consequence of its transformative character, revelation,
thirdly, has an impact on the commitments and behavior of those
who receive it. If revelation came simply as abstract propositional
truth or historical information, the act of faith by which it was
accepted could be a merely theoretical assent. But if revelation is
symbolic truth, the act by which it is accepted must express itself in
conduct. Faith must be an obedience whereby, as Vatican II puts it,
one "entrusts one's whole self freely to God."[26] Through faith the
Christian enters a community of believers and becomes bound to
it, as well as to its Lord, by ties of loyalty and trust.

Finally, thanks to its symbolic character, revelation gives insight
into mysteries that reason can in no way fathom. For Jews and
Christians, Eliade points out, "Yahweh is both kind and wrathful;
the God of the Christian mystics and theologians is terrible and gen-
tle at once, and it is this *coincidentia oppositorum* which is the starting point for the boldest speculations of such men as pseudo-
Dionysius, Meister Eckhardt, and Nicholas of Cusa."[27] Revelation is
itself a mystery inasmuch as it is the self-communication of the God
"who dwells in unapproachable light" (1 Tim 6:16). Contemporary
symbolic theology, as represented by Tillich, insists on the mysterious nature of revelation: "In being revealed [the transcendent] does
not cease to remain concealed, since its secrecy pertains to its very

essence; and when it is revealed it is so precisely as that which is hidden."[28] Vatican Council I had said as much when it declared: "Divine mysteries of their very nature so excel the created intellect that even when they have been given in revelation and accepted in faith, that very faith still keeps them veiled in a sort of obscurity, as long as 'we are exiled from the Lord' in this mortal life, 'for we walk by faith and not by sight' (2 Cor 5:6–7)."[29] The mysterious character of revelation, however, does not deprive it of intelligibility, for as Vatican Council I asserted in the paragraph just quoted, "reason, enlightened by faith, . . . achieves with God's help a certain understanding, and indeed a very fruitful one," of the divine mysteries.

## 4. Examples of Christian Symbolism

To illustrate the variety of revelatory symbols, some examples may be given. The symbolism of light affords an instance of cosmic or nature symbolism. By analogy light is closely connected with knowledge and revelation. Pervasive in many of the world religions, light symbolism held a central position in Zoroastrianism, Gnosticism, and neo-Platonism. It is prominent in the Qumran documents and in many parts of the Bible. Christ, according to John, declares himself the light of the world (Jn 8:12) and, according to Matthew, calls his disciples also the light of the world (Mt 5:14). The First Letter of John goes so far as to assert: God is light (1 Jn 1:5). For the ancients light, coming from mysterious heavenly bodies, was a numinous phenomenon, but, as Macquarrie points out, its numinous power has been somewhat diminished by the scientific understanding and technological control of light that human agents now possess. To restore something of the existential power belonging to this symbol, Macquarrie proposes substituting the concept of "openness," which, in his opinion, closely corresponds to it.[30]

A second kind of revelatory symbolism is more properly historical. One of the most central Christian symbols, by all accounts, is the Cross.[31] As a natural symbol, it conveys the ideas of encounter, crisis, and choice, as when we speak of "crossroads." It also signifies collision and opposition, with the connotation of "being crossed." As a wooden object, the Cross is a burden to be borne, as appears in the phrase, "to carry one's cross." In the context of the Gospels, it signifies meekness, obedience, and endurance under hardship. As an instrument of punishment, the Cross is a symbol of condemnation, pain, and death. In the case of Jesus, it signifies his heroic submission to the Father's will and his unlimited love for sinners such as ourselves. It represents also the Father's love in giving his own Son to be our ransom. From another point of view it symbolizes the enormity of human sin, and the climax of the history of human rebellion against God. As stained by the blood of Jesus, the Cross signifies the agency whereby we are reconciled to God and to one another. Representations of the empty Cross, or of the Cross from which Christ reigns, communicate the triumph of the Resurrection. To Constantine and the Crusaders the Cross became the emblem of victory. For the baptized Christian, the sign of the Cross expresses commitment to discipleship.

Sacramental worship provides still a third type of symbol. In a dense paragraph, John Macquarrie indicates something of the wealth of meaning in the Eucharist as a symbol:

> The Eucharist sums up in itself Christian worship, experience and theology in an amazing richness. It seems to include everything. . . . It combines Word and Sacrament; its appeal is to spirit and to sense; it brings together the sacrifice of Calvary and the presence of the risen Christ; it is communion with God and communion with man; it covers the whole gamut of religious moods and emotions. Again, it teaches the doctrine of creation, as the bread, the wine, and ourselves are brought to God; the doctrine of atonement, for these gifts have to be broken in order that they may be perfected; the doctrine of salvation, for the Eucharist has to do with incorporation into Christ and the sanctification of human life; above all, the doctrine of incarnation, for it is no distant God whom Christians worship but one who has made himself accessible in the world. The Eucharist also gathers up in itself the meaning of the Church; its whole action implies and sets forth our mutual interdependence in the body of Christ; it unites us with the Church of the past and even, through its paschal overtones, with the first people of God, Israel; and it points to the eschatological consummation of the kingdom of God, as an anticipation of the heavenly banquet. Comprehensive though this description is, it is likely that I have missed something out, for the Eucharist seems to be inexhaustible.[32]

All three of the symbols here used as examples may be said to possess an indefinite range of potential significations, many of them deeply ingrained in the archetypal forms of human consciousness. It would be futile to search in any of these symbols for some one lesson or articulate meaning. Because of their capacity to integrate a multitude of lofty speculations and half-felt sentiments, symbols have an integrative and reconciling power far greater than any explicit statement.

## 5. *Return to the Five Models*

In view of the remarkable correspondences between the attributes of revelation and those of symbolic communication, we are warranted in concluding at this point that the two are intimately associated. We must now test the symbolic theory by seeing whether it serves as a dialectical tool for reinforcing the sound points of each of our five models and for overcoming their respective weaknesses. I shall contend that the symbolic approach, properly understood, can incorporate what is valid in the five models and at the same time correct what is misleading in them. These models, in turn, can contribute to the symbolic theory by further explicating what is required for symbol to be truly revelatory.

### (a) *The Propositional Model*

To theologians who view revelation as propositional, the symbolic approach seems to imperil the truth of revelation. The danger is not altogether imaginary. There are positivistic reductionists who, following in the traces of Auguste Comte, maintain that symbol is nothing but a disguised way of talking about realities that can be accurately known through objective conceptual discourse. There are empirically-minded instrumentalists, such as Richard Braithwaite, who contend that the symbolic language of religion is nothing but a useful fiction intended to evoke distinctive ethical attitudes. The serious pursuit of truth, on either of these theories, would demand an abandonment of symbolic language in favor of direct speech concerning the realities to which the symbols refer.

Many proponents of the propositional model hold against the

symbolists one of the chief points that Eliade and Langer have urged
in its favor, namely the polysemy (or multivalence) of symbols.
Revelation, according to the propositionalists, must impart some
definite truth, or else it could not be believed. The powerful symbolism of the Bible, in their view, must be fully translated into literal
statements; otherwise, it could convey no definite meaning. Gordon
Clark, a Conservative Evangelical theologian, uses the very example
given above, namely, the Cross. He writes:

> Suppose the cross be selected as a Christian symbol, and suppose
> some flowery speaker should say, Let us live in the shadow of
> the cross. What can he mean? What does the cross symbolize?
> Does it symbolize the love of God? Or does it symbolize the
> wrath of God? Does it symbolize the influence of the church? If
> there are no literal statements to give information as to what the
> cross symbolizes, these questions are unanswerable.[33]

These remarks raise very sharply the question of the relationship between symbolic and propositional truth. Each of these
semantic forms, I have contended, has the capacity to convey meaning, which is found in the integration of subsidiaries through indwelling. In propositional speech the integration is easier either because of the particularity of the statement (which extends only to a
restricted sphere of reality) or because of its abstractness. Symbol
achieves the joint meaning of diverse and seemingly incompatible
particulars by an effort of imagination, whereby our tacit powers of
integration are aroused to an exceptional degree. By eliciting participation, a symbol can convey a richer and more personal apprehension of reality in its deeper dimensions than propositional language can do. Its distinctive mark is not the absence of meaning but
the surplus of meaning. Could one without recourse to symbolism
convey the wonders of a baby's birth, the horrors of a barbaric invasion, or the serenity of a quiet sunset? Are not these qualities as real
as those which can be reduced to measurements and numbers? If
our world is richer than statistics and bloodless abstractions, we
need a language with power of suggestion.[34] Even more is this true if
we would achieve awareness of the transcendent, which is the proper
theme of revelation. God, though utterly beyond description and
definition, is eminently real. Symbolic events and language can
mediate, albeit deficiently, something of God's reality. The reverence

shown by Evangelicals such as Clark for the Bible as a whole seems to indicate their capacity to appreciate the biblical symbolism.

A symbol can, of course, be expressed in a metaphor; a metaphor can be translated into a simile, and a simile to some extent explicated in propositional discourse. Thus the metaphor, "Jesus is the Good Shepherd" can be reexpressed: Jesus takes care of his followers as a shepherd takes care of his sheep; and this in turn can be explicated as implying "spiritual" nourishment, leadership, protection from enemies (human "wolves"). But the propositional explication, to the extent that it achieves literalness, leaves out things tacitly perceived through the symbol; it is incomplete, and by fragmenting the density of the symbol, blunts its power. Thus propositions are not an adequate substitute for symbols.

Propositional explication, to be sure, is not useless. Symbols, as we have noted, frequently require explication so as to clear up their ambiguity and prevent distortion. Christian doctrine sets necessary limits to the kinds of significance that can be found in the Christian symbols. Without doctrines we could hardly find in the Cross of Christ the manifestation of divine grace and redemption. But, as we shall later see, Christian doctrines are never so literal that they cease to participate in the symbolic. They live off the power of the revelatory symbols.

To Braithwaite and the instrumentalists we may concede that the symbolic language of religion recommends a way of life, endorses commitments, evokes gratitude, and instills an attitude of worship. But what is distinctive to religious symbolism is that it gives, or purports to give, religious insight. The peculiar character of "insight symbols," according to Wilbur Urban, "lies in the fact that they do not point to or lead to, but they lead *into;* . . . they are, or at least are supposed to be, a vehicle or medium of insight."[85] Even to accept the practical directives acknowledged by Braithwaite is implicitly to affirm that reality is of such a nature that the attitudes are warranted. The religious symbols, therefore, imply something about the real order. In the words of Ian Barbour, "It would be unreasonable to adopt or recommend a way of life unless one believes that the universe is of such a character that this way of life is appropriate. 'Useful fictions' are no longer useful if they are recognized as fictions or treated as 'parables' whose truth or falsity is taken to be irrelevant."[86]

Because of the cognitive content implicit in the originative symbols, revelatory symbolism is able not only to "give rise to thought" but also to shape the thought it arouses. The Cross reveals to the Christian something of the depths of God's love; the Resurrection, something of his power and fidelity. The doctrinal statements of Scripture and Christian tradition are in many ways tributary to the seminal symbols. Christology grows progressively out of the metaphorical titles conferred on Jesus, and classical ecclesiology meditates on the biblical images of the Church.

Yet the influence travels both directions. Doctrine enriches the meaning of the symbols, as we have already mentioned in connection with the Christian interpretation of Christ's Cross. As the process of doctrinal development goes on, the Church tests new proposals through its grasp of the total symbol-system (including the symbolism of creed and liturgy), through its long experience of the Christian life, through scholarly debate, and through the ongoing assistance of the Holy Spirit. In subsequent chapters we shall have to say more about the development of doctrine.

Crucial for the interpretation of symbols is the kind of participation in the community of faith described earlier in this chapter. The analogous discourse of theology derives its power and security from the vital indwelling of the speaker in the reality to which the symbols refer. When we speak of God as Father, Lord, Redeemer, and the like, our concepts are molded by a real existential relationship that cannot be conceptually thematized without the help of symbols given in revelation. Symbols that might appear to be ambiguous and open to misinterpretation receive a measure of definiteness from this kind of lived relationship. Certain interpretations of the symbols that might be speculatively possible appear as practically untenable. The Gospels bring out the various factors needed for a correct understanding of the parables of Jesus—a pure heart, uprightness of life, divine grace, prayerful union with God, authoritative guidance, and the support of a community of faith.

With this added explanation, it becomes apparent that symbolic mediation does not deprive revelation of its clarity and stability. The symbols are not indefinitely pliable. It is possible to submit oneself to their power, rather than wresting the symbols to one's own purposes. The Christian symbols, taken in the entire network that forms their context, and interpreted in the living community of faith, give secure directives for thought and conduct. Interpreted against the background of the symbols and of Christian life, certain conceptual formulations can be put forward as bearing the authority of revelation.

### (b) *The Historical Model*

Let us now consider how the symbolic approach to revelation is related to the historical. It would be possible to view these two approaches as antithetically opposed. The symbols, it might be thought, refer to the timeless and universal aspects of religion and thus are not essentially bound up with any particular historical events. Their evocative power, one might suspect, rests upon their correspondence to archetypes rooted in nature itself. Some proponents of the symbolic approach, concerned primarily with the literary analysis of the symbols, attach little importance to the facts of salvation history. They speak as though Christian faith had as its object not the God who became incarnate in Jesus of Nazareth but rather the biblical image of Jesus as the Christ.

Unlike these symbolists, I would insist on the profound affinity between the symbolic and historical approaches to revelation. The symbols of biblical and Christian faith, while they build on certain cosmic archetypes, are enriched and further specified through the historical memories of ancient Israel.[87] Persons standing within this tradition have solid reasons for cherishing this particular heritage. According to the biblical and Christian view, God is best known through those deeds of love by which he has disclosed himself in the history of Israel and in the career of Jesus. If love manifests itself principally by deeds, the actual occurrence of God's redemptive acts in this particular history is not immaterial. We know God far better through the significant actions he has performed than we could by fictitious symbols expressing what he might have done. Symbol, therefore, should not be equated only with fictitious representation.

How, then, does the symbolic theory qualify the historical, as outlined in Chapter IV? The historical model, in its more radical or consistent form, holds that revelation can be certainly known by rational inference from the nature of the events themselves. The symbolic approach, on the contrary, denies that the deeds of God can count as revelation unless they are symbols of his presence. To perceive them as symbols does not depend on an arbitrary attitude (such as R. M. Hare's celebrated "blik"). Rather, it is the appropriate response to the events themselves, which by their symbolic power grasp and mold the consciousness of the religiously oriented interpreter.

Understood in this way, the symbolic approach preserves the concreteness and realism for which we have commended the historical model. At the same time, it amends certain apparent weaknesses in some versions of that model. It does not demand that the events be of such a nature that their revelatory meaning can be strictly proved by academic research, but only that the religious inquirer be capable of discerning in them a divinely intended significance. The revelation, then, is not situated outside the interpreter's mind, as though it were a physical object, nor is it something added on to the event, coming from the subjectivity of the interpreter. Just as a literary text discloses to the literate reader a meaning which is really there, so a revelatory sign-event, to the religiously disposed observer, can convey a divine meaning that truly belongs to the event.

An objection to the historical model, as we have seen in Chapter IV, is the difficulty of explaining what is meant by a "mighty act of God." Is not God as creative cause at work in every cosmic and historical event? What could it mean for him to be specially at work? Does he bypass the agency of creatures and substitute himself for finite causes?

A full response to these difficult questions would go beyond the limits of the present study. The symbolic approach to revelation, however, may suggest a partial answer. According to the classical doctrine, God is omnipresent and is, indeed, at work in every action. To exert his causality, he does not need to come into the world from outside, as an interloper. As transcendent ground, he empowers created agents to move themselves.[38] For him to be specially at work, he does not need to be more active than at other times, but only to see to it that the effects correspond to his creative and redemptive purposes. When, through his omnipresent and encompassing causality, God brings finite reality into special affinity with himself, the effect is, in a special sense, his deed. These deeds are not simple manifestations of God's eternal qualities, as in the older liberal exemplarism, but transformative events giving new possibilities of life and salvation.

To hold that the characteristics of an effect can be determined by God as first cause without violation of the processes of secondary causality presumes that secondary causality is open to being directed in this way. From all that we know about the structure of reality, this does not seem unlikely. When I design a machine, I do not violate any laws of physics and chemistry, but I harness the forces already there to bring about an effect of a higher order, namely a device which by the joint activity of its parts can serve a specific human purpose. A similar principle of "marginal control"—to use Polanyi's term—is involved when a living organism makes use of physico-chemical processes in order to achieve a vital goal.[39] The principle of dual control seems to be such that it could be extended to the operations of a divine cause which would utilize, without infringing, the forces of nature. God, who is always at work in giving creatures the power to effect what is new, would, in addition, be directing the nature of the effect so that it becomes a sign of his intentions. Such acts of God, as we have suggested at the conclusion of Chapter IV, would possess the features of word and deed alike. They would be sign-events, recognizable through a process of interpretation which grasps the joint meaning of numerous clues.

The idea that God reveals through symbolic events makes it possible to retrieve many of the concerns underlying a more naive doctrine of miracle, such as one finds in the theological manuals of an earlier generation. A miracle need not involve a suspension of the laws of nature. As Karl Rahner remarks, nature is inherently open to being determined by, and incorporated into, a transcendent order of causality. Just as the laws of inorganic matter do not need to be suspended to make room for biological processes, so nature need not be violated in order to become the self-manifestation of God. As Rahner puts it:

> Similarly, the world in its material content must be conceived as open from the outset to the reality of the spirit and of faith seen as the total act of the innermost core of the spiritual person, and must be conceived as open to the reality of God. Hence the higher dimensions of the whole of reality come to appear in the lower dimensions of this reality by transforming them, but in such a way that the lower dimensions are preserved at the same time as the meaning and nature of the higher reality become visible within them.[40]

The symbolic approach, therefore, suggests ways of responding
to certain grave objections that have been raised against the historical model. It both modifies that model and retrieves what is valid in
it.

## (c) *The Experiential Model*

Turning now to our third model, we may compare the symbolic
approach with the mystical. The difference between the two seems
obvious. The symbolic theory holds that there is no revelation apart
from the created signs by which it is mediated. The mystical approach, on the contrary, affirms the possibility of an unmediated
perception of God or of the transcendent through interior, spiritual
union. If symbols are important for this school of thinkers, it could
only be because they prepare for, or express, an ecstatic peak experience that has no content except the ineffable Presence.

The mystical theory in this extreme form has few supporters.
The great tradition of Christian mysticism, as represented by John of
the Cross and Teresa of Avila, is very cautious in referring to an unmediated perception of God in this life. These saints, it would appear, are best interpreted as affirming that God makes himself
known by producing signs and effects of his presence in the soul. No
doubt it is possible for the mystic to be so drawn to God in love that
the symbols of his presence, so to speak, melt away. They may not
be attended to, but are they really absent? When the spiritual writers
speak of the touch and taste of God in the depths or substance of
the soul, and of the charity which goes out to God as he is in himself, they imply that the "immediacy" of God is not without a perceptible effect on the creature. Even the highest mystical experience,
which dispenses with normal mediations through concepts and images, still rests upon inner effects of grace that in some way mediate
the encounter itself.[41]

Authors such as Rahner, in their theology of revelation, speak
paradoxically of "mediated immediacy." This term aptly conveys the
dualism of the explicit and the implicit, the thematic and the
unthematic, the datum and the horizon in any revelatory experience.
What is immediate, for Rahner, is the self-communication of the divine, the experience of grace. But the inner presence of God cannot
be known and cannot achieve itself except insofar as it becomes

mediated, or mediates itself, in created symbols. The symbols, however, do arouse a genuine awareness of the divine itself—an awareness that always surpasses all that we can say about it.

The mystical tradition, by calling attention to the inner dimensions of the spiritual experience, complements and enriches the symbolic approach to revelation. The experientialists are right in insisting that revelation necessarily involves a real union between the human spirit and the God who bestows himself in grace. Further, they are correct in affirming that this union is always somehow conscious. In recognition of these points, we must now assert that the symbol itself, in its full dimensions, includes the experience of grace; for this experience provides the horizon necessary for any external symbol to be discerned as a divine communication. On the other hand, the experience of grace cannot be rightly interpreted, or recognized for what it is, without the help of symbols derived from the world known through sensory experience. Apart from such symbolic concretization, the rarified ecstasies of the mystic would not be sufficiently articulate to merit the name of revelation. In Rahnerian terminology, transcendental revelation and categorical revelation are not two separable entities but two dimensions of a single, complex reality.[42] Like form and matter, like soul and body, they are mutually dependent and mutually causative; they exist only in their coalescence. *Causae ad invicem sunt causae.*

The mystical component is particularly important for bringing out the negative factor in all thematizations of revelation. The mystic, aware of God as immediately present, is keenly sensitive to the inadequacy of all created images and analogies. More conscious than others that we know God only as one who escapes all categorization, the mystic celebrates the fact that we are conjoined with him in the utter darkness of faith. The mystical and symbolic dimensions of the divine-human encounter are complementary and yet opposed. Thomas F. O'Meara, in the following sentences, captures both the unity and the difference:

> Clearly, mystical experience is a process similar to the primal revelatory contact by God with every individual. . . . Yet the experiences, messages, and stories of mystical experience in the dark night do not tend to objectification; for authentic mystical experience terminates not in information but in ineffability. From the standpoint of clarity and community, mysticism is

rightly not given prominence as revelation; but from the viewpoint of intensity, the mystical experience is a *type* of primal,
subjective, revelatory experience. The normalcy and universality
of mysticism is a pointer to the omnipresence of grace. Yet
there are differences: for revelatory Presence in the history of
mankind tends to concreteness and explicitness in order to introduce the kingdom of God incarnationally, while in mysticism a
mature believer yields to a particular grace leading to darkness
and silence.[43]

### (d) *The Dialectical Model*

For the dialectical theologians, to whom we now turn, revelation is given not in symbol but in the word of God. Solicitous to
safeguard the divine transcendence, Barth was wary of anything that
might seem to involve God in the ambiguities of nature and history,
anything that might suggest an avenue from man to God, anything,
in fact, that would give scope to human creativity in the constitution
of revelation, or obscure the total sufficiency of the Bible, or imply
any real continuity between Christianity and the religions of the
world. For Barth, then, revelation is God's word, and "we have no
reason not to take the concept of God's Word primarily in its literal
sense. God's Word means that God speaks. Speaking is not a 'symbol' (as P. Tillich, *Rel. Verwirkl.*, 1930, p. 48 thinks)."[44] God's
word, in the fullest sense, is Jesus Christ, who transcends time and
history.

The alleged incoherence of the dialectical model, to which I
have several times alluded, comes principally from its polemical
relationship to the dominant rationalism of recent centuries. Protesting against the claim that reason can fit God and revelation into a
universal system, the dialectical theologians, inspired by Kierkegaard, spoke freely of paradox and of the absurd. Similar themes
reappear, in a less polemical context, in the symbolic approach. For
symbol, as we have noted, is capable of transcending differences
which, to discursive reason, appear unsurmountable. The symbolic
approach, like the dialectical, is at home with inscrutable mystery. It
refuses to reduce meaning and intelligibility to the narrow confines
of conceptual logic. This fundamental affinity between the two
approaches, however, does not eliminate all differences.

Writing in the full tide of "modernistic neo-Protestantism" (as he called it), Barth was understandably fearful that the category of symbol, applied to revelation, might compromise the divine transcendence and obscure the uniqueness of God's objective revelation in Christ. Tillich's doctrine of symbol, in particular, seemed to Barth to concede too much to Feuerbach. It could easily be taken to suggest that the symbols of revelation, emanating by necessity from the human consciousness under the impact of particular historical situations, might be mere projections of human need. In this framework God's word in Christ could easily be portrayed as "one symbol among many others."[45] In calling attention to these dangers, Barth assisted subsequent proponents of the symbolic approach, including many of those mentioned in the present chapter, to guard against any modernistic reductionism.

The theology of the word of God, as set forth by the Barthians, has many points in common with the kind of symbolic approach which has here been proposed. Against Absolute Idealism, the two schools agree that revelation, whether by word or symbol, must be a free and loving self-manifestation of God. Against mystical extravagance, they agree that revelation must be mediated by signs given in history—signs which Barth, in his later work, describes as sacramental embodiments of revelation.[46] Against the propositional model, they hold in common that the mediation must bring the believer into a living, personal contact with the divine. The two approaches agree, finally, against historicism that revelation cannot be objectively demonstrated from facts accessible to academic history. As something discerned by a spiritually attuned consciousness, revelation never truly exists outside of faith.

Does the symbolic approach lead to a doctrine of revelation in which Christ is no longer uniquely normative, but is reduced to "one symbol among others"? There can be no doubt that some symbolic theologians have moved in this direction. Whether that course is the only, or the best, development of the symbolic approach must await discussion in our next chapter, which will deal with Christology.

The word of God, as described by dialectical theologians, has a structure similar to that which we have attributed to symbol.[47] As the self-expression of the revealing God who addresses his creature by means of it, the word works mysteriously on human consciousness so as to suggest more than it can describe or define. It points beyond itself to the mystery which it makes present. The twisted imagery of the seer, the fiery denunciation of the prophet, and the joyful tidings of the apostle are alike imbued with a mysterious power to produce, as symbols do, the new life of which they speak. As the inspired words enter a stable tradition and become rooted, so to speak, in the collective consciousness of a believing people, they become still more palpably symbolic.

The revelatory word, indeed, may be described as a symbol which by its tenuousness and versatility almost escapes the conditions of materiality. Of all symbols it is the most spiritual and the most akin to the divine. As several authors have noted, the word has a special aptitude to represent that which cannot be attained except through negation.[48] The quasi-mystical experience of the divine, as already noted, manifests the inadequacy of all created analogies and therefore calls for negative statement. Consider, for instance, Paul's expression, "What no eye has seen, nor ear heard, nor the heart of man conceived, what God has prepared for those who love him" (1 Cor 2:9; cf. Is 64:4). The imagery is, so to speak, raised to a higher power by the negation, which indicates the excess of what is meant beyond all that can be positively said.[49]

The word, as the sign which articulates meaning, is a necessary complement to revelation through any other kind of symbol. The grosser symbolism of nature, deed, or artifact, potent though it may be, is too ambiguous to be the sole mediator of revealed religion. The symbol becomes revelation only when interpreted, and interpretation never occurs without a linguistic component. For public revelation, moreover, there must be external words, capable of being heard or seen. Such attesting words are necessarily symbolic, for otherwise they could not be conducive to a salvific union with the divine. Revealed religion does not simply take over the linguistic patterns that it finds. Rather, it creatively enriches and renews the speech that it adopts; it coins metaphors and thus gives rise to new symbolism.

### (e) The New Consciousness Model

In closing we may speak briefly of the relationship between the symbolic approach to revelation and the fifth model of revelation theology. In general, it may be said that there is a close correspondence. Partisans of the "consciousness" model commonly regard symbolic communication in one form or another (image, metaphor, parable, story, and the like) as the prime bearer of revelation.

It will readily be conceded that the symbolic approach safeguards the distinctive values of the fifth model. Since symbol, as we have seen, invites participation, a revelation imparted through symbol does not leave the recipient passive, but tends to elicit a high degree of spiritual activity. The plasticity of symbol gives it a power to speak to people of different sociocultural situations and to assure that revelance is not lost. Since there can be a measure of equivalence or complementarity among diverse symbol systems, the symbolic mode of communication is favorable to interfaith dialogue. In all these respects the symbolic approach supports the values characteristic of the awareness model.

For this very reason it must be seriously asked whether the symbolic approach can overcome the weaknesses already noted in the fifth model. The symbolic approach to revelation is commonly thought to imply subjectivism, relativism, and a reductionistic humanism. These charges would be justified if, as commonly supposed, symbols simply reflected the passing moods of the subject. But if the contentions of the present chapter are correct, symbol can have an objective density, imposing demands on the subject to pursue its meaning as a clue to the nature of reality. Religious symbols claim to be based on the permanent structures of being. The historical symbolism of biblical history, moreover, manifests the singular deeds of love whereby God has effectively transformed the possibilities of existence in the world. These symbols are not subject to arbitrary change and reinterpretation. The constellation of symbols transmitted within the Christian tradition imposes a discipline on new members of the Church as they are initiated into the world of meaning intended by the symbols. Dogma, however, can give stability and added power to the symbolism of primary religious discourse. The primacy of symbol does not justify any symbolic reductionism that would disallow the more reflective discourse of church doctrine and theology.

The symbols of Christian revelation, we have insisted, are not indefinitely pliable. Yet they allow a desirable margin of interpretation and application, and are modified and enriched by successive recontextualizations. The major biblical symbols are transmitted in the context of mutable secondary symbols, such as those employed in Christian art and liturgy. These secondary symbols, when they cease to make the intended impact, can be replaced by others, freshly generated by the religious imagination under the impact of the central symbols of faith.

The objection has been raised that if the symbols represent a breakthrough into a new stage of consciousness, every new advance of consciousness calls for a new set of symbols. As a result of successive replacements the very identity of Christian faith would in time be lost. Christianity would thus have the unity of a fluctuating movement rather than that of an enduring, self-identical faith. It might in time become obsolete and be replaced by a post-Christianity, theistic or atheistic as the case might be. Humanity, in the opinion of some, may be entering into a stage that leaves behind the symbolism of the traditional religions.

This hypothesis, however, is not self-evidently true. At the present point in our investigations we cannot rule out the possibility that religion might be a permanent feature of the human condition and that human and cosmic history might have a single origin and a single goal. If so, there might be a single central symbol that unsurpassably mediates the true meaning of existence and of human life. To explore this possibility it will be necessary to consider the symbol of Jesus as the Christ.

# Chapter X

# CHRIST THE SUMMIT OF REVELATION

## 1. *The Problem*

The New Testament, without using "revelation" as a technical theological term, does in effect designate Jesus as the supreme revelation of God. It teaches that "in these last days God has spoken to us by a Son, whom he appointed heir of all things, through whom also he created the world" (Heb 1:2). The Revealer-Son is described as bearing the very stamp of God's nature (Heb 1:3), as being the "image of the invisible God" (Col 1:15). Of him the Fourth Gospel says: "No one has ever seen God; the only Son, who is in the bosom of the Father, he has made him known" (Jn 1:18). In these and many other texts the preeminent and definitive character of the revelation given in Christ is evidently implied.

The special identification of revelation with Christ is almost a commonplace among modern theologians. Vatican II articulated a widespread consensus when it declared, in its Constitution on Revelation, "Jesus Christ is the Mediator and at the same time the fullness of all revelation."[1] In a key text the Council spoke of Christ as "the light of all the nations."[2]

Many theologians representing each of the five models agree that the revelation is supremely, or even exclusively, given in Christ. They differ, however, in how they understand this proposition. In the doctrinal model Jesus is seen as the divinely authoritative teacher—a predicate affirmed either of the Christ of Scripture or of the Christ of dogma. In the historical model the Christ-event is viewed as the culminating act of God in history, incomparably disclosing God's own attributes and intentions. In the experiential model, Jesus is regarded as having received the grace of unsurpassable and exemplary intimacy with the Father. In the dialectical model he is portrayed as God's word addressed in judgment and forgiveness to a sinful people. And in the consciousness model, Christ is viewed as the paradigm that restructures the human imagination as it opens itself to God's creative transcendence.

In the present chapter an effort will be made to see whether these differing approaches can be corrected or reconciled by utilizing the idea of revelation as symbolic communication. We shall therefore begin by exploring the concept of Christ as revelatory symbol.

## 2. Christ as Revelatory Symbol

The idea of Christ as symbol is not a part of classical Christology. In modern theology it has been popularized by authors such as Paul Tillich and H. Richard Niebuhr, both of whom saw a close connection between symbol and revelation. For Tillich, the biblical picture of Jesus as the Christ is the bearer of the New Being, and thus the medium of final revelation.[3] The revelatory meaning of the Christ is clarified by the two central symbols of the Cross and the Resurrection, each of which is supported by corroborating symbols such as the story of the Virgin Birth and the myth of the Second Coming. The Cross and the Resurrection, for Tillich, are not facts but symbols based on fact. Their revelatory character depends on their capacity to transmit the power of the New Being.

H. Richard Niebuhr, although he failed to elaborate a comprehensive philosophy of symbol, advocated a symbolic Christology. "Jesus Christ," he wrote, "is a symbolic form with the aid of which men tell each other what life and death, God and man, are like; but even more he is a form which they employ as an a priori, an image, a scheme or pattern in the mind which gives form and meaning to their experience."[4] In this context Niebuhr speaks of Jesus Christ as "a fundamental, indispensable metaphor."[5]

Although neither Paul Tillich nor H. Richard Niebuhr wished to dissolve the links between revelation and history or between revelation and doctrine, their teaching on symbol left these links rather tenuous. The case for speaking of Christ as symbol, already suspect on these grounds, is further weakened by the heritage of nineteenth-century positivism, which has interpreted symbols as noncognitive.

Symbols are often regarded as imaginative projections from the unconscious akin to dreams and illusions. Relying on the "hermeneutics of suspicion" promoted by Feuerbach, Marx, and Freud, many contemporary thinkers regard symbol as an ideological device whereby people prevent themselves or others from perceiving the objective situation.

The doctrine of symbol outlined in the last chapter gives some materials for a response. Symbols, whether real or mental, can initiate one into a wealth and intensity of meaning that could not be conveyed by merely indicative signs. Although symbols, like propositions, can sometimes distort, nothing in the nature of symbol prevents it from conveying truth. If ultimate reality is essentially mysterious, its true character will be better attainable through symbol than through conceptual and propositional discourse alone. To affirm that Christ is symbol, therefore, in no way denies that he is the very revelation of God.

A further difficulty arises from the fact that symbol is commonly regarded as being nonidentical with what it symbolizes. If Christ were a symbol of God, it is argued, he could not himself be God. To speak of Christ as symbol, therefore, is by implication to deny his divinity.

The question whether a symbol can be really identical with what it symbolizes requires careful analysis. Some symbols, which we may call "representative," refer the mind to things that are unreal or absent. A symbol such as a tombstone gathers up memories of a dead friend, but does not make the friend really present. Other symbols, however, indicate the presence of what they symbolize. We have earlier spoken of the human body as a symbol of the human spirit, which expresses itself through bodily acts and gestures. Of such "realizing" symbols Karl Rahner says: "The symbol is the reality, constituted by the thing symbolized as an inner moment of itself, which reveals and proclaims the thing symbolized, and is itself full of the thing symbolized, being its concrete form of existence."[6] "All beings," according to Rahner, "are by their nature symbolic, because they necessarily 'express' themselves in order to attain their own nature."[7]

In sacramental theology, it is commonly taught that Christ is "really present" in the sacramental elements and actions, such as the Eucharist. A sacrament is understood to be a material sign that communicates the real presence and power of a spiritual reality—the grace of Jesus Christ in the particular form signified by the sacrament in question. Not only is this true of individual sacraments (such as baptism and the Eucharist); it is true equally of the Church itself, which, as we shall seen in Chapter XIII, is a kind of general sacrament in which Christ makes himself dynamically present through the Holy Spirit.

If this be true, Christ himself may be called the "primordial sacrament" of God's saving presence in the world. Karl Barth, for instance, calls him the basic substance of the "sacramental reality of [God's] revelation,"[8] the "first sacrament, the foundation of eveverything that God instituted and used in His revelation as a secondary objectivity before and after the epiphany of Jesus Christ."[9] Many Catholic theologians speak in similar terms. According to Henri de Lubac, Christ is the sacrament of God and the Church is the sacrament of Christ.[10] Edward Schillebeeckx, speaking of Christ as "the sacrament of the encounter of God," explains that Christ "is not only the offer of divine love to man made visible but, at the same time, as prototype (or primordial model), he is the supreme realization of the response of human love to this divine offer."[11]

The terminology of sacrament generally has reference not so much to revelation as to the communication of grace and sanctification. For the communication of revelation, symbol is perhaps a better term than sacrament. If we take the term symbol in a strongly realistic sense, meaning a sign in which the thing signified is really present, Christ may be called the symbol of God par excellence. Such is in fact the teaching of Karl Rahner, who writes: "The Logos, the Son of the Father, is truly, in his humanity as such, the revelatory symbol in which the Father enunciates himself, in this Son, to the world—revelatory, because the symbol renders present what is revealed."[12] Christ, the God-man, he explains, "is at once God himself as communicated, the human acceptance of the communication, and the final historical manifestation of this communication and acceptance."[13] In Christ, therefore, the manifestation and that which is manifested ontologically coincide. The man Jesus Christ is both the symbol and the incarnation of the eternal Logos, who communicates himself by becoming fully human without ceasing to be divine.

Because any symbol involves an interlocking of two levels of meaning, a "realizing" symbol will involve two levels of reality. To say that the body is a symbol of the person implies that the person is not simply the body. In order to convey a surplus of meaning, the body must manifest the presence of the spiritual person, the "soul." The same may be said in the case of Christ as revelatory symbol. Christ's humanity is really identical with himself; it is not a mere mask for his divinity. But he is more than his humanity, and this more, according to Christian belief, is his divinity. According to Vatican II, Christ—and here the Council draws an analogy between Christ and the Church, which is likewise symbolic in structure—is a single "interlocked reality" (*realitas complexa*) comprising both a human and a divine element.[14] The classical doctrine of the "two natures" spells out in more conceptual language the implications of the symbolic character of Christ as God's concrete revelation in the flesh.

In what precedes we have concentrated on symbols that are not merely mental or fictional. Any symbolic reality (whether a "representative" or a "realizing" symbol, in Rahner's terminology) is an object or event so structured that it can, as a clue, offer insight into a deeper reality not knowable, at least with the same depth or intensity, without reliance upon itself. The whole form of Christ's human existence, from his Incarnation to his Cross and exaltation, is held to be a "realizing" symbol of God, present and active in this man. Paul seems to affirm this when he declares: "God was in Christ reconciling the world to himself" (2 Cor 5:19).

There is, however, a second aspect of symbol, frequently accented in modern Christologies. Influenced by the study of art and literature, many theologians look upon symbol as an imaginative projection of human possibilities. The symbol is regarded as a metaphorical or mythic expression of the mind, not necessarily corresponding to anything that actually exists. Without denying the distorting capacity of symbols, pointed out by the "hermeneutics of suspicion," contemporary theologians affirm that a symbol produced by the imagination need not be false or deceptive. Though fictional, it may reveal real possibilities that could not be grasped in a nonsymbolic way. Revelation, therefore, can come about not only through real events but also through inspired achievements of the human imagination. In biblical times prophets and apocalyptic visionaries were moved by the Holy Spirit to dream dreams and see visions disclosing possibilities that would otherwise have been hidden from human eyes. Is not the Kingdom of God in the preaching of Jesus an imaginative disclosure, under symbolic forms, of a world existing only in hope and promise?

Some contemporary authors look upon Christ as a revelatory myth or symbol forged by the believing community. Whereas in the nineteenth century positivistic historians tended to speak of the Jesus-myth as contravening the Christian claims, some twentieth-century theologians hold that the myth itself is a revelation of the highest possibilities of divinized humanity, and thus of God's purpose for creation.[15]

The realistic and the fictive approaches to symbol are not antithetical. If we assume that Jesus in his actual career was a real symbol of God's presence and of humanity's response, the kind of language that best expresses the true meaning of Jesus may well be metaphorical or mythical. For, as we have said, symbol discloses reality by arousing an imaginative integration of clues that could appear as incompatible and meaningless to merely discursive thought.

It is not our purpose here to construct a Christology based on the symbolic approach, but only to suggest what bearing such a Christology might have on the theology of revelation. This can best be done if, at the present stage, we return to our five models in order to consider how they can be illuminated or criticized with the help of a symbolic Christology, and how they might contribute to a Christology of this kind.

## 3. *The Symbolic Christ and the Christ of Doctrine*

The doctrinal model, in the two forms already studied, recognizes the absolute normativeness of Christ, who is depicted, by preference, as the divine teacher. The Bible is seen as an embodiment of Christ's doctrine, because the inspired word faithfully reflects the divine Logos, because Christ himself acknowledged the Old Testament as pointing to himself, and because the New Testament records what the apostles learned from Christ. In neo-Scholasticism and in some strands of Protestant orthodoxy, the teaching of the Church is recognized as an infallible or at least a reliable guide to the revelation given by Christ. Thus both the Bible and the Church are, under Christ, divine oracles, but Christ himself, as the divine teacher in person, stands above them. The doctrine of the New Testament and of Christian tradition concerning Christ as Son of God is used to support Christ's own doctrinal authority. As further confirmation of that divine authority, this model uses arguments from miracle and prophecy, especially from the supreme miracle of the Resurrection.

The symbolic approach does not require a wedge to be driven between symbol and doctrine, as though anything conceded to doctrine had to be subtracted from symbol. In the theory of symbol set forth in the last chapter, symbol has been presented as cognitive. Not only does it give rise to thought, it is reflected and prolonged in thought. As a very dense and vivid form of communication, symbol can be diffracted and analyzed in propositional statements. The Christological doctrines of the Bible and of the Church have emerged, in great part, through meditation on the Christian symbols. From the beginnings of Christianity, the symbols of faith were understood within a doctrinal context that included the teaching of the Hebrew Scriptures and that of Jesus himself.

We would part from the propositional theory, however, to the extent that it makes doctrine the primary form of revelation. Criticizing Origen on this score, Yves Congar points out that the revelation of Jesus "is not contained in his teaching alone; it is also, and perhaps we ought to say mainly, in what he *did*." Congar then adds: "The coming down of the Word into our flesh, God's acceptance of the status of a servant, the washing of the disciples' feet, the obedient love that led to the death of the Cross—all this has the force of a revelation and of a revelation *of God:* 'Philip, he that has seen me has seen the Father.' "[16]

The words of Jesus were no doubt revelatory. He revealed, as Vatican II tells us, not only by his deeds, his signs and wonders, and his death and Resurrection, but also by his words.[17] One of the four major strands of New Testament Christology, as analyzed by Helmut Koester, is a Wisdom Christology prominent in the Gospel materials taken from the Q tradition.[18] In this tradition the sayings of Jesus are treated as divinely authoritative, but we still do not have strictly propositional revelation, because Jesus taught by preference through parable and paradox. Thus it is misleading to speak of Jesus as an authoritative teacher according to the schematization of the propositional model.

The route from the symbolic realities of Christ's life and the metaphorical language of the early confessions to the conceptual discourse of systematic theology is long and tortuous. The early creeds, as many authors have noted, are formulated in the charged language of confession and worship. To speak of Jesus as the eternally generated Son, one in substance with the Father, is not to use the scientific language of metaphysics but, as Ian Ramsey shows, to evoke, in worship, a disclosure.[19] Credal expressions such as "God from God, light from light," though they move somewhat in the direction of abstraction, are still paradoxical and evocative rather than propositional.

Jean Galot, a strong defender of traditional orthodoxy, recognizes the rootedness of the Christological dogmas in the originative images of Scripture. "Is it not significant," he asks, "that the two most striking affirmations of the deed (*geste*) of Incarnation in Scripture [Phil 2:6–7 and John 1:14] come to us from primitive hymns? It is poetry inspired by adherence to Christ in faith and love that has best succeeded in grasping and depicting that invisible act which commands the earthly life of the Savior."[20] From this Galot draws the conclusion that theology must remain in close contact with aesthetic communication, for it is the perception of beauty that opens our eyes to the perception of divine love. "If we ask ourselves why certain propositions of abstract theology arouse not only indifference but repugnance, must we not blame the practice of expressing too dryly, to the exclusion of all emotion, a mystery that overflows with life and should bewitch us?"[21] Galot correctly maintains that the conceptual analysis of theology must incessantly return to the freshness of the biblical texts to retain its youth and vitality.

Galot's criticism of the arid conceptualism of scholastic orthodoxy thus reinforces the objections made from a very different point of view by Frans Jozef van Beeck, who speaks of "the inability of classical christology to do full justice to the life and death of Jesus" because of its assumption that real meaning consists in concepts.[22] The symbolic approach, without denying the value of propositions and concepts, provides a richer and more adaptable framework of meaning.

## 4. *The Symbolic Christ and the Christ of History*

In the doctrinal model the deeds and career of Jesus tend to be seen not as revelatory in themselves but as raw materials for revelatory teaching or as signs accrediting revealed doctrine. The historical model has the advantage over the doctrinal that events such as the Crucifixion and the Resurrection are perceived as embodying a meaning and a message from God.

The realistic doctrine of Christ as symbol or sacrament of God, set forth in the early pages of this chapter, evidently calls for a historical understanding of revelation. The life of Jesus in the flesh is God's actual, personal, and irrevocable self-communication to the world, and hence the supreme manifestation of what God chooses to be in free grace toward others. More specifically, we can say that Jesus' message of forgiveness, confirmed by his conduct, manifests God's unconditional love toward sinners. His wonderful deeds, in the context of his teaching, are sign-events showing forth the inbreaking of God's Kingdom through the personal presence of the Son of his love. The Crucifixion, as a symbolic reality, expresses the sacrificial character of God's redemptive love. The Resurrection symbolizes—again, by its very reality—the victory of that redemptive love over all that could oppose it, even death.

As noted in Chapter IV, there is within the revelation-as-history approach an internal dissension between those who seek to establish revelation by common historical method and those who, in faith, accept the biblical history as having a special character. Pannenberg, whose theology is more consistently historical, follows the first approach. He maintains that faith cannot establish any past events which are inaccessible to the historian as such.[23] The occurrence of the Resurrection of Jesus, as the culminating revelation, "is not made certain by faith but only by historical research, to the extent that certainty can be attained at all about questions of this kind."[24]

The other approach holds that the events of salvation history are known in faith, by acceptance of an authoritative prophetic interpretation, such as the Bible provides. This method, while it better safeguards the certainty of revelation, tends to make the connection between the events and their meaning seem rather extrinsic—a complaint directed against these theologians by the Pannenberg school.

The concept of symbolic history can be critically applied against both these schools, and can to some extent mediate between them. Symbolic events, as we have said, do not cogently demand a symbolic interpretation, but invite this. The meaning is not an inference from the qualities of the events taken as logical premises, but an insight achieved by a properly disposed subject tacitly relying on

the coherence of the clues. For the correct interpretation of revelatory events a prophetic grace or inspiration is a valuable, and in
some cases indispensable, qualification. Yet the interpretation is not
extrinsically imposed on the events. If the events are symbolic, they
in some sense contain their own meaning. God, as Pannenberg says,
speaks the language of events, but—as Pannenberg omits to say—
the communication is best interpreted by persons who are religiously
qualified by a grace-given affinity with the Revealer. The prophet is
par excellence the person equipped to read the "signs of the times"
and thus to recognize the hand of God in historical events. Once the
prophetic interpretation has been given, religiously attuned inquirers
can enter into the tradition of faith and perceive certain events as
self-expressions of God in history. Against Pannenberg it must be
urged that the technical academic historian has, as such, no competence to judge on the religious significance of past events and cannot
be asked to decide, by sheer historical method, whether God has
revealed himself in them. In events such as the Resurrection the
credibility of the event is so interwoven with its religious meaning
that the facts will inevitably be in dispute among those who differ in
their religious outlooks.[25]

Pannenberg distinguishes his own theory of indirect revelation
through history from any theory of symbolic revelation. "When a
symbol is supposed to have a divine content," he writes, "it is direct
revelation to the extent that it suppresses its own primary and un-
symbolic meaning in favor of its symbolism. In this sense, gnostic
revelation is direct, even though the divine spirit is communicated in
symbolic form."[26]

Yet Pannenberg himself, when he addresses the question of how
Christ is final revelation, comes rather close to a symbolic position.
In the Resurrection of Christ, he holds, "the distinction of the
revealing medium from God himself disappears."[27] The divinity of
Christ means God's "revelational presence" in him.[28] In the history
of Jesus the final consummation of all things appears proleptically,
in a manner contrary to appearance, and thus paradoxically.[29] From
our standpoint within history, Pannenberg admits, we cannot clearly
see what happened at Jesus' Resurrection. Until the Parousia "we
must speak favorably in thoroughly legitimate, but still only metaphorical and symbolic, form about Jesus' resurrection and the
significance inherent in it."[30] The Easter message, for Pannenberg,

rests on "the absolute metaphor of the resurrection of the dead, as well as the proleptic element that provides the basis of doxological statements about the God revealed in Jesus, which are metaphorical in their way."[31]

Although some of these statements refer to the transmission of the revelation rather than with its original occurrence, it is hard to see, on Pannenberg's own assumptions, how the original witnesses could have received the revelation if not by a kind of symbolic disclosure. If Pannenberg were to give greater scope to the symbolic, he might enrich his discussion of Easter by attaching greater importance to the personal traits of the one who rose, rather than by concentrating narrowly on the bare fact of the Resurrection.

## 5. The Symbolic Christ and Experiential Christology

Within the experiential model, as we have labeled it, there are considerable differences of opinion about the necessity of mediation and the mediatorial role of Jesus. Most theologians of this orientation would look upon Jesus as having possessed a singular, unsurpassable consciousness of union with God. They would also hold that the apostles, through Jesus, had revelatory experiences which are normative for the Chrastian community. We have already seen the views of authors such as Sabatier and Tyrell on these points.

For all its insistence on immediacy to God, this model does allow an important place for symbol. Revelation, for these authors, cannot be expressed except indirectly. The privileged recipients of revelation express their experience not through statements of a factual or conceptual character, but by symbolic words and gestures which can serve as occasions for others to undergo similar experiences. The Modernists, it will be recalled, accepted the Bible and the creeds of the Church not as containing revealed doctrine but as symbolic pointers to the Christian experience of God. Liberals such as Herrmann, anticipating his pupil Tillich, held that God touches the soul through the biblical image of Jesus. Christian revelation, for Herrmann, takes place in the inner transformation whereby the believer, affected by this image, comes to share in the inner life of Jesus.

The symbolic Christology set forth in this chapter can correct the experiential model at several crucial points. Some representatives of the experiential tendency show an excessive preoccupation with reconstructing the inner life of Jesus himself, as though his revelatory significance consisted in this alone. We do not wish to deny that his life of union with God was exemplary, and that he received revelatory and mystical illuminations. But, with the materials at our disposal, it is most difficult to reconstruct the conscious experiences of Jesus. What is chiefly revelatory about him is what emerged in his public life, his death, and his rising from the dead. These external events have their full revelatory value even though there may be divergences of opinion about the content of Jesus' personal consciousness.

Nor does the revelation we receive consist primarily in an immediate experience of our own union with God. Any such experience, taken in itself, would be too frail and transitory to serve as the basis for a personal life of faith, let alone for that of a stable community of faith and witness. According to the biblical and traditional understanding, the Christian revelation is a publicly accessible phenomenon, having its abiding center in the real, historical Christ.

Unlike the mysticism of experience, symbolic realism is able to give objectivity, coherence, and permanence to the Christian revelation. As symbolic communication, revelation has a two-level sacramental structure in which the perceptible sign is linked to the awareness of the mystery. This structure corresponds to the body-spirit structure of the human person. The divine, not being an object, cannot be directly apprehended. The human mind cannot know the transcendent except by turning to an external sign, which is historically and socially tangible. The revelation therefore has two dimensions, which may be called, in Rahner's terminology, transcendental and predicamental. The symbol through which God makes himself present is not a merely external fact but a quasi-sacramental reality. Thanks to the action of the Holy Spirit it becomes, as it were, transparent to the divine.

One may properly speak of the Christ-symbol, but the symbol should not be degraded into a mere occasion for revelation, whether originative or dependent. The symbol is an intrinsic element in the process and the result. The Christ-symbol, moreover, is not a free creation of the community, but is first of all a real event that brings the community into existence. If the community can transmit and interpret the symbol, that is only because the symbol previously forms and sustains the community.

## 6. *The Symbolic and the Proclaimed Christ*

We have seen in Chapter IX how the dialectical theologians, concerned to safeguard the absolute primacy of Christ in revelation, shy away from the category of symbol, which seems to them too general. Fearing that if Christ were viewed as symbol his divine uniqueness might be compromised, they prefer the category "word of God." This category emphasizes the divine freedom, the personal character of revelation, and the absence of any external likeness between God and the medium of his self-disclosure.

Rudolf Bultmann, inspired in part by the ideas of Martin Kähler, distinguished sharply between the Jesus of history and the Christ of faith. Revelation and salvation, for the Bultmannians, come through the preached Christ, the crucified and risen Lord, not through the Jesus painstakingly recovered by historical research. The proclaimed word, according to Bultmann, is a call for faith and decision. In the New Testament, the kerygma is presented in a mythological form, corresponding to the world view of late Judaism and early Gnosticism. Contemporary proclamation must divest the kerygma of its antiquated mythological trappings. In a radical reinterpretation, Bultmann attempted to present the Christian message with the help of Heidegger's existential philosophy.[32]

During the 1950s, there was a notable shift away from pure kerygmatic theology within the Bultmann school. The so-called post-Bultmannians (mostly former pupils of Bultmann himself) maintained that, while the empiricist history of the liberal school is powerless to catch the real significance of Jesus, modern existential history offers an avenue of approach to the revelatory self-understanding of Jesus. James M. Robinson, a member of this school, argued that whether Jesus is encountered through the kerygma or through existential history, the result is essentially the same. Both confront the reader with the same urgent demand for faith and personal decision.[33]

The shift of attention from the crucified and risen Lord to the Jesus of the public ministry could be welcomed as a healthy reaction against an excessively abstract understanding of the Easter kerygma. But the reaction could go too far if it were to suggest that the good news of Easter has nothing essential to add to the earthly career of Jesus. The events of Easter were surely revelatory to the first disciples, and if the pre-Easter story in the Gospels has revelatory value, it is partly because the Gospels are shot through with reflections of the Easter message.

A contemporary American theologian, Peter Hodgson, building skillfully on the work of Barth and Ebeling, continues to press for a word-centered Christology and for a theory of revelation through word. "Sight," he maintains, "reflects surfaces but sound communicates interiors without violating their interiority. . . . The only medium of relationship with God is that of the word, which allows him to remain hidden at the same time he unconceals himself."[34] Yet Hodgson does not understand the word simply as sound. He speaks freely of word-events, and includes under this heading the death of Jesus on the Cross.[35]

While admitting great value in this kind of word-theology, one may point out, with Tillich, that the "word of God" is itself a symbol.[36] If we follow Rahner's concept of symbol as "the expressive presence of the self as other," the word of God may even be called a divinely constituted symbol. "The theology of the Logos," Rahner holds, "is strictly a theology of the symbol, and indeed the supreme form of it."[37] To say that the Son is Logos is to say that he is the perfect image, the imprint, the radiance, and the self-expression of the Father. While it is true that the category of symbol can be abused to justify subjectivistic and naturalistic conclusions, the category of word is not secure against distortion. Word-theology, taken alone, could curtail the full realism of the Incarnation; it could convey the impression that the Word has become not flesh but only . . . word.

Thus it is not surprising that Barth, as he emerged from his dialectical period, leaned increasingly toward a sacramental Christology. "The humanity of Jesus Christ as such," he wrote, is the first sacrament."[38] The sacramental approach recalls the flesh-and-blood character of God's presence in the history of Jesus, and prevents any kind of Gnostic intellectualization or spiritualization of God's saving work. Barth's sacramentalism, as found in his later writings, harmonizes with the symbolic realism we have noted in authors like Rahner.

## 7. *The Symbolic Christ and "New Awareness" Christology*

The fifth model of revelation theology has major repercussions in Christology. In some versions of this model Jesus is seen as the point at which a new and final stage in history begins. In Teilhard de Chardin's evolutionary Christology Jesus appears as the bearer and goal of the upward movement of the universe toward the divine.[39] For Teilhard, Christ is the Omega point, the focus of union needed by the noosphere in order that it may achieve a creative breakthrough into a higher state of complexity and convergence. This intimate link between the Logos and the perfection of the universe Teilhard believed to be justifiable on New Testament grounds, thanks especially to the prologue to the Fourth Gospel and the Pauline Letters to the Colossians and Ephesians.

The Dutch Augustinian, Ansfried Hulsbosch, is in some ways a disciple of Teilhard. He divides the evolutionary process into four stages: matter without life, next plant and animal life, then human life, and finally the coexistence of the human family in union with Christ. Jesus is divine insofar as he is the man in whom God is uniquely revealed. Even his divinity is an unfolding of the capabilities that were latent in the potency of matter rather than a totally new insertion into the world.[40]

While distancing himself from Teilhard's evolutionary categories, which in his opinion suggest inevitability and irreversibility, William M. Thompson agrees that Jesus made possible a new and deepened experience of the divine immediacy, both restoring and transforming what the previous "axial" consciousness had made possible. By radicalizing the "axial" discovery of human personhood and autonomy, Christianity, he argues, is able to appropriate and even contribute to the discoveries of our modern technological age and to the projected future planetary age.[41]

The consciousness model is generally recognized as consonant with the symbolic approach to revelation. Symbol, we have seen, has a transforming effect on the subject, establishing new orientations and new relationships. If divine revelation is an entry into a new self-consciousness, one might expect that it would be accompanied by the emergence of new symbols. Gregory Baum, who may be taken as representative of the fifth model, holds that since "the divine mystery is the deepest dimension of human existence" it reveals itself in symbols. Understanding symbol to mean "a story or an event of a kind that reveals the hidden depth, in an encounter with which we undergo significant transformation," Baum declares that Christian truth is by nature symbolic.[42] It "reveals that hidden structure of human life and by so doing it significantly transforms the self-understanding of those who receive it."[43] This is notably true for the Christ-symbol. "We may even present Jesus Christ as the ultimate symbol in which the divine ground of the human and cosmic reality reveals itself."[44]

The consciousness model brings out the human relevance of the Christ-figure as presented in Scripture and tradition. Edward Schillebeeckx, who recognizes the legitimacy of this concern, calls attention to the symbolic power of the biblical story of Jesus:

> In the New Testament, the story of Jesus is experienced as the illuminating and transforming symbol which discloses to our understanding the depth-dimension of our finite existence. What was expressed in Jesus' words and deeds, his life and death, is evocative for our human experiences: it discloses our own existence to us; it illumines what authentic human life can be when we are aware that we are safe in the hands of the living God and can accept it as a challenge. . . . People come to know themselves (again) in Jesus the Lord. At the same time, the transforming power of this representative symbol calls us to a conversion in faith; in other words, this correlation is achieved in *metanoia* or conversion, and not in a simple alignment.[45]

What Schillebeeckx here asserts is in perfect harmony with the teaching of Vatican Council II on the manner in which the gospel concerning Jesus Christ, the image of the invisible God, speaks to "the most secret desires of the human heart" and brings "development, light, and peace" to the human enterprise.[46] The use of symbol in a consciousness Christology, when taken in conjunction with what is sound in the other models, can be compatible with a sincere affirmation of the traditional creeds.

What makes for trouble is the absolutization of the subjective element of the shift in consciousness, so that all Christian teaching is revelation only to the extent that it eventuates in this. When this position is taken, theology falls back into the subjectivism characteristic of model three. Such a distortion is apparent in some extreme examples of Modernism, such as Marcel Hébert's *Profession de Foi du Vicaire Savoyard* (1894). In the Christological article of his paraphrase of the creed, Hébert declared:

> And [I believe] in him in whom there was realized in an exceptional and unique degree the union of the divine with human nature . . . : Jesus Christ, whose striking superiority, impressing simple hearts, became symbolized for them by the idea of a virginal conception . . . , whose powerful action after his death . . . caused in the mind of the apostles and disciples the visions and appearances narrated in the Gospels, and is symbolized by the myth of a redemptive descent into hell and an ascension to the upper regions of the sky . . .[47]

As Edwyn Bevan remarks, Hébert obviously believed himself capable of seeing beyond the symbols and of grasping the plain truth that was intended by them.[48] Recurring to the distinction made above, one may say that Hébert was using myth as though it were allegory.

Something similar may be said of a recent collective work entitled *The Myth of God Incarnate,* which propounds the thesis that the Incarnation "is a mythological or poetic way of expressing his [Jesus'] significance for us."[49] According to John Hick, who is both editor of and contributor to this collection, the symbolic statement "that Jesus was God the Son incarnate is not literally true, since it has no literal meaning."[50] Hick then proceeds to translate what is intended by the mythical language of the creed:

> In the case of Jesus it gives definitive expressions to his efficacy as saviour from sin and ignorance and as giver of new life; it offers a way of declaring his significance to the world; and it expresses a disciple's commitment to Jesus as his personal Lord. He is the one in following whom we have found ourselves in God's presence and have found God's meaning for our lives. He is our sufficient model of true humanity in a perfect relationship to God. And he is so far above us in the "direction" of God that he stands between ourselves and the Ultimate as a mediator of salvation.[51]

Hick's conclusions regarding the Incarnation follow logically from his opinion that myth and symbol are "not indicative but expressive" and that their real point is "to express a valuation and evoke an attitude."[52] Charles Davis, in some recent writings, takes a similar position. "Christology," he writes, "was a remarkable achievement of the creative imagination as it strove to express the experience of the transcendent as felt overwhelmingly in the first Christian communities."[53] Davis believes that by acknowledging "the figurative nature of religious expression and the relativity of every human world, even when religious"[54] it may be possible to make room for "the legitimate demands of modern secularity."[55] The essential positions of Hick and Davis are widespread in the liberal Christianity of our day.[56]

The basic flaw in these approaches has been identified by Schillebeeckx. The Christological titles, he maintains, have both an objective and a projective side, though the two can never be totally separated. Theologians such as Davis, he contends, retain only the subjective, projective elements making Jesus a mere representation of particular possibilities of human life. Projection, Schillebeeckx admits, "certainly has a part to play, but . . . given the religious concern of scripture and tradition, this model is subject to critical correction from the divine element which really appeared in the person of Jesus."[57]

In conclusion, then, we may say that the idea of Christ as symbol, taken in a realist sense, serves as a valuable complement to the doctrinal, historical, and dialectical models, and can be enriched by incorporating the basic insights of these approaches. If, however, the Christ-symbol is taken only under its projective aspect, as in some versions of the third and fifth models, it comes into direct conflict with the other three models. Against the doctrinal, it holds that the traditional dogmas rest on a mistake about religious language. Against the historical, it interprets the stories about Jesus—including even the Incarnation and the Resurrection—only as inspired fiction. Against the dialectical, it holds that the Christ-symbol arises not through a binding revelation from above but through the creative powers of human religiosity in a particular sociocultural situation.

This subject-centered, agnostic, and relativist understanding of the Christian symbols, while perhaps irrefutable on its own premises, cannot be sustained when the testimony of the Bible and of Christian tradition are taken seriously. It erodes the distinctive witness of Christianity to the God "who so loved the world that he gave his only Son" (Jn 3:16). The positive contributions of the first, second, and fourth models come to the aid of the theologian who wants to do justice to both the realist and the projectionist aspects of the Christ-symbol.

Among the advantages claimed for the projectionist view of the Christ-symbol, by authors such as John Hick and Charles Davis, is its supposed value for interreligious dialogue. The question of Christ as the summit of revelation therefore leads directly to that of the relationship between Christianity and other living faiths.

# Chapter XI

# REVELATION AND THE RELIGIONS

## 1. *The Problem*

Before we analyze more particularly how God's revelation in Christ comes to Christians, we must deal with a wider question already broached in the closing pages of Chapter X. Many members of the human race have not known Jesus Christ and have not believed in him, at least explicitly. Does revelation come to them? If so, how is that revelation related to the revelation of God in Jesus Christ, of which we have been speaking?

These questions have been chiefly discussed in connection with the religions, especially those major religions which have, over the centuries, performed for millions of people functions broadly similar to those performed by Christianity for Christians. Religion typically involves prayer, worship, belief in higher powers, self-denial, and ethical commitment. If revelation is anywhere evident beyond the realm of Christian faith, it should be discernible in the religions.

In the case of one such religion, Christian faith has a fairly definite stance, based on the New Testament. Christ and the Church are seen as radicalizing the Law and the prophets. The religion of ancient Israel is viewed as a divinely given preparation for Christianity. The Bible, however, does not encourage a similarly favorable appraisal of paganism. It portrays the religions of the Egyptians and the Canaanites, the Greeks and the Romans, in a negative light bordering on caricature. Since the age of the apostles, Christian theology has vacillated between looking on other religions as providential preparations for Christianity and as idolatrous perversions. In recent discussion, as we shall see, still other options have emerged.

To clarify the intention of this chapter, several preliminary observations may be in order. In the first place, it should be obvious that the question is here being treated from the standpoint of Christian theology, not from that of a "nonaligned" history of religions. Even as theologians, moreover, we shall not here seek to appraise any given religious tradition in detail, but rather to see whether, in principle, the Christian theological warrants give us reason to think that revelation is present or absent in nonbiblical religions.

I say "nonbiblical" religions because the Christian can readily admit that Judaism and Islam, as "religions of the Book," contain revelation insofar as they accept sacred texts which Christians also recognize as Scripture. Although the relationships between these biblical faiths are complex and problematical, they will not here be the primary focus of attention. To pose our question in sharpest form, we shall concern ourselves with the presence or absence of revelation in other religions to the extent that they are untouched by historical contact with Judaism or Christianity. Eastern religions such as Hinduism and Buddhism present special problems since they do not make any claim to be founded on divine revelation; they are, in the phrase of Robley Whitson, not "overtly revelational."[1] Islam, by contrast, does claim to be founded on the word of God in the Qur'an, but this revelation has not been acknowledged by Christians as authentic.[2]

To define the term "religion" in a way that includes everything commonly so called, while excluding everything else, is notoriously difficult, perhaps impossible. Among the major world faiths, Hinduism and Islam fulfill the requirements of religion by any definition. Whether Buddhism is a religion could be disputed, and the same is even more obviously true of Confucianism. The fundamental issue of this chapter does not depend on precisely what qualifies as a religion. Since our concern is whether and how revelation is mediated under auspices other than those of Christian and biblical religion, we need not limit our attention to the religions. They have been selected for special consideration only because they would seem to be more likely bearers of revelation than philosophies such as neo-Platonism or ideologies such as Marxism.

Furthermore, it must be kept in mind that we are asking only about revelation. We are not trying to determine whether there is truth or ethical value in these other faiths, religions, ideologies, philosophies, or movements, nor are we seeking to lay down rules for fruitful interreligious dialogue, except insofar as presumptions about revelation could help or impede such dialogue.

Finally, we are not directly asking about who can be saved. Although revelation and salvation are presumably not unrelated, it would be inappropriate to assume at this point that the presence of revelation in a religion makes it a channel of salvation, for it could be that revelation is given therein only in a measure that suffices for condemnation.[3] Conversely, the absence of revelation in a religion does not by itself rule out the possibility that its adherents achieve salvation. It is at least theoretically possible that a Buddhist would have access to a saving revelation not through the Buddhist tradition but through the order of creation or through the voice of conscience. Or perhaps a case could be made for holding that one could make an act of saving faith through an upright will elevated by grace, without dependence on any specific revelation. To discuss the various theories of salvation would take us into a series of problems beyond the scope of this work.

The question of revelation in the religions might seem to be a very simple one, with a yes or no answer. Most theologians, however, answer with distinctions. Some say that without biblical revelation one may have natural revelation rather than supernatural, or general revelation rather than special, or cosmic revelation rather than historical, or general historical revelation rather than special historical revelation. If any kind of revelation is acknowledged, it must further be asked how this is related to biblical and Christian faith. Here again many different answers are possible. Some see all other revelation as preparatory to Christianity. Some think that it can only be a dim participation of what is given more fully in the Christian revelation. But others hold that the revelation in other religions is different from, and complementary to, that found in biblical religion. Then further differences arise between some who see the religions as being different perspectives on a revelation that is unitary, and others who see the different religions as holding different revelations in trust for the benefit of all. If so, each religion, including Christianity, could learn revealed truth from the others. Perhaps none could claim to be essentially superior to the rest.

The difficulty Christians experience in answering questions such as these is in substance theological. On the one hand, Christianity

proclaims Jesus Christ as the center, summit, and fullness of all revelation. On the other hand, Christianity is good news about God's
saving designs for humanity as a whole. It is not just good news for
Christians. Christianity contains, therefore, an inbuilt tension between particularism and universalism. Hence it is not surprising to
find some Christians saying that there is no revelation apart from
Jesus Christ, and others saying that God reveals himself to every
human being. Tensions such as these are evident in the way theologians speak about the relationship between revelation and the religions.

From the following survey, it will be apparent that the first, second, and fourth models, which tend to be reserved toward the
category of symbol, are the least inclined to admit revelation in the
world's religions. Models three and five, which favor the symbolic approach, find it easy to acknowledge that revelation is present in all
religions, but in so saying they frequently relativize the traditional
claims of Christianity.

## 2. The Propositional Model and the Religions

The propositional model, in its appraisal of the religions, is
concerned with the question whether they can receive revealed propositional truths in any way except through biblical revelation. This
question is answered in similar but slightly different ways in Conservative Evangelicalism and in Catholic neo-Scholasticism.

Conservative Evangelicals hold that special revelation is accessible only through the Bible, but they hold on the basis of certain
biblical texts, such as Acts 14:17, Acts 17:22–31, Romans 1:18–20,
and Romans 2:15, that God has not left himself without witness to
all peoples, which constitutes a kind of "general revelation." This
general revelation, however, is not salvific. The Lausanne Covenant,
a profession of faith issued by the International Congress on World
Evangelization in 1974, declares:

> We recognize that all men have some knowledge of God
> through his general revelation in nature. But we deny that this
> can save, for men suppress the truth by their unrighteousness.
> We also reject as derogatory to Christ and the Gospel every
> kind of syncretism and dialogue which implies that Christ
> speaks equally through all religions and ideologies.[4]

Waldron Scott, commenting on this text, holds that God does indeed reveal himself in nature, and that this light may well be reflected in the religions. "Yet people reject the awareness they have. They do not acknowledge God in truth. They utilize their religiosity to escape from God."[5] Gordon Clark holds that the contradictions among the pagan religions prove "the beclouding effects of sin upon the mind as it tries to discover God and salvation in nature."[6] Thus Conservative Evangelicalism, while it makes use of the distinction between general and special revelation, tends to look on extra-biblical religion not as revealed but as a "depraved answer to the revelation of God."[7]

Neo-Scholasticism characteristically makes the distinction not between general and special revelation but between natural and revealed religion, taking a moderately optimistic view of the former. Gerardus van Noort may be quoted as illustrative of this position:

> There are two types of religion: natural and supernatural. Natural religion stems necessarily from the very nature of God and of man, is known and regulated by reason, and leads to a natural goal. Supernatural religion rests upon some sort of revelation. Note, however, that supernatural religion does not destroy, or take the place of natural religion, but is added to it and perfects it.[8]

The fact that all peoples, from the most primitive to the most civilized, have always practiced religion can be explained, according to Monsignor van Noort, "only on the grounds that all peoples in this matter were following the dictates of sound reason."[9] But the religions that actually exist, he concedes, bear the marks of sinful corruption. They are found in "the perverted forms labeled fetishism, animism, manism, totemism, and so on."[10]

Some neo-Scholastics, including van Noort, fortify the idea of natural religion by appealing also to primitive revelation. On the basis of Scripture they hold that revelations were made to the first parents of the human race and to the patriarchs in the period before Moses.[11] Traces of this original revelation, they hold, are the best explanation for the nobility and purity of the religion found among some primitive peoples, even in our own day. In support of this, many authors allege the findings of the Viennese cultural anthropologist, Wilhelm Schmidt, S.V.D., in his monumental *Der Ursprung der Gottesidee* (twelve vols., 1921–55).

Contemporary ethnologists and historians of religion appear to be highly skeptical of the thesis, essential to the position of Schmidt, that the more primitive peoples were outstanding for their monotheism.[12] However that may be, the propositional model is too narrow in assuming that revelation outside the biblical religions would have to rest either upon rational deduction from the order of creation or upon some kind of primitive positive revelation, passed down in immemorial tradition. In contrast to other theories we shall examine, this model takes too little account of the workings of God in the history and experience of the unevangelized.

## 3. Revelation as History and the Religions

The second model, that of revelation as history, must likewise be discussed in two forms, salvation history and universal history. Oscar Cullmann, exemplifying the first approach, holds that the line of salvation history, from the beginnings to the time of Jesus Christ, became increasingly narrowed down to a representative minority until, with Jesus, only a single individual stood for the whole. Since the Resurrection of Jesus the line of salvation and revelation has expanded outward again from its midpoint in Jesus. The missionary proclamation of the Church gives meaning to the entire period of history from the Resurrection to the Parousia.[13] The Church, as the bearer of revelation, is "the instrument of the divine redemptive activity."[14] According to Cullmann the Church does not encounter in the pagan world people who have already accepted revelation, but on the contrary only those who have rejected it. He interprets Acts 17:22ff. and Romans 1:18ff. as teaching that "the Gentiles after Abraham, just as previously, close their minds to the revelation of God in the works of Creation."[15]

Jean Daniélou, who professes a modified salvation history approach, finds it possible to make some room for revelation in the nonbiblical religions. He holds that prior to the historical revelation given in biblical religion, God had already revealed himself universally through the cosmos, conscience, and the human spirit. The "cosmic covenant" between God and Noah, as attested by Genesis, chapter 9, extends, according to Daniélou, to all humanity. "The cosmic religion," he insists, "is not natural religion, in the sense that the latter means something outside the effective and concrete supernatural order. . . . The cosmic covenant is also a covenant of grace, but it is still imperfect, in the sense that God reveals himself therein only through the cosmos."[16] The Bible itself, he points out, celebrates the holiness of many "pagans," such as Abel, Enoch, Daniel, Noah, Job, Melchizedek, Lot, and the Queen of Sheba. Yet it must also be admitted, he says, that the religion of nature is invariably found, in the forms known to us, in a more or less corrupt condition.[17] Thus he feels authorized to make a sharp contrast between Catholic Christianity and all other religions:

> Thus, the essential difference between Catholicism and all other religions is that the others start with man. They are touching and often very beautiful attempts, rising very high in their search for God. But in Catholicism there is a contrary movement, the descent of God towards the world, in order to communicate His life to it. The answer to the aspirations of the entire universe lies in the Judaeo-Christian religion. The true religion, the Catholic religion, is composed of these two elements. It is the religion in which God's grace has made answer to man's cry. In other religions grace is not present, nor is Christ, nor is the gift of God. The vanity and illusion of syncretism lies in its belief that universality is a common denominator of all religions.[18]

Neither Cullmann nor Daniélou, therefore, seems to credit the idea of revelation in the non-Christian religions. Yet there is nothing in the concept of salvation history that requires the limitation of historical revelation to the biblical peoples. Even prior to the Noachic covenant, God, according to Ben Sirach, made an everlasting covenant with Adam and Eve (Sir 17:10). This was followed by a whole series of further covenants with Abraham, with Moses, with David, and ultimately with Jesus Christ. Each covenant may be interpreted as involving a revelation of God's care and intentions for his people. The successive covenants do not abrogate one another for, according to Paul, God's gifts are irrevocable (Rom 11:29). The "new and eternal covenant" in Jesus (1 Cor 11:25; Heb 8:13, 12:24) may be seen as a criterion by which all other covenants are to be measured and interpreted. The history of the covenants could perhaps provide the basis for a wider biblical theology of salvation history than is found in authors such as Cullmann and Daniélou, while not relativizing the Christian revelation. A number of recent authors, such as Hans Küng, Raimundo Panikkar, Heinz Robert Schlette, Eugene Hillman, and Donald Dawe, have asserted that all the nations are under a salutary cosmic covenant, but the consequences of this assertion for the theology of revelation remain as yet unclarified.[19]

The idea of revelation through universal history, championed by Pannenberg and his circle, might seem to offer great promise of finding revelation in nonbiblical religions. If God is conceived from the outset as related not simply to the history of a single elect people but to world history, he might be expected to disclose himself to all. Pannenberg, however, rejects the idea of revelation in a multiplicity of religions. Beginning from the Hegelian premise that universal history is an indirect revelation of God, he concedes that the meaning of universal history is knowable only at the end. This concession would seem to exclude all revelation within history were it not for the fact, recognized by Christians alone, that the end of universal history has already occurred proleptically in the Resurrection of Jesus from the dead. Pannenberg therefore agrees with Barth that revelation, as the self-disclosure of the one God, occurs only in Christ, in whom the divine breaks into the historical continuum.[20]

While reserving revelation to Christ, Pannenberg accords a special place to Israelite faith. Israel's history of promises, he says, is unique because it was open to future fulfillment, and indeed to that very fulfillment which occurred in Jesus. "In contradistinction to other peoples and their religions, Israel, in the light of its particular experience of God, learned to understand the reality of human existence as a history moving toward a goal which had not yet appeared."[21] By contrast, the myths of the religions are related to primordial time and thus closed to the future. These other religions, however, are not mere fabrications. They manifest in a confused manner the same reality which has revealed itself in Jesus.[22] Religious dialogue can strive to make the religions open to their own historical transformation, and thus also to the definitive manifestation of God in Christ. Concurrently such dialogue can prevent Christianity from clinging timidly to its own past forms and can actuate its inexhaustible assimilative powers.

Whereas Pannenberg, with his idea of revelation through universal history, restricts revelation to the Christ-event, Rahner, combining historical universalism with a symbolic approach to revelation, is able to find revelation in religion as such. Thanks to the Incarnation, Rahner maintains, the entire human family is constituted as God's people and is involved in a supernatural relationship with God. All men and women are called to eternal blessedness in Christ, whose grace is offered always and everywhere. Any naturally good act is elevated to the supernatural order by God's saving grace.

In view of his symbolic anthropology, already discussed in Chapter IX, Rahner holds that grace, when accepted, never remains suspended in a "metaempirical sphere," disconnected with the tangibility of history. On the contrary, grace will inevitably "try to objectify itself in explicit expressions of religion, such as in the liturgy and religious associations, and in protests of a 'prophetic' kind against any attempt by man to shut himself up in a world of his own categories and against any (ultimately polytheistic) misinterpretations of this basic grace-full experience."[23] Because religion is the normal way in which one's relationship to the absolute becomes thematized, supernatural grace cannot fail to show itself in the religions, even when accompanied, as might be expected, with distortions due to human sin and frailty.

In holding the salvific and revelatory character of the religions in general, Rahner does not relativize biblical revelation and Christianity. In his terminology, the religion of the Old and New Testaments constitutes the "special" history of revelation and salvation, inerrantly directed toward Christ, in whom God and the world enter into "absolute and unsurpassable unity."[24] Christ, the incarnate Word, is the absolute religious symbol in whom the aspirations of humanity for a definitive and irrevocable self-communication of God are fulfilled. The religions can be interpreted as expressions of a "searching memory" which somehow anticipates God's culminating gift in Jesus Christ.[25]

Rahner's theology of symbol as the revelatory self-expression of grace enables him to construct a theology of salvation history that gives not only salvific, but also revelatory, importance to the extrabiblical religions. In this respect Rahner goes beyond the typical representatives of the revelation-as-history model.

## 4. Revelation as Experience and the Religions

Theologians of the third model hold that a revelatory experience of God underlies all religions, and that they differ, not by hav-

ing different revelations, but by differently symbolizing the same re-
elation. While not affirming that all experiences of God are equally
pure or intense, or that all symbols are equally expressive, these
theologians regard the differences among the religions as accidental
rather than essential. The revelations accorded in different traditions
differ in degree rather than in kind.

Friedrich von Hügel, though he departs from the third model in
his firm commitment to the historical and institutional features of
Christianity, laid great stress on the mystical element. God, he held,
was experientially revealed in all religions, but this experience is
found "at its deepest and purest" in Christ.[26] Among the "great
Revealers and Incarnations of the prevenient love of the Other-than-
themselves," he wrote, "Jesus Christ holds the supreme, and indeed
the unique, place."[27]

Evelyn Underhill, the tireless explorer of mystical literature,
was convinced that mysticism has so far found its best map in
Christianity.[28] But the map, she added, is not the reality.

> Attempts, however, to limit mystical truth—direct apprehension
> of the Divine Substance—by the formulae of any one religion,
> are as futile as the attempt to identify a precious metal with the
> die which converts it into current coin. The dies which the mys-
> tics have used are many. . . . But the gold from which this di-
> verse coinage is struck is always the same precious metal; always
> the same Beatific Vision of a Goodness, Truth, and Beauty
> which is *one*. Hence its substance must always be distinguished
> from the accidents under which we perceive it: for this sub-
> stance has an absolute, and not a denominational, importance.[29]

For William Ernest Hocking, too, revelation was "the empirical
element in religious knowledge."[30] There is no religion, for him,
without a basis in revelation, and therefore it must be possible for
each religion to be reconceptualized in the light of the revelatory ingredients in the others. In such a rapprochement, he suggested, "the
concept of Christ is extended to include that unbound Spirit who
stands and has stood at the door of every man, and who, in various
guises, still appears to him who opens, both as an impersonal word
and as a personal presence."[31] In the coming world faith, as Hocking
envisaged it, the name of Jesus Christ would no longer be insisted
on.[32]

In many recent theologians an approach to extra-biblical religions is attempted on the basis of the patristic doctrine of Christ as

universal Logos. Paul Tillich, for example, held that all living religions rest upon revelatory experiences of the same omnipresent divine reality, differently symbolized in each. In one of his last works Tillich sought to show that the Buddhist symbol of Nirvana and the Christian symbol of the Kingdom of God are two ways of expressing the gulf between ultimate reality and the conditions of actual existence. Through a three-way dialogue, Tillich believed, the Eastern religions, the Western religions, and the new secular quasi-religions could achieve mutual enrichment and purification. "In the depth of every living religion there is a point at which the religion loses its importance, and that to which it points breaks through its particularity, elevating it to spiritual freedom and with it to a vision of the spiritual presence in other expressions of the ultimate meaning of man's existence."[33]

This combination of an absolutism of revelation with a relativism of symbols continues to be pressed by distinguished scholars of our day. John Hick, for example, maintains that since God is the God of the whole world, we must presume that the whole religious life of humanity is part of the continuous and universal human relationship to God.[34] The major religious traditions all rest on revelatory experiences of the absolute, but reflect this differently in view of the variety of cultural and historical conditions.[35] The unifying factor in all religions is God, about whom they revolve. The many different analogies of the divine reality may all be true, though expressed in imperfect human comparisons. Although we may not be able to bring about a single world religion, the new situation created by worldwide communications may lead to "an increasing interpenetration of religious traditions and a growing of them closer together."[36]

In this model, therefore, revelation is sharply distinguished from symbol. The revelation is seen as unitary and divine, the symbol systems as diverse and human. Jesus Christ is viewed as a Christian symbol, highly meaningful to Christians, but lacking the universal value of the experience of God to which the symbol points.

The limitations of this model for inner-Christian theology have already been mentioned in previous chapters. It may now be added that the attempt to separate the experience of revelation from symbol and concept is inhibiting for interreligious dialogue. As Hick, for example, is not unaware, there is an interpretative element in every experience of revelation. The effort to bypass the historical and cultural factors can therefore lead to an unwelcome reduction. Theism itself would be threatened since it has been in great measure shaped by the symbols and conceptual structures of biblical religion and Hellenistic philosophy, and is not widely accepted in the Eastern religions. Consistently applied, the effort to eliminate the culture-related specifics thus dissolves theocentrism as well as Christocentrism as a basis for dialogue. The common platform therefore becomes uncomfortably small.

## 5. Revelation as Dialectical and the Religions

Wary of the reductionistic trends in liberal and modernist theology, the dialectical theologians, under the leadership of Karl Barth, advocated an approach to the religions that would be deliberately controversial and critical rather than compromising and irenic. For these theologians Christ as the Word of God stands in judgment against all human achievements, including religion itself insofar as it proceeds from man. Leading from a position of strength, authors of the fourth model held that the supreme norm of all theology, including the theology of the religions, must be Jesus Christ in whom God had definitively disclosed himself.

Barth, in his Epistle to the Romans and in the first volume of his *Church Dogmatics* (part 2), eloquently set forth his position that revelation stands against all the religions, but that, in condemning, it heals and justifies, so that, in Christ, there can be a "true religion" rescued as a brand from the fire.[37] While rejecting any easy continuity between Christ and the religions, Barth's dialectical theology allowed for a kind of Hegelian *Aufhebung* (abolition and sublimation) of that religion upon which the light of Christ is made to shine. But he felt obliged to point out how even Amida Buddhism and Bhakti Hinduism, in spite of real anticipations of Pauline and Protestant Christianity, lack the one thing necessary for true religion, the name of Jesus Christ.[38]

Even in the last volumes of his *Church Dogmatics,* in which he emphasizes the far-reaching effects of Christ's reconciling action, Barth retains a posture of reserve. Religions such as Islam, he declares, are humanly and ethically imposing.

Missions presuppose both that they will be valued and taken
seriously, with a complete absence of the crass arrogance of the
white man, and yet also that they will not be allowed to exercise
any pressure on the Gospel but that this will be opposed to them
in all its radical uniqueness and novelty, with no attempt at
compromise or at finding points of contact and the like. Missions are valueless and futile if they are not pursued in strict acceptance of these two presuppositions, and therefore with a sincere respect and yet also an equally sincere lack of respect for
the so-called religions.[39]

Emil Brunner, who developed an "eristic" theology of the
religions, insisted that only the prophetic religions of the Near East
could be understood as making a serious claim to revelation.[40] But
the other living prophetic religions, Judaism and Islam, reject the
claims of Christianity, thus compelling a choice.[41] The claim of
Christianity to be the revelation given by God through Incarnation
sets it totally apart from both Judaism and Islam.[42] In the view of
Christian faith, Christ is both the fulfillment and the judgment of all
the religions. He fulfills them by being the truth, the advocate, the
sacrifice, and the ritual meal for which they seek in vain.[43] But he also
judges all the religions inasmuch as he shows up the falsehood in
their doctrines and the superstitious and cruel legalism of their practices. Called into being by God's self-manifestation in creation,
religion is always perverted by human pride and selfishness.[44]

The dialectical theology of the religions, as proposed by Barth
and Brunner, was applied to missiology by Hendrik Kraemer. His
book, *The Christian Message in a Non-Christian World,*[45] written at
the request of the International Missionary Council, was very
influential at the Tambaram Conference in India in 1938, and retains much influence in World Council circles to this day. Kraemer
held that the message of God, which is not adaptable to any religion
or philosophy, should be forthrightly announced, though always in a
manner intelligible and relevant to the evangelized. While not denying all signs of revelation in the religions, Kraemer focused on
Christ as God's only full revelation of himself. He was generally
critical of non-Christian religions as human achievements.

Dialectical theology is to be commended for its insistence that
Christians should bring the full resources of their faith to bear on
the encounter among the religions. Taking the teaching of the New

Testament at face value, and accepting the Trinitarian and Christological dogmas without equivocation, this theology holds to the incomparable richness of God's self-disclosure in his incarnate Word.
These theologians rightly remind us of the importance of signs and
testimonies which proclaim Jesus as universal Lord. Yet if God's
grace in Christ has a universal redemptive efficacy, as Barth seems
to admit, one might well suspect that all human religions, to the extent that they proceed from grace, might bear a mute or indirect testimony to God's Word in Christ. At this point Rahner's theory of
"searching memory" and the Logos theology of Tillich and others
might be able to supplement, and somewhat qualify, the more
polemical statements of Barth, Brunner, and Kraemer.

## 6. Revelation as New Consciousness and the Religions

The fifth model, it will be recalled, defines revelation dynamically in terms of its impact on human consciousness. Revelation is
seen as a divine summons to transcend one's present perspectives.
Since this summons is always correlated with the actual situation as
well as with the basic dynamism of the human spirit, revelation
comes in new ways in each period of history. In our own day, many
of these theologians assert, revelation involves a call to put aside the
limitations of cultural self-centeredness and to be open to the working
of the divine Spirit in alien cultures. Open to new currents in secular
and religious experience, Teilhard de Chardin, Gregory Baum, and
Paul Knitter have proposed radical revisions of conventional Christianity, with major implications for the dialogue between the religions.

Teilhard de Chardin was convinced that the present encounter
between the religions could not fulfill its promise unless the critique
of religion by secular humanism were taken into account. Yet secular humanism, lacking the transcendent focus provided by revelation, could not provide the kind of faith needed to sustain humanity
in the dawning planetary age. The Eastern religions, imbued with a
mystical sense of universal unity, provided a transcendent focus, but
failed to give meaning to human effort and evolutionary progress.
Christianity in its usual forms ("paleo-Christianity," Teilhard sometimes called it), suffered from some of the same unworldliness. He
therefore called for a "neo-Christianity," a "new mysticism," one

"for which we have as yet no name," to serve as a "privileged central axis" about which the religions might converge.[46]

> A general convergence of religions upon a universal Christ who fundamentally satisfies them all: that seems to me the only possible conversion of the world, and the only form in which a religion of the future can be conceived.[47]

Unlike the false monisms at work in Eastern and Western forms of pantheism, an authentic pan-Christism, according to Teilhard, could combine the Eastern concern for universal unity with the Western concern for individual dignity and freedom. In spite of some passing remarks to the effect that Christ must be reinterpreted in such a way as to "integrate those aspects of the divine expressed by the Indian god Shiva,"[48] Teilhard spoke more often of the limitations than of the merits of the "road of the East." When asked whether a Buddhist or a Hindu should become a Christian, he replied: "It would be better to try to carry its truth [that of your previous religion] with you, and transform it if you could, though of course sometimes this might not be possible."[49]

Baum, as we have seen, describes the acceptance of revelation as "an entry into a new self-consciousness and a new orientation toward the world."[50] Jesus "makes known to us God's redemptive involvement in the whole of human life."[51] Religion, as Marx and Freud pointed out, can be a screen shutting us off from responsible life in society,[52] but religious worship can also serve to protect us from the demonic power of sex, money, nation, and social philosophies. Without holding that nonbiblical religions are divine, we can find in them something "that offers salvation to men, detaches them from idolatry, elevates them to higher understanding, creates in them faith in a gracious transcendent reality, and initiates them into love and care for other people."[53]

Logos Christology, which viewed other religions as mere preparations for Christianity, is no longer adequate, according to Baum. The Church, he declares, must abandon its absolute claims, which inevitably breed aggression and conflict.[54] Each religion must strive to liberate itself, with the help of others, from its own idolatries.

> The Church's mission may then be understood as an on-going dialogue with other religions, designed to liberate all partners, including herself, from the ideological deformation of truth.

Through conversation and action men may learn to attach themselves to the authentic, life-giving and humanizing elements of
their religious traditions.[55]

Such an ideal, Baum maintains, will make it easy for people
belonging to each religion to make friends across the boundaries, to
share important experiences, to feel united in the same basic struggle, "and never think that anyone should change from one religion
to another."[56]

In the United States, another Roman Catholic, Paul Knitter, has
in several recent articles challenged the view that Christianity commits its adherents to the finality and superiority of God's revelation
in Christ. Such a tenet, he holds, is unjustifiable in terms of a modern approach to Scripture and a revisionist method in theology. It is
also disastrous for interreligious dialogue.[57] Following a consistent
consciousness theology, he argues that revelation and salvation occur
when the individual is "sucked into" a world constituted by myth and
symbol.

Myth-symbols save. Historical facts do not. . . . It is only when
we are grasped by and find ourselves responding with our whole
being to a symbol, myth, or story that we are encountering the
divine, touching and being touched by "the Ground of Being,"
and experiencing grace.[58]

Symbol and myth, Knitter maintains, are salvific not because
they correspond to some antecedent objective reality, but because
they reach into a person's innermost being, thereby renewing the
whole self. Once this is recognized, Christians no longer have to
take the symbol of the Incarnation as a factual statement. It is a
myth in the same sense as stories of the wonderful birth and exaltation of the Lord Buddha and the Lord Krishna. "If it is true that it
is the myth-symbol that saves, not historical facts as such, then
Christianity is placed essentially on the same level with other
religions."[59] Knitter adds: "Such insights will open new avenues in
the present-day dialogue among world religions."[60]

In Chapter X we have already commented on the opinion that
symbol is equivalent to myth, as a product of creative imagination,
and that the doctrine of the Incarnation, being mythical, cannot be
taken as a cognitive statement about Jesus himself. To hold that salvation is given by such a myth, rather than by the redemptive action

of God in his incarnate Son, radically shifts the center of Christian faith. Many contemporary theologians, with whom I associate myself, deny that such a transposition is called for by sound developments in hermeneutics or theological method. Charles Davis had good reason to write, not many years ago: "Frankly, I do not myself see how the universality and finality of Christ can be denied without emptying the Christian tradition of meaning."[61] For a Christian to say what Davis here says is not to deny that Christ is a symbol, or that the Christ-story is in some sense a myth, but it is to imply that the myth or symbol is disclosive of the meaning inherent in the Christ-event itself.

Could a Christian affirm that the same divine Lord whom Christians worship in Jesus is worshiped, under other symbols, by the devotees of the Lord Krishna and of the Lord Buddha? Fidelity to the Christian confession, it would seem, excludes the idea that there is any Lord except Jesus (cf. 1 Cor 8:6). In company with Lucien Richard, I would reject an extreme "archetype Christology" that would see the Jesus-story as "as the historicization of an archetype which is already found at work everywhere."[62] On the other hand, it need not be denied that the eternal Logos could manifest itself to other peoples through other religious symbols. Raimundo Panikkar, who proposes a "universal Christology," stands in continuity with a long Christian tradition of Logos-theology that goes back as far as Justin Martyr. On Christian grounds, it may be held that the divine person who appears in Jesus is not exhausted by that historical appearance. The symbols and myths of other religions may point to the one who Christians recognize as the Christ.

Would the interreligious dialogue be helped if Christians were to abandon the claim that Christ is universally and definitively normative? Obviously no dialogue would be possible if Christians demanded, as a condition of participation, that Christ be acknowledged by all as the supreme norm of truth. In an interreligious dialogue the particular convictions of any one party cannot be presumed as either true or false. For Christians antecedently to surrender their traditional claim might be injurious to the dialogue, since it might prevent them from making what is potentially their most important contribution.

Christians who are convinced of having in Jesus Christ hte definitive revelation can enter the interreligious dialogue with full consciousness of having something to contribute. But can they enter it with the expectation of having something to learn? According to the principles advanced in this chapter they can. They can expect to find signs and symbols of divine grace and human greatness in any major religious tradition. This is not a purely formal concession. The Christian cannot set limits to the heights of holiness and insight that God's grace may bring among those who do not recognize Christ as the incarnate Word.[63]

As living, incarnate symbol, Jesus Christ fulfills what is sound and challenges what is deficient in every religion, including Christianity. Christians, no less than others, are subject to him as norm. He detracts nothing from the revelatory meaning of other religions, nor do they detract from him. Even while questioning the adequacy of other religious symbols, Christ can place them in a new and wider frame of reference. As Carl Hallencreutz has said:

> For when confronted with Christ the symbols of the religious man are related in a new way to that "sacred reality" to which they have referred within their particular framework. They are brought together to their very centre and so "concentrated" that they can become new expressions of the richness of Christ.[64]

This recontextualization may be beneficial to all the religions, including Christianity. When the West, as a "Christian culture," was relatively isolated from contact with other religions, it may have been sufficient to construct Christology in terms of explicitly Christian symbols, but the present stage of world history seems to call for a further advance. The present encounter of the religions can have positive significance for the interpretation of what is revealed in Christ. In the words of Gabriel Fackre:

> There is a sound instinct in all of the models that respond to the new pluralism by attempting to reformulate the Christian doctrine of redemption in a more universal fashion. Doctrine does develop in response to new settings in which the Christian community finds itself. Plural shock can so impact our received theological traditions that we are led to a deeper insight into basic faith. But doctrine which develops does so always along the lines of the original trajectory. It renders more explicit which was implicit and coheres with the primal norm of the Gospel of Jesus Christ.[65]

We cannot accurately predict what we may learn from the dialogue that seems to be getting under way. There is no reason, however, to think that it will diminish the revelatory importance of Jesus Christ. It may well be that in the light of other revelatory symbols, the universal and abiding significance of Christ will be more strikingly manifested. Even though it already is the supreme and definitive self-disclosure of God, the Christ-symbol cannot be adequately appreciated for our time except in the context of many other symbols, including those of the extra-biblical religions. If disruptive change is avoided, the present encounter of the religions may well lead to an enrichment of the Christian symbolism and thus of the theology of revelation.

# Chapter XII

# THE BIBLE: DOCUMENT OF REVELATION

Having established that, for Christians, the central revelatory symbol, normative for all others, is Jesus Christ, we must further inquire how this symbol is accessible for believers who have not known Jesus in the flesh. The symbol of Jesus Christ has to be mediated to them through the Bible and the Church, which therefore become channels of revelation. In a general work on the theology of revelation, such as this, it will not be possible to give a full study of the use of the Bible and the Church in theology, but something must be said about how they serve to transmit revelation.

In each of the five models the Bible appears as a primary font or channel of Christian revelation. Yet the five differ greatly in how they depict the relationship between the Bible and revelation. Drawing upon the indications already given in earlier chapters, we shall here examine how these models stand with reference to certain standard questions, such as biblical inspiration, inerrancy, the canon, and the sufficiency of Scripture as a norm or source of church teaching and belief.

## 1. The Doctrinal Model and the Bible

In the first model, which equates revelation with propositional statements, the Bible is seen primarily as a source of doctrine. Attention is focused on the explicit teaching of Scripture, which is regarded as divine and inerrant. To vindicate the inerrancy of Scripture, appeal is made to the doctrine of inspiration, which is understood as a special impulse given to the biblical writers to write that —and only that—which God wants contained in the books. On the ground that God has inspired the entire text, it is taken as certain that everything the Bible says is true, for God, who is truth itself, could by no means be the author of falsehood.[1]

Within the propositional model, there are differences between the Protestant and Catholic positions. Protestant representatives of the model regard the Bible as self-attesting, self-sufficient, and self-interpreting. Since it is self-attesting, the canon validates itself, and does not have to be certified by ecclesiastical authority. Since the Bible is sufficient, there is no need to look outside the biblical books for any revealed truth. Church doctrine can only repeat and clarify what has already been taught in the Bible. And since, finally, the Bible is self-interpreting, the faithful have no need of any other agency to tell them what the Bible means.[2]

In the Catholic form of the propositional model the canon of Scripture does not rest on Scripture alone but, at least partly, on the teaching of the Church, which identifies the canonical books with the help of tradition. The Bible is not a sufficient source of doctrine, for there are some revealed truths (including the list of canonical books) known only through tradition. The Bible, moreover, cannot be rightly understood outside the Church, which is divinely commissioned and equipped to give an authoritative interpretation. The Bible, therefore, is not to be left to the private interpretation of individuals.[3]

Within both the Protestant and Catholic families there have been heated debates about the precise nature of inspiration. Some have held that inspiration extends only to the ideas and contents of the Bible, whereas others maintain that the very words themselves were given by divine inspiration. In either case, God, as the source of the ideas in the biblical books, is held to be the author. The human writers are said to be secretaries or, according to some theologians, instrumental authors. The distinction between principal and instrumental author raises further questions which were subtly debated in the scholastic manuals. These debates continue even today within certain conservative circles, both Protestant and Catholic.[4]

In the biblical theology of the mid-twentieth century a variant on the propositional model emerged, according to which the locus of inspiration and authority was shifted from the formal teaching of the Bible to the themes and concepts found in the canonical books. Biblical theologians, both Protestant and Catholic, produced learned studies of the biblical vocabulary, exploring terms such as *dabar* (word), *emeth* (truth), *shalom* (peace), and *ruah* (spirit).[5] These studies frequently contrasted the biblical categories, which were considered concrete and dynamic, with Greek thought forms, which were alleged to be metaphysical and static. The biblical theology movement did a great deal to revitalize theology in the decades following World War II, but it came under attack in the mid-sixties, when a number of scholars questioned the distinctiveness, coherence, and authority of the biblical concepts.[6]

## 2. *The Historical Model and the Bible*

The historical model of revelation theology, as we have noted, comes in two rather different forms. In its "salvation history" form, it works with the biblical concept of history, which is taken as normative.[7] Biblical history, according to this theory, recounts the acts of God in dealing with his chosen people. The Bible gives a divinely authoritative account of particular events which, as interpreted in the Bible, are revelation. Although inspiration is not much discussed by the leading authors of this school, the inspiration of the Bible, on this theory, may be seen as the ability of the authors to recognize, interpret, and present the events wherein God graciously disclosed himself.[8] The Bible is considered trustworthy, even inerrant, not in every detail but in its narration of sacred history. Protestants and Catholics who follow this approach continue to disagree about the sufficiency of Scripture, the criteria of canonicity, and the principles of interpretation. As in the doctrinal model, so in the *Heilsgeschichte* model, Protestants affirm the sufficiency of Scripture, whereas Catholics rely on church tradition as a necessary supplement to the Bible, even though perhaps derivative from it.

The second form of the historical model makes little appeal to inspiration and inerrancy, if it does not actually reject these ideas. It holds that revelation is given in the events themselves as recovered through a critical reading of the Bible. The Bible is seen not as an inspired and inerrant book, but as the most original source at our disposal for reconstructing the revelatory events. In particular, the event of Jesus Christ is seen as normative for Christian faith.

Wolfhart Pannenberg, a Protestant representative of this "critical history" approach, argues that it is necessary to probe behind the biblical texts in order to find the unity of Scripture, for the texts themselves do not agree. "The unified 'historical content' of Scripture, which, for Luther, was the basis of its authority, is for our historical consciousness no longer to be found in the texts but only behind them, in the figure of Jesus who is attested in the very different writings of the New Testament in very different and incongruous ways."[9] From a Catholic point of view, Hans Küng maintains that the Bible has normative value for faith only when it is used as a source of gaining access to the actual Jesus of history and his original message.[10]

In this second form of the historical model, the inveterate debates between Protestants and Catholics about the sufficiency of the Bible lose much of their importance. The Bible is normative because, and insofar as, it is a reliable report about the saving events. The exact limits of the canon are not considered crucial. The living tradition of the Church is not employed as a source of historical information about the revelatory events, but it may be consulted for indications how the message may best be proclaimed.

## 3. The Experiential Model and the Bible

Theologians who espouse the experiential model are perhaps those least committed to the Bible as revelation. Many of them strongly deny that Scripture is a quarry of revealed doctrine. Auguste Sabatier, for instance, writes: "As soon as the distinction is made in our consciousness between the word of God and the letter of holy Scripture, the first becomes independent of all form and of all external guarantee."[11] Yet Sabatier relies on the Bible in order to establish the supremacy of the revelation that took place in the consciousness of Jesus. C. H. Dodd, who comes close to the experiential model in some of his early writings, praises the prophets as religious geniuses. "In the Founder of Christianity," he asserts, "religious genius reached its highest point and passed into something greater still."[12] The Bible has authority for Dodd because the biblical authors write out of their experience of God in the soul, or of God's dealings in what happened to them and their people.[13]

Almost alone among representatives of this model, George Tyrrell insists on the distinction between revelatory experience and inspiration. The category of revelation, he holds, extends in the strict sense to the former alone, but in ·a broad sense includes inspiration as well. Inspiration is the added gift whereby certain recipients of revelation, in the period before the death of the last apostle, were impelled to translate their revelatory experiences into literary symbols capable of evoking similar experiences in their readers. Since the period of normative inspiration ended with the death of the last apostle, Tyrrell maintains, the deposit of Christian revelation is complete and incapable of being further developed.[14]

Paul Tillich criticizes both the propositional and the historical models from a standpoint similar to that of the experiential theologians.[15] He resolutely opposes any use of the Bible as an authoritative source of historical or theoretical knowledge. Protestant biblicism, he holds, is mistaken in making the Bible as such the norm, even the sole norm, of faith and theology. The norm is rather the power of the New Being, manifest in Jesus as the Christ. The Bible transmits this powerful revelatory picture; it is an icon of the holy. The inspiration of the New Testament writers was their acceptance of Jesus as the Christ, and with him, of the New Being. The Old Testament, in Tillich's estimation, is not directly normative for Christians.

Tillich, to be sure, is not a pure representative of the third model.[16] He severely criticizes the Schleiermacher school for looking on religious experience as source and norm. For Tillich, experience is only the medium through which the revelation comes. But since he makes the medium inseparable from the norm, religious experience becomes for him functionally determinative. The Bible is the document of revelation insofar as it proceeds from, and is evocative of, revelatory experiences. These experiences he describes in individualistic, existential terms heavily dependent on Rudolf Otto's religious phenomenology. "The major question that must be put to Tillich's entire theological enterprise is whether, by shifting the center of importance in his theology from the proposal of belief to a proposal of attitude, he throws Christian proclamation shaped by his theology seriously out of line with New Testament proclamation."[17]

## 4. *The Dialectical Model and the Bible*

In the dialectical model primary importance is attached to the kerygma, the word about Jesus that is preached in the Church.

Barth, in the early volumes of his *Church Dogmatics,* develops a doctrine of Scripture that harmonizes with the dialectical model as we have described it. For him the Bible, as the written form of the word, is "written proclamation"; it is "the deposit of what was once proclamation by human lips." He writes: "Scripture as the commencement and present-day preaching as the continuation of one and the same event" belong to a single series.[18] Barth accepts the inspiration of Scripture, and indeed its verbal inspiration, but he adds: "The literally inspired Bible was not at all a revealed book of oracles, but a witness to revelation."[19] Communicating God's word in the alien form of fallible human words, the Bible simultaneously reveals and conceals. Verbal inspiration means for Barth "that the fallible and faulty human word is as such used by God and has to be received and heard in spite of its human fallibility."[20] The Bible for Barth is not, properly speaking, the "revealed word"—a term he reserves to the Christ to whom the Bible and church proclamation bear witness—but is the fundamental attestation through which the Church has access to the revealed word. The Bible is God's word when and insofar as God freely chooses to speak through it.[21]

The canonical books of Scripture, then, are the books in which the Church has heard the word of God, and in which she expects to hear it again. The identity of the sacred books, for Barth, rests upon no extrinsic criterion but simply upon the fact that God's word manifests itself through these books and not through others. In this sense the Bible is *autopistos* (self-attesting). "The Bible constitutes itself as the canon."[22]

The Church's assertion that she has heard God speaking in certain books does not give absolute assurance that at some future date God might be heard not in these books but in others. Barth therefore maintains that the canon of Scripture is only relatively closed. In the sixteenth century certain biblical books which had previously been regarded as Scripture were excluded from the canon by the Reformers, and in the future the canon could conceivably be expanded or contracted again.[23]

Whereas Barth and his followers tend to emphasize the need of the Church to subject itself to the thought-forms of the Bible in order to hear God's word in it, Bultmann and his disciples, in another version of dialectical theology, emphasize the task of the Church to translate the biblical message into terms that can be understood today. Bultmann's program of demythologization may be positively interpreted as a proposal for existential interpretation.[24] What is normative and revelatory in the Bible, for Bultmann, is the human self-understanding that it conveys. For the Bultmannians, as for the Barthians, revelation occurs in an encounter with God's word as attested by the Bible.

## 5. *The Consciousness Model and the Bible*

Unlike partisans of the first and fourth models, adherents of the fifth do not look for revelation in the Bible considered as an objective deposit. For them revelation occurs in contemporary experience as illuminated by biblical and other paradigms. Revelation as an ongoing process generates continually new meanings for the Bible. Whereas Tillich described experience not as a source but as a medium of revelation, the new consciousness theology regards experience as a source—understanding experience, however, not empirically as mere sense data but as including an element of interpretation.

Gregory Baum, an important representative of this position, speaks of two modes of divine self-communication, corresponding to the two divine processions as Word and Spirit. The Church and the faithful, he asserts, are in touch with God's truth not only through the Scriptures but also through their personal experience of God's presence. Scripture, then, cannot be described as *norma normans non normata,* as though it were an objective datum against which all other things could be measured. "The Church's experience," he writes, "may well open up new perspectives, pose new questions, and lead Christians after rereading the Scriptures to new insights which as such are not found in the Scriptures."[25] Yet these new insights have to be tested, criticized, and confirmed by the Scriptures, which yield their "salvational meaning" when reread and reinterpreted in the light of the experience of the believing community. The outer word given in Scripture can thus help the believer to "discover what God's inner Word is saying in the depth of his own life and the experience of the community."[26]

The contemporary American Protestant, Ray L. Hart, speaks in similar terms. He holds that our current experience is illumined and configured by certain events in the past which have power to interpret our present situation.[27] These paradigmatic events, however, are not accessible in themselves, but only as "inverbalized." The events of biblical history, enshrined in the imaginative language of Scripture, are, in his view, decisive. Scripture he describes as "the primal schematization of revelation as fundament, and therefore as the indispensable heuristic for bringing revelation under circumspection anew." Consequently, he adds, "it is with scripture that theology perpetually recommences."[28]

Edward Schillebeeckx in his recent work seeks to incorporate the best features of the "new consciousness" model into a synthesis enriched by his previous efforts to integrate the neo-Thomistic and "salvation history" approaches.[29] His present position may be summarized somewhat as follows.[30] The inspiration of Scripture originally meant the capacity of certain writings to inspire the religious community to discover its own identity. The authority of Scripture was originally the inspiring significance of the new experiences of salvation communicated through these texts. Subsequently, the argument was inverted. The Scriptures were held to possess formal authority because they had been inspired by God. This logical inversion, however, was not illegitimate. Because the whole Christian movement was inspired by Jesus as God's emissary, the New Testament (and analogously the rest of Scripture) could be viewed as divinely inspired.

By the canon Schillebeeckx understands the foundational texts which the Christian community has acknowledged as normative for its own identity. By its decision concerning the canon the Church forged for itself an instrument wherewith to integrate neophytes pedagogically, ethically, and socially into the group whose identity was defined in relation to these texts. Although the boundaries of the canon remained somewhat vague, the Church's determination of the canon proved over the centuries to have been not only necessary but highly successful. The Bible, Schillebeeckx concludes, may be regarded as a "fragment of grace."[31] Every development in the Church must be within the bounds of the *memoria Iesu* set forth in the New Testament.[32]

This does not mean for Schillebeeckx that individual statements in the Bible are to be uncritically accepted. The biblical authors themselves criticize one another's work.[33] What currently passes for a conservative interpretation of Scripture is in fact an innovation; it is a reaction against the new challenge of historical critical con-

sciousness, and is in that sense a "modernism." Schillebeeckx himself favors a "postcritical" approach that aims to rehabilitate the
sign-value of stories which we today cannot credit as factually
historical.[84]

To begin with the Bible alone as an absolute starting point is, in
Schillebeeckx's opinion, impossible.[85] We have no choice but to read
the Bible in a contemporary context and against the background of
our remembered past.[86] Because the Bible itself mirrors the faith-ex-
periences of the early Christian congregations there is truth in both
the Protestant formula of "Scripture alone" and the Catholic formula of the Church as norm. Protestants and Catholics today can
agree that the New Testament is uniquely authoritative as "the
Church's 'charter' or foundation document."[87]

## 6. Symbolic Communication and Biblical Rhetoric

What, then, is the relation between Scripture and revelation? Is
the Bible a divinely authoritative book, propositionally containing
God's very word (Model one)? Does it give access to events in which
revelation is signified (Model two)? Does it express and induce immediate experiences of the divine in the depths of the human psyche
(Model three)? Does it simultaneously reveal and conceal the God to
whom it bears witness in fallible human language (Model four)? Or
does it provide paradigms that enable us to interpret our own history
and situation in the light of God's plan and purposes (Model five)?

With the prospect of resolving some of the differences between
existing theories, we may turn to our basic theme of revelation as
symbolic communication. As we have noted, God communicates
both through symbolic realities and through the inspired images
whereby believers express the meaning they have found in those
realities. Can the inspiration and truth of the Bible be better understood in terms of these two types of symbol?

Austin Farrer puts the accent on the imagery of Scripture. "The
stuff of inspiration," he writes, "is living images."[38] The images, insofar as they were alive and moving in the minds of the biblical
writers, gave rise to inspired literature. Not all of Scripture, however, is inspired. Those parts of it which contain straight historical
narrative are more properly called informative about saving facts
than inspired—yet the line is difficult to draw because, Farrer adds,

"the effects of inspiration are widely seen over the historical paragraphs."[39]

In restoring the rights of imagination, Farrer has rendered a signal service. Biblical revelation does not have to be in every case propositional; it can be carried by inspired images. But the images, Farrer recognizes, are not self-sufficient; they are revelatory because connected with real events. "Certainly the events without the images would be no revelation at all, and the images without the events would remain shadows on the clouds."[40]

One reservation regarding Farrer's theory of inspiration may here be expressed. Is it necessary to exempt the historical passages, insofar as these literally describe what happened? If the events pertain to the history of God's dealing with his people, the impulse to give them literary expression could well be inspiration. For inspiration, as understood in contemporary theology, it is not essential that images or ideas be infused by God into the minds of the sacred writers. It is enough that the process of composition be shaped by the revelatory events, so that as a result God's self-disclosure is authentically and reliably recorded.

Revelation and inspiration, then, may be seen as intrinsically related. Revelation, as it takes root in human minds and lives, finds its way into literary sedimentation. To the extent that the revelation dominates the process of literary objectification, the books are inspired. In some cases, the authors may have been moved to teach, even in propositional form, past events and their meaning. In other cases they may have been impelled to express themselves in poetry, drama, promise, or exhortation. Inspiration extends to each of these categories no less than the others. It embraces all the means whereby the people of God, at a given state of its development, was moved to objectify itself and its faith in writings that could be normative for the faith of later generations.[41]

Traditionally associated with the doctrine of inspiration are the assertions that God is author of the Bible and that the Bible is God's word in written form. These expressions, though they can easily lead to fundamentalistic misinterpretations, can be rightly understood. Essentially the term "author" means responsible producer. God is first and foremost author of his people. But at a time when writing had become a decisive means of establishing and maintaining community, authorship of a community of faith involved, as an intrinsic moment, the production of writings expressive of that faith. In willing to be the author of a people of faith in a literate age, God concomitantly willed to be "author" of the religious writings. Even more evidently is this true if God willed the community at a certain moment of its history to be the repository of God's permanently normative revelation of himself in his Son.[42]

It is not easy to specify the exact kind of causality which God exercises in bringing about the composition of the books. His action has traditionally been regarded as that of a principal efficient cause, utilizing the human writers as instruments. Modern theology, insisting that the biblical writers were not God's secretaries but "true authors,"[43] shies away from the category of instrumental causality. As I have previously suggested, Polanyi's category of marginal control could be useful in this connection.[44]

The authorship of Scripture is a particular instance of the larger question how God's causality in the order of grace, rather than diminishing human responsibility, increases it. If we keep in mind that God is immanent to the whole of creation, and is active whenever any created cause is active, it becomes less difficult to see how God's grace can be truly present and active without curtailing the human activity of those who "cooperate." Grace is God's vital self-communication, and hence what proceeds from a graced consciousness proceeds from God himself. The symbolic self-expression of the people to whom God communicates himself, insofar as it signifies what God communicates of himself, is also his self-expression. The writings whereby the people of God and its spiritual leaders articulate what grace enables them to perceive or imagine may be called, in a more than metaphorical sense, God's word.

This symbolic theory of inspiration is helpful, I believe, for understanding the formation of the canon. The canon of Scripture was not drawn up by an arbitrary decision of the Church or by a miraculous dictation of a list of the inspired books. The selection was made by the Church as it pondered the quality of the books themselves. In appraising what was to become the New Testament, the Church relied upon its prior familiarity with God, gained through the Hebrew Scriptures and the apostolic tradition. As the canon became more complete, the Church had more ample criteria for assessing the canonicity of the remaining books. In drawing up the canon, the Church was simultaneously making a judgment on the books and expressing its own self-understanding. For the Church to have accepted different books would have been to identify itself differently.[45]

In accepting the canonical books, the Church does not subject itself to a heteronomous norm, yet it does renounce full autonomy. By taking on the identity that the Scripture gives it, the Church consciously submits to a call from God to become a particular kind of people. To quote David Kelsey: "To say 'this is our scripture' is to say 'These are the texts that present to us the promise and call that define our communal identity.' It is a 'self-involving' expression."[46] Rahner speaks in much the same terms: "The Church, filled with the Holy Spirit, recognizes by 'connaturality' that a given writing belongs among those which accord with her nature."[47] "The concrete, fully realized essence of the Church includes the Scriptures; they are a constitutive part of her."[48]

The Bible is normative for the Church, and in committing itself to that norm the Church implicitly asserts that the Bible is in some sense inerrant. For the Church could not consistently bind itself to a norm that it judged unreliable. To say that the Bible is canonical is not necessarily to say that every sentence in the Bible is error-free, but it is to confess that the Bible, properly used, imparts saving truth. Because and insofar as it is God's word, it can be relied on to bring the Church into deeper communion with him.

The Bible is a many-dimensioned work. It contains doctrinal statements, historical claims, existential symbols, poems, parables, dramas, ethical precepts, apocalyptic threats, and eschatological promises. Bitter disputes have raged as to where, if at all, the unity is to be sought. Is it in doctrine, in historical continuity, in mystical disclosure, in existential demand, in a horizon of hope, or elsewhere? The dialectical theologians, like Luther before them, find the Bible's unity in the person of Christ, to whom the Old Testament points as one to come and the New Testament as one who has come. This thesis, however, brings with it some difficult hermeneutical problems regarding passages, in the New Testament as well as in the Old, that do not seem to refer to Jesus. Almost inevitably, it leads either to irresponsible exegesis or to erecting a "canon within the canon."

A more comprehensive unifying category, suggested by our symbolic approach, might be the self-expression of God. The Bible as a whole may be said to "render God" in the sense that it depicts who he is and how he wills to be toward his creatures.[49] "The fundamental identity description of God," writes George Lindbeck, "is provided by the stories of Israel, Exodus, and Creation. This identity description is then completed or fulfilled by the stories of Jesus' life, death, and resurrection, but the latter stories must be read in the context of what went before."[50] To say this is not to deny that Jesus is, as Barth puts it, "the image and reflection of the divine Yes to man and his cosmos."[51] The accounts of the creation, the Exodus, and the history of Israel, for the Christian, receive their full meaning in the context of the Christ-event.

As a human historical document, the Bible can be read by anyone with the requisite literary and historical skills, but as "rendering God," it requires skills of a religious order. To integrate the biblical clues in such a way as to find God in them, we must have skills of the same order, though not necessarily of the same degree, as the inspired authors. Above all, we must direct our attention to God rather than focally to the clues in themselves. "Signs or words," as Thomas Torrance observes, "fulfill their semantic function properly when we attend away from them to the realities they signify or intend." Applying this to the Bible, he goes on to say that the Bible "effaces itself before the immediacy and compulsion of God's self-revelation."[52]

## 7. Return to the Models

In insisting on the doctrinal component the propositional model makes a valid and important point. The Bible cannot be reduced to symbols having a purely existential impact. Even though revelation arises, as we have contended, from evocative communication, it does not remain fixed at the preconceptual stage. In biblical times, Israelites and Christians already expressed their faith in confessional formulas, historical claims, and finally, in doctrinal assertions of a more reflective character. If we had no confidence in the propositional teaching of the Bible, we could hardly put our trust in the persons and events of biblical history, or even in the God to whom the Bible bears witness.

The doctrinal approach, though sound within certain limits, needs to be supplemented by the symbolic because the truth of the

Bible is much richer than its propositional teaching. God is personally present by his redemptive grace when the symbolic events of redemptive history are rightly interpreted and when the symbolic language of the Bible is read. Even the propositional statements are the self-expression of individuals and communities transmitting their personal and corporate faith. The various schools and writers who contribute to the biblical tradition may be seen as reflecting, always inadequately, a faith that is beyond the comprehension of any human witness. Their individual statements must be interpreted according to their relationship to the developing faith of God's people. The older inerrantism, which tended to fix on individual statements taken out of historical and canonical context, was too atomistic.

The biblical theology of the mid-twentieth century, by calling attention to the developing biblical themes, escaped from the rigidity of the older propositional approach and came very close, on many points, to the symbolic understanding of Scripture which is here being advocated. Many of the biblical word-studies of that period were in effect studies of the developing symbols. By contemplating the Old Testament beginnings in the light of the long history of modification and fulfillment, the biblical theology of our own century rehabilitated ancient themes such as the "spiritual exegesis" of the church Fathers and the *lectio divina* of the medieval monks, who sought to read the Bible in light of the present experience of the Holy Spirit. Although not exempt from certain exaggerations, this biblical theology achieved solid gains that will probably be better appreciated when the recent wave of criticism is put in perspective.

The historical model, like the doctrinal-conceptual, can be advantageously combined with the symbolic. If God reveals himself through history, he does so by means of symbolic events, and if these events are to be revelatory for later generations, they must be recounted in language that carries their salvific meaning. The "salvation history" movement strove in its way to preserve the unity between the revelatory events and the revelatory language of Scripture. Recent historical-critical investigation, by reconstructing the successive steps from the original revelatory events, through the various stages of proclamation and oral transmission, to the final canonical accounts, has greatly enriched our understanding of the texts. In the light of such critical study it becomes easier to recognize the many levels of significance in a single discourse or incident as initially reported, as handed down in the tradition, and as taken up by the biblical authors.

Two extremes are to be avoided. The one would be the tendency, observable in some historical-critical scholarship, to reduce everything to hard facts, as though the faith-interpretation and the literary symbolism were unessential or even misleading. In view of what has been said about doctrine and imagery, it should be evident that the revelation would be nonexistent or incomplete without these ingredients.

The other extreme would be to say that since myth and symbol are revelatory, facts are never important. In our chapter on symbol we have pointed out that the facts too can be symbols, and that in the case of God's saving providence, the facts about what he has done often have far greater revelatory power than fantasies about what he might have done.

The biblical authors, to be sure, are not greatly concerned with drawing a precise line between history and parable, literal statement and metaphor, though passages such as 2 Peter 1:16 (on the non-mythical character of the Transfiguration) can occasionally be found. Even the professional exegete, with all the technical apparatus of modern scholarship, is often incapable of making a clear distinction. In Scripture God has given us, first of all, a religious testimony, and only secondarily a historical source. We can know the general outlines of God's saving work, and certain particular facts, but on many points our yearning for exact information must remain unsatisfied.

The experiential model as developed in the early decades of the century was too much under the sway of individualist, empiricist psychology. It ignored the necessary links between experience and expression, between the achievements of genius and social environment. A more adequate epistemology, pointing up the essentially historical and social character of revelation, can complete and correct many of the theses of this model. Sabatier and the Modernists, and more recently Tillich, were on firm ground in holding that the symbolic language of Scripture arises out of revelatory experience and that such language can induce revelatory experiences in those who read in faith. These points can be even more effectively made in terms of a theology that gives greater cognitive weight to religious symbols. The experientialists tend to overlook the revelatory value of propositional statements which reflect and live off the original revelatory events.

The dialectical model, in its approach to the Bible, brings out a dimension too easily obscured in the symbolic—namely, that the revelatory power of Scripture depends on the continued presence and activity of God in the situation in which the Scripture is read or proclaimed. Seen in this light, the Bible may be called not simply a letter from God (as some ancient church writers called it) but a mode of God's present self-communication. The inspiration of Scripture, then, means more than the inspiration of its writers. Barth did well to emphasize that God, working through the Bible, inspires the heralds and hearers of the word. In somewhat Barthian language, Vatican II endorsed this idea: "For in the sacred books, the Father who is in heaven meets His children with great love and speaks with them; and the force and power in the word of God is so great that it remains the support and energy for her sons, the food of the soul, the pure and perennial source of spiritual life."[53]

These important insights, for which contemporary theology is indebted primarily to the dialectical theologians, are not opposed to the symbolical theory of communication proposed in the present work. If it be true that the human body, with its speech and gestures, is a living symbol of the person, it is no less true that the Bible, in which God "inverbalizes" or "inscripturates" himself, is an efficacious symbol of God who inspires it. As a medium of encounter, it transmits a deeper and richer meaning than could be conveyed by ordinary conceptual speech. As a divinely inspired symbol, the Bible renders God as agent. Barth and his followers, with their theocentric hermeneutic, remain far closer to the evident intentions of Scripture than do the Bultmannians with their thoroughgoing existential reduction.

The "new consciousness" model seeks to avoid the objectivism, privatism, biblicism, and sacralism to which other models are subject. This model is to be valued for its insistence that God is never just the God of religious experience or sacred history, of the Bible or of the Church. As Lord of the world, God is to be sought in the totality of life and experience. Having said this, the theologians of the fifth model generally go on to admit that we could not recognize this God in our own history were it not for the paradigmatic events and prophetic interpretations given in Scripture. The consoling and provocative memories of biblical history illuminate our own struggles and aspirations. The consciousness model, when understood in the light of symbolic communication, has affinities with the historical, inasmuch as the "disclosure situations" of biblical history provide a framework in which we can find new meaning in our own lives.[54]

The fifth model tends to stress fluidity of interpretation. The reader, whose horizons are set by contemporary experience, goes to the Bible to find materials that can speak, or be made to speak, to the current situation. While this may be a valuable procedure, it is one that can, in principle, be applied to any worthwhile literature. The distinctive character of a classical or canonical text, as Hans-Georg Gadamer has shown, is its ability to interpret itself and to say something to every generation.[55] The Bible, as a canonical text, is not just a quarry of materials to be shaped according to the perspectives of the reader. As the dialectical theologians insist, it is an instrument in the hands of God, who addresses his Church by means of it. The Bible forms the consciousness of its own readers, brings its own horizon with it, and thereby shapes a tradition of interpretation. The Christian reader, dwelling within that tradition, will allow the Bible to establish its own framework of meaning, forming, reforming, and transforming its own readers. The Bible's proved capacity to enlarge and stabilize the vision of those who submit to its power is one of the reasons why it has come to be accepted as inspired.

Once this has been acknowledged, one must also say, with Gadamer, that the meaning of the classical text and of its symbols is never static. We approach the text not with romantic archaism, as though we had to recapture the meaning in the mind of the first writers, but from a distance, as we read from the context of a changed world. Since we are different, we understand the text in a different way, or we do not understand it at all. The lapse of time is not just a chasm to be overcome, but is the occasion for productive understanding. Time filters out many factors that would obscure the true meaning of the text, affords perspective, and brings out implications that would previously have been imperceptible.[56]

The radical shift of world views between the ancient and the contemporary periods establishes the need and the possibility of hermeneutics, as the term is understood today. The contemporary meaning of a canonical text must be positively related both to the text and to the modern reader. Such a meaning must stand in continuity with, and grow out of, the tradition of meaning arising from the impact of the text on previous generations. The biblical symbols of marriage and family, deserts and animals, kings and warriors, even when they do not exactly correspond to the conditions of our own life, remain powerfully evocative.

The kind of reinterpretation here described would not be feasible unless there were a common horizon between the communities that formed and transmitted the text and the community that reads it today. For many classics the common horizon is chiefly constituted by our shared human nature. In the case of Scripture, Christian faith asserts, and Christian experience confirms, a yet greater commonality. Christians of every generation are conscious of possessing the same grace-given relationship to God that was disclosed with incomparable power in the appearance of Jesus as the Christ. The "new and eternal covenant" established in Jesus Christ is the basis of a common horizon that perdures. And if the various Old Testament convenants still stand, or are fulfilled, they too have undying relevance. The Church, in its passage through time, is able to educe new meanings and old from the stories, symbols, and teachings of Scripture.

The biblical symbols, then, should continue to be cultivated, but should not tyrannize the modern reader, as though their acceptance involved an abandonment of modernity. Our horizons of meaning must be brought to the text, tested and modified by encounter with it. Historical consciousness, as Gadamer says, distinguishes the horizon of the text from that of the interpreter, and limits itself to neither horizon. Through an exercise of imagination, one strives to achieve what Gadamer calls "a fusion of horizons."[57]

Inevitably our discussion of the Bible has brought us to the question of the Church. The Bible, as we understand it, is an ecclesial book, insofar as it establishes the identity of the Church, nurtures that identity, and calls the Church to its true mission. This chapter therefore prepares us to turn our attention now to the question of revelation and the Church.

# Chapter XIII

# THE CHURCH: BEARER OF REVELATION

Jesus Christ, the great symbol of revelation, is not accessible except insofar as there are signs that point to him in the world today. One such sign is the Bible, which embodies the teaching of Jesus and the testimony of the early Church to him. In our last chapter we have seen that the Bible is an essentially ecclesial book, since it was produced, at least to a great extent, by the Church, since it has been gathered up and authenticated by the Church, since it is primarily designed for the use of the Church, and since the Church is the community in which the Bible is normally interpreted, whether officially or unofficially. It is also true that the Bible serves as a norm for the Church, and even, to some extent, a corrective norm. Hence the relationship between Bible and Church is complex.

The relationship of the Church to the Bible is only one of the ways in which its relationship to revelation has been conceived. Each of the five models has its own way of depicting the Church-revelation relationship. Relying in part on what has been said in earlier chapters, we may here recall, and in some respects amplify, the characteristic positions.

## 1. *The Church and Revelation According to the Five Models*

In the first model the Church is seen primarily as guardian or teacher of revelation, conceived as a deposit committed to the safekeeping of the Church according to the biblical precept, "O Timothy, guard what has been entrusted to you" (1 Tim 6:20; cf. 2 Tim 1:14). The differences between the Protestant and Catholic forms of the doctrinal model relate chiefly to the means by which revelation is transmitted.

As previously indicated, the Protestants who espouse this model, notably the Conservative Evangelicals, insist that the whole of revelation is given in the Bible, which has authority over the Church. Carl Henry, a leading representative of this position, writes: "The church is neither the locus of divine revelation, nor the source of divine inspiration, nor a seat of infallibility. Rather, the church has the task of transmitting, translating, and expounding the prophetic-apostolic Scriptures."[1] He rejects what he takes to be the Catholic position, namely, that the Church is an ongoing locus of revelation.[2]

Against the common Catholic assertion that the Church exercises authority over the Scriptures in drawing up the canon, Protestants of the propositional school maintain that in specifying its canonical Scripture the Church simply points out the foundation on which it is built. "It is the Canon as it was entrusted to the Church by Christ and the apostles as its *depositum custodi,* which the Church continues as the standard and rule for its faith and life."[3]

The Catholic expression of the propositional model, while insisting no less than the Protestant on the completeness of the revelation given in apostolic times, holds that the Church learns the revelation primarily through tradition. According to Canon George Smith:

> It would be true, in a sense, to say that there is but one source of revelation—namely, divine Tradition—understanding thereby the body of revealed truth handed down from the Apostles. . . . Nevertheless, since a great and important part of that tradition was committed to writing and is contained in the inspired books of Holy Scripture, it is the custom of the Church to distinguish two sources of revelation, Tradition and Scripture . . .[4]

"The only certain guide as to the inspiration and canonicity of all the books of Sacred Scripture," writes Smith, "is the authoritative pronouncement of the Church."[5] The Church, through the living teaching office conferred upon it by Christ, infallibly teaches what is contained in the twofold deposit of revelation. Although no addition can be made to the original revelation given in apostolic times, the magisterium can unfold or develop what is implicitly contained in the original deposit, and does so when it proclaims new dogmas.

The historical model is similar to the doctrinal insofar as it sees the Church simply as handing on a revelation already given, though the two models, of course, differ sharply in the way in which they depict the original bestowal of revelation. The task of the Church, according to the historical model, is to preserve the memory of the great deeds of God in past history, and especially the memory of the Christ-event as God's climactic deed.

As noted in previous chapters, there are two main subtypes of the historical model. The first, represented by Cullmann and the "salvation history" school, sees revelation as given in the events of biblical history together with the inspired interpretation given by the prophets and apostles. The second, represented by Pannenberg and the "universal history" school, sees revelation as given in the events themselves, independently of any authoritative interpretation.

Of these two approaches the first tends to attribute greater importance to the Church as bearer of the word. According to Cullmann the period between the Ascension and the final return of Christ is the period of the Church. "The Church is the earthly center from which the full Lordship of Christ becomes visible."[6] In the Church, where the Holy Spirit is now active, the redemptive work of Christ continues to occur through miracle and sacrament.[7] The Church is the place in which all the writings of the New Testament arose, and from within which they are best understood.[8]

For Cullmann, however, revelation comes to a conclusion in biblical times. The decisive event has taken place in Jesus Christ and has been given its decisive interpretation in the witness of the apostles.[9] The postapostolic Church is bound to the apostolic faith and hence to the Bible as the canonical expression of that faith. In drawing up the canon, says Cullmann, the Church "by what we might call an act of humility . . . submitted all subsequent tradition to be elaborated by itself to the superior criterion of the apostolic tradition, codified in the Holy Scriptures."[10]

Pannenberg's theology of universal history is primarily directed against biblicist and kerygmatic word-theologies that would subject human reason to an authority to be accepted without rational scrutiny. These word-theologies, which speak of revelation as something occurring in the present, are perceived as overlooking the historical character of both revelation and Church. The essence of the Church, for Pannenberg and his circle, must be grasped in relation to, and in continuity with, the event of Jesus Christ, in whom God's revelation culminated.[11]

Revelation, from this perspective, is known through history, and thus through the exercise of historical reason. The Spirit dwells in Christians not as a special principle of supernatural knowledge, nor as giving them "some special ecclesiastical light and authority."[12] Far from being "an independent occurrence of revelation," writes Pannenberg, the experience of the Spirit is given only in and with the acceptance of historical revelation.[13] "The sermon by itself," he maintains, "is not revelation, but the report of the revealing history and an explication of the language of fact, which is implicit in this history."[14] The Church is not in communion with Christ by some inner spiritual experience but by being dedicated to the Kingdom which was preached and inaugurated by him.[15]

In the experiential model the historical dimension is subordinated to present experience. In certain forms of liberal Protestantism personal piety was stressed almost without reference to either history or Church. But in certain representatives of this model, such as the Catholic Modernists, the Church plays a central role. Loisy criticizes Sabatier and Harnack for their religious individualism. For him the essential issue between Protestantism and Catholicism is "whether it is for the individual Christian himself to build up his own faith and all his religion with the aid of Scripture, or whether Christian faith and religion ought not to be and are not rather a perpetual and universal work, to which each contributes and from which each derives benefit."[16] Loisy finds the Christian revelation in the collective life of the Church, which undergoes continuous change and development from its roots in the apostolic age. "All this development proceeds from the innermost life of the Church, and the decisions of authority only sanction, so to speak, or consecrate, the movement that arises from general thought and piety."[17]

Tyrrell, while accepting in substance Loisy's experiential notion of revelation, stresses the unsurpassable character of the apostolic experience and the abiding authority of the biblical and creedal symbols handed down from apostolic times. "Of this normative apostolic revelation, this prophetic vision of the Kingdom of God, the Church is, according to Catholic teaching, the divinely assisted guardian."[18] The spirit of Christ unfolds itself through the corporate activity of the whole people of God. "To interpret the Church's collective mind," he holds, "is the office of bishops, councils, and popes. . . . They are witnesses to, not creators of, the Church's faith and practice."[19]

The dialectical model, rejecting both the liberal reliance on scientific history and the modernist appeal to religious experience, depicts revelation as closely related to the authoritative witness of the Church. This is notably the case with Karl Barth in his *Church Dogmatics*. Unlike Jesus Christ, the Church, for Barth, is not revelation in the objective sense of the term, but it is, under Scripture, the great sign or token of revelation.[20] It has revelatory power not by itself but by reason of him to whom it attests.[21] In its objective aspect the Church has the nature of a sacrament; it is a visible sign or symbol of the revelation which is given through it.[22]

From another point of view, the Church is the subjective reality of revelation; it is revelation as received through the outpouring of the Holy Spirit.[23] The reception of revelation occurs first of all in the Church and only secondarily in individuals who believe through its ministrations.[24] The Church is a visible as well as an invisible reality, and under both aspects it is from God.[25]

Because the Church is not the objective revelation but is under the revelation that comes to it from the Scriptures, the Church has only an indirect and relative authority.[26] Dogmatic theology, listening to the word of God as its norm, must continually invite the teaching Church to correct its proclamation in light of the revelation itself.[27]

Notwithstanding his high ecclesiology, therefore, Barth would agree with other dialectical theologians that the Church becomes truly Church only when God is pleased to speak in and through it. Bultmann is typical of the dialectical school when he writes:

> As the word is God's word only as an event, the Church is genuine Church only as an event which happens each time here and now; for the Church is the eschatological community of the saints, and it is only in a paradoxical way identical with the ecclesiastical institutions which we observe as social phenomena of secular history.[28]

Emil Brunner is representative of the dialectical movement when he writes that Christ's revelation "is a living, present event, which takes place in and through the Church."[29] In his later work, however, Brunner makes a very sharp distinction between Church (*Kirche*), as an organization, and *Ecclesia,* as a community of faith. To the latter alone does he attribute positive theological value.[30]

The relationship between revelation and the Church in the fifth model is predicated on the position that history is not just a sequence of external events but, at a deeper level, a progressive molding of human consciousness. Some, like Teilhard de Chardin, see a new breakthrough in the history of consciousness as having occurred in Jesus Christ, who releases new energies of love.

For theologians of this orientation, God is redemptively present in human history as a whole. As seen by Teilhard, the ferment in the spiritual history of our times is happening for the sake of the Church, the new Jerusalem. "Accept it, this sap," he exhorts the Church, "for without its baptism, you will wither, without desire, like a flower out of water; and tend it, since, without your sun, it will disperse itself wildly in sterile shoots."[31]

Elsewhere Teilhard de Chardin writes that through the contemporary phenomenon of "ultrasocialization" the Church is able to "form itself little by little, collecting under their most sublime form all the spiritual energies of the Noosphere." The Church may therefore be described as "the reflexively christified portion of the world" and as "the central axis of universal convergence."[32]

According to Gregory Baum, God's ongoing self-communication in his word brings about a reconceptualization of revelation and in this way produces "a new self-consciousness of the Church."[33] Creatively reinterpreting its own past teaching, the Church refocuses the gospel:

> We see here clearly the creative moment in the divine tradition of the Church. What goes on in the Church in the faithful traditioning of the Gospel in a changed environment is not a simple repetition of the primitive message, it is not even reducible to the primitive message by purely logical means; what is involved here is an indefinable moment, the work of the Spirit in the community, by which the Church judges that a certain experience in which she shares, coheres with the Gospel once for all received by the apostles, and hence gives witness to the selfsame divine Word. As the Church listens to this divine Word present in history, she lays hold of the Gospel in a new way. The Word of God coming toward the Church from her encoun-

ter with history enables her to see her divine message from a new viewpoint as addressing itself to a new issue, and having a new central impact. And this is precisely what we have called the re-focusing of the Gospel.[34]

In this task of reinterpretation, the Church, according to Baum, is continually assisted by the Holy Spirit, so that it is able to discern the signs of the times and to profit from dialogue with people of all conditions and persuasions. Freed from the burden of its own past doctrines, it is able to reinterpret its dogmatic heritage in ways that make sense to a new age.[35]

When he speaks of refocusing the gospel, Baum does not mean easy accommodation to the dominant culture. On the contrary, he is conscious that at many times the Church has had to raise its voice in prophetic protest against current trends, as happened, for instance, in Nazi Germany at the time of the Barmen Declaration. In every age the Church must "find the central message and thrust of divine revelation which makes it the salvational reply to the present question that threatens to undo human life."[36] Newly fashioned creeds, he asserts, can "protect the faithful against the errors that pervade the culture in which they live" and guard them from "the corroding influence of the worldly environment."[37] In 1968 Baum found fault with the proposed new creed of the United Church of Canada for failing to warn against "the powers of destruction that threaten human life" and neglecting to announce God's eschatological judgment.[38]

As this survey of positions indicates, disagreements remain about the Church's relationship to revelation. Does it receive new revelation or only transmit a revelation given in the remote past? If the latter, is the revelation totally contained in the Bible alone? Does the Church transmit revelation by formal teaching or by incarnating it in its corporate life and worship? Does revelation continue to occur in the proclamation and worship of the Church? Does the individual believer receive revelation immediately from God or only mediately through the ministry of the Church? Is the Church maintained in the gospel by a "charism of unfailing truth" or does it sometimes stray and have to be brought back again by prophetic protest, by biblical exegesis, or by historical research? On questions such as these there is as yet no general consensus among Christian theologians.

## 2. *Symbolic Mediation and the Church*

At this point it may be appropriate to ask what light can be shed on the disputed questions by the idea that revelation is symbolic communication. How would such communication occur in and through the Church?

The idea of the Church as sign has been familiar to apologists and theologians for many centuries, and was given new currency by Cardinal Victor Dechamps in the midnineteenth century. Referring to a text in Isaiah, Vatican I took up the theme of the Church as the "sign raised up among the nations."[39] It called attention to the properties of the Church as one, holy, catholic, and enduring (apostolic) as indications of the Church's divine origin. Bishop Konrad Martin, the reporter for the Deputation on Faith, declared to the Fathers at the Council that the Church is, so to speak, "divine revelation in concrete form."[40]

Vatican II moved beyond the apologetic concern for sign to the more theological notion of sacrament. In the first paragraph of the Constitution on the Church, where the Church is described as a sacrament of unity, the concept of sacrament is explicated as implying both sign and instrument. The Church is thus described as an efficacious sign, one that effects what it signifies. In all this the Council was adhering closely to the classical definition of sacrament as an "effective sign of grace."[41]

The idea of the Church as sacrament has been elaborated by many contemporary theologians, including Otto Semmelroth, Karl Rahner, and Edward Schillebeeckx.[42] They point out that a sacrament, as distinct from a mere indicative sign, implies the real presence of that which is signified. If the Church is a sacrament of Christ, that is because Christ is truly present in it, communicating his life to the members of the Church. As Schillebeeckx wrote in one of his early books, "The Church is the visible shape of salvation, the sign filled with the reality it signifies."[43]

In terms of the theology of revelation set forth in the past few chapters, the sacramental model of the Church has major implications. Just as Christ is a real symbol of the godhead, so, analogously, the Church is a real symbol of Christ. "As Christ appears as a *theophany,* so," according to René Latourelle, "the Church appears as a *Christophany*."[44] The parallelism is only an analogy. Christ is a divine person, but the Church is not a divine person. It is a community of human persons kept in union with Christ by the abiding presence of the Holy Spirit, the Spirit of Jesus.[45] To the extent that it lives up to the law of its own being, the Church is a sign and reflection of Christ, who directs it and dwells in it by his Spirit.

It goes without saying that the Church is never a perfect sign. Made up of human beings who are frail and sinful, it is to some extent a countersign. In its historical and empirical realization, it always falls short of the divine idea of what it ought to be. To quote Schillebeeckx again, "The Church is great and glorious, but not on account of its earthly strength and achievements; in it Christ's redeeming grace always triumphs in spite of human weakness. It is in this weakness that the divine power comes into its own and becomes visible as divine. The Church is therefore not only the object of our faith; it is also the test of our faith."[46] It has a "dia-bolic" as well as a "sym-bolic" aspect.

More specifically, the Church is a symbol of Christ insofar as by its configuration it points to him and actualizes what God tells us through his Son. This may be illustrated with respect to the four classical attributes of the Church as one, holy, catholic, and apostolic. By being *one* the Church signifies the unitive power of Christ's love; by being *holy,* the sanctifying efficacy of that love; by being *catholic,* the universality of God's saving will in Christ; and by being *apostolic,* the irrevocable character of God's redemptive act in Christ. Without the Church as representative symbol, we would not be able to know Christ as he really is. The Church reveals God not so much by what it says about him as by what it is. Yet insofar as its existential condition falls short of what it ought to be, the Church discloses its own essential character by confessing its shortcomings and by holding aloft its unachieved ideals.

This sacramental vision of the Church implies a certain orientation to the questions about the relationship between Church and revelation which we have found to be disputed.

Revelation is complete in Jesus Christ, since there can be no disclosure above or beyond that whereby God fully and unsurpassably communicates himself to the world in the life, teaching, death, and glorification of his Son. In Chapter X we have already commented on the teaching of Vatican II to the effect that Christ is "the

Mediator and at the same time the fullness of all revelation."[47] The Church as sacrament of revelation has no reason for existence except to express and communicate the meaning of the Christ-event.

Still, it may be said that revelation is not complete without the Church. If there were no community of believers, revelation as a transaction would be cut short. For revelation, as a communication from God to human beings, destined for their conversion and redemption, achieves itself only when it is received and responded to in faith.

The Church, rather than its individual members, is the prime recipient of revelation. In its history of salvation and perdition, of grace and sin, humanity exists and acts socially—that is to say, as a network of people in relationships. A sacrament, and hence the Church as sacrament, is a socially constituted and communal symbol of grace as present and transforming individuals into a people. Sacraments have a dialogic structure insofar as they are administered in mutual interaction, so that individuals can achieve together, in their interrelatedness, new levels of life and meaning that they could not achieve in isolation. Every sacrament binds the individual in new ways to the Church, which is the great sacrament. Only in connection with the Church, the community of believers, does the individual have access to the revelation of God in Christ.

From this perspective it is not too much to say with Bishop Martin at Vatican I that the Church, in a sense, *is* revelation—a statement that Barth, with the proper qualifications, also makes. Insofar as the Church is recipient, it may be called "subjective revelation," but insofar as it is sign or symbol, it is objective revelation—not in original, but in dependent, form. What was originally given through the prophets and apostles continues to be given, with dependence on the origins, through the Church.

The question of ongoing revelation will be more fully examined in our next chapter. At this point it may suffice to say that the communication of revelation continues to occur. Even today, according to Vatican II, God speaks through the signs of the times;[48] he is present and active "in the happenings, needs, and desires" of the age and culture.[49] They are signs to the Church, and the Church, in responding, perfects itself as a sign of Christ to the world.

The Church does not know God's revelation in Christ without dependence on Scripture and apostolic tradition. In order to avoid betraying the gospel, the Church and its leaders must avail themselves of the means given. Yet the promised assistance of the Holy Spirit is such that Christians may confidently hope that the Church will never forsake the gospel or cease to make it available. In spite of the sinfulness and fallibility of its members, taken as individuals, we may rest assured that the Church itself will continue to be, albeit imperfectly, a sacrament or symbolic presence of Christ.

A preeminent sign of Christ's presence with his Church, according to the sacramental view, is Christian sanctity. The revelatory significance of the saints has not been lost on Protestants. Nathan Söderblom, an ecumenical Lutheran, lamented that the doctrine of the saints had been neglected in "Evangelical-Catholic Christendom." "A saint," he declared, "is he who reveals God's might. Saints are such as show forth clearly and plainly in their lives and in their very being that God lives."[50] A generation later, Paul Tillich, criticizing the prevalent word-theology, sought to restore within Protestantism a better appreciation of the meaning of sainthood. Saints he defined as "the persons who are transparent to the ground of being [Tillich's term for God] which is revealed through them and who are able to enter a revelatory constellation as mediums."[51] Even the faith and love of ordinary Christians, he added, "can become sign-events for those who are grasped by their power and creativity."[52] Tillich was concerned to show how the "Protestant principle" could protect the idea of sainthood from the danger of demonic profanization.[53]

Official Roman Catholic teaching, notably in Pius XII's encyclical on the Mystical Body (1943) and Vatican II's Constitution on the Church, Chapter VII, has emphasized the importance of the saints as signs of the holiness of the Church in various circumstances. According to Karl Rahner, they embody the essence of the Church in new and unpredictable ways. "They are the initiators and creative models of the holiness which happens to be right for, and is the task of, their particular age. They create a new style."[54] Von Balthasar connects sanctity with living tradition. "The saints are tradition at its most living, tradition as the word is meant whenever Scripture speaks of the unfolding of the riches of Christ."[55] Bernard and Francis, Ignatius and Teresa "were like volcanoes pouring forth molten fire from the inmost depths of Revelation."[56] Just as the apostolic office presents an abstract, doctrinal interpretation of revelation, so the saints, by their lives, give a concrete exegesis of the gospel. Their holiness testifies not to their own personal achievement but to the Lord whom they seek to serve. Of any saint it may be said: "He was not the light, but came to bear witness to the light" (Jn 1:8).

### 3. Application to the Five Models

In the perspectives of the preceding discussion of the Church as sacrament of revelation, we may now reconsider the views on the relationship between revelation and Church implied in the five models.

The first model brings out the importance of doctrine for clarifying the ambiguities in symbolic communication, whether verbal or nonverbal. To the propositional model we may concede that the teaching of the Scriptures, rightly interpreted, is an inviolable norm. These writings were adopted and are retained as canonical because the Church finds them to be normative expressions of its own faith. The dogmas of the Church—at least for Catholic Christianity—are likewise, in their own order, inviolable.[57] Neither the authority of Scripture nor that of church teaching, emphasized in this model, detracts from the importance of the symbols conveyed through Scripture and tradition.

Against some forms of propositionalism, it must be pointed out that the doctrines of the Church need not in every case be demonstrable from clear statements in Scripture. The Bible transmits revelation not only in propositional form, but even more fundamentally in the form of metaphors, parables, stories, or, more generally, that of symbolic-evocative communication. Already in biblical times, theologians such as Paul meditated on the symbolic events of the Incarnation, Crucifixion, and Resurrection in order to penetrate the Christian meaning of life, suffering, and death. The propositional model has tended to neglect the deposit of symbols as an ever-fertile source of meaning and of doctrine.

Opposing the propositional model, Temple, Tillich, and a host of others have asserted that there are no revealed doctrines. Quite evidently, the doctrines of the Church are produced by human reflection, but so was the Bible and so is revelation in any articulate form. In comparison with visual and literary symbolism, doctrine is a relatively abstract style of statement, and is to be understood with reference to the more concrete and figurative style of discourse from which it is, in great part, derived. But with this qualification, one may hold that right doctrine, insofar as it accurately mirrors the meaning of the original message, is, in its content, revealed. God's revelation achieves itself through human concepts and words.

The dispute between the Conservative Evangelicals and the neo-Scholastics about the sufficiency of the Bible can be at least partly transcended in the symbolic approach. The primary question, for such an approach, is not what is propositionally contained in the deposit, but how to use the patrimony of symbols and statements so that the power of the original revelation can assert itself. Scripture and tradition have each their own importance. Scripture, though not simply a body of propositions, is a fixed and permanently normative verbal deposit. Tradition, fluid in form, is primarily a process of transmission. The dynamic character of tradition was well expressed by the World Conference on Faith and Order at Montreal in 1963: "Thus we can say that we exist as Christians by the Tradition of the Gospel (the *paradosis* of the *kērygma*) testified in Scripture, transmitted in and by the church through the power of the Holy Spirit."[58] Vatican II, about the same time, asserted, in its important chapter on tradition:

> Now what was handed on by the apostles includes everything which contributes to the holiness of life, and the increase in faith, of the People of God, and so the Church, in her teaching, life, and worship, perpetuates and hands on to all generations all that she herself is, all that she believes.[59]

Vatican II looked for authentic tradition not so much in formal statements as in "the practice and life of the believing and praying Church."[60]

In this dynamic perspective, the problem of Scripture and tradition becomes more tractable. There can be no question of the Church carrying on without tradition. Authentic tradition must of course be established by sound criteria, but the criteria cannot be rightly used by those who do not live within the tradition. Neither the interpretation of Scripture nor the decisions of ecclesiastical authority are independent of tradition. In the language of Vatican II:

> It is clear, therefore, that sacred tradition, sacred Scripture, and the teaching authority of the Church, in accord with God's most wise design, are so linked and joined together that one cannot

stand without the others, and that all together and each in its
own way under the action of the one Holy Spirit contribute
effectively to the salvation of souls.[61]

Since our theme is revelation rather than the development of
doctrine, we cannot here probe more deeply into the question of authentic teaching. For present purposes it may suffice to point out, on
the one hand, the necessity for the Church to abide in the revelation
that came to expression in the canonical Scriptures, and on the other
hand, the fact that the revelation is more inclusive than the propositional teaching of Scripture. In discerning the cognitive import of the
stories and symbols, the individual Christian and the teaching office
may profit from the tradition, confident that the Holy Spirit is with
the Church in the process of transmission. The pastoral leadership
of the Church has special responsibilities for authenticating sound
doctrine and warning against deviations.

The historical model properly calls attention to the Church's
subordination to the foundational redemptive events and to the biblical accounts of these events. The sacramental view of the Church,
with its symbolic approach to revelation, can accept the positive
affirmations of both the "salvation history" and the "universal history" schools, but calls attention to the importance of the Church as
the proper symbolic environment for the actualization of the ancient
patrimony. Cullmann, though he saw the importance of worship and
mission in the "age of the church," tended to depreciate the continuing role of the Holy Spirit in the developing tradition, and thus
depicted the Bible too much as an alien norm to be critically applied
against ecclesiastical tradition. While this critical function should be
admitted, Daniélou would seem to be correct in protesting that Cullmann was too archaistic and failed to appreciate "the positive worth
of current history, consisting of the growth of the mystical body
through the work of the Spirit."[62]

Similar criticisms have been directed against Pannenberg from
the Roman Catholic side. In the judgment of F. J. van Beeck, he reacts excessively against "the kerygmatic theologians' emphasis on
the presence of the living Lord to the Church as the abiding source
of her faith."[63] The believer's knowledge of Christ, consequently,
"has no truly ecclesial dimension; nowhere in Pannenberg's book
[Jesus—God and Man] is there a hint that present worship and

witness—and the knowledge involved in them—are the ways in which the Christian experiences the actual presence of the risen Lord."[64] For symbolic communication it is essential that the recipient be in a situation that permits the symbols to have a transforming impact. Life within the Church as a locus of faith and worship provides the necessary preunderstanding for interpreting the story of Christian origins.

The third model highlights the specifically religious mission of the Church—to establish a personal relationship between the believer and God. Sabatier, Loisy, and Tyrrell saw the importance of the symbols of revealed religion in preparing for an experience of the divine. But many Modernists and experientialists tend to look upon the religious symbols too extrinsically, as if they were mere pointers that lose their value as soon as the immediate experience is achieved. A sacramental ecclesiology, by insisting on the real presence of Christ in the Church and its sacraments, can offer a corrective at this point. A healthy Christian spirituality will not lead to pietistic isolation but to full participation in the corporate life of the Church. Recognizing ecclesiastical office as a symbolic prolongation of Christ's own presence in his capacity as teacher and lord, sacramental ecclesiology will give due weight to the gospel precept, "Whoever hears you hears me" (Lk 10:16), but will, at the same time, avoid confusing the ecclesiastical magisterium with Christ, whom it sacramentally represents. A symbolic realism that accepts the cognitive value of religious symbols will appreciate the importance of religious experience but will show that such experience is to be governed by the doctrinal norms of Model one, the defining historical events of Model two, and the Christological engagement typical of Model four.

The dialectical model converges with the symbolic insofar as both acknowledge the mediatory role of the Church. The insistence on the Church's sinfulness, characteristic of this model, need not be taken as contradicting the sacramental ecclesiology here proposed, for the confession of its own emptiness is one of the ways in which the Church can proclaim God's surpassing goodness. But there can be some exaggeration here. At least from a Roman Catholic perspective, it seems important to recognize the effectiveness of God's grace in Christ, constituting the Church as a sign of truth and holiness in the world. In the theology of Bultmann and of the early Barth this theme is scarcely present.

In Catholic sacramentalism the Church is seen not simply as addressing a paradoxical message at the world, but as ministering in the name of Christ to the human hunger for truth and meaning. Precisely as sacrament of Christ, the Church continues his role as teacher and healer. The symbolic mode of originative religious discourse confronts the Church with the task of unfolding the many-faceted truth implicit in the primary symbolic communication. Christian doctrine is a constitutive feature of the Church as it carries out its mission. Dialectical theology, especially in its Bultmannian form, stresses proclamation almost to the exclusion of doctrine, existential actuality almost to the exclusion of historical continuity.

The "new consciousness model" has arisen in response to the pluralism of the electronic age. Affected by radical historical consciousness, the proponents of this model are eager to liberate the Church from what Baum calls "the burden of a dogmatic heritage that has become irrelevant."[65] To this end, Baum contends that religious truth is always symbolic. Dogmas, he says, are not to be taken literally. Properly understood, they communicate new consciousness, not new ideas. The gift of God's ongoing self-communication to the Church, which Baum is prepared to christen "infallibility," enables the Church to reinterpret its own symbols according to the demands of new historical situations.

An extreme Modernism, divorcing the truth of symbol from the truth of dogma, would hold that dogmas are infinitely pliable, so that the same dogma would be understood in mutually contradictory ways at different times and in different places. If this were implied in symbol, we should have to deny that dogmas are symbolic. But they are symbolic in the sense that they communicate more than can be contained in clear concepts. According to the old scholastic maxim, "an article of faith is a perception of the divine truth toward which it tends."[66] The propositionalism of the rationalistic age lost sight of the dynamic aspect of dogma, treating it rather as a picture or scale model that could be substituted for the reality to which it referred. Dogmas should never be allowed to become objects in which the understanding comes to rest. They must function disclosively.

With Thomas Torrance, one may say that dogmas are "fluid axioms"—fluid not in the sense that they can be made to mean anything, but in being ever open to greater refinement, enrichment, and renewal in the light of the further manifestations of God. Forged under the impact of revelation, they are structures through which God's truth can disclose itself in new and surprising ways. The anticipatory conceptions used in dogmatic speech are lenses through which we glimpse the transcendent. To make proper use of the concepts and formulations, we must not look at them in themselves, but rely on them to attend to the divine reality in which we believe. Used in this way, dogmas are genuinely cognitive.[67]

In summary, the sacramental vision of the Church has immense importance for the theology of revelation. Looking upon the Church as the symbolic presence of Christ, who is himself the symbolic presence of the Word in human flesh, this vision preserves the realism of revelation. It safeguards the social character of revelation and yet makes room for the responsible participation of the individual believer, led by the grace of the Holy Spirit. It supplies a living, objective norm and at the same time assures an immediate, personal relationship to God on the part of every Christian. For all these values to be secure, it is essential that the Church be understood neither as a merely human construction nor as a merely invisible communion, but as a sacrament; that is to say, as a visible presence of the invisible Christ, who communicates his life by means of it. The symbolic words and actions of the Church, perceived in faith, are signs and sacraments of the encounter with God.

# Chapter XIV

# REVELATION AND ESCHATOLOGY

## 1. *The Problem*

Since Christians find revelation preeminently in Jesus Christ as attested by the Scriptures, they spontaneously associate revelation with antiquity. For this reason we must raise the question whether the revelation has been fully given in the events to which the Scriptures bear witness, or whether it continues to occur. In particular it must be asked whether God may be expected to reveal himself more fully in the age to come.

The New Testament itself speaks of revelation in three tenses. In some texts, revelation is identified with something that has taken place—for instance the manifestation of Jesus as the Christ to Peter (Mt 16:17) and to Paul (Gal 1:12). In Jude 3 and in many passages in the Pastoral Epistles "the faith" or revelation is identified with an objective "deposit of faith" to be preserved and handed down (1 Tim 6:20; 2 Tim 1:12, 14).

In other texts, the New Testament speaks of revelation as something that continues to occur after the departure of Jesus. The Fourth Gospel alludes to the revelatory task of the Paraclete, who will give testimony to Jesus and lead the disciples into truth beyond that which Jesus could declare (Jn 15:26; 16:13). Elsewhere in the New Testament the apostles and Christian prophets are depicted as receiving fresh revelations. The entire book of the Apocalypse is cast in the form of a series of revelations received by the seer of Patmos.

In still other passages, terms such as *apocalypsis* (revelation), *epiphaneia* (manifestation), and *phanerōsis* (disclosure) are used with verbs in the future tense to refer to the final appearance of

Christ at the Parousia (e.g., 1 Cor 1:7; 2 Thess 1:7; Col 3:4; 1 Tim 6:14; Tit 2:13; Heb 9:28).

In patristic and medieval theology, it was common to speak of revelation as a process that continued to occur in the Church, notably in the lives of the saints and in charismatic events such as general councils. Since the Reformation, however, the tendency of both Protestants and Catholics has been to look on revelation as having been given in its fullness to the apostolic Church, and as being handed down through Scripture and tradition.

In the twentieth century, efforts have been made to construct theologies of history that make room for ongoing revelation since biblical times. Concurrently, the biblical renewal and certain pessimistic assessments of history have prompted attempts to recover the eschatological dimension of revelation.

Theologically, it is unacceptable to look upon revelation as a miscellany of curious insights purportedly bestowed on privileged minds. Revelation is inseparably connected with the new creation. If Christ is revelation it is because he is the Omega, in whom all things will achieve their consummation. The appearance of the Messiah and the bestowal of the Holy Spirit are, biblically speaking, eschatological events. Revelation, therefore, either coincides with the end of history or anticipates that end. Within time, revelation is given only under the form of promise or anticipation of a fuller revelation yet to be given. In all five models of revelation theology, revelation is closely connected with the eschaton. Yet they depict that relationship in radically diverse ways, and the diversity gives rise to certain problems.

## 2. Eschatological Revelation in the Five Models

In the propositional model, revelation is treated primarily under the aspect of a verbal and doctrinal deposit. Among theologians of this orientation, it is almost axiomatic that revelation came to an end with the death of the last apostle.[1] Since that time, there can be no public revelation, although private revelation to certain individuals for the direction of their lives is not excluded. The deposit is to be handed down by the Church without change, although restatements and new explanations may be added to guard against misinterpretations. The course of history since biblical times is not a source of new revelation, and thus is theologically without interest. Nothing that happens in history can add any new meaning nor can it alter or detract from what was given before the end of the apostolic age.

The connection between revelation and eschatology is seen in terms of the content. Revelation teaches us about the age to come; it arouses hope for the face-to-face vision of God that is to be given when Christ returns in glory or when the individual, after death, comes into the immediate presence of God. The "beatific vision," though it could be called revelation, is not commonly treated under that rubric. Eschatology becomes a separate theological treatise, scarcely related to the theology of revelation.

The historical model must be considered in each of its two forms. According to Cullmann and the salvation-history school, revelation is essentially linked to the stages of redemptive history. The Jews looked forward to a messianic revelation that would bring history to its close. Christ, however, became the midpoint of history, not its end. In the interim period between the Resurrection and the Parousia, nothing new is disclosed. The final consummation is already known; the victory is assured, but the process of "mopping up" the enemy continues.[2] Daniélou, who follows Cullmann's essential position, calls attention to the disparity between the history of revelation and world history: "Here we face a characteristic paradox of Christianity. Although the time-process continues, and the last day, or chronological end of the world, is in the future, yet the ultimate reality is already present, in the person of the incarnate Word; there is not, because there cannot be, anything beyond this."[3]

In Pannenberg, likewise, the end of all things has already come about in the resurrection of Jesus from the dead. Nothing essentially new is to be expected. The whole cosmos must eventually come to the point marked out by Jesus' Resurrection. Revelation, therefore, is already complete. The final consummation will confirm what Christians have always known.

By contrast to the first two models, the third almost totally suppresses the eschatological—or rather collapses it into immediate experience. Schleiermacher, anticipating this position, wrote rather sarcastically about those who pretend to believe in future immortality. The true immortality, he held, can be possessed within time. "In the midst of finitude to be one with the Infinite and in every moment to be eternal is the immortality of religion."[4] Evelyn Underhill, typifying this model of revelation theology, maintains that the mystics of all religions are in contact with the same divine reality, "always the same Beatific Vision of a Goodness, Truth, and Beauty which is *one*."[5] The idea that eternal life consists in awareness of the presence of God is a commonplace for authors such as Ferdinand Ebner and Paul Tillich.

The dialectical model, spurning all mystical aspirations as a mere temptation, finds revelation only in the form of a paradoxical presence of God in history. Yet God, it insists, never becomes a part of history. Revelation is at every moment an eschatological occurrence, for it discloses the eternal "transcendent meaning" of all moments of time, insofar as they stand at the frontier of the eternal.[6] This view, set forth in Barth's *Epistle to the Romans,* was stated in a more existential style by Bultmann, for whom Christian preaching, with its call to faith, is eschatological. He clearly divorces eschatology from the sweep of global history:

> It is the paradox of the Christian message that the eschatological event, according to Paul and John, is not to be understood as a dramatic cosmic catastrophe but as happening within history, beginning with the appearance of Jesus Christ and in continuity with this occurring again and again in history, but not as the kind of historical development which can be confirmed by any historian. It becomes an event repeatedly in preaching and faith. Jesus Christ is the eschatological event not as an established fact of past time but as repeatedly present, as addressing you and me here and now in preaching.[7]

In the early Barth and in Bultmann, no less than in the mystical experientialists, the eschaton is cut loose from any beliefs about human immortality and the future consummation of the world.

In the fifth model revelation is eschatological because it implies that the Omega has entered history and is bringing it to a close. For Teilhard de Chardin, who identified Omega with Christ, revelation has its unity not from its content but from the direction in which it points. Many theologians of this tendency find that the biblical paradigms continue to offer useful guidance, but Juan Luis Segundo observes that, as history goes on, these paradigms become continually less serviceable. The task of carrying on the process of revelation is entrusted to history itself. "The Spirit of Christ, that is, the dynamic, intrinsic result of the revelatory education process, ensures a process that will lead to the full and complete truth." This is biblically grounded, according to Segundo, for Paul's concept of faith "entails the freedom to accept an educational process that comes to maturity and abandons its teacher to launch out into the provisional and relative depths of history (Gal 4:1ff.; Rom 8:19–23; 1 Cor 3:11–15)."[8]

For theologians of the fifth model, therefore, the end is already at work within history, thanks to the gift of the Holy Spirit. Revelation answers the deepest human aspirations. The Kingdom of God is progressively revealed as history approaches its end through the building of a human society of peace and plenty.

## 3. Symbolic Mediation and Eschatology

In order to refine, correct, and in some degree harmonize these different perspectives we may have recourse to the idea of symbolic communication. Such communication occurs at different stages in Christ, as the primary event of revelation, in the time of the Church, in which the revelation continues to be given, and at the final consummation, in which, according to Vatican Council II, "the mystery of the Lord . . . will be revealed in total splendor."[9]

The time of revelation is par excellence the time of Jesus Christ, in whose person and life revelation found its supreme symbol. Insofar as he is the incarnation of the eternal Word, he is a real symbol; insofar as he communicates grace through the gift of his Spirit, he is an efficacious symbol. As a real, efficacious symbol Christ is, as already mentioned, the sacrament of God.

The coming of God into the world in Jesus Christ is not a mere incident in the unfolding of processive time. Modifying the "transcendental eschatology" of his dialectical phase, Karl Barth, in his *Church Dogmatics,* explains how Christ by his coming transforms time.[10] The time of revelation is God's time for us; it is the time of fulfillment, the time that fulfills and redeems our lost time. The life of the incarnate Word is not eternity, but it renders eternity present in a hidden way. In our own language we might say that Christ's time is the symbol and sacrament of eternity. It is worldly time qualified by the hidden presence of the eternal.

Although the career of Jesus is pointed toward the Paschal mystery, which terminates in his glorious resurrection, it does not first become revelation at the moment when Christ rose from the dead and ceased to be present in history. To hold this would be to dehistoricize revelation, and to render its very existence questionable. For if revelation is not given in history, it is not given. By rejecting the category of the symbolic, Pannenberg undermines the reality of revelation, but as we have noted in a previous chapter, he ultimately salvages revelation by accepting something very like the notion of symbol.[11]

The time after the Ascension, beginning with the apostolic age, is called by Barth the "time of recollection." The term might suggest that revelation requires us to look backward rather than forward, but Barth points out that the recollection of Christ, who is not bounded by worldly time, turns us toward the future. Because we have revelation behind us, he says, we have it in front of us. Since Christ is the *Eschatos,* the revelation of Christ is revelation of the coming God.[12]

Just as Christ has a two-level symbolic structure (human-divine and, consequently, temporal-eternal), so, analogously, does the Church. Vatican II, as we have seen, spoke of the Church as a "complex reality," both visible and spiritual.[13] It is a sacrament—an efficacious symbol in which the Kingdom of God is already present "in mystery."[14] Extending Barth's conception of qualitatively different sorts of time, Hans Urs von Balthasar holds that the Church exists in a time proper to itself. "In this communion between the Lord and his Church," he writes, "there comes into existence a kind of time which is sacramental, and most especially eucharistic."[15] In a mysterious way the Church is always contemporaneous with Christ and thus, through him, with the eternal. By the mystery of its own existence, the Church brings the eschaton into time. Von Balthasar links the sacraments especially with the forty days of the Lord's risen life on earth:

> The time of the sacraments has an eschatological orientation in common with that of the forty days: each is in a different way a pledge of eternity. But whereas the forty days anticipate the coming revelation with a certain unobscured clarity, our sacramental encounters with the Lord point towards it in a veiled manner. As the Cross anticipates the Last Judgment, so the forty days are a foretaste of eternal life. And because these are

the inauguration of sacramental time, they give it an eschatological orientation. This, again, is a special work of the Holy Spirit.[16]

The time of the Church, therefore, is a sacramental, eucharistic time, in which the Lord is present in mystery through the Holy Spirit who has been given. Does this mean that God continues to reveal himself in the Church? Some distinctions seem to be necessary. The Constitution on Divine Revelation, after stressing the completeness of revelation in the career of the Incarnate Word, including his death and resurrection and the "sending of the Spirit of truth," added: "The Christian dispensation, therefore, as the new and definitive covenant, will never pass away, and now we await no further new public revelation before the glorious manifestation of our Lord Jesus Christ (cf. 1 Tim 6:14 and Tit 2:13)."[17]

This formulation did not meet with the satisfaction of all the council Fathers. An amendment was proposed to the effect that it should be expressly stated that revelation was closed (clausam esse) with the death of the apostles. The Doctrinal Commission, however, rejected this amendment on two grounds: first, because the intention of the proposed amendment has already been met in the statement just quoted; and, secondly, because the proposed formulation raised "difficulties of various kinds."[18] No doubt the Commission was referring to the ambiguity in the terms "closed" and "death of the apostles."[19]

For the reasons already indicated, the Council avoided saying that revelation continues in the history of the Church. But it did say, in the Constitution on the Liturgy, that Christ himself "speaks when the Holy Scriptures are read in the Church,"[20] and, in the Constitution on Revelation, that God "uninterruptedly converses with the Bride of His beloved Son; and the Holy Spirit, through whom the living voice of the gospel resounds in the Church, and through her, in the world, leads unto all truth those who believe and makes the word of Christ dwell abundantly in them (cf. Col 3:16)."[21]

Vatican Council II, therefore, clearly taught that the Holy Spirit is active in continuing to communicate the revelation already given. This continued communication corresponds to what some theologians would call continuing, dependent, or repetitive revelation.

Granted that God addresses the Church through the Scriptures and the sacraments, does God not speak also through creation and through secular history? Archbishop Söderblom, among others, maintained that God continues to reveal himself through both these channels. The Bible itself teaches us, he asserted, "that our God is a living, a still living God, who has not become older and less active than in earlier days. . . . God reveals himself as much in the vicissitudes of nations as in the institutions of religion. . . . It may be that political changes and social movements mean a mightier revelation of God than the undertakings of the Church."[22] Söderblom mentioned the Danish churchman Nikolai Grundtvig as a prophetic genius who was able to interpret the "signs of the times" with the inspiration of the Holy Spirit.[23]

Without teaching explicitly that God reveals himself through nature and current history, Vatican Council II recognized the revelatory importance of both. It asserted, for example: "All believers of whatever religion have always heard His [God's] revealing voice in the discourse of creatures."[24] And in a number of texts, picking up a favorite term of Pope John XXIII, it referred to the "signs of the times."[25] The term is used in a general way in the Pastoral Constitution: ". . . The Church has always had the duty of scrutinizing the signs of the times and interpreting them in the light of the gospel."[26]

From its biblical origins (Mt 16:3–4), the term "signs of the times" might seem to have reference to the approaching end. In the usage of John XXIII and Vatican II, however, the term was applied more broadly to "authentic signs of God's presence and purpose in the happenings, needs, and desires in which this People [of God] has a part along with other men of our age. For faith throws a new light on everything . . ."[27] Among the signs of the times Vatican II especially mentioned the ecumenical movement,[28] the recognition of the freedom of religion as a civil right,[29] and the growing solidarity of all peoples.[30]

Although the Council may perhaps be accused of an overoptimistic appraisal of the secular developments of the day, it did not go to the length of saying that these developments were a divine revelation or that the gospel should be reinterpreted in the light of them. Rather, it stressed that the signs of the times were themselves to be interpreted in the light of the gospel in which the revelation is fully given. The preaching and writing of the prophets and the apostles, and of those who stood in solidarity with them, are trustworthy and spiritually efficacious because they are dominated and controlled by the redemptive events which they attest and interpret, and because they are composed, as we have seen, under the inspiration of the Holy Spirit. The literary productions of the early community, accepted as canonical by the Church, are abiding norms for subsequent generations in their efforts to interpret the questions of a later day.

The term "signs of the times" can remind Christians of their responsibility to keep alert to new developments. The stirring of God's Spirit in the world—raising up outstanding witnesses to justice, peace, and other values of the Kingdom of God—often brings the Church to new awareness of what lay dormant in its faith. These secular movements are not new and independent revelations; they do not add anything strictly new to the revelation already given in Christ, but they point up aspects and implications of that revelation which might otherwise have been overlooked. Judged ultimately by their conformity to Christ and the gospel, movements inspired by the Spirit of God have symbolic power to transform the consciousness of properly attuned persons.

Some theologians have tried to find evidences of God's purposes in the general patterns of postbiblical history. Even classical instances of such a theology of history, such as those authored by Augustine, Bossuet, and Hegel, have led to conflicting and ambiguous results. Von Balthasar, in a paragraph that repays meditation, gives some reasons for supposing that such efforts will never succeed:

> Church time as the era of the Holy Spirit is, in contrast to the Old Testament and the era of Christ, not time in which revelation grows and takes place, but time in which the unsurpassable fullness of revelation establishes and expresses itself. During the time of growing revelation significance can be derived from the dimension of its becoming—from Abraham to Christ there is something like true development and unfolding going on, and equally in the lifetime of Christ, even in his death and resurrection. However, when the attained fullness begins to be disseminated, an historical law of its dissemination cannot be established. Hence, all attempts to write a theological history of Church time which is not only phenomenal, but also noumenal, must prove unavailing. Not that this time is one of static repose

or else a spiritual, charismatic chaos. But the order of the Holy
Spirit is so much the order of divine freedom and infinity, that it
cannot be translated into the categories of world and human history. The lines that we can draw may show divine wisdom in
many ways. They may be plausible, and even obvious, in their
way, but they will never show more than a fragment of the
infinity of significance, which as such cannot be grasped by us.[31]

With regard to the period between the apostles and the Parousia, therefore, we may affirm that God continues to communicate
awareness of himself through the Holy Spirit, and in that sense to
reveal. But the signs and symbols of this communication are not new
revelation in the sense of providing anything that could serve as an
additional or independent norm of faith, over and above Christ and
the gospel. The signs of the times must be discerned in the light of
the gospel, and only then can they serve to elucidate or confirm
what is in principle a part of the gospel itself.

A recurrent problem in the chapters on Christ, the religions, the
Bible, and the Church has been the abiding validity of the Christian
symbols. This problem shows up in a particularly acute way in relation to temporal change. Symbols, as Tillich put it, are born and die.
What is to assure us that the most basic biblical and Christian symbols, including the symbol of Jesus Christ, will not be superseded? If
other symbols were substituted for the Bible and for Jesus Christ,
would not Christianity cease to exist? Must Christianity face with
equanimity the prospect of its own demise?

The point has already been made that the humanity of Jesus is
objectively a symbol, insofar as God has uniquely expressed himself
in that humanity which was personally united to himself, the eternal
Logos. But it might still be objected that this symbol could cease to
communicate anything to people who have been culturally conditioned in certain ways. The objection, however, rests on the assumption that time has its own character, and that God, in entering time,
must submit to its conditions. The message of the gospel is quite
different. Revelation tells us that God is lord of time and that, by
entering time, he redeems it. Because Jesus Christ is the Alpha and
the Omega, he embraces all time and overcomes its relativity. "Jesus
Christ is the same yesterday and today and for ever" (Heb 13:8).
The Church, as founded and sustained by him, is the eschatological

community. It belongs not only to time but to eternity. The risen Christ remains with it all days "to the close of the age" (Mt 28:20).

To accept this message is to allow one's views of time and the future to be transformed, but such transformation is possible and even necessary. Apart from Christ, time appears to carry with it the threat of annihilation. The rapid change characteristic of our own era threatens all our convictions and values, and undermines our identity. The ceaseless imperative to adapt ourselves to new conditions aggravates, rather than alleviates, the problem of "future shock." As Pannenberg says, this demand "deprives man of his dignity by turning him into an alienated, though possibly useful, element of the megamachine society."[32] Christian revelation, by opening up the eschatological future, endows us with an indestructible identity and makes us potentially equal to all vicissitudes. Faith in the Incarnation and the Resurrection means conviction that the future will fulfill what has already been given, rather than abolish it. In Christ we already possess, in symbol and mystery, a share in the final Kingdom.

The gospel, admittedly, can never be communicated without making use of the transitory languages and cultural forms of particular peoples. These cultural forms must neither be shunned nor idolized. In particular cases, it will often be difficult to draw the line between accommodations that are necessary in order to make the gospel accessible to a given people and others that would mutilate the gospel. Since the Christian revelation was given in a particular history, some of its symbols are unalterable. New symbolism, while it should be encouraged, must not obscure the unity of the universal Church, its abiding identity, and its constitutive relationship to Jesus of Nazareth as its living Lord. A program of thoroughgoing trans-symbolization, that would excise these biblical and traditional symbols, would therefore be unacceptable.

In recent literature there is much concern for "world unification," "cosmification," or, as some call it, "transculturalization." Biblical eschatology fosters cosmic consciousness by its symbols of new creation, resurrection from the dead, and the restoration of all things in Christ. Understood in this light, the Christ-symbol, far from being an obstacle, can be a help for transcultural unity. Through his death and resurrection Jesus, according to Karl Rahner, becomes liberated from the particular cultural circumstances of his earthly life and inserted into cosmic history.[33] Belief in the risen Christ, as William M. Thompson suggests, can provide a transcendent principle, operative within history, that draws humanity toward greater universalization.[34]

The crucial importance of the eschatological dimension in revelation raises the question whether and to what extent we can speak from within time about the events that will bring history to a close. Some Millenarians and pre-Millenialists have attempted to write detailed scenarios of the climax of history on the basis of their personal exegesis of texts such as the Apocalypse.[35] Such efforts have all too often been based on ignorance of the biblical literary forms. In his study of the hermeneutics of eschatological assertions, Karl Rahner argues persuasively that the accounts of the end-time in Scripture are always couched in imagery taken from intrahistorical experience rather than from the phenomena of the future taken in themselves. The various biblical images, he shows, if taken as exact predictions, cannot be harmonized.[36]

At the opposite extreme are the Christian existentialists who refuse to say anything about the end of history except that the biblical images, if taken seriously, can induce Christian attitudes such as hope and courage for the present. Some political and liberation theologians, taking a leaf from the works of Marxists such as Ernst Bloch, hold that the biblical concept of the Kingdom of God is a utopian projection that can make us critical of existing institutions and inclined toward revolutionary praxis.[37]

Gregory Baum, in a brief summary of his views on heaven and hell, has this to say:

These teachings . . . are not information about a future world but a message about the present-as-well-as-the-future. They initiate us into a new consciousness. They mediate divine salvation. Heaven, then, stands for God's victory over sin and evil, operative in our midst at this time but achieving its completion only at the end. The doctrine of hell reminds us of the chaos from which God's grace saves us. It makes us aware of the possibility of total loss, of making ourselves so completely deaf to the divine Word that we shall no longer be able to hear God's voice when he addresses us in mercy. The doctrine of heaven and hell reveals to us the seriousness which lies in moral decisions. Heaven and hell indicate the dimensions of man's possibilities.[38]

One's judgment on a passage such as this will depend very much on how one views the cognitive import of symbol and metaphor. In formulating doctrines about events beyond historical time, we must stretch our conceptual capacities to the limit, and we are always in danger of failing to keep the right mean between excessive literalism and agnosticism. The metaphors do imply distinctively biblical and Christian doctrinal affirmations such as those found in the articles of the creed on the return of Christ, the final judgment, the resurrection of the body, and everlasting life. These and other eschatological beliefs, unlike the blueprints of the apocalypticists, echo a constant refrain in the Scriptures; they are coherent with the gospel as a whole, and have stood the test of time in the life and witness of the Church. When taken as referring to real events, such beliefs have significant impact on Christian behavior.

According to Scripture and church teaching, revelation will be most fully given at the close of the history of the individual and of the world. We look forward in hope to what is called in the Bible a face-to-face vision wherein we shall know even as we are known (1 Cor 13:12). Yet even this language is metaphorical, for we have no way of positively conceiving what is proper to a state exceeding our present possibilities. On philosophical grounds it seems evident that the so-called beatific vision cannot give exhaustive or comprehensive knowledge of God, for he immeasurably surpasses the capacity of every finite intellect, however graced.[39] Thus there can be no strict parity between God's knowledge of us and our knowledge of him. God, moreover, cannot be objectively seen, for he is not an object. As transcendent, he is the horizon against which all actual and possible objects are conceived and known. It is reasonable to infer, therefore, that the "beatific vision" will not be mere spectator knowledge, but rather knowledge by participation. We shall know God inasmuch as we dwell in him, and he in us. The indwelling of the divine persons in the justified can provide, even in this life, a faint anticipation of the knowledge that will flower under the light of glory.

The biblical imagery of the final consummation brings out the bodily and social aspects of heavenly blessedness. Scripture speaks of heaven as a kingdom, a city, a banquet, a wedding feast, and the like. Since the late Middle Ages theology has tended to depict the state of glory in unduly static, individualistic, and spiritualistic terms, as though each of the saints were totally preoccupied with a purely private contemplation of the divine essence. More recent theological developments, which may be seen reflected in Chapter VII of Vatican II's Constitution on the Church, can help to restore the dynamic, social, and integrally human dimensions.

Does the blessed vision of heaven leave room for symbolic mediation, or is such mediation needed only for revelation under the conditions of earthly existence? Until recently Catholics, relying on late medieval theology, and particularly on the Constitution of Pope Benedict XII (A.D. 1342), would commonly have held that the immediacy of the beatific vision rules out any symbolic mediation.[40] Some recent theologians, however, have suggested that Christ remains in some sort mediator even for the blessed in heaven. The humanity of Jesus, according to Karl Rahner, is not simply a support needed for us to achieve union with God here on earth. On the contrary:

> Jesus, the Man, not merely *was* at one time of decisive importance for our salvation, i.e., for the real finding of the absolute God, by his historical and now past acts of the Cross, etc., but —as the one who became man and has remained a creature—he is *now* and for all eternity the *permanent openness* of our finite being to the living God of infinite, eternal life. . . . One always sees the Father only through Jesus.[41]

Juan Alfaro develops this line of argument at greater length.[42] At the end of time, he asserts, Christ will "come" in a manifest way, so that the blessed may enjoy beatitude through perfect union with him. In the life of glory, therefore, the saints will participate in the splendor of the risen Christ, in whom the fullness of the godhead dwells corporeally (cf. Col 1:15, 19; 2:9). By perceiving the radiant humanity of Christ through their sensory faculties the blessed will be perfectly disposed for the immediate vision of God as the necessary complement to that perception. The light of glory, immediately bestowed upon them, will so transform their minds that they will be able to see the glory of God reflected in the face of Jesus (cf. 2 Cor 4:6). The vision of God in Christ will be linked to the vision of the world, now gloriously transformed in such wise as to reflect the splendor of Christ himself. The cosmic and Christic dimensions of the final vision do not conflict with, but rather reinforce, the immediacy of the blessed to God.

Although we inevitably lisp and stammer when speaking about the final vision, which lies far beyond all that can be conceived on earth, the idea of symbolic communication is useful for bringing together the themes of immediacy to God and of social-bodily mediation, both of which belong to the patrimony of biblical and Christian faith. Just as there is an element of immediacy in the "mediate" knowledge of faith (which always depends on God's self-gift in interior grace), so there may be an element of mediation in the glorious vision, notwithstanding its "immediacy." The combination of mediacy and immediacy is best maintained in the kind of symbolic realism which has been found important for the understanding of revelation set forth in the last few chapters. A reciprocal interaction occurs between the immediate presence of God to the human spirit and the external symbols which mediate that immediacy.

## 4. *Critique of the Five Models*

The propositional model has the merit of preserving the cognitive import of the biblical and traditional affirmations concerning the events of the end-time. This type of eschatology, when applied to the theology of revelation, has practical fruitfulness insofar as it sustains moral effort, reinforces Christian commitment, and thereby enhances the corporate life and mission of the Church.

Some excesses in this type of eschatology must be obviated. Overlooking the symbolic character of the biblical statements, propositionalists are inclined to interpret them too literalistically and thus to take positions which lack coherence and plausibility. This type of eschatology, moreover, is not fully faithful to the Bible, for while rightly seeing the end-time as promised in word, it neglects the way in which the eschaton is actually anticipated in the Christ-event, as shown in the second model, and in the communal existence of the Church. Looking on revelation as a static, objective deposit, it fails to reckon with the immediate presence of the Holy Spirit in the current actualities of proclamation and secular history, as emphasized respectively in the fourth and fifth models. Propositionalism also disregards the immediacy of God's transforming presence in the minds and hearts of those open to his grace, as set forth in the third model.

The second model is to be valued for bringing out the eschatological dimension of the actual, historical Christ-event. This emphasis is faithful to the Bible and gives added impact and credibility to the Easter message. But the second model labors under some weaknesses of its own. In both its salvation-history and universal-history forms, it tends to ignore the real newness and theological importance of what has happened since Easter and what is still to happen when history comes to a close. As Jürgen Moltmann says, "The Christian expectation is directed to no other than the Christ who has come, but it expects something new from him, something that has not happened so far."[43] Pannenberg's merely noetic horizon of Jewish apocalyptic expectation, according to Moltmann, must be further expanded to make room for what Moltmann calls the horizon of transformative truth, the "world-transforming outlook in terms of promise and missionary history."[44] As Moltmann also remarks, Pannenberg's eschatology causes the Cross of Jesus to recede in favor of the Resurrection. It lacks an *eschatologia crucis*.[45]

These shortcomings in the historical model can perhaps be remedied by recognizing that the Resurrection of Jesus, while it symbolically precontains the end of history, does not preempt the end. The category of symbol, moreover, enables us to appreciate the eschatological significance of the whole career of Jesus, including his suffering as well as his risen life. The risen life, unfortunately for Pannenberg's theory of revelation as history, begins just at the point where history leaves off, but the symbolic manifestations occur within history. Only in symbol can time and eternity be intertwined.

The third model is basically correct in its perception that the Ultimate can really be experienced in this life, thanks to the immediate self-communication of God in grace. God's intimate presence to the human spirit can impart a real participation of eternal life here and now.

Some experientialist theologians, however, write as though the experience of the divine were self-certifying and self-interpreting. They take too little account of the need for a personal and communal framework of symbols and doctrines in order to give a determinate meaning to the otherwise vague experience of the transcendent. In their concern for present experience, they minimize the biblical themes of promise and hope. Concentrating on individual experience, they fail to stress the importance of mission and ministry in order that the promised Kingdom may effectively transform the world.

The fourth model, to its credit, brings out the eschatological significance of Christian proclamation, in which God is already active in judgment and salvation. The dialectical theologians correctly affirm that God's presence in the word of Scripture or proclamation is a paradoxical presence-in-absence. In so saying, they rightly give a quasi-sacramental value to the Church's ministry of the word, even though they sometimes give insufficient emphasis to the real presence of the Lord in the sacraments.

Against Bultmann and against Barth in his earlier dialectical phase, it may be objected that the "transcendental eschatology" of Kant has been allowed to overshadow the Christian message. As Barth himself later confessed, his commentary on Romans failed to make it sufficiently clear that he meant to speak of God "and not of a general idea of limit and crisis." In his exegesis of Romans 13:11–12, he admitted, he had overlooked the distinctive feature of the passage, namely, "the teleology which it ascribes to time as it moves forward towards a real end."[46] Without this confidence in God's future accomplishments, Christian hope is severely curtailed. In preference to the paradoxes of dialecticism, we would propose symbolic realism as better preserving the links between the Paschal mystery, which is recalled, the ministry of word and sacrament, which is experienced, and the coming fullness, which is anticipated in hope.

The fifth model, better than any of the others, brings out the eschatological dimension of the history of Church and world. It correctly acknowledges that the eschaton, having entered time in the Incarnation of the Son and the sending of the Spirit, actively impels history toward its future consummation. The "new awareness" theology overcomes the danger of biblical archaism and ecclesiastical constriction. It prompts the Christian to be alert for signs of God's presence and bidding in current events both in and beyond the Church.

Without rejecting this model, one may properly warn against certain dangers. In some theologians there is a risk that the Christ-event is relativized and that Scripture, instead of being used critically against current ideologies, is used only selectively to support one's preconceived positions. In a carefully balanced review of Segundo's methodology Gregory Baum remarks: "What he neglects is the critical impact of Scripture and tradition on the initial experience"—this is to say, on the experience of participation in contemporary social movements.[47]

Another danger in this model is that the divine promises may be reduced to mere symbols of what happens in personal conversion or what is demanded for the building of a just society. The eschatological symbolism of the biblical events and promises, we have maintained, is not merely a disguised way of talking about transitory realities; it conveys true, though veiled, knowledge about what lies beyond. A firm hope in the final consummation, in combination with a salutary awareness of the possibility of final perdition, can give a new perspective on the things of time, and new motivations for personal and social conduct.

# Chapter XV

# THE ACCEPTANCE OF REVELATION

## 1. *The Problem*

Faith, as we have suggested in Chapter VIII, is a term having many meanings. In different theological systems it is variously identified with belief, fidelity, obedience, commitment, trust, and the like. To explore all these Christian attitudes and to construct a coherent theology of faith would take us far beyond the scope of the present work, which deals only with the theology of revelation. We shall here discuss faith only insofar as, in some systems, it is considered to be the act whereby revelation is accepted. In order not to preclude other systems, we speak in the title of this chapter not of faith, but rather of the acceptance of revelation.

The acceptance of revelation appears to involve a dilemma. Either revelation can be rationally verified or it cannot. If it can, it does not transcend the powers of reason and, at least after being verified, it ceases to merit the name of revelation, having been assimilated into the sphere of verified knowledge. But if revelation cannot be verified, it is indistinguishable from illusion and thus not recognizable as revelation.

Since patristic times, philosophers and theologians have generally addressed this problem by referring to two types of mental activity: faith and reason. Four basic positions are common.

According to the first position, assent must always be based on reason, which responds to evidence. To assent to anything on the basis of authority without personal verification would seem to be a violation of the morality of knowledge. Revelation, then, is rejected as an infraction of the order of the universe and infringement of the autonomy of the human mind. This extreme rationalist position is rare among philosophers, and may be said to be absent among theologians.

In the second position, faith is viewed as an inferior type of knowledge, lacking in clarity and certitude. Summarizing John Locke, Polanyi says: "Belief is here no longer a higher power that reveals to us knowledge lying beyond the range of observation and reason, but a mere personal acceptance which falls short of empirical and rational demonstrability."[1] Some nineteenth-century Roman Catholic theologians, under the influence of Hegel, developed a system in which revelation, initially accepted in faith, is subsequently transformed into clear, demonstrated knowledge. This "semirationalism," along with the extreme rationalism of the unbelievers, was repeatedly condemned by Rome in the course of the nineteenth century.[2]

The third major position ranks revelation above reason. According to this view, human reason is competent only within the limited sphere of worldly matters. Revelation shows up the limitations of reason and brings its pretensions under judgment. Revelation cannot be validated by reason; it must be accepted in blind faith, even though it be absurd. This view, often called fideism, has been associated with theologians such as Tertullian, Peter Damian, Martin Luther, and Søren Kierkegaard, though it is debatable how far each of these authors corresponds to the type. In our own century certain biblical and dialectical theologians have been accused of fideism.

The fourth position attempts to achieve a kind of balance between faith and reason, often through a system of mutual priorities. Reason is identified with the innate power of the intellect to know, and in that sense is regarded as the presupposition of revelation (which could not be communicated to a nonrational being). But revelation, when it occurs, proposes mysteries that exceed the comprehension of reason, and thus demands the submission of faith. Once it has submitted, reason can profitably reflect on what it now knows. Although it may not be able to give cogent proofs or achieve clear comprehension of the revealed mysteries, reason can see their inner coherence and their capacity to illuminate things naturally known. Thus the contents of revelation, though not strictly verifiable, are shown to be rationally credible.

Augustine laid the groundwork for this fourth position in many of his statements on authority and reason. He wrote, for instance: .

> There are two different methods, authority and reason. Authority demands belief and prepares man for reason. Reason leads to understanding and knowledge. But reason is not entirely absent from authority, for we have got to consider whom we have to believe, and the highest authority belongs to truth when it is clearly known.[3]

Vatican Council I, attempting to find a middle path between rationalism and fideism, espoused essentially the Augustinian position, as filtered through Thomas Aquinas. In one form or another, this position is widely prevalent among contemporary theologians, Protestant as well as Catholic. But, as our survey of the five models will disclose, elements of the other positions are still current.

## 2. *Assent and the Propositional Model*

The propositional model, especially in its neo-Scholastic form, gives a central role to deductive reason. The neo-Scholastics have great confidence in the power of rational thought to establish the antecedent possibility and suitability of revelation, as well as to draw up criteria whereby revelation, when it comes, can be verified. Canon George D. Smith may be taken as representative. The human mind, he declares, cannot make an authentic act of faith unless it has first established with certainty the truths which are the basis of faith. "It is not enough to conjecture with some degree of probability that there is a veracious God and that he has made a revelation. While doubt concerning the preambles of faith remains, the act of faith cannot be reasonable. No man believes reasonably unless he has first seen that he must believe."[4]

According to this theory even children and uninstructed persons must, before they believe, attain a kind of "relative certitude" of the fact of revelation—a certitude proportioned to their abilities, excluding prudent doubt. This rational process terminates in a judgment of credibility—that is, a judgment that it is eminently reasonable to believe—and thus paves the way for the act of faith whereby, under the leading of divine grace, one unreservedly assents to the revelation itself. In faith we believe not on the basis of the evidences of credibility but on the authority of God who reveals.[5]

Among the evidences of credibility, miracles are considered especially important. In the words of Canon Smith: "If a true miracle, which is the word of God alone, is performed by a man *as a sign that his teaching is divine,* it argues an extraordinary intervention of divine power to vindicate his claim, and, since the true God cannot confirm falsehood, the argument is peremptory."[6]

In the apologetical literature of the neo-Scholastic period, historical method plays a prominent part. Once a person has come to perceive that the Gospels are generally reliable as historical sources, one may proceed, according to Monsignor Van Noort, to establish theses such as the following: "Christ declared that He had been sent by God to teach men the truth, that His teaching was divine, and that it must be accepted by man. . . . We know that His testimony was true because of: (a) His extraordinary holiness; (b) the fulfillment of His prophecies; (c) His numerous miracles; (d) His resurrection from the dead."[7]

Vatican Council I, in 1870, on some points endorsed the tenets of neo-Scholasticism, while avoiding the technical phraseology of that particular system.[8] The Council taught that faith and reason, having their source in the same God, can never disagree;[9] that the act of faith, while essentially the gift of God,[10] is consonant with reason, inasmuch as God has adorned his revelation with many external signs and proofs, especially miracles and prophecies;[11] and that the contents of revelation, while surpassing everything that reason can properly demonstrate or fully comprehend,[12] have a certain intelligibility when pondered by reason under the guidance of faith itself.[13]

A persistent objection against the neo-Scholastic position has been that the historical evidence in favor of the Christian revelation, impressive though it may be, can hardly be judged to yield more than a very high probability for scholars, let alone for children and uneducated persons. The certitude of faith, however, is held to be so firm that one would be obliged to lay down one's life for it. To bridge this "credibility gap," the neo-Scholastics appeal to the interior workings of grace. Grace, they assert, gives light to the mind so that it can find certitude where others would find no more than probability. But without further explanation, this solution is unconvincing. How can an inner light supply for a lack of external evidence? If it can supply, why is the evidence needed at all? This is a problem to which we shall have to return later in the present chapter.

Some Protestant Evangelicals, in the late nineteenth and early twentieth centuries, adopted a scholasticism not unlike that of their Catholic contemporaries. Aligning himself with Calvin and especially with Melanchthon, Benjamin Warfield accepted the classic demonstrations of the existence of God. He maintained that faith, as a conviction regarding truth, must be founded on rational evidence, and hence on the perception of objectively valid arguments proving the credibility of the biblical testimony. The Holy Spirit, he held, prepares the heart to respond to the evidence, but in no way takes the place of such evidence. Apologetics, as the scientific study and presentation of the Christian evidences, plays an important part in the Christianizing of the world. "Other religions may appeal to the sword, or seek in some other way to propagate themselves. Christianity makes its appeal to right reason, and stands out among all religions, therefore, as distinctively 'the Apologetic religion.' "[14]

In Warfield's apologetics Christian evidences establish the divine origin and authority of the Bible. Miracles, in particular, attest the credibility of the inspired authors as God's messengers. Although the evidence for biblical inspiration is not in the strict logical sense demonstrative, this evidence, according to Warfield, "is about as great in amount and weight as 'probable' evidence can be made," and thus the conviction to which it leads "should be practically equal to that produced by demonstration itself."[15]

In contemporary Evangelical orthodoxy there is a certain division of opinion between one school of authors who, like John Warwick Montgomery, seek to vindicate the biblical revelation by means of historical proofs from empirically accessible data[16] and others who, like Carl F. H. Henry, begin with the presupposition that the Bible is divinely inspired and inerrant. Henry holds that human dependence on the divine, and the distortions resulting from the Fall, make it impossible to gain rational truth about God and the possibility of revelation without the help of special revelation. Beginning with the Judaeo-Christian revelation (as he calls it), Henry takes the Bible as the primary and sufficient criterion of truth—a criterion not measured by any empirical tests, whether from science, history, or personal experience. But to apply this criterion, Henry insists, one need not be a believer. Any rational person, he holds, can apprehend the inner consistency of the biblical message and the consistency between the Bible and the Church's teaching.[17]

How does one decide that the Bible is to be used as the norm? Denying that reason ever operates without presuppositions, Henry frankly lays down the divine veracity of the Bible as the presupposition of evangelical Christianity. Having adopted this presupposition, however, one can show up the inconsistency of rival faiths, whether secular or religious. Consistency, according to Henry, is a negative criterion that cannot be denied. Whenever I meaningfully affirm anything I inevitably commit myself to reject whatever is inconsistent with it.[18]

To the Bible as positive norm and consistency as negative norm, Henry adds, as a subordinate criterion, what he calls coherence. By this he means that "the revealed facts of the Christian system of truth can indeed be coherently correlated with all other information, including empirical data involving chronology, geography, history, and psychological experience as well."[19] The nature of truth, according to Henry, is such that the Christian revelation "offers a more consistent, more comprehensive and more satisfactory explanation of the meaning and worth of life than do other views."[20] Christianity is hypothetically open to falsification in the sense that it would be refuted if one could disprove the existence of God, the bodily resurrection of Jesus, or the "works" attributed to Jesus in the Bible.[21]

In their handling of the argument from miracles, Montgomery and Henry differ. Montgomery, like the neo-Scholastics, holds that strict historical method suffices to prove the biblical miracles. Henry, from his presuppositionalist perspective, comments:

> Montgomery is right about divine revelation in historical acts, supremely in the resurrection of the crucified Jesus, but he expects more from historical method than it can yield. The historical redemptive acts are no more self-interpreting than are other historical acts, and their factuality cannot be defended apart from their divinely given meaning.[22]

Just as the neo-Scholastics attribute cognitive value to interior grace, so the Conservative Evangelicals, especially those in the Calvinist tradition, attach great importance to the "inner testimony of the Holy Spirit." In Warfield's day, Amsterdam theologians such as

Abraham Kuyper and Herman Bavinck were maintaining that one could not become convinced of the truth of the Christian message without the special grace and illumination of the Spirit. In reply Warfield asserted that faith rests on rational grounds, and that the special help of the Holy Spirit was needed only for fiducial faith— that is to say, for saving trust in the God who reveals.[23] Carl Henry takes the position that rational argument is sufficient to make the truth of revelation known, and that the gifts of the Holy Spirit are required only for personal assurance and appropriation, "enlivening the Scriptures as God's Word to us, through them."[24]

## 3. Assent and the Historical Model

The distinguishing feature of the historical model, it will be recalled, is not its reliance on history for proof, but its claim that historical deeds, rather than words about them, are the heart of revelation. In its "salvation history" form this model attributes rather less importance to apologetics than do most of the propositional theories. It holds that the revelation originally given in events is primarily accessible in the biblical narrative. But how are we to know that the events really happened as described and were rightly interpreted by the biblical authors? Oscar Cullmann, disavowing any approach through apologetics, appeals to the power of the biblical story to bring conviction. "We come to faith," he writes, "when we are so overwhelmed by salvation history as such that we cannot help regarding ourselves as included in it, and we must therefore consciously align ourselves with it." True and living faith in the events, he contends, is inseparable from trust in the biblical witnesses, the prophets and apostles. Without any prior rational argument we find ourselves simply swept into the dynamic current of history to which the decisive biblical events belong.[25]

Pannenberg, the leading exponent of the theory of revelation as universal history, holds against the propositional and salvation-history schools that revelation is not to be believed on the basis of faith but known on the basis of reason. In contrast to many Lutherans and Calvinists he asserts that no inner illumination above and beyond the light of reason is necessary to grasp the reality of revelation.[26] Once one has established by reason the fact of revelation, and firmly assented to it, it becomes possible to make an act of faith in the sense of trustful self-commitment to the God who has revealed himself.[27]

Since the Enlightenment, Pannenberg holds, it is irresponsible to accept the teaching of Scripture on the ground that the biblical authors have divine authority. We are no longer faced with the simple choice between believing a historical report on the motive of authority and disbelieving it. Thanks to critical methodology we can rationally reconstruct the past events using the accounts as clues rather than as authorities. All historical writings, including the Bible, have become open to critical examination.[28]

Logically and normally, Pannenberg asserts, one's decision concerning revelation will not be an act of blind trust but will be founded on a rational assessment of evidence.[29] Such a foundation is lacking in Bultmannian kerygmatic theology, which grounds faith in proclamation without establishing that the proclamation is anything more than a child of faith. Equally unfounded is the experiential theology of Schleiermacher and Gerhard Koch, who appeal respectively to an experience of redemption and to an encounter in worship, both of which could well be illusory. For Pannenberg, the certainty of faith, while it must stand the test of present experience, is grounded entirely on what happened in the past, as known to historical reason.[30]

Reason, Pannenberg acknowledges, always operates on presuppositions concerning the future. Faith, which is explicitly directed toward the eschatological future, as anticipated in the resurrection of Jesus, can remind reason of its own absolute presuppositions and thus assist reason to be fully transparent to itself.[31]

## 4. Assent and the Experiential Model

The problem of relating reason and revelation, which looms so large in most theological systems, hardly exists in the experiential model. For in this model, as we have seen, revelation has no contents not immediately given in the experience of encounter with God. A typical representative of this position, Auguste Sabatier, denies that revelation is a communication of immutable doctrines which must be steadfastly maintained. The object of revelation, he holds, can only be God himself, and as a consequence no proof can be regarded as necessary:

> I see very clearly that the revelation of God never needs to be proved to any one. The attempt would be as contradictory as it is superfluous. Two things are equally impossible: for an irreligious man to discover a divine revelation in a faith he does not share, or for a truly pious man not to find one in the religion he has espoused and which lives in his heart.[32]

The Catholic Modernists, who tended to look upon revelation as an immediate datum of experience, sought to develop an apologetics that would foster the experience of faith. Tyrrell, for example, argued that every human person is equipped with a religious sense "whose developments, healthy or unhealthy, furnish an experimental criterion of belief, one whose verdict is often not less considerable than that of a strictly intellectual criterion."[33] In his *Lex Orandi* he sought, by applying the "criterion of life, of spiritual fruitfulness," to give an experimental proof of Christianity.[34]

The Modernists were not generally opposed to the idea of miracle, but they objected to the neo-Scholastic view of miracle as a scientifically ascertainable extrinsic sign. Rather, they held that miracles were to be discerned as aspects of revelation itself. Von Hügel, for example, spoke of an experience of miracle in which one immediately apprehends that the divine Spirit, in acting on the soul, can affect the very body in its physical conditions and environment. Miracle, he argued, pertains to the spiritual experience of mankind, but it cannot be strictly demonstrated by science, for science cannot be asked to ascertain that which, by definition, lies beyond its own competence.[35]

Although distinctions have to be made between one author and another, the encyclical *Pascendi,* in 1907, seems to have caught the general tenor of the movement when it declared that for Modernists "the goal that it [apologetics] sets for itself is this: to lead a person who lacks faith in such a way as to induce that experience of the Catholic religion which, according to Modernist tenets, is the sole foundation of faith."[36] In rejecting this trend the encyclical reaffirmed the validity of the reigning apologetics, which argued from miracles and prophecies as extrinsic signs. Thus the Oath Against Modernism (1910) required submission to the proposition:

"I admit and recognize the external signs of revelation—that is, divine facts, and primarily miracles and prophecies—as most certain signs of the divine origin of the Christian religion, and I hold that these signs are very suitable to the understanding of all ages and all human beings, even those of today."[37]

## 5. *Assent and the Dialectical Model*

The relationship between revelation and reason is more strained in the dialectical model than in any other. For the early Barth and his colleagues human reason was intrinsically corrupted by the Fall, with the result that sinners could make no positive approach to faith by their own powers, including the power of reason. Apologetics, considered as a rational preparation for faith, was therefore ruled out. Faith could not arise except as a sheer gift, unsupported by reason, but justified and authenticated by God's word. Even after faith was given, revelation could not be vindicated by any criteria independent of faith itself. Consistently with this position, Rudolf Bultmann could write:

> May we then say that God has "proved" Himself by the "facts of redemption" (*Heilstatsachen*)? By no means. For what we call facts of redemption are themselves objects of faith and are apprehended as such only by the eye of faith. They cannot be perceived apart from faith, as if faith could be based on data in the same way as the natural sciences are based on data which are open to empirical observation. To be sure, the facts of redemption constitute the grounds of faith, but only as perceived by faith itself.[38]

Emil Brunner likewise held that the evidence of faith "does not belong to the sphere of rational argument, but to the knowledge of faith."[39] The argument for revelation, he wrote, "does not lie in the sphere of rational knowledge but in the sphere of that divine truth which can be attained only through divine self-communication, and not through research of any kind."[40]

Within faith, according to this model, it is possible to achieve only an elusive kind of knowledge, in which a yes and a no are kept in constant tension. Totally other, God cannot be fitted into the categories of human thought, and thus theology cannot speak of God except in paradoxes.

## 6. Assent and the Consciousness Model

The consciousness model, as compared with the dialectical, takes a far more positive view of human powers. Revelation is seen as fulfilling in a transcendent way the dynamism inherent in creation itself. Paul Tillich, for example, looked upon revelation as an experience of ultimate concern which enabled the mind to overcome the mutual estrangement of faith and reason and to reestablish the true nature of each. Reason, then, does not have to subject itself heteronomously to the contents of revelation. Revelation fulfills reason and carries it beyond the limits of its finitude.[41]

Influenced by the existentialism of his day, Tillich made a sharp contrast between "ecstatic" (or "theonomous") reason and "technical" (or "formal") reason, resulting in rather disconnected spheres of knowledge. Another architect of the fifth model, Teilhard de Chardin, held that revelation, although deriving from a different source, completes and perfects scientific and technical knowledge. Teilhard's synthetic enterprise is well described by Christopher Mooney:

> What Teilhard was searching for always was an approach to the mystery of man which would enable him to dispense with looking at the human person alternately from a scientific, philosophic and theological point of view. He wanted to be able to pass in a single movement from one mode of knowledge to another, from the data of reason on its various levels to the data of Christian revelation, and to do so with ease and without confusion.[42]

The Christ of revelation, for Teilhard, gave added support and clarity to his scientific hypothesis of a definite goal (Omega) directing the evolutionary process. Revelation thus became a kind of superscience proportioned to the new consciousness brought into the world by Christ.

Contemporary representatives of the fifth model, as noted in previous chapters, look on revelation not as a static content but as a dynamic and continuing process. The human mind, animated by the self-gift of the Absolute, acquires a new horizon from which it constantly reinterprets its own religious past, assesses the signs of the times, and moves into the future to which the Spirit is calling it. When confronted by problems of credibility, these theologians feel free to reinterpret the doctrinal patrimony in ways that correspond to the "legitimate demands" of the reigning secular mentality.

To summarize the five models, we may say that the dialectical theologians and some partisans of salvation history are wary of harmonizations between faith and reason. The dialectical theologians, at times, gloried in speaking of revelation as the "absurd" and "absolute paradox." In other models, revelation is viewed as consonant with reason or at least with the highest exercise of reason. Reason, however, is understood in different ways. In the first model, it is viewed as a power to draw necessary conclusions from evident premises—in other words, as syllogistic or deductive reason. In the second model, as represented by Pannenberg and his circle, reason is understood as a power to recover the facts of history and to construct a coherent, forward-looking, universal vision. For the experientialists, reason is an intuitive faculty which apprehends the data of immediate experience. Finally, for the "new consciousness" theologians, revelation addresses itself to an "ecstatic" or self-transcending reason and thereby overcomes the myopia of ordinary discursive thought. The contents of revelation are subject to continual reinterpretation.

## 7. *Assent and Symbolic Communication*

By adverting to the symbolic character of revelation we may find it possible to escape certain dilemmas and overcome certain clashes among the models. Symbolic knowledge, it will be recalled, is here used to include a wide spectrum of figurative or nonliteral communication, whether by word or by deed. Symbols, by their evocative power, arouse the imagination and invite participation. As contrasted with literal discourse, symbol induces a kind of indwelling in the world of meaning to which it points. Symbols frequently make known a meaning too deep or comprehensive for clear articulation; they arouse tacit awareness of things too vast, subtle, or complex to be grasped in an explicit way; they bridge contrasts that defy conceptual integration.

Revelation, we have maintained, initially occurs by way of symbol and is transmitted within a symbolic context. In revealing, God

manifests himself and his intentions by acting as transcendent cause
to produce clues or symbols pointing to a meaning he intends. In
certain privileged moments prophets or other gifted persons, existentially involved in disclosure situations, perceive that God is so
manifesting himself. The symbols, as such, are not open to dispassionate analysis, but exert a dynamic, transforming influence on the
consciousness of those who apprehend them. Symbolic revelation
thus occurs by a transaction analogously similar to that whereby
human persons manifest themselves through signs, with the important difference that human persons are in principle visible, whereas
God is not.

How is reason involved in this disclosure process? The discernment is not an achievement of formal or explicit reasoning, such as
takes place in mathematical or syllogistic logic. Many authors, such
as John Henry Newman[43] and Michael Polanyi,[44] insist that real assents and creative discoveries are rarely, if ever, effected by formal
reasoning, which is incapable of transcending the categories from
which it sets out. Such insights and convictions are commonly the
fruit of informal reasoning and of operations which Newman—with
a somewhat unhelpful term—ascribed to the "illative sense." Revelatory knowledge rests on the tacit integration of clues which to
conventional thought might appear disconnected and incoherent. By
arousing the imagination, the affections, and the heuristic impulses,
symbols initiate and direct a process whereby the mind, relying
partly on unspecifiable clues, perceives radically new patterns and
meanings in particular constellations of data. If such tacit inference
is ranged under the heading of reason—as Newman and Polanyi
would wish it to be—we may properly claim that the transmission of
revelation through symbol involves the use of reason. Even so, the
moment of illumination is an unexpected gift that comes when it
will.[45] Theologically speaking, the discernment of revelation is a
grace.[46]

The validation of symbolic knowledge is notoriously difficult.
Symbol can be a means of entering into a world of fantasy only
tenuously linked to the realities of experience. Faith, however,
claims that the Christian symbols interpret, without distorting, the
real order. Yet the world of meaning disclosed by the symbols, since
it is inaccessible without them, cannot be verified by strictly empirical tests.

What cannot be empirically verified, however, may be capable of experiential validation. The most powerful index of reality will frequently be the sense that the pattern of meaning corresponds not only to the symbols that brought it into focus but to a vast multitude of clues drawn from the totality of experience. This is what we mean when we say that a given account rings true. A tacit discovery may furthermore be confirmed (or disconfirmed) by its applicability to a range of questions not envisaged when the discovery was made. Major discoveries, centuries after they were originally made, give rise to new and unpredictable insights, conferring intelligibility on data that would otherwise appear meaningless and confusing. This is the case with religious as well as scientific and philosophic teachings. But religious teachings, in addition, are confirmed when they motivate their adherents to live up to their own highest ideals and to behave as they spontaneously feel that they must.

Experiences such as these, corroborated by many individuals of differing background and temperament, and by the corporate judgments of the total community of faith, can give an assurance to religious discoveries not inferior to what passes for proof in the practical affairs of daily living. Acceptance of revelation is achieved and manifested within a living community of faith in which the insights of all the members are exchanged and subjected to mutual criticism, so that illusions can be detected and exposed.

Along lines such as these it may be possible to escape the dilemma proposed at the beginning of this chapter. Revelation cannot be verified by explicit processes of measurement and inference. Yet it can be distinguished from illusion, for it can be assessed by a multitude of clues which Newman, in his *Grammar of Assent,* called "too various for direct enumeration, too personal and deep for words, too powerful and concurrent for refutation."[47] If we know more than we can say, and if we know tacitly more than we know explicitly, it should not be surprising that in matters of personal faith the evidences should sometimes be of a sort that cannot be marshaled for forensic debate.

## 8. *Critique of the Five Models*

In the light of these reflections we may appropriately consider certain values and weaknesses of the five models in their bearing on the question of assent to revelation.

Some propositionalists, such as Gordon Clark and Carl Henry, are strongly opposed to symbol and myth as vehicles of religious truth. "To insinuate any objective intellectual import into a symbolic or mythical view," writes Henry, "involves a confusion of categories and ignores either myth or logic."[48] His objection is that if the symbol has cognitive content, its truth is literal, and if it does not, it conveys no truth. These stark alternatives can be transcended by an epistemology that makes room for tacit awareness and informal inference.

In seeking to make the "laws of logic" the final norm for religious truth, the propositionalists often overlook the difficulty of subsuming the mysteries of faith under the laws of human logic. Paul was emphatic on the incapacity of reason, as the Greeks understood that faculty, to authenticate the gospel (1 Cor 1:18–2:16). The power of Christian proclamation, heralding the good news of the death and resurrection of Jesus, can greatly modify what reason holds to be coherent.

In the attention they gave to miracles as "signs of credibility" the older apologists were not wholly mistaken, but their deductivist approach to miracles was unconvincing. Three weaknesses in the standard presentations may be noted.[49]

First, the historicity of the biblical miracles is difficult to establish. Modern biblical criticism has made it clear that the biblical accounts, for the most part, are not intended to be exact descriptions of what a camera or tape recorder would have registered. They are traditional narratives reflecting the faith-interpretation of the religious community. In some cases, perhaps in most, the miracle stories in the Bible are primarily intended to bring home to the reader the religious significance of the persons and events. Such narratives have more dogmatic and explicative than apologetical and demonstrative value.

Secondly, the tendency of orthodox apologetics has been to look upon the miracles too exclusively as exceptions to the laws of nature. The biblical authors themselves saw the miracles rather as sign events; that is to say, as events which by their inherent character showed forth the attributes of God and the qualities of the coming Kingdom. The apologetics we are here criticizing made too sharp a dichotomy between revelation by word and authentication by events. Deeper familiarity with Scripture shows that the words and events are intrinsically connected, in such a way that the words are powerful and the events meaningful. Miracles are words in action, visible words.

Thirdly, the orthodox apologetics tended to exaggerate the capacity of deductive reason to establish the divine agency in miracles. Even if a miracle were to occur before one's eyes, it could not be accredited except by an act of personal judgment. It cannot be cogently proved that a law of nature has been violated or that, if violated, the deviation was due to the intervention of God. In its essentials the critique of the argument from miracles by Maurice Blondel, Edouard Le Roy, and the "Modernist" authors (using this term in a broad sense) still seems to stand.[50] In the words of a contemporary apologist, Henri Bouillard: "No historical proof could suffice to establish that these facts [i.e., miracles] manifest the presence of God and the advent of his Kingdom, unless these are spiritually discerned from the standpoint of a personal commitment."[51]

A symbolic epistemology, which looks on miracles as symbolic events, does better justice to their apologetic value. Miracles are shaking, transforming events that modify the point of view, and hence the critical standards, of persons involved in them. Wrought in the power of the Holy Spirit, miracles communicate a share in the power of the Spirit so that they can be discerned as signs from God.

In expounding the neo-Scholastic and Conservative Evangelical positions, we alluded to the role of grace and of the Holy Spirit in both these theological systems. Does the Holy Spirit, we asked, give conviction beyond what the evidence warrants? According to the symbolic approach, there can be no question of attributing conversion partly to the force of the evidence and partly to the gift of the Spirit. The Spirit, communicated through the sign-events, produces an affinity or connaturality which enables the witness to perceive the divine significance.

Notwithstanding their hostility to apologetics, authors of the salvation-history school rightly emphasize the power of the biblical narrative to effect conviction. As Cullmann notes in a passage we have quoted, salvation history takes us up into itself and transforms us. In their attachment to the ancient Semitic categories, Cullmann and the biblical theologians lay themselves open to the charges of uncritical naiveté, archaism, and fideism. But they are correct in their recognition that the biblical words, concepts, and categories retain exceptional symbolic power. These theologians' approach to the dynamics of conversion could be confirmed and fortified by deeper study of the principles of symbolic communication.

Pannenberg and the advocates of "universal history," reacting against the irrationalism of authoritarian theologies of the word, sometimes write as though a detached critical study of the biblical texts, undertaken by purely secular historians, could lead to a firm conviction that Jesus rose from the dead and that Christianity is the absolute religion. To this, many object that nonbelievers, using the techniques of academic history, cannot establish the reality of revelation. The truth of revelation is not *known* without being *believed*.

The symbolic approach, by contrast, calls attention to the need of a religious framework of inquiry in order for the theological interpretation to be plausible and meaningful. To recognize the divine signs in history requires that one have a positive openness to the meaning conveyed by the signs. Such openness being presupposed, historical and biblical scholarship can assist in the conversion process. It can give a sharper presentation of the revelatory events and thus enable one to replicate, in some sort, the faith-experience of the original witnesses. This experience will depend on an appreciation of the symbolic power of the revelatory events, too little emphasized by Pannenberg and his associates.

The third model identifies the evidence of credibility with the revelatory experience itself. In the presence of the divine, it is held, we experience a joy and consolation that are not of this world, and thereby receive assurance of the authenticity of the revelation. In terms of a symbolic theory of knowledge, this need not be denied. Symbol, as we have contended, does not simply impart information about objective facts. It invites participation in the experience out of which the symbols were born. Religious symbols mediate that which they signify. The unalloyed peace and joy that flood the hearts of those who give themselves to God in faith can be, for some, equivalent to proof.

The experiential model is, however, in need of a corrective. Authors of this orientation, while recognizing the value of symbolic expression, tend to overlook the importance of symbolic mediation. By seeking a wholly unmediated experience of God, one can easily fall prey to illusions. Only when we allow our attention to be focused by the symbols on their meaning do we enjoy, concomitantly, the sense of the presence of God.

The dialectical theologians, for their part, do well to point out the limitations of conceptual thought and its impotence to rise to a living knowledge of God. It is quite true that, as these theologians say, the truth of revelation cannot be affirmed from a position outside of faith. It would be contradictory for a nonbeliever to assert that the Christian message is true. Even from a standpoint within faith, moreover, reason cannot achieve a clear conceptual integration of all the data of revelation.

These and many other points, effectively made by the dialectical theologians, are no less evident from the symbolic perspective. The word of God, proclaimed in faith, may be characterized as a symbolic event. It can induce a fundamental change of horizon—an intellectual as well as a moral and religious conversion. God's word, made present through revelatory symbols, shows up the inadequacy of the unbeliever's cognitive framework and challenges the presumption of all who seek to criticize revelation from a merely human point of view.

In derogating from the powers of reason the dialectical theologians often relied on a narrow and rationalistic conception of reason itself. Barth and Brunner in their later work gave increasing attention to the inherent intelligibility of the revealed message and to the capacity of faith to give a coherent account of itself. They constructed impressive syntheses of dogmatic theology but they did not sufficiently explore the dynamics of conversion, as the process whereby one responsibly comes to faith in the word of God. The epistemology of symbolic communication, as outlined in the present chapter, might help to supply for this lacuna.

More successfully than any of the other models, the fifth respects the dynamic character of human reason, which functions according to different patterns in different contexts. Instead of viewing reason as a static faculty, always the same in every time and place, it sees reason as concretely affected by the history of sin and redemption. It situates reason within the total quest of the human spirit for meaning and truth. Like the symbolic approach, the consciousness model envisages a transformation of human reason through the revealing presence of God.

For many representatives of the consciousness model, religious symbolism is the vehicle of revelation. Gregory Baum, for example, pleads for a symbolic as opposed to an objectivist understanding of divine revelation. "Revelation," he writes, "is here [i.e., in Christianity] a set of symbols that illuminates the ambiguity of life and discloses the graciousness situated at the heart of the cosmos."[52] And elsewhere he declares: "The symbolic approach understands revelation in symbolic terms (the word is here used in its strong sense) and the Christian religion as a set of symbols, which people assimilate and celebrate, and out of which they define their lives and create their world."[53]

Some exponents of the consciousness model give the impression that the symbols of revelation are freely constructed, expressive, but not cognitive. We have in earlier chapters shown this to be the case with R. B. Braithwaite, Charles Davis, and others. Robert Bellah, who classifies himself as a symbolic realist, regards the biblical symbols as expressive of ultimate reality, but not as founding a historically oriented faith.[54] Gregory Baum rightly questions Bellah's bypassing of history. "The symbolic approach to Christian theology," he writes, "acknowledges that something marvelous and unaccountable really happened in history which, when accompanied by a new word, revealed to people the meaning of their lives and enabled them to recreate their social existence. And this happened through symbols."[55]

It is perhaps a weakness of the fifth model that even Baum, who here acknowledges the historical grounding of the Christian symbols, speaks of their significance in existential and sociopractical terms. From a wider basis that takes account of the contributions of other models, it is possible to give symbols a cognitive import that goes beyond the existential and practical spheres. Nothing in the nature of symbolic communication requires us to say less than is affirmed in the Fourth Gospel: "This is eternal life, that they may know thee the only true God, and Jesus Christ whom thou has sent" (Jn 17:3).

## Chapter XVI

# REVELATION AT ITS PRESENT VALUE

## 1. *Recapitulation*

Our study of revelation in the preceding chapters has been limited in scope. Writing as fundamental theologians, we have not tried to construct a full theology of revelation. We have said enough to serve as a grounding for the dogmatic enterprise, but only in dogmatic theology would it be possible to complete and refine many points here left vague or untouched. Dogmatic theology would be able to say a great deal more about revelation in relation to the three divine persons, to Christ, to the Church, and to sinful and redeemed humanity. Seeking not to intrude upon other theological treatises, we have not attempted to specify in any exact way how revelation is attributable to the Father, the Son, and the Holy Spirit, how the human consciousness and statements of Jesus are related to revelation, how the Church authoritatively teaches revelation, or how revelation is connected with grace and salvation. Questions such as these, we believe, can only be resolved in a wider dogmatic context. A fundamental theology of revelation, while providing materials that are helpful to the dogmatic task, cannot by itself complete that task.

Although our approach has not been dogmatic, it has been self-consciously theological. We have not sought to fashion a concept of revelation as it might appear to someone for whom revelation was merely an abstract possibility. Just as the epistemologist writes of knowledge as one who already knows, so the theologian writes of revelation as already accepting it. We have written throughout as believers in God's revelation as it comes through the Bible, through Christian tradition, and especially through Jesus Christ. Our project has been to translate the vague, implicit awareness of revelation that we possess as Christians into a relatively clear and reflexive knowledge that would enable us to answer the questions what revelation is and how it occurs.

After surveying five models of revelation theology in Chapters III through VII, we resolved in Chapter VIII to correct the specific weaknesses of each model while seeking to preserve their valid insights. Such a critical retrieval did not seem possible without recourse to a dialectical tool that would help to identify what was sound and what deficient in the rival models. As a dialectical tool we selected in Chapter IX the concept of symbolic mediation. Without contending that revelation is the same as symbol, we described revelation as the self-manifestation of God through a form of communication that could be termed, at least in a broad sense, symbolic.

Our understanding of symbol was not a purely generic one, but was itself shaped by Christian conviction and refined in dialogue with the five models. In light of this procedure, we adopted a position that may be called symbolic realism. Five important points regarding symbol are characteristic of this position.

First, revelatory symbols are not pure creations of the human imagination. The basic symbols of Christian revelation, we maintained, are the persons, events, and other realities whereby God brings into existence the community of faith we call the Christian Church. On the basis of this self-manifestation, God may inspire believers to construct images that are helpful for understanding and communicating what has been given, but the figures of speech and the literary imagery are secondary to the real symbols out of which they emerge.

Secondly, Christian revelation is not simply the product of human interpretation of the natural symbols contained in cosmic nature. Through specific actions at definite points in time and place, the universal symbolism of nature is taken up into the biblical and Christian tradition and thereby given added depth and significance. In Chapter IX we considered the interplay of nature and history in three examples: the symbolism of light, of the Cross, and of the Eucharist.

Thirdly, symbols do not necessarily point to things strictly other than themselves. Although there must be at least a formal distinction between the symbol and what it points to, the symbol and the symbolized may constitute "a single interlocked reality," as Vatican Council II said of the two natures of Christ and of the two aspects of the Church.[1] Just as the human body is really one with the spiritual person who comes to expression through it, so according to Christian theology, the man Jesus Christ is one with the Word of God. So, likewise, with differing modes of union, the Church is one with the Spirit of Christ, and the sacraments are, in still another way, one with the divine persons present and active in them. Jesus in his human nature, the Church in its social structure, and the sacraments in their visible aspect may all be described, in their several ways, as "realizing symbols"—symbols that contain and mediate the reality they signify.

Fourthly, revelatory symbols do not simply arouse emotions, strivings, fantasies, and ideals. They point to, and provide insight into, realities inaccessible to direct human experience. Although they are not scale models, pictures, or descriptions of what they signify, such symbols denote and disclose what is ontologically real.

Revelatory symbols, fifthly, have a twofold truth. They have "symbolic truth" insofar as they express, communicate, or produce a transformed consciousness. But the truth of the symbol is not merely its symbolic truth.[2] In reflection, symbols give rise to true affirmations about what is antecedently real. Revelatory symbols, being dense and concrete, can generate an inexhaustible brood of affirmations. Yet the symbols are not indefinitely malleable. Only some statements can claim to be grounded in the symbols; certain others are excluded by the symbols, rightly understood.

With the help of symbolic realism we may at this point formulate certain conclusions about revelation, suggested in Chapter IX and confirmed in subsequent chapters. Our first set of conclusions will be negative, our second set positive, with reference to the five models. Negatively, then:

1. Revelation does not initially occur in the form of propositions, still less that of prefabricated propositions miraculously inserted into the human mind. Nor can revelation be adequately transposed into any determinate set of propositions. The statements in Scripture and tradition represent valid though limited aspects of revelation as seen from particular points of view.

2. Revelation is not a series of events in the remote past, recoverable only through historical-critical method. While historical

investigation can always be useful, it does not by itself yield revelation. Granted the nature of the biblical materials, and the antiquity of the events, dispassionate, academic history is rarely capable of reconstructing the revelatory events in detail. The process whereby revelatory meaning is discerned in the events is not a matter of formal inference, but a synthesis of subsidiarily known clues. The events of biblical history, as seen in the framework of Scripture and Christian tradition, are disclosive of God.

3. Revelation is not an ineffable mystical encounter between God and the individual soul. While mystical experiences of union may sometimes be authentic, they do not by themselves yield a determinate revelation. For them to be interpreted in a theistic or Christian sense, one must rely on the mediation of Christian symbols, traditions, and doctrines.

4. Revelation is not an unintelligible word or an absurd message to be accepted in a blind leap of faith. It has a content beyond the mere fact of revelation itself. It does not occur in a time wholly incommensurable with chronological time nor without continuity with other events in history.

5. Revelation is not a mere invitation or impulse to adapt one's attitudes and behavior to the needs of a particular phase of the evolutionary process. The meaning of revelation does not change so radically from one age to another as to contradict the previous meaning.

These negative conclusions may be balanced by the following positive statements, embodying themes from each of the five models.

1. Revelation has cognitive value that can be expressed, to some extent, in true propositions. The truth of these propositions is permanent and universal in the sense that, if they are ever authorized by revelation, they at no time or place become false in their own terms. The propositions help to establish the context in which the symbols yield their revelatory meaning.

2. The chief symbols of biblical and Christian revelation are given in a specific history mediated to every generation through the canonical Scriptures, read in the light of living and ongoing tradition. The events, attributable in their specificity to God as agent, convey a divinely intended meaning, discernible with particular clarity and assurance by prophetically endowed interpreters.

3. By evoking participation, the revelatory symbols mediate a lived, personal communion with God, which is, in its way, immediate. This may be described as an experience of God or of grace, provided that God or grace is not depicted as an object to be encountered but as a horizon within which inner-wordly objects are encountered.

4. The words of Scripture and Christian proclamation are dynamic. They are, under favorable circumstances, imbued with the power of God who speaks and acts through them. The word is an event as well as a content, and the word-event exceeds all that can be said about it in clear propositional speech. Especially when the revelatory events are seen as visible words, the word takes on characteristics like those we have attributed to symbol.

5. Revelation is not merely speculative truth. It has implications for human existence and conduct. Demanding obedience, it brings with it a new horizon, a new consciousness. The full significance of revelation can be perceived only by those who respond, with personal commitment, within a community of faith.

In Chapters X through XV we considered six specific areas of revelation theology: Christ, the religions, the Bible, the Church, eschatology, and the acceptance of revelation. In Chapter X we observed how the concept of symbol harmonizes with the traditional Christian doctrine that God gave a universally valid and definitive revelation of himself in Christ. In so holding one need not, and should not, deny that the Christ-symbol needs to be illuminated by the cosmic symbolism of nature and the historical symbolism of various epochs and cultures. In order to clarify the unsurpassable power of the Christ-symbol, we drew upon the theological idea of sacrament as a symbol wherein the reality signified is truly and actively present. The doctrine of Christ as incarnate Word, we found, enriches and confirms the symbolic approach to revelation.

In Chapter XI we confronted some difficult questions regarding the possibility of admitting, from a Christian point of view, the existence of revelation in other religions. We concluded that, although it might be too much to speak of the non-Christian religions as revealed, symbols of revelation may be recognized in such religions. By dialogue the Christian theologian may profitably strive to relate the symbolism of these religions to Jesus Christ as the central symbol of the Christian faith. In the perspectives of Christian theology such dialogue may be seen as contributing to a better understanding both of Christ and of the other religions.

In Chapter XII we examined, in the context of our symbolic approach, the positions of various theological schools regarding the Bible as the primary font or document of revelation. We concluded that the traditional doctrines of the inspiration and canonical authority of the Bible—and even, in a certain sense, the doctrine of inerrancy—can be understood and defended by adverting to the symbolic character both of the events recorded in the Bible and of the literary devices whereby the biblical authors transmit the significance of the events. The epistemology of symbolic knowledge, we found, throws light on biblical hermeneutics.

We then turned in Chapter XIII to the connection between revelation and the Church. This connection, we maintained, is clarified if the Church is viewed not simply as a teacher or even as an indicative sign, but as a genuine sacrament of Christ—that is to say, a symbolic reality in which Christ continues to be present and active. Notwithstanding the weakness of the members of the Church, the revelation given once-for-all in Christ continues to be given through the Holy Spirit in the Church as the primordial sacrament of Christ in the world. To those who dwell spiritually in the Church as the home of faith, the Christian symbols take on existential meaning and become a source of light amid the perplexities of life.

In Chapter XIV we took up the question whether revelation has already become complete or, on the contrary, is to be considered as something promised. We maintained that, while the biblical symbols and especially the symbol of Jesus Christ have abiding normative value, the interpretation of the received symbols and the fashioning of new symbols continues to occur in sacred and secular history (as two dimensions of one indivisible history) and will reach a transcending consummation at the end of time. Although traditional theology has spoken of an unmediated face-to-face encounter with God in the "beatific vision," it seems possible and proper to look on the risen Christ as symbolically mediating even the vision of God forever enjoyed by the blessed.

Finally, in Chapter XV, we explored the utility of the symbolic approach for resolving the theological disagreements regarding the acceptance of revelation. While noting that symbolic knowledge is evocative, and that it appeals more to tacit than to explicit reason, we maintained that symbolism is not on that account noncognitive, still less irrational. Revelation, although it cannot be verified by deductive or empirical tests, can be validated by criteria of the kind that are applied to other forms of symbolic knowledge—for example, the interpretation of a poem or the discernment of a man's character or intentions from his facial expression and gestures. In this way it proved possible to forge a viable path between the opposite extremes of rationalism, which would insist on formal demonstration, and fideism, which would seek to dispense with all rational grounds of credibility.

## 2. Contemporary Difficulties Reviewed

In the light of the theory of revelation developed in the intervening chapters we may now profitably return to the eight objections to revelation set forth in Chapter I. These objections, it may be noted, came to the fore during what has been called the "critical period" of Western thought, between the time of Descartes and that of Bertrand Russell. As Polanyi observes, "It has been taken for granted throughout the critical period of philosophy that the acceptance of unproven beliefs was the broad road to darkness, while truth was approached by the straight and narrow path of doubt."[3] The method of doubt, which Polanyi regards as central to critical thought, "trusts that the uprooting of all voluntary components of belief will leave behind an unassailed residue of knowledge that is completely determined by the objective evidence."[4] The objections to the idea of revelation raised by critical philosophy, sociology, and psychology, while they tell rather decisively against certain precritical concepts of revelation, may be able to assist the postcritical theologian to gain a sharper concept of revelation. Postcritical thinking does not simply reject the critical enterprise, but recognizes that the critical movement, while serving to demolish some superstitions, suffered from a certain naiveté of its own. The critics too easily assumed that truth could be established on the basis of self-evident principles. Contemporary thinkers such as Polanyi and Ricoeur call for a postcritical method that aims, in Ricoeur's words, "to go beyond criticism by means of criticism, by a criticism that is no longer reductive but restorative."[5] Such a postcritical approach can make due allowance for tacit awareness and symbolic communication.

With this preliminary observation we may turn once more to the eight objections.

1. *Philosophical agnosticism* relied heavily on the Kantian assumption that knowledge was confined to the sphere of sensory phenomena and their interrelations as seen with the help of certain transcendental regulative ideas. Many idealists and transcendental philosophers, building on Kant's own theory of the categories of speculative and practical reason, have argued that the ineluctable tendency of the mind to pose questions about suprasensible realities proves the impossibility of restricting the competence of thought to the phenomenal order. With these critics we agree that agnosticism and positivism rely on a theory of knowledge too narrowly modeled on the mathematical and physical sciences.

According to Kant, "an intuition of intelligible objects is not given to man, but only a symbolic knowledge."[6] By this statement Kant himself may have intended to question the cognitive value of human ideas about suprasensible realities, but in the light of the postcritical evaluation of symbol and tacit knowledge, Kant's own observation may be used as the point of departure for a response to the agnosticism of the positivists. Symbolic awareness, we have argued, can open the mind to realities that transcend the empirical and thereby satisfy man's deeper intellectual cravings.

2. *Linguistic analysis* has sometimes denied that language about God and the supernatural has any meaning. Generally speaking, such denials were characteristic of the early stages in which the philosophy of language was dominated by positivists such as A. J. Ayer, who identified meaning with empirical verifiability. Since that time many philosophers of language, influenced by the later work of Wittgenstein, have greatly extended and nuanced the concept of meaning. A few theologians, such as John Hick, have had recourse to the concept of "eschatological verification" to defend the meaningfulness of theological discourse.[7] In the present work a different direction has been taken, relying on the cognitive value of symbols and the importance of the tacit dimension. Religious symbols, insofar as they enable the mind to integrate data that might otherwise seem disconnected or incompatible, are eminently meaningful. If

meaning consists in the integration of clues, and if integration depends on tacit knowledge, it follows that meaning is never directly verifiable by empirical tests. The verification theory is to that extent in need of amendment.

3. *Modern epistemology,* it is true, tends to blur the distinction between acquired and revealed knowledge, but the reality of revelation in no way depends upon the existence of a clear line of demarcation. In a sense it is true that all revelation is acquired by the subject who receives it, and must, as Maurice Blondel insisted, "correspond in some way to a need of development."[8] Revelation may be understood from the point of view of the recipient as knowledge or awareness gained through the special assistance of God as he freely manifests himself through tangible clues. Revelation, in this perspective, is not a set of truths fallen from heaven, but rather a dimension or component of mental activity elicited by God's self-presentation through symbolic mediation. Revelation never exists by itself in a chemically pure state. To admit this is not to deny that the human mind, under the impact of God's revealing action, may be able to exceed its normal capacities and to affirm, in a humanly conditioned way, the very thing that God is manifesting to it. Because of the transcendence of the human spirit, the mind is capable of being self-critical and of recognizing the limited character of the images and concepts it employs. In so doing thought, so to speak, transcends itself.

4. *Empirical psychology* has shown how difficult it is to ground one's faith in supposedly direct communications from on high received in paranormal psychic states. This advance imperils certain precritical concepts of revelation. Especially in times past, it was not uncommon to speak of visions, auditions, and the like as revelations. But the concept of revelation that has been dominant in fundamental theology since the origins of that discipline (about the eighteenth century) has not relied in an essential way on this psychological approach. It has focused rather on the interpretation of historical persons and events, seen as symbols and mediators of God's gracious self-communication. Parapsychological phenomena have been considered under the rubric of "private revelation" in treatises on spiritual and mystical theology.

5. *Biblical criticism,* by calling into question a naive interpretation of certain specific words and deeds to God, has contrib-

uted to the maturation of revelation theology. Few modern theologians adhere to the fundamentalistic views of revelation and miracle that the critical study of Scripture has undermined. Among those who adopt a symbolic approach to revelation, the Bible may be seen as the word of God in the sense that it symbolically expresses and mediates the faith whereby the biblical authors were vitally in communion with God. Through symbolic deeds recounted in symbolic language, the Bible vividly depicts the mysterious manner in which God has made himself present through historical persons and events, as well as through community interpretation. God, as symbolic cause, does not substitute himself for created efficient causes (as some theories of miracle and inspiration might seem to imply). Rather, he directs the processes of inner-worldly causality so that certain words and events become effective signs of his loving self-communication.[9] When human agents are caught up in the life of grace, they become living symbols through which God speaks and acts. With the help of a religious interpretation of the symbolic words and deeds of the Bible, the modern believer may enter into communication with God.

6. *The history of doctrine* does indeed establish that certain truths once widely accepted as revealed are no longer so regarded. This fact could be disturbing to those who believe that religious doctrines can be neatly dichotomized into some which are revealed and others which are not. The difficulty is less acute in the symbolic approach to revelation we have followed. Revelation comes into being through symbolic persons and events and is initially expressed through symbolic forms of communication. Through careful reflection on these originative expressions it is possible to hammer out doctrines which articulate authentic aspects of the meaning of the symbols. Such formulated statements, however, will never be exempt from human and historical influences. Constant critical reflection will be needed to determine which traditional assertions remain acceptable in their original form. The Holy Spirit, continuously active in the Church, supplies the creativity needed to reexpress, in the conceptuality and language of a new age, the revelatory meaning of the earlier formulations.

That Christian doctrine should exhibit certain historical fluctuations is thus neither scandalous nor surprising. The relative stability of the doctrinal tradition, which continues to uphold definitions handed down in the early centuries, invites confidence in the dogmatic teaching of the Church of modern times. Even within shifts of language and conceptuality, an intelligible content perdures.

7. *Comparative religion* raises problems of the kind discussed in Chapter XI. We have seen that the propositional, historical, and dialectical models, in pure form, tend to be unfavorable to revelation outside the biblical religions. The symbolic approach, however, provides a framework for respectful dialogue in which each religion can acknowledge and profit from the revelatory ingredients in other religions. To reject the idea of revelation, far from facilitating reconciliation among the religions, would remove one of the chief points of agreement among many or most religions. Judaism, Christianity, and Islam are united in the conviction that God has revealed himself through his word in history. Many Eastern religions, while not using the vocabulary of revelation, cultivate the memory of certain outstanding religious personalities and the study of certain religious writings as privileged channels of enlightenment and of access to the transcendent. Revelation, therefore, is a valuable theme for dialogue among the religions.

It is to be expected that some tension will exist among religions as it does among philosophic and scientific schools. Such tension, creatively harnessed, can be a source of ferment and progress. It need not, and must not, be allowed to degenerate into hatred or violence. Without repudiating its own foundations Christianity cannot deny the permanent and universal significance of Jesus Christ as the preeminent "real symbol" of God's turning to the world in merciful love. The Christ-symbol, like other religious symbols, can always be better understood and presented with the help of elements derived from other faiths and traditions, and can contribute to the better understanding of these elements.

8. *Critical sociology* has done well to point out the ideological factors at work in institutional religion. Unceasing vigilance is necessary to detect these sinister forces. Revelation, because of its inherent authority, is always in danger of being turned into an instrument of human pride and ambition. These vices, however, are not averted by the rejection of revealed religion. Individual and collective egoism can be motivating forces behind any social and intellectual movement, whether it be religious, nonreligious, or antireligious. The symbols of revealed religion, by calling attention to the sinful

tendencies of human nature, have helped to expose the workings of ideology in religion as well as elsewhere, and to bring these aberrations under judgment. The Cross, as the central symbol of Christianity, is a standing revelation of the power of sin and of the demand for repentance and conversion. Combined with the Resurrection, this symbol prevents believers from falling into cynicism and despair, as they might otherwise be tempted to do. By reminding them that God's grace is more powerful than the world's sin, these symbols inspire their adherents with courage to combat the perversions of ideology.

### 3. Christianity Without Revelation?

In our opening chapter we made use of the writings of Karl Jaspers and F. Gerald Downing to show that acute criticisms of the concept of revelation can be mounted from within the Christian tradition. In the light of the positions developed in the present study we may now respond more fully to the positions of these two authors.

Jaspers, in his *Philosophical Faith and Revelation,* the work on which we chiefly relied, might seem to be rejecting not only a particular concept of revelation but the very idea of revelation itself. In other works, however, he is more favorable to certain concepts of revelation. In a published dialogue with Rudolf Bultmann he contrasts two kinds of faith in revelation, the orthodox and the liberal. Orthodoxy, as he portrays it, holds that God reveals himself in an exclusive way to certain particular peoples, that revelation is permanently fixed in the past, that it must be uncritically accepted on the authority of human witnesses, that it excludes human inquiry and speculation, that it makes puppets of its adherents, and that it breeds intolerance and fanaticism. Liberal faith, however, takes the position "that the revelation of truth is a mystery, a series of sudden illuminations in the history of the mind; it recognizes that we are ignorant of how men arrived at this revelation, and that some of its elements have not yet been comprehended."[10] Furthermore, he says, "Liberalism recognizes faith in revelation, including belief in the truth of the redemptive history as a possible truth valid for him who believes it—insofar as the believer does not, by his deeds and words, draw consequences destructive to the freedom of men who find themselves directly before God, nor attempt to coerce others by violent means."[11]

Confronted by these alternatives, few Christians would wish to espouse the position Jaspers calls orthodox. The acceptance of revelation, as proposed in this study, demands immediacy to God, reflection, and free commitment. Rightly understood, revelation instills tolerance for the conscientious religious quest of every individual and group. Far from being a fixed object in the world, revelation involves a mysterious personal encounter with Transcendence. It invites exploration and is always susceptible of deeper penetration. Never confined to any one time or place, the revealing God, it would appear, is at work always and everywhere.

When Jaspers contends that transcendence discloses itself only obliquely in "ciphers," he might seem to be converging with a symbolic theory of revelation. Essential being, he holds, is revealed through ciphers, wherein it becomes immediately present.[12] Yet the agreement is far from complete. Jaspers' particular philosophical stance, with its Kantian and existentialist roots, precludes the idea that God could make himself present, in a permanent or cognitively significant way, in any particular person, event, or institution. As previously mentioned, Jaspers' position is contestable on philosophical grounds. Some of his own contemporaries, such as Gabriel Marcel, found philosophical existentialism highly compatible with revealed religion.[13]

As for Gerald Downing, he nowhere expressly denies that Christianity rests on revelation. His view is rather that "a positive claim [to revelation], though possible, can only be a heavily qualified one."[14] While agreeing with Braithwaite that the Christian, in speaking of God, is using "directly or indirectly the language of commitment,"[15] he holds, contrary to Braithwaite, that the "myths" of biblical religion imply, for the believer, not only a commitment to live "agapeistically" (as Braithwaite would have it), but the belief that God has really acted in Christ with a love prior to our own.[16] According to Christian faith, he later affirms, "God has acted most characteristically in Christ" and "has expressed himself most fully in Jesus' life, death, and resurrection."[17] Going beyond the instrumentalists' view that religious myths are merely useful symbols, Downing asserts that they are designed to tell us something about God and his relation to the world.

In the end, therefore, Downing concedes in effect that Christianity makes a claim to what the majority of theologians call revelation. Downing's contention that the Christian, in speaking of God, is using "directly or indirectly the language of commitment" need not be denied. But, as we have contended in Chapter IX, following Ian Barbour, commitment to a way of life implies at least a tacit conviction that reality is of such a nature as to warrant the commitment. The question whether Jesus is to be followed is inseparable from the question who Jesus is—a question insistently put to us by the Gospels (cf. Mk 8:28 par). In general, commitment and reality-claims cannot be played off against each other. A deeper investigation would show that it is only within a framework of commitment that truth can be affirmed at all.[18]

Downing's disinclination to use the term "revelation" for anything that falls short of the clear, eschatological disclosure reserved for the end-time is understandable. As we have pointed out in Chapter XIV, the term does apply par excellence to the final manifestation of God. But there seems to be no sufficient reason for departing from standard theological usage in employing the term also to designate the provisional, symbolic self-communication of the divine that is available under the conditions of earthly existence.

## 4. Functions of the Concept of Revelation

In Chapter I it was noted that in modern theology revelation has been seen as serving three major functions: to ground the faith of the Christian, to direct the mission of the Church, and to undergird theological argument. If the concept of revelation is to be restructured in accordance with the symbolic approach recommended in this work, questions arise as to whether revelation can still perform these three traditional functions or whether it takes on new and different functions.

1. The first function touches on the relationship between revelation and faith. In the precritical era revelation was rather unreflectively identified with a large body of materials by which it was thought to be mediated. An argument from any portion of the Bible, from the creed, or even from the Fathers, in the absence of weighty objections, was taken to be an argument from revelation. Faith was

understood to be a submission of the mind to the doctrine contained in the Christian sources.

As the critical movement advanced, theologians sought to find an unshakable basis for faith that would be secure against all doubt, at least on the part of church members. Protestants frequently found such a basis in Scripture alone; Catholics, in the dogmas of the Church. For practical purposes these authoritative sources were equated with revelation, which was identified, by the reigning propositional school, with formulated truth.

This position labors under a logical weakness. If truth exists formally in the mind which judges, and not in the pages of books, revelation, it would appear, cannot be formally contained in written sentences.[19] Since the Kantian "turn to the subject," revelation has frequently been located only in the minds of believers. Some critical theologians, as we have seen, make faith prior to revelation, and even demote revelation to the status of second-order language. James Mackey, for instance, calls revelation "a metaphorical or mythical description of the literal truth of faith," investing the latter with divine authority.[20]

In a symbolic approach it would seem possible to restore the role of revelation as normative for faith without lapsing into the uncritical objectivism of the early modern period. Revelation, in the symbolic or postcritical view, can be seen as the immanent norm within faith itself. Faith and revelation are regarded as reciprocally prior to each other.

On the one hand, revelation precedes faith inasmuch as, before anyone can believe, there must be symbols wherein God expresses what he is, and wills to be, for the world. These symbols, before their meaning is understood and accepted, are virtual revelation. When believers accept revelation, they allow their minds to be determined by the meaning they find in the symbols. Thus revelation shapes their faith.

On the other hand, faith exists before revelation inasmuch as the symbols do not yield their meaning except to religious inquirers or believers who are actively committed to the search for truth. The quest itself involves a kind of implicit faith—a confidence that the search is not a futile one and that God's revelation, if it exists, can be recognized. When the search has succeeded, faith actively receives revelation and provides it, so to speak, with a dwelling place in the mind. Since revelation cannot exist as such outside a created mind, revelation may be said to presuppose faith.

The view here set forth should not be confused with the opinion that revelation *is* faith.[21] The two, we would rather say, are polar opposites. Revelation is, in principle, an apprehension in which the mind rests satisfied. Faith, however, is a stretching forth of the mind toward an insight not yet given, or not clearly given. Faith, as a kind of trustful probing, animates the quest for revelation; it sustains the process of discovery. To the extent that revelation is given, the appetite of faith is both stimulated and assuaged. Faith therefore stands in dialectical tension with revelation. The completeness of revelation, were it ever given (as the asymptotic goal toward which faith aspires), would do away with the very possibility of faith.[22]

The symbolic approach seeks to escape both subjectivism and objectivism. Unlike subjectivism it holds that faith does not create its own object but defers to a revelation that comes from God through meaningful symbols. Unlike objectivism it holds that revealed truth has no formal existence outside the faith of those who submit to the power of the symbols. Faith, as the subjective attitude, and revelation, as the affirmed content, coexist and constitute each other by their mutual union.

Within the perspectives of a symbolic epistemology, it is still correct to say that faith is grounded in revelation, provided one adds that revelation, conversely, is grounded in faith. God, as encompassing cause, produces both the symbols that speak to faith and the faith that discerns the symbols.

2. If revelation has no formal existence outside of faith, how can the Church appeal to revelation as the basis of its mission, and how can it use revelation as a norm for judging controversies about the faith? In addressing these questions we shall supplement what has been said in Chapter XIII on Revelation and the Church.

The mission of the Church is not derived from some command that exists, fully constituted, before the Church does. All authoritative formulations of the Church's mission, including the great mandate of Mt 28:19–20, are warranted by the Church itself. Matthew's Gospel, composed within the Church, expresses in symbolically charged language the Church's belief concerning its own origins. By including this passage in its canonical Scriptures, the postapostolic

Church authenticates it as a reliable expression of what the Church knows itself to be. It regards its own self-consciousness, both past and present, as the work of the Lord who continually calls the Church into existence. Thus the missionary mandate, though it receives its authoritative formulation from the Church, is in some sense prior to the Church. As in the case of faith and revelation just considered, we are dealing here with mutual priorities.

The same principles hold for the resolution of doctrinal disputes within the Church. Such disputes cannot be settled by simple appeal to an objective norm that in no way depends on the Church. Rather, the Church strives, by prayerful meditation on its own inmost reality, to discern what is or is not consonant with the law of its being. The Church apprehends revelation by pondering on the symbolic persons and events that shape its self-consciousness. It scrutinizes the testimony of Scripture and tradition, but does not use these sources in a mechanical, objectivistic way, as though they could supply ready-made divine answers to current problems. Only when interpreted with living faith do the sources deliver living revelation.

In a symbolic and postcritical approach, then, revelation may still be taken as the final criterion for establishing the mission of the Church and for settling questions about doctrine. Revelation, however, is an immanent ground, not an external one. In appealing to revelation the Church turns to the symbolic sources of its own life and submits to the direction they give, confident that in so doing it is being faithful to the God who reveals.

3. If the Church cannot ascertain its mission or resolve questions of doctrine except by plumbing the depths of its own self-consciousness, where can theology find a firm basis on which to found its conclusions? In classical theology revelation has been regarded as the source and norm that sustains theology as the "science of faith." Can this position still be defended?

In the precritical period theologians commonly held that revelation was objectively contained in testimonies continuously handed down from apostolic times.[23] They believed it possible, by making the necessary distinctions, to harmonize everything asserted in the Bible, the creeds, the writings of the Fathers, and the acts of the councils. No significant differentiation was made between revelation and what these sources said, though in cases of irresolvable conflict it might be necessary to distinguish various levels of authority among the sources. Criticism was not totally absent, especially in the evaluation of theological and philosophical theorems, but it played a minor role in the search for the revealed datum.

In the critical period theologians became greatly preoccupied with the problem of error in the matter of revelation itself. They anxiously sought for uncontestable sources of authority, and advanced a variety of proposals.

Orthodox Protestantism, followed by Conservative Evangelicalism, has treated the Bible as the sole authority, in the sense that any other authority must be judged by the Bible. In some less sophisticated circles all statements in Scripture, even when read out of context and without the tools of modern criticism, are viewed as revealed truths. Apologetics is used to vindicate the Bible as a "divine armory" of proof-texts.

In Catholic dogmatic theology, the dogmas were frequently treated as "divinely revealed truths." They were used as premises for a deductive system in which conclusions were drawn by syllogistic reasoning with the help of naturally known truths as added premises. The conclusions, normally, were seen as having only the authority of the weaker premise. This method of dogmatic-scholastic theology, which became popular in the seventeenth century, lives on in recent neo-Scholasticism.[24]

In liberal Protestantism a more thoroughgoing attempt was made to incorporate modern critical thinking, at the expense of certain forms of authority. Some attempted to substitute the authority of the historical Jesus, as known by scientific historiography, for the crumbling authority of Scripture, but this maneuver raised more doubts than it settled. Seeking to be faithful to the intentions of liberal Protestantism, Schubert Ogden denies that faith and biblical authority have any probative value in theology. "If the claims of Christianity are meaningful and true at all," he writes, "they are so only because or insofar as they are also warranted somehow by our common experience and reason, or, at least, our common *religious* experience and reason, simply as human beings."[25] The theologian, according to Ogden, cannot properly argue from the authority of Scripture or the faith of the Church.

Postcritical theology takes a different route. Recognizing that every discipline, whether in the arts or in the sciences, depends on commitment to a community, its leaders, and its methods, this theology works unabashedly within the circle of faith. Adhering to the Christian symbols, as interpreted in the tradition and in the faith and praxis of the Church today, the theologian seeks to retrieve the wealth of meaning and wisdom contained in the multiple sources that were at the disposal of earlier theologians. Scripture and tradition are used not atomistically to provide logical premises for deductive arguments, but organically and imaginatively to provide symbols and clues so that the mind of the believer can be ever more fully attuned to the truth of revelation.

How, then, is revelation related to theology? In the symbolic or postcritical approach, revelation is accepted, at least by tacit faith, from the beginning. Insofar as it places explicit trust in the Church, with its normative sources, symbols, and traditions of interpretation, theology takes shape as a specific discipline with a distinct methodology. Revelation, rather than being presupposed as fully known from the start, is progressively elucidated as theology carries out its task. As the joint meaning of all the clues and symbols whereby God communicates himself, revelation is the source and center, the beginning and the end, of the theological enterprise.

# NOTES

## References in Notes

DS – *Enchiridion symbolorum, definitionum et declarationum de rebus fidei et morum,* edited by H. Denzinger; 32nd ed., revised by A. Schönmetzer (Freiburg im Breisgau: Herder, 1963).

The Documents of Vatican II are cited according to their Latin titles, namely:

*Apostolicam actuositatem*—Decree on the Apostolate of the Laity
*Dei Verbum*—Dogmatic Constitution on Divine Revelation
*Dignitatis Humanae*—Declaration on Religious Freedom
*Gaudium et spes*—Pastoral Constitution on the Church in the Modern World
*Lumen gentium*—Dogmatic Constitution on the Church
*Sacrosanctum Concilium*—Constitution on the Sacred Liturgy
*Unitatis redintegratio*—Decree on Ecumenism

### PREFACE

1. R. Latourelle, *Théologie de la Révélation* (Bruges: Desclée de Brouwer, 1963).
2. R. Latourelle, *Theology of Revelation* (Staten Island: Alba House, 1966).

### CHAPTER I
### THE PROBLEM OF REVELATION

1. The terms "Eastern religions" and "Western religions" are here taken in their conventional sense. The so-called Western religions were Near Eastern and Semitic in their origins, and Islam still remains predomi-

nantly such. Christianity and Judaism have in many places interpene-
trated with the culture of the West, without however becoming definitively or exclusively tied to that culture. See A. T. van Leeuwen,
*Christianity in World History: The Meeting of the Faiths of East and
West* (London: Edinburgh House Press, 1964), esp. pp. 35–45.

2. On the development of the apologetic notion of revelation since the
seventeenth century, see Peter Eicher's study, "Offenbarung als apolo-
getische Kategorie," in his *Offenbarung: Prinzip neuzeitlicher Theologie*
(Munich: Kösel, 1977), pp. 73–162; also Max Seckler, "Aufklärung and
Offenbarung" in *Christlicher Glaube in moderner Gesellschaft* (*En-
zyklopädische Bibliothek,* Teilband 21) (Freiburg: Herder, 1980), pp.
5–78. In his *Ecclesial Reflection: An Anatomy of Theological Method*
(Philadelphia: Fortress, 1982), Edward Farley shows that this development had deep roots in the classical tradition of Jewish and Christian
faith since biblical times.

3. Vatican Council I, Constitution *Dei Filius,* chap. 3 (DS 3008).

4. Emil Brunner, *Revelation and Reason* (Philadelphia: Westminster,
1946), p. 3.

5. Anselm, *Proslogium,* "Preface," in S. N. Deane (ed.), *St. Anselm:
Basic Writings* (La Salle, Ill.: Open Court, 1962), p. 2.

6. Thomas Aquinas, *Summa theologiae,* Part I, q. 1, a. 1. Cf. his *Summa
Contra Gentiles,* Bk. IV, chap. 25, and his *In Boet, de Trin.,* q. 2, a. 3,
ad 7.

7. K. Rahner, "Theology. I. Nature," in K. Rahner (ed.) *Encyclopedia
of Theology: The Concise "Sacramentum Mundi"* (New York: Seabury,
1975), p. 1687.

8. H. Bavinck, *The Philosophy of Revelation. The Stone Lectures for
1908–1909* (Grand Rapids, Mich.: Eerdmans, 1953), p. 20.

9. Ibid., p. 24.

10. W. Kasper, "Offenbarung Gottes in der Geschichte. Gotteswort in
Menschenwort," in B. Dreher and others (eds.), *Handbuch der Ver-
kündigung,* vol. 1 (Freiburg: Herder, 1970), pp. 53–96, p. 53.

11. K. Jaspers, *Philosophical Faith and Revelation* (New York: Harper
& Row, 1967), p. 17.

12. Ibid., p. 18.

13. Ibid., p. 8.

14. Ibid., p. 10.

15. Ibid., pp. 19–20.

16. Ibid., p. 333.

17. Ibid., p. 21. Cf. K. Jaspers, *The Perennial Scope of Philosophy* (New
York: Philosophical Library, 1949), p. 38.

18. *Philosophical Faith and Revelation,* p. 340.

19. Ibid., p. 342.

20. Ibid., p. 357.

21. Ibid., p. 126. Cf. pp. 141–45.

22. Ibid., p. 145.

23. Ibid., p. 325.

24. Ibid., pp. 110–12.

25. Ibid., pp. 17, 330–34.

26. Ibid., p. 116.

27. Relying on the previous work of P. Ricoeur, H. Dufrenne, and others, Cornelio Fabro expresses some sharp criticisms in his *God in Exile* (New York: Newman, 1968), pp. 894–907. Alan M. Olson, in his *Transcendence and Hermeneutics: An Interpretation of the Philosophy of Karl Jaspers* (The Hague: Nijhoff, 1979), considers the criticisms made by Bultmann, Ricoeur, and Gadamer.

28. K. Barth, *Church Dogmatics,* vol. III/4 (Edinburgh: T. & T. Clark, 1961), p. 479. Cf. K. Jaspers, *Philosophical Faith and Revelation,* pp. 325–29.

29. K. Jaspers, *Philosophical Faith and Revelation,* p. 9.

30. Ibid., p. 336.

31. F. G. Downing, *Has Christianity a Revelation?* (London: SCM Press, 1964), p. 185.

32. Ibid., p. 186.

33. Ibid., p. 286.

34. Ibid., p. 289.

35. Ibid., p. 10.

36. Ibid., p. 46.

37. Ibid., p. 160, citing H. D. McDonald, *Ideas of Revelation* (London: Macmillan, 1959), p. 2.

38. *Has Christianity a Revelation?,* pp. 198, 208, 219, etc.

39. G. O'Collins, *Foundations of Theology* (Chicago: Loyola University Press, 1971), p. 145. Cf. his *Fundamental Theology* (Ramsey, N.J.: Paulist, 1981), pp. 56–57.

40. G. O'Collins, *Foundations of Theology,* p. 142.

41. On the difficulties of demonstrating the truth or credibility of Christian revelation within the perspectives of the nonbeliever, see A. Dulles, "Fundamental Theology and the Logic of Conversion," *Thomist* 45 (1981), pp. 175–93.

42. For an exchange on this subject, see John Connelly, "The Task of Theology," *Proceedings of the Catholic Theological Society of America* 29 (1974) pp. 1–59, with responses by Schubert Ogden (pp. 59–66) and David Tracy (pp. 67–75).

43. Cf. M. Polanyi, *Personal Knowledge* (New York: Harper Torch-books, 1964), pp. 53–65.

44. The nature and status of fundamental theology are much discussed in recent literature. Of great importance is H. Stirnimann, "Erwägungen zur Fundamentaltheologie," *Freiburger Zeitschrift für Philosophie und Theologie* 24 (1977), pp. 291–365. For information concerning recent views see the articles of J.-P. Torrell and R. Latourelle in G. O'Collins and R. Latourelle (eds.), *Problems and Perspectives in Fundamental Theology* (New York: Paulist, 1982).

45. Although these seven criteria of fundamental theology are of my own devising, they partly coincide with criteria proposed by others. Langdon Gilkey, in *Naming the Whirlwind* (Indianapolis: Bobbs–Merrill, 1969), pp. 460–65, discusses the following three warrants: fidelity to the symbolic forms of the community and the tradition; relation to common secular experience; ability to generate categories that are illuminating for the whole of life.

David Tracy, in *Blessed Rage for Order* (New York: Seabury, 1975), esp. pp. 64–87, proposes criteria such as: (1) meaningfulness, in the sense of disclosive power in relation to actual experience; (2) coherence, i.e., the internal intelligibility of fundamental concepts; (3) appropriateness, in the sense of faithfulness to the meanings embodied in the tradition; and (4) adequacy in illuminating the conditions and possibilities of ordinary experience.

Langdon Gilkey in *Reaping the Whirlwind* (New York: Seabury, 1976), p. 373, note 1, and p. 378, note 33, compares his own present positions with those of Tracy.

Still more recently, in *The Analogical Imagination* (New York: Crossroad, 1981), Tracy distinguishes sharply between the criteria appropriate for fundamental, systematic, and practical theology. Church tradition, he holds, is a warrant in systematics but not in fundamental theology, which must employ "the approach and methods of some established academic discipline to explicate and adjudicate the truth-claims" under examination (p. 62).

My own criteria for fundamental theology are closer to Tracy's criteria for systematic theology. The reasons for my divergence from Tracy are indicated in the article referred to in note 41 above.

For additional literature on criteria see John McIntyre, *The Shape of Christology* (Philadelphia: Westminster, 1966), chap. 3; A. A. Glenn, "Criteria for Theological Models," *Scottish Journal of Theology* 25 (1972), pp. 296–308; and Ian Barbour, *Myths, Models, and Paradigms* (New York: Harper & Row, 1974), pp. 142–46; and D. A. Lane, *The Experience of God* (New York: Paulist, 1981), pp. 22–27.

46. Thus one may transfer to the criteria of fundamental theology what Michael Polanyi says of the premises of science: "Indeed when we try to apply any of these formulations for deciding a great question in science, we find that they prove ambiguous precisely to the extent of allowing both alternatives to be equally arguable." (*Personal Knowledge*, p. 165.)

### CHAPTER II
### THE USE OF MODELS IN REVELATION THEOLOGY

1. A. Dulles, *Revelation Theology: A History* (New York: Herder & Herder, 1969).

2. On private revelations, see L. Volken, *Visions, Revelations, and the Church* (New York: Kenedy, 1963), K. Rahner, "Visions and Prophecies," *Inquiries* (New York: Herder & Herder, 1964), pp. 88–188; P. De Letter, "Revelations (Private)," *New Catholic Encyclopedia*, vol. 12, pp. 446–48.

3. E. Troeltsch, *The Social Teaching of the Christian Churches*, 2 vols. (New York: Macmillan, 1931; German original, 1911).

4. H. R. Niebuhr, *Christ and Culture* (New York: Harper Torchbooks, 1956), pp. 43–44.

5. Cf. A. Dulles, *Revelation Theology*, pp. 171–75.

6. Ibid., pp. 177–80. For a similar approach, developed at greater length, see Friedrich von Hügel, *The Mystical Element of Religion*. (New York: Dutton, 1923), vol. 1, chap. 2, "The Three Elements of Religion," pp. 50–82.

7. Cf. A. Dulles, *Models of the Church* (Garden City, N.Y.: Doubleday & Co., 1974), chap. 11, "The Church and Revelation," pp. 166–78.

8. Matthew Lamb, *Solidarity with Victims: Toward a Theology of Social Transformation* (New York: Crossroad, 1982), p. 99.

9. Ibid., p. 87.

10. I. G. Barbour, *Myths, Models, and Paradigms* (New York: Harper & Row, 1974), p. 16.

11. Ibid., p. 30.

12. Ibid., p. 34.

13. Ibid., p. 38.

14. Cf. Vatican I, *Dei Filius*, chap. 4 (DS 3016).

15. Ibid.

16. S. Pepper, *World Hypotheses: A Study in Evidence* (Berkeley: University of California Press, 1942).

17. N. Bohr, *Atomic Theory and the Description of Nature* (Cambridge: At the University Press, 1934), p. 96; quoted by I. G. Barbour, *Myths, Models, and Paradigms*, p. 75.

CHAPTER III
MODEL ONE: REVELATION AS DOCTRINE

1. Among Evangelicals who depart somewhat from the positions of Conservative Evangelicalism as here defined one might mention prominent living American authors such as Dewey M. Beegle, Paul K. Jewett, Jack B. Rogers, Donald K. McKim, and Donald G. Bloesch. Bloesch, who argues for a kind of "catholic evangelicalism," discusses a variety of "evangelical" tendencies in his *Essentials of Evangelical Theology,* vol. 1 (San Francisco: Harper & Row, 1978), pp. 7–23.

2. B. B. Warfield, *Revelation and Inspiration* (New York: Oxford University Press, 1927), pp. 15–28.

3. Ibid., p. 28.

4. Ibid., p. 48.

5. B. B. Warfield, *The Inspiration and Authority of the Bible* (2nd ed., Philadelphia: Presbyterian and Reformed Publishing Company, 1948), p. 442.

6. C. Pinnock, *Biblical Revelation—Foundation of Christian Theology* (Chicago: Moody Press, 1971), p. 80. Some of Pinnock's more recent articles express dissatisfaction with the term "inerrancy." For discussion, see C. F. H. Henry, *God, Revelation, and Authority,* vol. 4 (Waco, Texas: Word, 1979), pp. 177–81.

7. J. A. Quenstedt, *Theologia didactico-polemica,* vol. 1 (Leipzig, 1702), p. 71; quoted by Emil Brunner, *Revelation and Reason* (Philadelphia: Westminster, 1946), p. 274, note 2.

8. A. Calov, *Systema locorum theologicorum,* vol. 1 (Wittenberg, 1655), p. 608; quoted by R. D. Preus, *The Theology of Post-Reformation Lutheranism* (St. Louis: Concordia, 1970), p. 357.

9. C. F. H. Henry, *God, Revelation, and Authority,* vol. 2 (Waco, Texas: Word, 1976), p. 87.

10. Ibid., p. 12. Cf. vol. 3 (Waco, Texas: Word, 1979), pp. 449, 453, 455.

11. G. Clark, *Karl Barth's Theological Method* (Nutley, N.J.: Presbyterian and Reformed Publishing Company, 1963), p. 150. Cf. C. F. H. Henry, *God, Revelation, and Authority,* vol. 3, p. 456.

12. F. Schaeffer, *The God Who Is There* (Chicago: Inter-Varsity Press, 1968), p. 93. Cf. C. F. H. Henry, *God, Revelation, and Authority,* vol. 3, p. 457.

13. C. Pinnock, *Biblical Revelation,* p. 66. Cf. C. F. H. Henry, *God, Revelation, and Authority,* vol. 3, p. 457.

14. J. I. Packer, "Contemporary Views of Revelation," in C. F. H. Henry

(ed.), *Revelation and the Bible* (Grand Rapids, Mich.: Baker Book House, 1958), p. 90.

15. J. I. Packer, *"Fundamentalism" and the Word of God* (Grand Rapids, Mich.: Eerdmans, 1958), pp. 91–92.

16. Specifics concerning the views here summarized are available in C. F. H. Henry, *God, Revelation, and Authority,* vol. 4.

17. B. B. Warfield, *Selected Shorter Writings,* vol. 2 (Phillipsburg, N.J.: Presbyterian and Reformed Publishing Company, 1973), p. 120.

18. G. H. Clark, *Religion, Reason, and Revelation* (Philadelphia: Presbyterian and Reformed Publishing Company, 1961), pp. 107–8.

19. C. F. H. Henry, *God, Revelation, and Authority,* vol. 3, p. 487.

20. C. F. H. Henry, *God, Revelation, and Authority* vol. 4, p. 279.

21. Ibid., p. 284. Henry draws in this connection on the work of Bernard Ramm, *The Witness of the Spirit* (Grand Rapids, Mich.: Eerdmans, 1960).

22. C. Pesch, *Praelectiones dogmaticae,* vol. 1 (5th ed., Freiburg: Herder, 1915), no. 151, p. 116.

23. Vatican I, *Constitution on Catholic Faith,* chap. 2 (DS 3005–6). Cf. C. Pesch *Praelectiones dogmaticae,* vol. 1, nos. 170–76, pp. 125–28; also M. Nicolau, "De Revelatione christiana," *Sacrae theologiae summa,* vol. 1 (Madrid: B.A.C., 2nd ed., 1952), part II, nos. 76–89, pp. 110–22.

24. H. Dieckmann, *De Revelatione christiana* (Freiburg: Herder, 1930), no. 198, p. 137.

25. Ibid., no. 199, pp. 138–39; Dieckmann's italics.

26. Ibid.

27. C. Pesch, *Praelectiones dogmaticae,* vol. 1, no. 151, p. 115. Cf. H. Dieckmann, *De Revelatione christiana,* no. 197, p. 137; nos. 215–17, pp. 150–52; and R. Garrigou–Lagrange, *De Revelatione per Ecclesiam catholicam proposita,* vol. 1 (4th ed., Rome: Ferrari, 1945), p. 141.

28. H. Dieckmann, *De Revelatione christiana,* nos. 202–3, pp. 140–41.

29. M. Nicolau, "De Revelatione christiana," part II, no. 53, p. 93.

30. Vatican I, *Constitution on Catholic Faith,* chap. 3 (DS 3011).

31. *Oath Against Modernism* (DS 3542).

32. See M. Nicolau, "De Revelatione christiana," part II, nos. 149–85; pp. 158–85.

33. The role of the infused light of faith is acutely discussed by R. Garrigou–Lagrange, *De Revelatione,* vol. 1, pp. 427–81, and by J. Alfaro, *Fides, Spes, Caritas* (Rome: Pontificia Universitas Gregoriana, 1963), pp. 281–91, and on the "instinctus interior," pp. 445–58. Each of these authors gives abundant citations from St. Thomas.

34. Pius XII, *Humani generis,* no. 25 (DS 3884).

35. Ibid., no. 29 (DS 3885).

36. Vatican I, *Constitution on Catholic Faith*, chap. 2 (DS 3006).

37. Cf. Leo XIII, Encyclical *Providentissimus Deus* (1893) (DS 3292).

38. M. Nicolau, "De Sacra scriptura," *Sacrae theologiae summa*, vol. 1, part IV, no. 176, p. 1044.

39. G. van Noort, *Dogmatic Theology*, vol. 3, *The Sources of Revelation* (Westminster: Newman, 1961, 1963), no. 191, p. 205. See also M. Nicolau, "De Revelatione christiana," part II, no. 58, p. 97; "De Sacra scriptura," part IV, no. 103, p. 1006.

40. "Pari pietatis affectu ac reverentia," Council of Trent, Sess. IV (1546), *Decretum de libris sacris et de traditionibus recipiendis* (DS 1501).

41. G. van Noort, *Dogmatic Theology*, vol. 3, no. 138, p. 139.

42. *God, Revelation, and Authority*, vol. 1, pp. 238–39.

43. "The mechanism of commitment is such that it is commitment to a particular explanation or formulation of meaning and to the stream of collective experience or religious organization that bears it. In its most intense and typical form it is total, undifferentiated, and unreserved attachment. . . . Commitment to a high-demand meaning movement also seems to produce a missionary zeal, a warmth and eagerness to share the newfound meaning with others, which can be admirable," Dean M. Kelley, *Why Conservative Churches Are Growing* (New York: Harper & Row, 1972), pp. 158–59.

44. Ray L. Hart, *Unfinished Man and the Imagination* (New York: Herder & Herder, 1968), p. 80; Hart's italics.

45. Some of the difficulties from modern biblical scholarship are indicated in R. E. Brown, *The Critical Meaning of the Bible* (Ramsey, N.J.: Paulist, 1981), chap. I.

46. The Congregation for the Doctrine of the Faith, in its 1973 Declaration, *Mysterium Ecclesiae*, made a guarded admission of the need to reinterpret previous statements of the official magisterium: "It sometimes happens that some dogmatic truth is first expressed incompletely (but not falsely) and at a later date, when considered in a broader context of faith or human knowledge, it receives a fuller and more perfect expression. . . . Finally, even though the truths which the Church intends to teach through her dogmatic formulas are distinct from the changeable conceptions of a given epoch and can be expressed without them, nevertheless it can sometimes happen that these truths may be enunciated by the Sacred Magisterium in terms that bear traces of such conceptions." See translation in *Catholic Mind*, vol. 71, no. 1276 (Oct. 1973), p. 59.

47. M. Blondel, *History and Dogma* (New York: Holt, Rinehart and Winston, 1964), pp. 265–66.

48. Ibid., p. 266.

49. M. Polanyi, *Personal Knowledge* (New York: Harper Torchbooks, 1964), p. 53.

50. Pius XII, *Humani generis,* nos. 30, 36 (DS 3886). The concept of theology conveyed by the words here quoted is somewhat broadened by the concession that theology becomes sterile unless it continually rejuvenates itself by a return to the sources, which contain inexhaustible treasures.

CHAPTER IV
MODEL TWO: REVELATION AS HISTORY

1. J. Baillie, *The Idea of Revelation in Recent Thought* (New York: Columbia University Press, 1956), pp. 49–50.

2. D. H. Kelsey, *The Uses of Scripture in Recent Theology* (Philadelphia: Fortress, 1975), p. 32.

3. J. Barr, "Revelation Through History in the Old Testament and in Modern Theology," in M. E. Marty and D. G. Peerman (eds.), *New Theology No. 1* (New York: Macmillan, 1964), p. 62. This is a reprint of Barr's inaugural address at Princeton Seminary, December 1962, originally published in *Interpretation: A Journal of Bible and Theology* 17 (1963), pp. 193–205. See also J. Barr, "The Concepts of History and Revelation," *Old and New in Interpretation* (London: SCM Press, 1966), chap. III, pp. 65–102.

4. "Revelation and Its Mode," Lecture 12 of *Nature, Man and God* (London: Macmillan, 1935), pp. 301–27.

5. W. Temple in J. Baillie and H. Martin (eds.), *Revelation* (London: Faber & Faber, 1937), p. 107. Cf. *Nature, Man and God,* p. 312.

6. G. E. Wright, *God Who Acts: Biblical Theology as Recital.* Studies in Biblical Theology No. 8 (London: SCM, 1952), p. 12.

7. Ibid., p. 107.

8. Ibid., p. 84.

9. Ibid., pp. 23–24.

10. Ibid., p. 57.

11. Ibid., p. 83.

12. Ibid., p. 43. Cf. G. E. Wright, *The Book of The Acts of God* (Garden City, N.Y.: Doubleday & Co., 1959), p. 73.

13. Ibid., p. 86.

14. O. Cullmann, *Christ and Time* (Philadelphia: Westminster Press, 1950; rev. ed., 1964). Cf. O. Cullmann's *Salvation in History* (New York: Harper & Row, 1967), in which he restates his position in comparison with the view of various other theologians. The views of Cullmann on salvation history are summarized in Mary C. Boys, *Biblical Interpreta-*

*tion in Religious Education* (Birmingham, Ala.: Religious Education Press 1980), pp. 34–49.

15. *Salvation in History*, p. 90.

16. See, for instance, ibid., p. 98.

17. Ibid., pp. 55, 154, 156.

18. *Christ and Time*, p. 98.

19. J. Daniélou, *The Lord of History* (Chicago: Regnery, 1958), p. 111.

20. For an account of Troeltsch's critique of salvation history see T. W. Ogletree, *Christian Faith and History* (Nashville, Tenn.: Abingdon, 1956), pp. 32–37.

21. W. Pannenberg, "Redemptive Event and History," in his *Basic Questions in Theology*, vol. 1 (Philadelphia: Fortress, 1970), pp. 41–42. See also Pannenberg's "Introduction" in W. Pannenberg and others, *Revelation as History* (New York: Macmillan, 1968), esp. pp. 18–19.

22. W. Pannenberg, "Response to the Discussion," in J. M. Robinson and J. B. Cobb, Jr. (eds.), *Theology as History* (New York: Harper & Row, 1967), pp. 247–48.

23. *Revelation as History*, p. 137. Cf. W. Pannenberg, *Faith and Reality* (Philadelphia: Westminster, 1977), pp. 61–63.

24. *Revelation as History*, pp. 135–39.

25. Ibid., pp. 152–55. Cf. *Theology as History*, pp. 256–58.

26. *Revelation as History*, pp. 139–45.

27. B. B. Warfield, *Revelation and Inspiration* (New York: Oxford University Press, 1927), pp. 12–13.

28. Cf. J. Barr, "Revelation Through History," pp. 65, 70.

29. Ibid., p. 66.

30. Ibid., p. 72.

31. Ibid., p. 73.

32. L. Gilkey, "Cosmology, Ontology, and the Travail of Biblical Language," *Journal of Religion* 41 (1961), pp. 194–205.

33. A. Darlap, "Fundamentale Theologie der Heilsgeschichte," *Mysterium Salutis. Grundriss heilsgeschichtlicher Dogmatik,* vol. 1 (Einsiedeln: Benziger, 1965), pp. 3–156; K. Rahner, "History of the World and Salvation-History," *Theological Investigations*, vol. 5 (Baltimore: Helicon, 1966), pp. 97–114.

34. W. Pannenberg, *Jesus—God and Man* (Philadelphia: Westminster, 1968), p. 89. See the whole section, "Jesus' Resurrection as a Historical Problem," pp. 88–106.

35. J. Moltmann, *Theology of Hope* (London: SCM Press, 1967), p. 82.

36. C. F. H. Henry, *God, Revelation, and Authority*, vol. 2 (Waco, Texas: Word, 1976), p. 303.

37. C. Braaten, *History and Hermeneutics* (New Directions in Theology,

vol. 2) (Philadelphia: Westminster, 1966), pp. 46–47. It is not clear to me whether Braaten fully accepts the objection here expressed.

38. W. Pannenberg, *Jesus—God and Man*, p. 107.

39. E. Schillebeeckx, "Revelation-in-Reality and Revelation-in-Word" in his *Revelation and Theology*, vol. 1 (New York: Sheed & Ward, 1967), pp. 33–41. Also R. Latourelle, *Theology of Revelation* (Staten Island: Alba House, 1966), pp. 315–20, 348–51.

40. *Dei Verbum*, art. 2.

41. P. C. Hodgson, *Jesus—Word and Presence* (Philadelphia: Fortress, 1971), p. 96. Hodgson is here summarizing the views expressed by Maurice Merleau–Ponty in his *Phenomenology of Perception* (London: Routledge & Kegan Paul, 1962).

42. Otto Procksch, Rudolf Bultmann, and Gerhard Ebeling are summarized by Hodgson as holding the "word" in the Hebrew Scripture is a "happening word" and thus a "word-event." Hodgson also points out, with references to Heidegger, that the Greek term *logos* (word) originally had the character of *power* just as clearly as did the Hebrew *dabar*. See *Jesus—Word and Presence*, pp. 74–79.

CHAPTER V

MODEL THREE: REVELATION AS INNER EXPERIENCE

1. A. Sabatier, *Outlines of a Philosophy of Religion Based on Psychology and History* (London: Hodder & Stoughton, 1897), p. 34.

2. N. Söderblom, *The Nature of Revelation* (Philadelphia: Fortress, 1966), p. 41.

3. G. Tyrrell, *Through Scylla and Charybdis* (London: Longmans, Green, 1907), p. 281.

4. *Outlines*, p. 65.

5. Ibid., p. 54.

6. W. R. Inge, *Faith and Its Psychology* (New York: Scribner's, 1910), pp. 239–40.

7. W. Herrmann, *Der Begriff der Offenbarung*, p. 22; quoted by A. E. Garvie, *The Ritschlian Theology* (Edinburgh: T. & T. Clark, 1902), p. 201.

8. *Der Begriff*, pp. 10–11. Cf. A. E. Garvie, *The Ritschlian Theology*, p. 199.

9. K. Rahner, "Mysticism," *Encyclopedia of Theology: The Concise "Sacramentum Mundi"* (New York: Seabury, 1975), p. 1010. For a fuller discussion of the significance of the experience of grace for the theology of revelation, see P. Fransen, "Divine Revelation: Source of Man's Faith," in P. Surlis (ed.), *Faith: Its Nature and Meaning* (Dublin: Gill & Macmillan), pp. 18–52.

10. K. Rahner, "Mysticism," p. 1010.

11. K. Rahner, "Observations on the Concept of Revelation," in K. Rahner and J. Ratzinger, *Revelation and Tradition* (New York: Herder & Herder, 1966), pp. 9–25, esp. pp. 14–17; also K. Rahner, *Foundations of Christian Faith* (New York: Seabury, 1978), pp. 129–31, 148–52, 171–72. In "The Experience of God Today" [*Theological Investigations*, vol. 11 (New York: Seabury, 1974), p. 164], Rahner holds that the unthematic experience of God is "the ever living source of that conscious manifestation which we call 'revelation.'"

12. *Outlines*, p. 35.

13. Ibid., p. 47.

14. W. E. Hocking, *The Meaning of God in Human Experience* (New Haven: Yale University Press, 1963), p. 448.

15. Ibid., p. 457.

16. F. Schleiermacher, *On Religion: Speeches to Its Cultured Despisers* (New York: Harper Torchbooks, 1958), p. 90.

17. F. Schleiermacher, *The Christian Faith* (New York: Harper Torchbooks, 1963), vol. 1, p. 77.

18. *Outlines*, p. 60.

19. Ibid., pp. 322–25.

20. Ibid., p. 46.

21. G. Tyrrell, *Through Scylla*, pp. 326–27 et passim.

22. Ibid., pp. 334–35.

23. Ibid., pp. 329–30. Cf. F. M. O'Connor, "George Tyrrell and Dogma," *Downside Review* 85 (1967), pp. 16–34, 160–82, esp. pp. 164–66.

24. *Meaning of God*, p. 459.

25. E. Underhill, *The Essentials of Mysticism* (New York: E. P. Dutton, 1960), p. 4.

26. See note 7 above.

27. W. Herrmann, *The Communion of the Christian with God* (Philadelphia: Fortress, 1971), pp. 197–99.

28. *Nature of Revelation*, p. 78.

29. Ibid., p. 82.

30. Ibid., p. 78.

31. Ibid., p. 85.

32. C. H. Dodd, *The Authority of the Bible* (first published, 1929; New York: Harper Torchbooks, rev. ed., 1960), p. 27.

33. Ibid., pp. 264–65.

34. Ibid., p. 34.

35. Ibid., p. 264.

36. Ibid., p. 37.

37. *Outlines*, p. 63.

38. Ibid., p. 64.

39. *Nature of Revelation*, p. 157.

40. *Outlines*, pp. 35–36.

41. Ibid., pp. 62–63.

42. G. Tyrrell, *Lex Orandi* (London: Longmans, Green, 1904), p. xxxi; also his "Revelation as Experience," *Heythrop Journal* 12 (1971), p. 147.

43. *Lex Orandi*, p. 209.

44. *Faith and Its Psychology*, p. 136. Cf. p. 81.

45. *Nature of Revelation*, p. 118.

46. *Authority of the Bible*, p. 271.

47. C. F. H. Henry, *God, Revelation, and Authority*, vol. 4 (Waco, Texas: Word, 1979), p. 284, (quoted above, chap. III, note 21). Cf. C. F. H. Henry's "Supplementary Note: Calvin on the Spirit's Work of Illumination," pp. 290–95.

48. *Meaning of God*, p. 451.

49. *Authority of the Bible*, p. 271.

50. Cf. G. Tyrrell, *Through Scylla*, p. 284.

51. C. H. Dodd, *The Bible Today* (first published, 1946; Cambridge: At the University Press, paperback reprint, 1961), pp. 106–7.

52. F. Schleiermacher, *On Religion*, p. 91.

53. W. James, *The Varieties of Religious Experience* (New York: Mentor Books, 1958), p. 326.

54. Ibid., p. 387.

55. A. H. Maslow, *Religions, Values, and Peak-Experiences* (Columbus: Ohio State University Press, 1964), pp. 19–20, 28.

56. W. James, *Varieties*, p. 195. Cf. pp. 366, 389; italics his.

57. On the necessity of transcending the psychological approach, see W. Pannenberg, "Toward a Theology of the History of Religions," *Basic Questions in Theology*, vol. 2 (Philadelphia: Fortress, 1971), pp. 96–118.

58. Söderblom himself acknowledged: "The comparative study of religions in general leaves the question about revelation open," *The Living God* (London: Oxford University Press, 1933), p. 384. The same is true of an empirical psychology of religious phenomena.

59. See John E. Smith, *Experience and God* (New York: Oxford University Press, 1968); Paul Marceau, "The Christian Experience of God," *Communio* 4 (1977), pp. 3–18.

60. John E. Smith, *Experience and God*, p. 52.

61. Ibid., p. 66.

62. E. Schillebeeckx, *Interim Report on the Books* Jesus *and* Christ (New York: Crossroad, 1981), p. 11.

63. Ibid., p. 13: and more fully in E. Schillebeeckx, *Christ—The Experi-*

*ence of Jesus as Lord* (New York: Seabury, Crossroad, 1980), pp. 49–54.

64. E. Schillebeeckx, *Jesus—An Experiment in Christology* (New York: Seabury, Crossroad, 1979), pp. 392–93, 548–49.

65. *Interim Report*, pp. 15–16.

66. Louis Dupré, "Experience and Interpretation: A Philosophical Reflection on Schillebeeckx' *Jesus* and *Christ*," *Theological Studies* 43 (1982), pp. 30–51, esp. pp. 43–44.

67. Ibid., p. 45.

CHAPTER VI

MODEL FOUR: REVELATION AS DIALECTICAL PRESENCE

1. K. Barth *Church Dogmatics*, Vol. I/1 (Edinburgh: T. & T. Clark, 1975), p. 304.

2. Ibid., p. 320. Cf. pp. 175, 330, 363.

3. R. Bultmann, *Existence and Faith* (New York: Meridian Books, 1960), p. 30.

4. R. Bultmann, *The Gospel of John* (Philadelphia: Westminster, 1971), p. 161.

5. Ibid., p. 361.

6. E. Brunner, *Revelation and Reason* (Philadelphia: Westminster, 1946), p. 24.

7. Ibid., p. 171.

8. K. Barth, *Church Dogmatics*, vol. IV/3, first half (Edinburgh: T. & T. Clark, 1961), p. 97.

9. K. Barth in J. Baillie and H. Martin (eds.), *Revelation* (London: Faber & Faber, 1937), p. 53.

10. Ibid.

11. *Existence and Faith*, p. 75.

12. *Revelation and Reason*, p. 112; *The Christian Doctrine of God* (*Dogmatics*, vol. 1) (Philadelphia: Westminster, 1950), p. 15.

13. This is not to deny that God addresses humanity through the cosmos —a theme affirmed with various nuances by Brunner, Bultmann, and eventually by Barth himself. On Barth's handling of this theme see Hans Urs von Balthasar, *The Theology of Karl Barth* (New York: Holt, Rinehart and Winston, 1971), pp. 140–42.

14. *Church Dogmatics*, vol. II/1 (Edinburgh: T. & T. Clark, 1957), p. 168.

15. E. Brunner, "Die Offenbarung als Grund und Gegenstand der Theologie" (1925), in J. Moltmann (ed.), *Anfänge der dialektischen Theologie*, part I (Munich: Kaiser, 1966), pp. 311–12.

16. R. Bultmann, "Faith (New Testament)" in R. Bultmann and A. Weiser, *Faith* (Bible Key Words) (London: A. & C. Black, 1961), p. 86.

17. *Church Dogmatics,* vol. I/1, p. 409. Cf. J. Baillie and H. Martin, *Revelation,* pp. 74–75.

18. E. Brunner, "Gesetz und Offenbarung" (1925) in J. Moltmann, *Anfänge,* p. 29.

19. *The Gospel of John,* p. 605.

20. Ibid., p. 47.

21. In J. Baille and H. Martin, *Revelation,* p. 67. Cf. *Church Dogmatics,* vol. I/1, pp. 131–33.

22. K. Barth, *The Word of God and the Word of Man* (New York: Harper Torchbooks, 1957), esp. chap. 6, "The Word of God and the Task of the Ministry, pp. 183–217.

23. *Church Dogmatics,* vol. I/2 (Edinburgh: T. & T. Clark, 1956), pp. 529–30.

24. E. Brunner, *Truth as Encounter* (Philadelphia: Westminster, 1964), p. 137.

25. P. K. Jewett, *Emil Brunner's Theology of Revelation* (London: James Clarke & Co., 1954), p. 74.

26. *The Gospel of John,* pp. 606–7 (commenting on Jn 14:6). Cf. p. 164.

27. *Existence and Faith,* p. 85; italics Bultmann's.

28. Ibid., p. 100.

29. Ibid., p. 90.

30. P. K. Jewett, *Brunner's Theology of Revelation,* p. 135.

31. R. Bultmann, *Jesus Christ and Mythology* (London: SCM Press, 1960), p. 71.

32. *Existence and Faith,* p. 79.

33. Ibid., p. 89. Cf. *Gospel of John,* p. 607.

34. *Church Dogmatics,* vol. I/2, p. 249.

35. *Revelation and Reason,* p. 33.

36. "Die Offenbarung als Grund," p. 317.

37. *Existence and Faith,* p. 79.

38. K. Barth, *Protestant Theology in the Nineteenth Century* (Valley Forge, Pa.: Judson Press, 1975), p. 442.

39. *Church Dogmatics,* vol. I/1, p. 305.

40. *Revelation and Reason,* pp. 205–6.

41. "Gesetz und Offenbarung," p. 295.

42. *The Gospel of John,* p. 266 (commenting on Jn 5:37–38).

43. K. Barth, *Epistle to the Romans* (London: Oxford University Press, Galaxy Books, 1968), p. 203.

44. Ibid., p. 204. On the subsequent disappearance and reappearance of

the term "Urgeschichte" in Barth's theology, one may consult E. Jüngel, *The Doctrine of the Trinity* (Grand Rapids, Mich.: Eerdmans, 1976), pp. 75–76.

45. E. Brunner, *The Mediator* (London: Lutterworth, 1934), pp. 355–56.

46. This point is effectively made by A. Richardson, *History Sacred and Profane* (Philadelphia: Westminster, 1964), pp. 132–33.

47. R. Bultmann, *Theology of the New Testament,* vol. 1. (New York: Scribner's, 1951), p. 26.

48. On these terms in Fuchs and Ebeling, see J. M. Robinson, "Hermeneutic Since Barth," in J. M. Robinson and J. B. Cobb, Jr., (eds.), *The New Hermeneutic* (New York: Harper & Row, 1965), pp. 57–58.

49. The Barthian point of view is reflected in Wilhelm Vischer, *The Witness of the Old Testament to Christ* (London: Lutterworth, 1936).

50. Luther gives these titles to Christ in his *Lectures on Galatians* (1535). See *Martin Luthers Werke: kritische Gesamtausgabe,* vol. 40[1] (Weimar: H. Böhaus, 1911), pp. 458–59; English trans. in *Luther's Works,* vol. 26 (Philadelphia and St. Louis: Concordia, 1963), p. 295. Discussion of this principle may be found in P. Althaus, *The Theology of Martin Luther* (Philadelphia: Fortress, 1966), pp. 79–81.

51. Cf. G. Ebeling, *Dogmatik des christlichen Glaubens,* vol. 1 Tübingen: Mohr, 1979), p. 252.

52. The "new Protestantism" of Barth, Brunner, and Bultmann was vehemently rejected by Cornelius Van Til in his *Christianity and Barthianism* (Philadelphia: Presbyterian and Reformed Publishing Company, 1962), and continues to be criticized in standard works such as C. F. H. Henry's *God, Revelation, and Authority,* vols. 1–4 (Waco, Texas: Word, 1976, 1979).

53. D. H. Kelsey, *The Uses of Scripture in Recent Theology* (Philadelphia: Fortress, 1975), p. 209.

54. H. U. von Balthasar, *Theology of Karl Barth,* p. 71.

55. L. Gilkey, *Naming the Whirlwind* (Indianapolis: Bobbs–Merrill, 1969), p. 97.

56. Ibid., pp. 92–95; also V. A. Harvey, *The Historian and the Believer* (New York: Macmillan, 1966), pp. 127–63.

57. In his *Church Dogmatics,* vol. I/2, pp. 12–13, Barth severely attacks the nineteenth century "positive" theologians who separated off *Heilsgeschichte* as a section of universal history. For Barth's own position, see esp. pp. 56–58.

58. The positions of Fritz Buri and Schubert Ogden are summarized by V. A. Harvey, *The Historian and the Believer,* pp. 165–68.

59. On the post-Bultmannians see H. Zahrnt, *The Historical Jesus* (Lon-

don: Collins, 1963); also V. A. Harvey, *The Historian and the Believer*, pp. 168–203.

60. G. E. Wright, *The Old Testament and Theology* (New York: Harper & Row, 1969), chap. 1.

61. K. Barth, *Church Dogmatics*, vol. I/2, p. 326. Already in his *Epistle to the Romans* (pp. 183–84), Barth had said: "Religion is the ability of men to receive and to retain an impress of God's revelation; it is the capacity to reproduce and give visible expression to the transformation of the old into the new man—so that it becomes a conscious human expression and a conscious and creative human activity."

62. Emil Brunner consistently held that the primacy of revelation does not exclude, but positively demands, both *analogia fidei* and *analogia entis*. In the cases of Bultmann and Barth, their move from dialectical to analogous discourse is more qualified and more debatable, but the argument for such a move has recently been restated in David Tracy, *The Analogical Imagination* (New York: Crossroad, 1981), pp. 415–21, 425–26.

63. "Creator and creature are to be perfect, each in its own way, because between them no similarity can be found so great but that the dissimilarity is even greater," Lateran Council IV, chap. 2 (DS 806).

CHAPTER VII
MODEL FIVE: REVELATION AS NEW AWARENESS

1. H. de Lubac, *Teilhard de Chardin: The Man and His Meaning* (New York: Mentor Omega, 1965), p. 168; also in H. de Lubac, *The Religion of Teilhard de Chardin* (New York: Desclee, 1967), p. 182. The quotation is from Teilhard's unpublished *Introduction à la vie chrétienne*.

2. The last three quotations are from Teilhard de Chardin, "Outline of a Dialectic of Spirit," *Activation of Engery* (London: Collins, 1970), p. 148.

3. P. Teilhard de Chardin, *Christianity and Evolution* (New York: Harcourt Brace Jovanovich, 1971), p. 143; cited in R. W. Kropf, *Teilhard, Scripture and Revelation* (Rutherford, N.J.: Fairleigh Dickinson University Press, 1980), p. 264.

4. Ursula King, *Towards a New Mysticism: Teilhard de Chardin and Eastern Religions* (New York: Seabury, 1980), p. 178.

5. R. W. Kropf, *Teilhard*, p. 273.

6. Ibid., pp. 276–79.

7. Ibid., p. 283.

8. Ibid., p. 287.

9. Ibid., pp. 289–90.

10. K. Rahner, "Observations on the Concept of Revelation," in K. Rahner and J. Ratzinger, *Revelation and Tradition* (New York: Herder & Herder, 1966), p. 12.

11. Ibid., pp. 14–15.

12. K. Rahner, "Theology and Anthropology," in T. P. Burke (ed.), *The Word in History* (New York: Sheed & Ward, 1966), pp. 1–23.

13. T. F. O'Meara, "Toward a Subjective Theology of Revelation," *Theological Studies* 26 (1975), pp. 401–27, esp. p. 415.

14. Ibid., pp. 420–21, quoting K. Rahner, "Revelation," *Theological Dictionary* (New York: Herder & Herder, 1965), p. 411.

15. G. Moran, *Theology of Revelation* (New York: Herder & Herder, 1966), pp. 50–51.

16. G. Moran, *The Present Revelation* (New York: Herder & Herder, 1972), p. 265.

17. Ibid., p. 111. Cf. p. 118.

18. G. Baum, *Faith and Doctrine* (New York: Newman, 1969), p. 27.

19. G. Baum, Foreword to A. M. Greeley, *The New Agenda* (Garden City, N.Y. Doubleday & Co., 1973), p. 16.

20. G. Baum, *Faith and Doctrine*, p. 27.

21. G. Baum, Foreword to A. M. Greeley, *New Agenda*, pp. 25–29; also G. Baum contribution to J. Kirvan (ed.), *The Infallibility Debate* (New York: Paulist, 1971), esp. pp. 18–26.

22. P. Tillich, *Systematic Theology* vol. 1 (Chicago: University of Chicago Press, 1951), p. 145.

23. Ibid., p. 110.

24. Ibid.

25. L. Gilkey, *Naming the Whirlwind* (Indianapolis: Bobbs–Merrill, 1969), p. 296.

26. Ibid., p. 465.

27. Ibid., p. 450.

28. R. W. Kropf, *Teilhard*, p. 284.

29. E. R. Baltazar, *Teilhard and the Supernatural* (Baltimore: Helicon, 1966), p. 177.

30. E. R. Baltazar, *God Within Process* (New York: Newman, 1970), pp. 175–78.

31. R. L. Hart, *Unfinished Man and the Imagination* (New York: Seabury, Crossroad, 1979), p. 182.

32. Ibid., pp. 281–83.

33. Ibid., p. 283.

34. Ibid., p. 289; quoting F. Schleiermacher, *Christian Faith*, p. 50.

35. E. Fontinell, *Toward a Reconstruction of Religion* (Garden City, N.Y.: Doubleday & Co., 1970), pp. 84, 258.

36. Ibid., pp. 100–4.

37. G. Moran, "The God of Revelation," in D. Callahan (ed.), *God, Jesus, Spirit* (New York: Herder & Herder, 1969), p. 11.

38. R. W. Kropf, *Teilhard*, pp. 289–90.

39. E. R. Baltazar, *Teilhard and the Supernatural*, p. 177.

40. G. Baum, *Man Becoming* (New York: Herder & Herder, 1970), p. 34. Cf. G. Baum, "Vatican II's Constitution on Revelation," *Theological Studies* 28 (1967), pp. 51–75.

41. *Man Becoming*, p. 101.

42. Ibid., p. 116.

43. L. Dewart, *The Future of Belief* (New York: Herder & Herder, 1966), p. 116, note 26.

44. Ibid., p. 99.

45. Ibid., p. 112.

46. G. Moran, "The God of Revelation," p. 7.

47. G. Moran, *The Present Revelation*, p. 125.

48. R. L. Hart, *Unfinished Man*, pp. 281–83.

49. Ibid., p. 304.

50. Ibid., p. 306.

51. E. Fontinell, *Toward a Reconstruction*, p. 106.

52. G. Baum, Foreword to *New Agenda*, p. 30.

53. W. M. Thompson, *Christ and Consciousness* (New York: Paulist, 1966), p. 50.

54. Vatican II, *Gaudium et spes*, no. 11.

55. G. Baum, *Man Becoming*, p. 27.

56. G. Baum, *New Horizon* (New York: Paulist, 1972), p. 56.

57. G. Moran, "The God of Revelation," p. 11.

58. Vatican II, *Gaudium et spes*, no. 36.

59. T. F. O'Meara, "Toward a Subjective Theology," p. 418; italics in original.

60. G. Moran, *Design for Religion* (New York: Herder & Herder, 1970), p. 40.

61. *Christ and Consciousness*, p. 172.

62. J. Hick, "Jesus and the World Religions," J. Hick (ed.), *The Myth of God Incarnate* (Philadelphia: Westminster, 1977), p. 180.

63. J. Hick, *God and the Universe of Faiths* (London: Macmillan, 1973), p. 141.

64. G. Moran, *Present Revelation*, p. 43.

65. Ibid., p. 45.

66. Ibid.

67. J. P. Mackey, *Problems in Religious Faith* (Dublin: Helicon, 1972) p. 191. A somewhat similar observation had been made earlier by Alan Richardson in his *History Sacred and Profane* (Philadelphia: Westminster, 1964), p. 224, note 1: "We do not here speak of 'revelation,' since this is an interpretative concept used by dogmatic theologians and apologists." Richardson, adhering to the more phenomenological terms of I. T. Ramsey, spoke rather of "disclosure situations," "discernment of meaning," and "commitment."

68. J. P. Mackey, "The Theology of Faith: A Bibliographical Survey (and More)," *Horizons* 2 (1975), pp. 207–37, esp. p. 235.

69. W. M. Thompson, *Christ and Consciousness,* p. 170.

70. Ibid., p. 172.

71. Ibid., p. 174, note 18. Cf. p. 163.

72. G. Baum, *New Horizon,* p. 56.

73. Teilhard de Chardin criticized William James's *Varieties of Religious Experience* and Aldous Huxley's *Perennial Philosophy* for treating the religious problem as a strictly individual one, intelligible outside the context of an evolving humanity. See R. W. Kropf, *Teilhard,* pp. 270–71.

74. *Gaudium et spes,* no. 5.

75. Ibid., no. 7.

76. Text in DS 3542.

77. J. P. Mackey, "The Theology of Faith," p. 213.

78. We shall return in later chapters to the questions of the culmination of revelation in Jesus Christ and the presence of revelation in the non-Christian religions.

79. J. Maritain, *The Peasant of the Garonne* (New York: Holt, Rinehart and Winston, 1968), p. 54.

80. Ibid., p. 119, with quotations from Etienne Gilson and Charles Journet to the same effect.

81. K. Barth, *Letters 1961–1968* (Grand Rapids, Mich.: Eerdmans, 1981), p. 117.

82. As cited above, note 72.

### CHAPTER VIII
### THE MODELS COMPARED

1. M. Polanyi, *Personal Knowledge* (New York: Harper Torchbooks, 1964), pp. 110–17.

2. H. R. Niebuhr, *The Meaning of Revelation* (first published, 1941; New York: Macmillan paperback ed., 1960), p. 80.

3. Ibid., p. 138.

4. B. Lonergan, *Method in Theology* (New York: Herder & Herder, 1972), chap. X, "Dialectic," pp. 235–66.

5. Ibid., p. 241. Cf. K. Rahner, *Hearers of the Word* (New York: Herder & Herder, 1969), p. 24.

6. John Calvin spoke of the Holy Scriptures as the spectacles which focus our blurred vision and gather up for us "the otherwise confused knowledge of God in our minds." *Institutes of the Christian Religion,* Book I, chap. 6, no. 1. In Chapter 14, no. 1, he repeats this image and adds that of a mirror. Vatican Council II taught that sacred tradition and sacred Scripture together resemble "a mirror in which the pilgrim Church on earth looks at God, from whom she has received everything, until she is brought finally to see Him as He is, face to face (cf. 1 Jn 3:2)," *Dei Verbum,* art. 7.

## CHAPTER IX
### SYMBOLIC MEDIATION

1. Quoted from an unpublished manuscript in Stephen Happel, "Response to William Van Roo," *Proceedings of the Catholic Theological Society of America* 32 (1977), p. 119.

2. W. B. Yeats, "William Blake and His Illustrations to the Divine Comedy," *Collected Works,* vol. 6 (Stratford-on-Avon: Shakespeare Head Press, 1908), p. 138.

3. P. Ricoeur, *The Symbolism of Evil* (Boston: Beacon, 1969); see esp. the Introduction and Conclusion. Also, P. Ricoeur, "The Hermeneutics of Symbols and Philosophical Reflection," *International Philosophical Quarterly* 2 (1962), pp. 191–218.

4. R. H. Wheelwright, *Metaphor and Reality* (Bloomington: Indiana University Press, 1962), p. 94.

5. M. Polanyi and H. Prosch, *Meaning* (Chicago: University of Chicago Press, 1975), pp. 69–75.

6. W. M. Urban, *Language and Reality* (London: Allen & Unwin, 1939), pp. 433, 470–71.

7. R. H. Wheelwright, *Metaphor and Reality,* pp. 92–98; P. Ricoeur, *Interpretation Theory* (Fort Worth: Texas Christian University Press, 1976), pp. 45–69.

8. John Macquarrie, *God-Talk* (London: SCM Press, 1967), p. 169, quoting W. M. Urban, *Humanity and Deity* (London: Allen & Unwin, 1951), p. 89. Cf. W. M. Urban, *Language and Reality,* pp. 591–92.

9. Cf. P. Ricoeur, *Interpretation Theory,* pp. 55–56.

10. Norman Perrin, *Jesus and the Language of the Kingdom* (Philadelphia: Fortress, 1976), p. 202.

11. Mircea Eliade, *Patterns in Comparative Religion* (New York: Sheed & Ward, 1958), p. 447.

12. For a more developed statement of the argument from Scripture, see John E. Smith, *Reason and God* (New Haven: Yale University Press, 1961) pp. 227–47. Smith draws here on the earlier work of Wilbur M. Urban and others.

13. A. Richardson, *History Sacred and Profane* (Philadelphia: Westminster, 1964), pp. 223–27.

14. L. Monden, *Faith: Can Man Still Believe?* (New York: Sheed & Ward, 1970), p. 10.

15. N. Perrin, *Jesus and the Language of the Kingdom* (Philadelphia: Fortress, 1976), p. 33.

16. The three properties of symbol discussed in the following paragraphs may be compared with the six examined by M. Eliade in his "Methodological Remarks on the Study of Religious Symbolism" in M. Eliade and J. M. Kitagawa, eds., *The History of Religions* (Chicago: University of Chicago Press, 1959), pp. 98–103. According to Eliade, religious symbols (1) disclose modalities of the real not evident in ordinary experience, (2) refer to real structures of the world, (3) are multivalent, (4) reveal perspectives in which heterogeneous realities can be articulated into a whole, (5) make it possible to express paradoxical situations otherwise inexpressible, and (6) addresses situations in which human existence is engaged.

17. N. Mitchell, "Symbols Are Actions, Not Objects," *Living Worship* 13/2 (Feb. 1977), pp. 1–2.

18. Victor White, *God and the Unconscious* (Cleveland, Ohio: Meridian, 1952), pp. 233–34.

19. Cf. A. Dulles, "Symbol in Revelation," *New Catholic Encyclopedia* 13 (1967), pp. 861–63.

20. P. Tillich, *Dynamics of Faith* (New York: Harper, 1957), p. 42.

21. T. Carlyle, *Sartor Resartus,* part 3, chap. 3; quoted by R. H. Wheelwright, *Metaphor and Reality,* pp. 95–96.

22. M. Polanyi and H. Prosch, *Meaning,* pp. 66–71.

23. P. Ricoeur, *Symbolism of Evil,* p. 348.

24. M. Eliade, *Patterns in Comparative Religion,* pp. 455.

25. M. Eliade, "Methodological Remarks," pp. 99–100.

26. *Dei Verbum,* art. 5.

27. *Patterns in Comparative Religion,* p. 419.

28. P. Tillich, "Die Idee der Offenbarung," *Zeitschrift für Theologie und Kirche* NF 8 (1927), p. 406. Cf. L. Dupré, *The Other Dimension* (Garden City, N.Y.: Doubleday & Co., 1972), p. 293.

29. *Dei Filius,* chap. 4 (DS 3016).

30. J. Macquarrie, *God-Talk*, p. 206-11.

31. On the multivalence of the symbol of the Cross, see S. K. Langer, *Philosophy in a New Key* (Cambridge: Harvard University Press, 3rd ed., 1969), pp. 284-85; also T. Fawcett, *The Symbolic Language of Religion* (Minneapolis: Augsburg, 1971), pp. 21-25. In "Christ on the Cross: A Study in Image" *Liturgy* 23/5 (Sept. 1978), pp. 26-29, Diane Apostolos Cappadona shows how different aspects of the Crucifixion have come to the fore at different stages of the history of Christian iconography.

32. J. Macquarrie, *Paths in Spirituality* (London: SCM Press, 1972), p. 73.

33. G. H. Clark, "Special Divine Revelation as Rational," in C. F. H. Henry (ed.), *Revelation and the Bible* (Grand Rapids, Mich.: Baker, 1958), pp. 39-40.

34. This point was well made in a review of William L. Shirer's *Rise and Fall of the Third Reich* in *Time*, Oct. 17, 1960: "The story of Adolf Hitler and his works is curiously resistant to the historian's approach. Such massive evil can scarcely be conveyed by facts, figures, and chronology. What is needed is another Dante with a genius for portraying hell, or a new Wagner who can translate horror into myth and spell out the dread meanings in a *Götterdämmerung* finale. Surrealist imagination, not research, may one day tell the definitive story; in the meantime, there are books."

35. W. M. Urban, *Language and Reality*, p. 415.

36. I. G. Barbour, *Myths, Models, and Paradigms* (New York: Harper & Row, 1974), p. 58.

37. R. L. Hart points out the interweaving of archetypal symbolism and "historical master images" in the biblical and theological tradition. See his *Unfinished Man and the Imagination* (New York: Seabury, 1979), pp. 290-305.

38. On God's transcendent-immanent causality, see K. Rahner, *Hominization* (New York: Herder & Herder, 1965), pp. 62-93; also P. Schoonenberg, *The Christ* (New York: Herder & Herder, 1971), pp. 13-49.

39. The concept of "boundary control" or "marginal control" is frequently discussed by Michael Polanyi. See, for instance, his *Knowing and Being* (edited by Marjorie Grene) (Chicago: University of Chicago Press, 1969), pp. 225-30.

40. K. Rahner, "The Saving Force and Healing Power of Faith," *Theological Investigations*, vol. 5 (Baltimore: Helicon, 1966), p. 467.

41. On the sense in which mysticism does or does not involve an immediate experience of God there has been extended controversy. For an opin-

ion that seems to do justice to the various aspects, see J. Maritain, *The Degrees of Knowledge* (New York: Scribner's 1959), p. 261, note 3.

42. K. Rahner, *Foundations of Christian Faith* (New York: Seabury, 1978), p. 171.

43. T. F. O'Meara, "Toward a Subjective Theology of Revelation," *Theological Studies* 36 (1975), pp. 401–27, quotation from p. 427.

44. K. Barth, *Church Dogmatics* I/1 (Edinburgh: T. & T. Clark, 1975), p. 132.

45. Ibid., p. 63.

46. *Church Dogmatics,* vol. I/2 (Edinburgh: T. & T. Clark, 1956), p. 223; vol. II/1 (Edinburgh: T. & T. Clark, 1957), p. 53.

47. William P. Loewe acutely remarks that although Barth "ignores the mediating role of religious symbol . . . it turns out that the criterion really operative in his appeal to 'facts' lies in the felt meaningfulness of religious symbol" ("The Cross: Barth and Moltmann," *Thomist* 41 [1977], p. 527).

48. E.g., K. Rahner, *Hearers of the Word* (New York: Herder & Herder, 1969), pp. 154–55.

49. Cf. R. Otto, *The Idea of the Holy* (New York: Oxford University Press, 1958), p. 34.

CHAPTER X
CHRIST THE SUMMIT OF REVELATION

1. Vatican II, *Dei Verbum,* art. 2. Cf. arts. 4 and 7.

2. Vatican II, *Lumen gentium,* art. 1.

3. P. Tillich, *Systematic Theology,* vol. 1 (Chicago: University of Chicago Press, 1951), p. 133; also esp. vol. 2 (1957), passim.

4. H. R. Niebuhr, *The Responsible Self* (New York: Harper & Row, 1963), p. 154.

5. Ibid., p. 156.

6. K. Rahner, "The Theology of the Symbol," *Theological Investigations,* vol. 4 (Baltimore: Helicon, 1966), pp. 221–52; quotation from p. 251.

7. Ibid., p. 224.

8. K. Barth, *Church Dogmatics,* vol. II/1 (Edinburgh: T. & T. Clark, 1957), p. 53.

9. Ibid., p. 54.

10. H. de Lubac, *Catholicism* (London: Burns, Oates, and Washbourne, 1950), p. 29.

11. E. Schillebeeckx, *Christ the Sacrament of the Encounter with God* (New York: Sheed & Ward, 1963), p. 18.

12. K. Rahner, "Theology of the Symbol," p. 239.

13. K. Rahner, "Observations on the Concept of Revelation," in K. Rahner and J. Ratzinger, *Revelation and Tradition* (New York: Herder & Herder, 1966), p. 15.

14. Vatican II, *Lumen gentium*, art. 8.

15. "To say that Jesus is a religious myth or symbol, albeit the most important religious symbol in the Western world, is not to deny him reality. There is nothing more real than men's symbols and myths. To say that Jesus is a symbol does not say that his life and message are legend. Quite the contrary, it is the very core of the myth of Jesus that his life and message were real historical phenomena . . ." A. M. Greeley, *The Jesus Myth* (Garden City, N.Y.: Doubleday & Co., 1971), p. 13. James P. Mackey, in *Jesus the Man and the Myth* (New York: Paulist, 1979), likewise uses the terms symbol and myth in a nonreductive sense.

16. Y. Congar, *The Revelation of God* (New York: Herder & Herder, 1968), pp. 70–71; italics in original.

17. Vatican II, *Dei Verbum*, art. 4.

18. H. Koester, "The Structure and Criteria of Early Christian Beliefs," in J. M. Robinson and H. Koester, *Trajectories Through Early Christianity* (Philadelphia: Fortress, 1971), pp. 205–31. Koester's hypothesis is followed by E. Schillebeeckx, *The Christ* (New York: Seabury, Crossroad, 1980), pp. 405–38.

19. I. T. Ramsey, *Religious Language* (New York: Macmillan, paperback ed., 1963), pp. 175–201.

20. J. Galot, *Vers une nouvelle christologie* (Gembloux: Duculot–Lethielleux, 1971), p. 52.

21. Ibid., p. 53.

22. F. J. van Beeck, *Christ Proclaimed* (New York: Paulist, 1979), p. 103.

23. W. Pannenberg, *Jesus—God and Man* (Philadelphia: Westminster, 1968), p. 109.

24. Ibid., p. 99.

25. For the different perspectives of the academic historian and the religious believer, see M. Blondel, *History and Dogma* (New York: Holt, Rinehart and Winston, 1964), pp. 219–87. I have sought to apply some of these distinctions to New Testament apologetics in my *Apologetics and the Biblical Christ* (Westminster, Md.: Newman, 1963), making some points to be mentioned below in Chapter XV.

26. W. Pannenberg, *Revelation as History* (New York: Macmillan, 1968), p. 15.

27. W. Pannenberg, *Jesus—God and Man*, p. 130.

28. Ibid., pp. 127–33.

29. Ibid., p. 157.

30. Ibid., p. 397.

31. Ibid., p. 187.

32. There are countless books on Bultmann and his demythologizing program. Still useful is John Macquarrie, *The Scope of Demythologizing: Bultmann and his Critics* (New York: Harper Torchbooks, 1960).

33. James M. Robinson, *A New Quest of the Historical Jesus* (London: SCM Press, 1959), p. 92. For this and other developments within the Bultmann school one may consult, for example, Michael L. Cook, *The Jesus of Faith: A Study in Christology* (New York: Paulist, 1981). For my own earlier assessment, see "Jesus as the Christ: Some Recent Protestant Positions" in my *Revelation and the Quest for Unity* (Washington, D.C.: Corpus, 1968), pp. 245–65.

34. P. C. Hodgson, *Jesus—Word and Presence* (Philadelphia: Fortress, 1971), p. 128.

35. Ibid., pp. 202–17. Cf. pp. 96–97 as quoted above in Chapter IV.

36. P. Tillich, *Systematic Theology*, vol. 1 (Chicago: University of Chicago Press, 1951), pp. 122, 157–59.

37. K. Rahner, *Theological Investigations*, vol. 5 (Baltimore: Helicon, 1966), p. 235.

38. K. Barth, *Church Dogmatics*, vol. II/1, p. 54. For commentary, see E. Jüngel, *The Doctrine of the Trinity* (Grand Rapids, Mich.: Eerdmans, 1976), pp. 47–55.

39. On Teilhard de Chardin's Christology, see C. F. Mooney, *Teilhard de Chardin and the Mystery of Christ* (New York: Harper & Row, 1965). Ursula King in *Towards a New Mysticism: Teilhard de Chardin and the Eastern Religions* (New York: Seabury, 1980) ably presents the "Christian pantheism" of Teilhard, pp. 115, 161–62, et passim.

40. A. Hulsbosch, "Jezus Christus, gekend als mens, beleden als Zoon Gods," *Tijdschrift voor Theologie* 6 (1966), pp. 250–73, summarized in R. North, "Soul-Body Unity and God-man Unity," *Theological Studies* 30 (1969), pp. 27–60. See also the more severe criticisms of J. Galot, *Vers une nouvelle christologie*, pp. 5–15, 41–116, and those of T. Citrini, *Gesù Cristo Rivelazione di Dio* (Venegono Inferiore [Varese]: Scuola Cattolica, 1969), pp. 271–78, 286–91.

41. W. M. Thompson, *Christ and Consciousness* (New York: Paulist, 1977), pp. 10–11, 90–91.

42. G. Baum, *Religion and Alienation* (New York: Paulist, 1975), p. 240.

43. Ibid., p. 241.

44. Ibid., p. 119.

45. E. Schillebeeckx, *Interim Report on the Books* Jesus *and* Christ, (New York: Crossroad, 1981), p. 60.

46. Vatican II, *Gaudium et spes,* art. 21. Cf. art. 22.

47. Quoted in Jean Rivière, *Le Modernisme dans l'Eglise* (Paris: Letouzey et Ané, 1929), p. 143.

48. E. Bevan, *Symbolism and Belief* (first published, 1938; London: Collins, 1962), p. 226.

49. J. Hick (ed.), *The Myth of God Incarnate* (Philadelphia: Westminster, 1977), p. ix.

50. Ibid., p. 178.

51. Ibid.

52. Ibid.

53. C. Davis, "Religion and the Sense of the Sacred," *Proceedings of the Catholic Theological Society of America* 31 (1976), pp. 87–105.

54. Ibid., p. 103.

55. Ibid., pp. 91–92.

56. In *The Case for Liberal Christianity* (San Francisco: Harper & Row, 1981), Donald E. Miller advocates a "symbolic formist" approach to Christology and the creeds, derived from H. Richard Niebuhr in combination with elements from the sociology of knowledge of Peter Berger, Robert Bellah, and others.

57. E. Schillebeeckx, *Interim Report,* p. 28.


CHAPTER XI

REVELATION AND THE RELIGIONS

1. R. E. Whitson, *The Coming Convergence of World Religions* (New York: Newman, 1971), p. 145.

2. Wilfred Cantwell Smith proposes a sense in which Christians might be able to admit that the Qur'an is the word of God. See, most recently, his *Towards a World Theology* (Philadelphia: Westminster, 1981), pp. 163–64. On the basis of a study of the Hindu sacred books, Ishanand Vempeny holds that the "non-biblical Scriptures are truly yet analogically inspired by God" in "Conclusion" to his *Inspiration in the Non-Biblical Scriptures* (Bangalore: Theological Publications in India, 1973), pp. 177–78.

3. Paul Knitter in his "European Protestant and Catholic Approaches to the World Religions," *Journal of Ecumenical Studies* 12 (1975), pp. 13–28, points out (pp. 21–22) that P. Althaus, C. J. Ratschow, and other Lutherans admit the existence of revelation but not the availability of salvation in religions which do not preach faith in Christ. He could have added, perhaps, that for Barth the adherents of these religions can apparently receive salvation without revelation.

4. Text in J.D. Douglas (ed.), *Let the Earth Hear His Voice* (Minneapolis: World Wide Publications, 1975), pp. 3–4.

5. W. Scott, " 'No Other Name'—An Evangelical Conviction," in G. H. Anderson and T. F. Stransky (eds.), *Christ's Lordship and Religious Pluralism* (Maryknoll, N.Y.: Orbis, 1981), p. 66.

6. G. H. Clark, "Special Divine Revelation as Rational," in C. F. H. Henry (ed.), *Revelation and the Bible* (Grand Rapids, Mich.: Baker Book House, 1958), p. 27.

7. G. C. Berkouwer, "General and Special Divine Revelation" in C. F. H. Henry (ed.), *Revelation and the Bible*, p. 17.

8. G. van Noort, *The True Religion* (*Dogmatic Theology*, vol. 1) (Westminster, Md.: Newman, 1969), p. 9.

9. Ibid., p. 15.

10. Ibid., p. 28.

11. Ibid., pp. 29, 107.

12. G. van der Leeuw, *Religion in Essence and Manifestation* (New York: Harper Torchbooks, 1963), pp. 160–61.

13. O. Cullmann, *Christ and Time* (Philadelphia: Westminster, 1950; rev. ed., 1964), p. 157.

14. Ibid., p. 167.

15. Ibid., p. 183.

16. J. Daniélou, *Holy Pagans of the Old Testament* (Baltimore: Helicon, 1957), p. 20.

17. J. Daniélou, *The Lord of History* (Chicago: Regnery, 1958), p. 119.

18. J. Daniélou, *The Salvation of the Nations* (Notre Dame: University of Notre Dame Press, 1962), p. 8. For a similar position contrasting the descending movement of divine revelation with the ascending movement of human religion, see H. U. von Balthasar, "Catholicism and the Religions," *Communio* 5 (U.S. edition) (1978), pp. 6–14.

19. See, for instance, D. G. Dawe, "Christian Faith in a Religiously Plural World," in D. G. Dawe and J. B. Carman (eds.), *Christian Faith in a Religiously Plural World* (Maryknoll, N.Y.: Orbis, 1978), pp. 13–32.

20. W. Pannenberg, "Introduction" to *Revelation as History* (New York: Macmillan, 1969), pp. 6–8.

21. W. Pannenberg, "Toward a Theology of the History of Religions," *Basic Questions in Theology*, vol. 2 (Philadelphia: Fortress, 1971), p. 113.

22. Ibid., p. 115.

23. K. Rahner, "History of the World and Salvation-History," *Theological Investigations*, vol. 5 (Baltimore: Helicon, 1966), pp. 97–114; quotation from p. 105.

24. Ibid., p. 107.

25. Cf. K. Rahner, "Christianity and the Non-Christian Religions," ibid., pp. 115–34; K. Rahner, *Foundations of Christian Faith* (New York: Seabury, 1978), pp. 311–21.

26. F. von Hügel, *Essays and Addresses on the Philosophy of Religion,* Second Series (New York: E. P. Dutton, 1926), p. 39.

27. F. von Hügel, *The Reality of God and Religion and Agnosticism* (New York: E. P. Dutton, 1931), p. 146.

28. E. Underhill, *Mysticism* (London: Methuen, 12th ed., rev., 1930), p. 104.

29. Ibid., p. 96.

30. W. E. Hocking, *Living Religions and a World Faith* (New York: Macmillan, 1940), p. 166.

31. W. E. Hocking, *The Coming World Civilization* (New York: Harper, 1956), pp. 168–69.

32. Ibid., pp. 169–70.

33. P. Tillich, *Christianity and the Encounter of the World Religions* (New York: Columbia, 1963), p. 97.

34. John Hick, *God and the Universe of Faiths* (London: Macmillan, 1973), p. 101.

35. Ibid., p. 106.

36. Ibid., p. 107.

37. K. Barth, *Church Dogmatics,* vol. I/2 (Edinburgh: T. & T. Clark, 1956), p. 356.

38. Ibid., pp. 340–44.

39. K. Barth, *Church Dogmatics,* vol. IV/3, Second Half (Edinburgh: T. & T. Clark, 1962), p. 875.

40. E. Brunner, *Revelation and Reason* (Philadelphia: Westminster, 1946), p. 227.

41. Ibid., pp. 229–32.

42. Ibid., p. 236.

43. Ibid., p. 270.

44. Ibid., pp. 261–64.

45. Third ed., London: James Clarke, 1956. The first edition of 1938 was introduced by a glowing foreword by William Temple, then Archbishop of York.

46. Ursula King, *Towards a New Mysticism: Teilhard de Chardin and Eastern Religions* (New York: Seabury, 1980), pp. 181–89.

47. Teilhard de Chardin, *How I Believe* (New York: Harper & Row, 1969), p. 85.

48. U. King, *Towards a New Mysticism* p. 181.

49. Ibid., pp. 225–26.

50. G. Baum, *Faith and Doctrine* (New York: Newman, 1969), p. 27; see above, chap. VII, note. 20.

51. G. Baum, "The Religions in Catholic Theology," in his *New Horizon* (New York: Paulist, 1972), p. 105.

52. Ibid., pp. 102–3.

53. Ibid., p. 96.

54. G. Baum, "The Jews, Faith, and Ideology," *Ecumenist,* vol. 10, no. 5 (July–Aug. 1972), p. 74.

55. Ibid.

56. Ibid., p. 76.

57. P. Knitter, "World Religions and the Finality of Christ: A Critique of Hans Küng's *On Being a Christian,*" *Horizons* 5 (1978), pp. 151–64.

58. P. Knitter, "Jesus–Buddha–Krishna: Still Present?" *Journal of Ecumenical Studies* 16 (1979), pp. 651–71, esp. p. 657.

59. Ibid., p. 664.

60. Ibid.

61. C. Davis, *Christ and the World Religions* (New York: Herder & Herder, 1971), p. 127.

62. Lucien Richard, *What Are They Saying About Christ and World Religions?* (Ramsey, N.J.: Paulist, 1981), p. 67.

63. Cf. K. Rahner, "The Charismatic Element in the Church" in his *The Dynamic Element in the Church* (New York: Herder & Herder, 1964), p. 63.

64. C. F. Hallencreutz, *New Approaches to Men of Other Faiths* (Geneva: World Council of Churches, 1970), pp. 93–94.

65. Gabriel Fackre, "The Scandals of Particularity and Universality," *Mid-Stream: An Ecumenical Journal* 22 (1983), pp. 32–53; quotation from pp. 46–47.

CHAPTER XII

THE BIBLE: DOCUMENT OF REVELATION

1. The phrasing of the last two sentences echoes the statements on inspiration and inerrancy in Leo XIII's *Providentissimus Deus* (1893), which is foundational for twentieth century neo-Scholasticism (text in DS 3291–93). James I. Packer exemplifies a tendency within the Conservative Evangelical position when he states: "There are no words of God spoken to us at all today except the words of Scripture (direct revelations having now ceased). Conversely, all scriptural affirmations are in fact divine utterances, and are through the Spirit apprehended as such by faith," *"Fundamentalism" and the Word of God* (Grand Rapids, Mich.: Eerdmans, 1958), p. 119.

2. For positions akin to these, see the Conservative Evangelical works summarized in Chapter III.

3. Views such as these were endorsed by the *Schema De Fontibus Revelationis* drawn up by the Preparatory Commission for the First Session of Vatican Council II (1962).

4. For the history of debates on this subject consult, on the Catholic side, B. Vawter, *Biblical Inspiration* (Philadelphia: Westminster, 1972) and, on the Protestant side, J. B. Rogers and D. K. McKim, *The Authority and Interpretation of the Bible* (San Francisco: Harper & Row, 1979).

5. The most monumental achievement reflecting, on the whole, this point of view is the ten-volume *Theological Dictionary of the New Testament* edited by G. Kittel and G. Friedrich (German original, 1949–78; Eng. trans., Grand Rapids, Mich.: Eerdmans, 1964–76).

6. For criticism of the "biblical theology" movement, see B. S. Childs, *Biblical Theology in Crisis* (Philadelphia: Westminster, 1970) and J. Barr, *The Bible in the Modern World* (New York: Harper & Row, 1973).

7. Catholic and Protestant representatives of the salvation history model are critically discussed in M. C. Boys, *Biblical Interpretation in Religious Education* (Birmingham, Ala.: Religious Education Press, 1980).

8. Among Catholic proponents of salvation history, several have written on the concept of biblical inspiration; for example, David M. Stanley, R. A. F. Mackenzie, and John L. McKenzie.

9. W. Pannenberg, "The Crisis of the Scripture Principle," in his *Basic Questions in Theology*, vol. 1 (Philadelphia: Fortress, 1970), p. 7. Pannenberg repeats the same point in *Jesus—God and Man* (Philadelphia: Westminster, 1958), pp. 24–25.

10. See H. Küng, "Toward a New Consensus in Catholic (and Ecumenical) Theology," in L. Swidler (ed.), *Consensus in Theology?* (Philadelphia: Westminster, 1980), pp. 1–17, esp. pp. 6–8.

11. A. Sabatier, *Outlines of a Philosophy of Religion Based on Psychology and History* (New York: J. Pott, 1902), pp. 53–54.

12. C. H. Dodd, *The Authority of the Bible* (New York: Harper Torchbooks, 1960), p. 37.

13. Ibid., p. 269.

14. See G. Tyrrell, *Through Scylla and Charybdis* (London: Longmans, Green, 1907), p. 324 et passim.

15. P. Tillich, *Systematic Theology*, vol. 1 (Chicago: University of Chicago Press, 1951), pp. 34–52.

16. See his section, "Experience and Systematic Theology," ibid., pp. 40–46.

17. D. H. Kelsey, *The Fabric of Paul Tillich's Theology* (New Haven: Yale University Press, 1967), p. 195. See also A. Dulles, "Paul Tillich and the Bible," in *Revelation and the Quest for Unity* (Washington, D.C.: Corpus, 1968), pp. 220–44.

18. K. Barth, *Church Dogmatics,* vol. I/1 (Edinburgh: T. & T. Clark, 1975), p. 102.

19. Ibid., vol. I/2 (Edinburgh: T. & T. Clark, 1956), p. 521.

20. Ibid., p. 533.

21. Ibid., vol. I/1, p. 117.

22. Ibid., vol. I/1, p. 107. Cf. I/2, p. 537.

23. Ibid., vol. I/2, pp. 597–602.

24. See above, chap. X, sec. 6.

25. G. Baum, "The Bible as Norm," *The Ecumenist,* vol. 9, no. 5 (July–Aug. 1971), p. 75; reprinted in his *New Horizon* (New York: Paulist, 1972), p. 44.

26. Ibid., p. 77; *New Horizon,* p. 49.

27. R. L. Hart, *Unfinished Man and the Imagination* (New York: Seabury, 1979), p. 283.

28. Ibid., p. 104.

29. E. Schillebeeckx, *Revelation and Theology,* vol. 1 (New York: Sheed & Ward, 1967), esp. pp. 167–95.

30. E. Schillebeeckx, *Christ: The Experience of Jesus as Lord* (New York: Seabury, 1980), chap. II, "The Authority of the Canonical New Testament," pp. 65–71.

31. Ibid., p. 70.

32. E. Schillebeeckx, *Jesus: An Experiment in Christology* (New York: Seabury, 1979), p. 60.

33. Ibid., p. 59.

34. Ibid., p. 79.

35. *Christ,* p. 71.

36. *Jesus,* p. 59. Cf. pp. 35, 44.

37. *Jesus,* p. 59.

38. A. Farrer, *The Glass of Vision* (Westminster, Md.: Dacre Press, 1948), p. 44.

39. Ibid., p. 52. In this connection it is worth noting that Old Testament books which Christians call historical were known to the Jews as belonging to the Law and the Former Prophets.

40. Ibid., p. 43.

41. In this paragraph I am presenting, in essentials, the position of Karl Rahner in his *Inspiration in the Bible* (rev. trans., New York: Herder & Herder, 1964). R. E. Brown accuses Rahner of "collapsing inspiration into revelation," but I would prefer to say that he is calling attention to the intrinsic connection between the two. For reasons not clear to me

Brown denies that a passage such as the first nine chapters of 1 Chronicles could be "a literary objectification of a faith that is a response to revelation." See R. E. Brown, *The Critical Meaning of the Bible* (Ramsey, N.J.: Paulist, 1981), p. 7. Cf. *Theological Studies* 42 (1981), pp. 8–9.

42. See Rahner, *Inspiration in the Bible*, for a fuller development of the idea of God as the "author" of Israel and the apostolic Church.

43. This term appears in Vatican II, *Dei Verbum*, art. 11.

44. See above, chap. IX, sec. 5(b).

45. James Sanders, in his *Torah and Canon* (Philadelphia: Fortress, 1972), has shown the connection between the canon and the identity of the community. See also D. H. Kelsey, *The Uses of Scripture in Recent Theology* (Philadelphia: Fortress, 1975), pp. 104–5, 164–67.

46. D. H. Kelsey, "The Bible and Christian Theology," *Journal of the American Academy of Religion* 48 (1981), pp. 385–402, esp. p. 393.

47. K. Rahner, *Inspiration in the Bible*, p. 70

48. Ibid., p. 50.

49. According to Kelsey, Barth characteristically construes Scripture as a set of narratives that render God as agent. See D. H. Kelsey, *The Uses of Scripture*, pp. 39–50.

50. G. A. Lindbeck, "The Bible as Realistic Narrative," in L. Swidler (ed.), *Consensus in Theology?* (Philadelphia: Westminster, 1980), pp. 81–85; quotation from p. 85.

51. K. Barth, *Church Dogmatics*, vol. IV/2 (Edinburgh: T. & T. Clark, 1958), p. 180.

52. T. F. Torrance, *Reality and Evangelical Theology* (Philadelphia: Westminster, 1982), p. 96.

53. Vatican II, *Dei Verbum*, art. 21.

54. Alan Richardson persuasively defends the position that "the distinctive character of Israel's history was that it was built around a series of disclosure situations, which through the activity of prophetic minds became interpretative of Israel's historic destiny and ultimately of the history of all mankind," *History Sacred and Profane* (Philadelphia: Westminster, 1964), p. 224.

55. H.-G. Gadamer, *Truth and Method* (New York: Seabury, 1975), p. 255.

56. Ibid., pp. 261–67.

57. Ibid., p. 273.

CHAPTER XIII
THE CHURCH: BEARER OF REVELATION

1. C. F. H. Henry, *God, Revelation, and Authority*, vol. 2 (Waco, Texas: Word, 1976), p. 15.

2. Ibid., vol. 4 (1979), p. 221, note 2.

3. H. Ridderbos, "The Canon of the New Testament," in C. F. H. Henry (ed.), *Revelation and the Bible* (Grand Rapids, Mich.: Baker Book House, 1958), p. 201.

4. G. D. Smith, *The Teaching of the Catholic Church* (New York: Macmillan, 1962), vol. 1, p. 28.

5. Ibid., p. 30.

6. O. Cullmann, *Christ and Time* (Philadelphia: Westminster, 1950; rev. ed., 1964), p. 154.

7. Ibid., pp. 155–56.

8. O. Cullmann, *Salvation in History* (New York: Harper & Row, 1967), p. 327.

9. Ibid., p. 294.

10. O. Cullmann, "The Tradition," in his *The Early Church* (Philadelphia: Westminster, 1956), pp. 59–99; quotation from p. 90. Here and in *Salvation in History*, pp. 300–4, Cullmann is replying to Jean Daniélou, whose criticism will be noted later, note 62.

11. R. Rendtorff, "The Problem of Revelation in the Concept of the Church," in W. Pannenberg and others, *Revelation as History* (New York: Macmillan, 1968), pp. 159–81.

12. W. Pannenberg, *Theology and the Kingdom of God* (Philadelphia: Westminster, 1969), p. 74. Cf. p. 86.

13. W. Pannenberg, *Faith and Reality* (Philadelphia: Westminster, 1977), p. 65.

14. W. Pannenberg, *Revelation as History*, p. 155.

15. *Theology and the Kingdom of God*, p. 76.

16. A. Loisy, *The Gospel and the Church* (Philadelphia: Fortress, 1976), p. 209.

17. Ibid., p. 178.

18. G. Tyrrell, *Through Scylla and Charybdis* (London: Longmans, Green, 1907), p. 327.

19. Ibid., p. 355. Cf. C. J. Healey, "Tyrrell on the Church," *Downside Review*, vol. 91, no. 302 (Jan. 1973), pp. 35–50.

20. K. Barth, *Church Dogmatics*, vol. I/2 (Edinburgh: T. & T. Clark, 1956), p. 500.

21. K. Barth, contribution to J. Baillie and H. Martin (eds.), *Revelation* (London: Faber & Faber, 1937), pp. 41–81, esp. p. 69.

22. *Church Dogmatics*, vol. I/2, p. 231.

23. Ibid., p. 233.

24. Ibid., p. 211.

25. Ibid., pp. 210–14.

26. Ibid., p. 538.

27. Ibid., p. 797.

28. R. Bultmann, *Jesus Christ and Mythology* (London: SCM Press, 1960), pp. 82–83.

29. E. Brunner, *Revelation and Reason* (Philadelphia: Westminster, 1946), p. 137.

30. J. J. Smith, *Emil Brunner's Theology of Revelation* (Manila: Loyola House of Studies, 1967), pp. 97–113.

31. P. Teilhard de Chardin, *The Divine Milieu* (New York: Harper, 1960), p. 138.

32. P. Teilhard de Chardin, "Comment je vois" (unpublished manuscript), p. 15. Cf. E. Rideau, *The Thought of Teilhard de Chardin* (New York: Harper & Row, 1967), p. 597.

33. G. Baum, *The Credibility of the Church Today* (New York: Herder & Herder, 1968), p. 174.

34. Ibid., pp. 164–65.

35. G. Baum, contribution to J. J. Kirvan (ed.), *The Infallibility Debate*, p. 30.

36. G. Baum, *Faith and Doctrine* (New York: Newman, 1969), pp. 107–8.

37. G. Baum, "A New Creed," *The Ecumenist*, vol. 6, no. 5 (July–Aug. 1968), pp. 164–67, esp. p. 164.

38. Ibid., p. 167.

39. Is 11:12, quoted by Vatican I in its Constitution on Faith, chap. 3 (DS 3014).

40. J. D. Mansi, et al. (eds.), *Sacrorum Conciliorum nova et amplissima collectio*, 51:314b; quoted by R. Aubert, *Le problème de l'acte de foi*, 2nd ed. (Louvain: Warny, 1950), pp. 193–94.

41. According to the Council of Trent the sacraments contain and confer the grace which they signify; sess. VII, canons 6 and 8 (DS 1606, 1608).

42. On the idea of the Church as sacrament, see Leonardo Boff, *Die Kirche als Sakrament* (Paderborn: Bonfacius Druckerei, 1972); more briefly, A. Dulles, *Models of the Church* (Garden City, N.Y.: Doubleday & Co., 1974), chap. IV.

43. E. Schillebeeckx, *Christ the Sacrament of the Encounter with God* (New York: Sheed & Ward, 1963), p. 204.

44. R. Latourelle, *Christ and the Church: Signs of Salvation* (Staten Island: Alba House, 1972), p. 267.

45. The Church is particularly related to the Holy Spirit in the work of Heribert Mühlen. See his *Una Persona mystica*, 3rd ed. (Paderborn: 1968).

46. E. Schillebeeckx, *Christ the Sacrament*, p. 205.

47. Vatican II, *Dei Verbum*, art. 2.

48. Vatican II, *Gaudium et spes,* art. 4.

49. Ibid., art. 11. Cf. art. 26 on the presence of God's Spirit in the growing awareness of human dignity in our day.

50. N. Söderblom, *The Living God* (London: Oxford University Press, 1933), p. 386.

51. P. Tillich, *Systematic Theology,* vol. 1 (Chicago: University of Chicago Press, 1951), p.121.

52. Ibid., p. 52.

53. See esp. *Systematic Theology,* vol. 3 (Chicago: University of Chicago Press, 1963), pp. 237–43.

54. K. Rahner, "The Church of the Saints," *Theological Investigations,* vol. 3 (Baltimore: Helicon, 1967), p. 100.

55. H. U. von Balthasar, *A Theology of History* (New York: Sheed & Ward, 1963), p. 105.

56. Ibid. See also M. Kehl and W. Löser (eds.), *The von Balthasar Reader* (New York: Crossroad, 1982), pp. 378–80.

57. The question whether and how a given ecclesiastical pronouncement can be identified as an infallible dogma is a complex one requiring many ecclesiological considerations that cannot be adequately handled here. I have dealt with this question in *A Church to Believe In* (New York: Crossroad, 1982), chap. IX.

58. P. C. Rodger and L. Vischer (eds.), *The Fourth World Conference on Faith and Order* (New York: Association Press, 1964), no. 45, p. 52.

59. Vatican II, *Dei Verbum,* art. 8.

60. Ibid.

61. Ibid., art. 10.

62. J. Daniélou, *The Lord of History* (London: Longmans, Green, 1958), p. 10.

63. F. J. van Beeck, *Christ Proclaimed* (New York: Paulist, 1979), pp. 314–15.

64. Ibid., p. 315.

65. For the ideas in this paragraph see esp. *The Infallibility Debate,* pp. 24–30.

66. "Articulus fidei est perceptio divinae veritatis tendens in ipsam," Thomas Aquinas, *Summa theol., Pars I–II,* q. 1, a. 6, *sed contra.*

67. T. F. Torrance, *Reality and Evangelical Theology* (Philadelphia: Westminster, 1982), p. 50. Cf. pp. 64, 71, 96, etc.

CHAPTER XIV

REVELATION AND ESCHATOLOGY

1. Rejecting Modernism, the Holy Office in 1907 condemned the proposition, "The revelation that constitutes the object of Catholic faith was not

completed with the apostles"—*Lamentabili sane,* prop. 21 (DS 3421). What is here denied is not the continued occurrence of revelation but the fact that, if it occurs, it is constitutive of the object of Catholic faith. The constitutive period of revelation is regarded as having ended with the apostolic age.

2. O. Cullmann, *Christ and Time* (Philadelphia: Westminster, 1964), pp. 91–93.

3. J. Daniélou, *The Lord of History* (Chicago: Regnery, 1958), p. 190.

4. F. Schleiermacher, *On Religion* (New York: Harper Torchbooks, 1958), p. 101.

5. E. Underhill, *Mysticism,* 12th ed. (London: Methuen, 1930), p. 96.

6. K. Barth, *The Epistle to the Romans,* 6th ed. (New York: Oxford University Press, Galaxy Books, 1968), pp. 497–501.

7. R. Bultmann, *The Presence of Eternity* (New York: Harper, 1957), pp. 151–52.

8. J. L. Segundo, *The Liberation of Theology* (Maryknoll, N.Y.: Orbis, 1976), pp. 121–22.

9. Vatican II, *Lumen gentium,* art. 8, last sentence.

10. K. Barth, *Church Dogmatics,* vol. I/2 (Edinburgh: T. & T. Clark, 1956), p. 635.

11. See above, chap. X, sec. 4.

12. K. Barth, *Church Dogmatics,* vol. I/2, pp. 116–17.

13. *Lumen gentium,* art. 8, first paragraph.

14. Ibid., art. 3.

15. H. U. von Balthasar, *A Theology of History* (New York: Sheed & Ward, 1963), p. 95.

16. Ibid., p. 96.

17. *Dei Verbum,* art. 4.

18. *Acta synodalia sacrosancti Concilii Oecumenici Vaticani II,* vol. IV, periodus quarta, pars I (Vatican City: Typis polyglottis, 1976), p. 345 (*expensio modorum* of Nov. 20, 1964). Cf. vol. III, periodus tertia, pars III (publ. 1974), p. 77.

19. The question of continuing revelation was again discussed in connection with the drafting of the U.S. National Catechetical Directory, no. 53. For commentary on the resulting text, see W. P. Loewe, "Revelation: Dimensions and Issues," *Living Light* 16 (1979), pp. 155–67, esp., pp. 163–67.

20. *Sacrosanctum Concilium,* art. 7.

21. *Dei Verbum,* art. 8. Cf. art. 21: "For in the sacred books, the Father who is in heaven meets his children with great love and speaks with them . . ."

22. N. Söderblom, *The Living God* (London: Oxford University Press, 1933), p. 379.

23. Ibid., pp. 374–75.

24. *Gaudium et spes,* art. 36.

25. The term "signs of the times" was first used by Pope John XXIII in his Apostolic Constitution, *Humanae Salutis,* of December 25, 1961, convening Vatican Council II. He wrote: "We make ours the recommendation of Jesus that one should know how to distinguish the 'signs of the times' (Mt 16:3), and we seem to see now, in the midst of so much darkness, not a few indications which augur well for the fate of the Church and of humanity" [W. M. Abbott (ed.), *Documents of Vatican II* (New York: America Press, 1966), p. 704, trans. modified]. John XXIII returned to the theme in his opening allocution at Vatican II (October 11, 1962; cf. Abbott, pp. 712–13), and yet again in the headings of the modern-language versions of his encyclical *Pacem in Terris* (April 11, 1963) in J. Gremillion (ed.), *The Gospel of Peace and Justice* (Maryknoll, N.Y.: Orbis, 1976), pp. 209–32.

26. *Gaudium et spes,* art. 4.

27. Ibid., art. 11.

28. *Unitatis redintegratio,* art. 4.

29. *Dignitatis humanae,* art. 15.

30. *Apostolicam actuositatem,* art. 14.

31. H. U. von Balthasar, *A Theological Anthropology* (New York: Sheed & Ward, 1967), pp. 118–19.

32. W. Pannenberg, "Future and Unity," in E. H. Cousins (ed.), *Hope and the Future of Man* (Philadelphia: Fortress, 1972), pp. 60–78, quotation from p. 74.

33. K. Rahner, *On the Theology of Death,* 2nd English edition; revised, 1965, p. 63.

34. W. M. Thompson, *Jesus, Lord and Savior* (New York: Paulist, 1980), p. 264. See also his article, "The Risen Christ, Transcultural Consciousness, and the Encounter of the World Religions," *Theological Studies* 37 (1976), pp. 381–409.

35. For a sampling of such predictions see William Martin, "Waiting for the End," *Atlantic Monthly,* vol. 249, no. 6 (June 1982), pp. 31–37.

36. K. Rahner, "The Hermeneutics of Eschatological Assertions," *Theological Investigations,* vol. 4 (Baltimore: Helicon, 1966), pp. 323–46, esp. p. 335.

37. In asserting that the idea of the future Kingdom functions as utopia, many of these authors are careful not to deny that it also corresponds to a coming reality. See, for instance, G. Gutierrez, *A Theology of Liberation* (Maryknoll, N.Y.: Orbis, 1973), pp. 232–39; E. Schillebeeckx, "The Magisterium and the World of Politics," in J. B. Metz (ed.), *Faith*

*and the World of Politics* (*Concilium*, vol. 36) (New York: Paulist, 1968), pp. 19–39, esp. pp. 32–36.

38. G. Baum, "Eschatology," in George Dyer (ed.), *An American Catholic Catechism* (New York: Seabury, Crossroad, 1975), p. 95. Baum's eschatology is unfavorably criticized in E. J. Fortman, *Everlasting Life After Death* (Staten Island: Alba House, 1976), pp. 110–12.

39. Cf. K. Rahner, "The Concept of Mystery in Catholic Theology," *Theological Investigations*, vol. 4. (Baltimore: Helicon, 1966), esp. p. 56.

40. According to Benedict XII, the blessed "vident divinam essentiam visione intuitiva et etiam faciali, nulla mediante creatura in ratione obiecti visi . . . ," *Benedictus Deus* (DS 1000).

41. K. Rahner, "The Eternal Significance of the Humanity of Jesus for our Relationship with God." *Theological Investigations*, vol. 3 (Baltimore: Helicon, 1967), p. 44.

42. J. Alfaro, "Cristo Glorioso, Revelador del Padre," *Gregorianum* 39 (1958), pp. 222–70.

43. J. Moltmann, *Theology of Hope* (London: SCM Press, 1967), p. 229.

44. Ibid., p. 83. Cf. pp. 84–94.

45. Ibid., p. 39.

46. K. Barth, *Church Dogmatics*, vol. I/2, p. 635. On the basis of concessions such as these Moltmann presses for still further revisions in Barth's concept of revelation, in the direction of a future-oriented eschatology. See *Theology of Hope*, pp. 50–58. The shift in Barth's thought should not be exaggerated. As early as 1935 he set forth a strongly futurist eschatology in his *Credo* (New York: Scribner's, 1962), pp. 161–72.

47. G. Baum, "The Theological Method of Segundo's *The Liberation of Theology*," *Proceedings of the Catholic Theological Society of America*, vol. 32 (1977), p. 122.

CHAPTER XV
THE ACCEPTANCE OF REVELATION

1. Michael Polanyi, *Personal Knowledge* (New York: Harper Torchbooks, 1964), p. 266.

2. The views of Georg Hermes were condemned under Gregory XVI (DS 2730–40); those of Anton Günther and Jakob Frohschammer under Pius IX (DS 2828–31, 2850–61).

3. Augustine, *Of True Religion*, xxvi. 45, trans. J. H. S. Burleigh (Chicago: Regnery Gateway, 1959), p. 41.

4. George D. Smith, *The Teaching of the Catholic Church,* vol. 1 (New York: Macmillan, 1962), p. 10.

5. Ibid., pp. 10–24.

6. Ibid., p. 13.

7. G. van Noort, *The True Religion* (Westminster, Md.,: Newman, 1959), p. 127.

8. For a thorough analysis of the teaching of Vatican I on faith and reason, see H. J. Pottmeyer, *Der Glaube vor dem Anspruch der Wissenschaft* (Freiburg: Herder, 1968).

9. Vatican I, Constitution *Dei Filius,* chap. IV (DS 3017).

10. Ibid., chap. III (DS 3010).

11. Ibid., (DS 3013).

12. Ibid., chap. IV (DS 3015).

13. Ibid., (DS 3016).

14. B. B. Warfield, *Selected Shorter Writings,* vol. 2 (Phillipsburg, N.J.: Presbyterian and Reformed Publishing Company, 1973), pp. 99–100.

15. B. B. Warfield, *The Inspiration and Authority of the Bible,* 2nd ed. (Philadelphia: Presbyterian and Reformed Publishing Company, 1948), pp. 218–19.

16. Cf. J. W. Montgomery, *The Shape of the Past* (Ann Arbor, Mich.: Edwards Brothers, 1968). Montgomery emphasizes God's unambiguous presence in history, somewhat as does his fellow-Lutheran Pannenberg, but unlike Pannenberg he argues from historical premises to the trustworthiness of the Gospels, and ultimately to their inerrancy.

17. C. F. H. Henry, *God, Revelation, and Authority,* vol. 1 (Waco, Texas: Word, 1976), pp. 229–32.

18. Ibid., p. 235.

19. Ibid., p. 237.

20. Ibid., p. 238.

21. Ibid., p. 270.

22. Ibid., vol. 2 (Waco, Texas: Word, 1976), p. 330. Cf. J. W. Montgomery, *Where Is History Going?* (Grand Rapids, Mich.: Zondervan, 1969), Appendix D, "Faith, History and the Resurrection," pp. 225–39.

23. B. B. Warfield, *Selected Shorter Writings,* vol. 2, p. 106.

24. C. F. H. Henry, *God, Revelation, and Authority,* vol. 1, p. 260. Cf. pp. 228, 270.

25. O. Cullmann, *Salvation in History* (New York: Macmillan, 1968), pp. 323–25; quotation from p. 323.

26. W. Pannenberg, *Revelation as History* (New York: Macmillan, 1968), pp. 135–37.

27. Ibid., pp. 138–39.

28. W. Pannenberg, *Theology and the Kingdom of God* (Philadelphia: Westminster, 1969), pp. 95–96.

29. W. Pannenberg, "Insight and Faith," *Basic Questions in Theology*, vol. 2 (Philadelphia: Fortress, 1971), pp. 31–33.

30. W. Pannenberg, *Jesus—God and Man* (Philadelphia: Westminster, 1968), pp. 25–28.

31. W. Pannenberg, "Faith and Reason," *Basic Questions*, vol. 2, pp. 46–64, esp. p. 64.

32. A. Sabatier, *Outlines of a Philosophy of Religion* (New York: J. Pott, 1902), pp. 35–36.

33. G. Tyrrell, *Lex Orandi* (London: Longmans, Green, 1903), p. ix.

34. Ibid., p. xxxi.

35. F. von Hügel, *Essays and Addresses on the Philosophy of Religion*, First Series (London: J. M. Dent, 1921), pp. 57–58.

36. Pius X, Encyclical *Pascendi* (1907) (DS 3499).

37. Pius X, Motu proprio *Sacrorum antistites* (DS 3539).

38. R. Bultmann, *Jesus Christ and Mythology* (London: SCM Press, 1958), p. 72.

39. E. Brunner, *Revelation and Reason* (Philadelphia: Westminster, 1946), p. 205.

40. Ibid., p. 206.

41. P. Tillich, *Dynamics of Faith* (New York: Harper, 1957), pp. 76–78.

42. C. F. Mooney, *Teilhard de Chardin and the Mystery of Christ* (New York: Harper & Row, 1966), p. 66.

43. J. H. Newman, *Essay in Aid of a Grammar of Assent*, chap. IX, no. 3 (Garden City, N.Y.: Doubleday Image, 1955), pp. 296–97, on the incapacity of reasoning to achieve discovery. In Chapter IV, no. 3 (pp. 86–92), he speaks of the failure of argument to bring about a real assent.

44. "Formal processes of inference cannot thrust toward the truth, for they have neither passion nor purpose. All explicit forms of reasoning, whether deductive or inductive, are impotent in themselves; they can operate only as the intellectual tools of man's tacit powers reaching toward the hidden meaning of things," M. Polanyi, "Faith and Reason," *Journal of Religion* 41 (1961), pp. 237–47; quotation from p. 243.

45. Cr. M. Polanyi, ibid., p. 247: "The discoverer works in the belief that his labors will prepare his mind for receiving a truth from sources over which he has no control."

46. Cf. A. Dulles, "Revelation and Discovery," in W. J. Kelly (ed.), *Theology and Discovery: Essays in Honor of Karl Rahner, S.J.* (Milwaukee: Marquette University, 1980), pp. 1–29.

47. J. H. Newman, *Grammar of Assent*, chap X, part 2, no. 10, p. 379.

48. C. F. H. Henry, *God, Revelation, and Authority,* vol. 1, p. 65.

49. I have written at greater length on historical method and New Testament apologetics in *Apologetics and the Biblical Christ* (Westminster, Md.: Newman, 1963).

50. Cf. F. Rodé, *Le Miracle dans la controverse moderniste* (Paris: Beauchesne, 1965).

51. H. Bouillard, "De l'apologétique à la théologie fondamentale," *Dieu connu en Jésus Christ. Les Quatre Fleuves* 1 (Paris: Ed. du Seuil, 1973), pp. 57–70; quotation from p. 69.

52. G. Baum, Foreword to A. M. Greeley, *The New Agenda* (Garden City, N.Y.: Doubleday & Co., 1973), p. 16.

53. G. Baum, *Religion and Alienation* (New York: Paulist, 1975), p. 252.

54. R. N. Bellah, *Beyond Belief* (New York: Harper & Row, 1970), pp. 220–21, 246–57.

55. G. Baum, *Religion and Alienation,* p. 253.

## CHAPTER XVI
### REVELATION AT ITS PRESENT VALUE

1. "Una realitas complexa," *Lumen gentium,* art. 8.

2. The distinction between "symbolic truth" and the "truth of the symbol, is made by Wilbur M. Urban in *Language and Reality* (London: Allen & Unwin, 1939), p. 444.

3. Michael Polanyi, *Personal Knowledge* (New York: Harper Torchbooks, 1964), p. 269.

4. Ibid.

5. Paul Ricoeur, *The Symbolism of Evil* (Boston: Beacon Press, paperback ed., 1969), p. 350.

6. Immanuel Kant, *On the Form and Principles,* 2, 10; *Gesammelte Schriften* (Berlin, 1902–42), vol. 2, p. 396. Cf. F. Copleston, *A History of Philosophy,* vol. 6, part 1 (Garden City, N.Y.: Doubleday Image, 1964), p. 229. On the ambiguity of symbol in Kant's philosophy of religion, see M. Despland, *Kant on History and Religion* (Montreal: McGill-Queen's University Press, 1973), pp. 149–53, 232, 242, 260–61.

7. J. Hick, *Faith and Knowledge,* 2nd ed. (Glasgow: Collins Fontana Books, 1974), pp. 176–99.

8. M. Blondel, *Letter on Apologetics* (New York: Holt, Rinehart and Winston, 1964), p. 152.

9. In this connection see what was previously stated about the "acts of God" in Chapter IX, sec. 5(b), and about inspiration in Chapter XII, sec. 6.

10. K. Jaspers in K. Jaspers and R. Bultmann, *Myth and Christianity* (New York: Noonday Press, 1958), p. 41.

11. Ibid., p. 47.

12. K. Jaspers, *Truth and Symbol* (New York: Twayne, 1959), pp. 49 and 56.

13. Helmut Ogiermann, after pointing out such differences even among existentialist philosophers, concludes: "Thus the basic problem is not the opposition between philosophy and revealed religion but between opposed philosophies," "Die Alternative 'Philosophie oder Offenbarung' nach Karl Jaspers," in K. Rahner and O. Semmelroth (eds.), *Theologische Akademie*, vol. 1 (Frankfurt a. M.: Knecht, 1965), pp. 27–52, esp. p. 48.

14. F. G. Downing, *Has Christianity a Revelation?* (London: SCM Press, 1964), p. 7.

15. Ibid., p. 183.

16. Ibid., p. 185.

17. Ibid., p. 288.

18. Cf. M. Polanyi, *Personal Knowledge*, pp. 299–324.

19. Speaking of certain seventeenth-century theologians, Bernard Lonergan remarks: "They seem to have thought of truth so objective as to get along without minds." See "The Subject," *A Second Collection* (Philadelphia: Westminster, 1974), pp. 71–72.

20. See the discussion of J. P. Mackey and others in Chapter VII, sec. 6, above. Mackey's idea that first-order language is literal and second-order language mythical almost reverses what John Hutchison had in mind when he coined these terms. See J. A. Hutchison, *Language and Faith* (Philadelphia: Westminster, 1963), p. 227.

21. W. M. Thompson as cited in Chapter VII, sec. 6, above.

22. In the preceding paragraph I reiterate some thoughts from my article, "Revelation and Discovery" in W. J. Kelly (ed.), *Theology and Discovery* (Milwaukee: Marquette University, 1980), p. 25.

23. According to Bernard Lonergan premodern theologians "assumed not only an unbroken tradition of faith but also unchanging modes of apprehension and conception." See "Theology and Man's Future," *Second Collection*, p. 136.

24. On the origins of "dogmatic" theology as a distinct discipline in the seventeenth century, see Y. Congar, *A History of Theology* (Garden City, N.Y.: Doubleday & Co., 1968), pp. 178–79. The idea of dogma as a revealed truth did not come into common Catholic usage until the nineteenth century. See A. Dulles, *The Survival of Dogma* (New York: Crossroad, 1982), pp. 157–58.

25. S. Ogden, "Sources of Religious Authority in Liberal Protestantism," *Journal of the American Academy of Religion* 44 (1976), p. 409.

AVERY DULLES, S.J., is a professor of theology at the Catholic University in Washington, D.C. and a past president of the Catholic Theological Society of America. He is the author of several books including *The Survival of Dogma, Models of the Church, The Resilient Church* and *Revelation Theology: A History*.